Asian Management in Transition: Emerging Themes

Edited by

Samir R. Chatterjee

and

Alan R. Nankervis

palgrave
macmillan

First published in 2007 by
PALGRAVE MACMILLAN
Houndmills, Basingstoke, Hampshire RG21 6XS and
175 Fifth Avenue, New York, N.Y. 10010
Companies and representatives throughout the world.

PALGRAVE MACMILLAN is the global academic imprint of the Palgrave
Macmillan division of St. Martin's Press, LLC and of Palgrave Macmillan Ltd.
Macmillan® is a registered trademark in the United States, United Kingdom
and other countries. Palgrave is a registered trademark in the European
Union and other countries.

ISBN-13: 978–0–230–00774–1
ISBN-10: 0–230–00774–0

This book is printed on paper suitable for recycling and made from fully
managed and sustained forest sources.

A catalogue record for this book is available from the British Library.

A catalog record for this book is available from the Library of Congress.

10 9 8 7 6 5 4 3 2 1
16 15 14 13 12 11 10 09 08 07

Printed in China

To my late parents, Jibon Ranjan Chatterjee and Binapani Chatterjee, for being role models through their life choices which embraced the Asian Virtues of duty paradigm as exemplified in *Niscam Karma* – hard work, connectedness and compassion.

Samir R. Chatterjee

To Lesley and Bryan, my Yin and Yang.

Alan R. Nankervis

Contents

List of tables

List of figures

About the editors

Samir Ranjan Chatterjee was born and educated in India. He currently holds a professorship in International Management at Curtin University of Technology, Australia. Besides Australia, he has researched, consulted and taught in USA, China, Japan and many other countries in Asia and Europe over the past three decades. He was an advisor to the UNDP in setting up the management education in Mongolia from 1994 to 1998, advisor to ADB in the Higher Education sector reform in Indonesia in 2003–04 and one of the programme leaders for managerial training for senior officials of the Ministry of Finance and Ministry of Foreign Affairs and Trade in China funded by the Australian Government. His distinguished fellowships include the American Graduate School of International Management, Indian Institute of Management, Calcutta, University of Ljublijana in former Yugoslavia, E.M Lyon in France, and University of Hokkaido in Japan. He has written six books, over twenty book chapters and more than a hundred referred scholarly journal papers and international conference proceeding papers.

Alan Ray Nankervis is an Associate Professor of Human Resource Management at the Royal Melbourne Institute of Technology University, Melbourne, Australia. He is the co-author of many books and scholarly articles on strategic human resource management, Asian human resource management, performance management, and services management, and has taught, consulted and conducted research in Singapore, Indonesia, China, Malaysia and Thailand.

List of chapter contributors

Dr. Brian Sheehan has been a senior academic in a number of universities in Thailand over the past decade. He was the Dean of the International Programme at Rangsit University. Before that, he had taught in a number of Business Schools in Australia and is the former Dean of the Business School of Phillip Institute of Technology, Melbourne and Associate Dean of the Faculty of Business at RMIT University (Chapter 9).

Dr. Lee Ngok is a senior academic in Hong Kong where currently he is the Executive Director of Vocational Training Council. He had held senior positions in Hong Kong University including the Directorship of the School of Professional and Continuing Education (SPACE). He has written widely on political, social, cultural and managerial transformations in China (Chapter 3).

Dr. Helen Singleton is a Research Associate of the School of Management, Curtin University of Technology. She has done significant research on Asian business culture, especially on Indonesia (Chapters 7 and 10).

Dr. Richard Grainger is currently the Head of School of Management at Curtin University of Technology. He specialises in East Asian management issues and has contributed a large number of research papers on Japanese and Korean management (Chapters 5 and 6).

Dr. Stephen Choo is currently a Senior Research Fellow in the Graduate School of Management at the University of Western Australia. He has researched extensively on the entrepreneurial developments in South East Asia (Chapter 8).

Mr. Subramaniam Ananthram lectures on management in the School of Management, Curtin University of Technology. His research focus is on the managerial challenges associated with globalisation in service organisations in Asia (Chapter 6).

Dr. Tadayuki Miyamoto lectures on international management in the School of Management, Curtin University of Technology. His research focus has been in the areas of services management in Asia-Pacific with a particular interest in Japan (Chapter 5).

Dr. Victor Egan lectures on management in the School of Management, Curtin University of Technology. He has spent extended period in Thailand researching in the comparative management practices of construction and engineering organisations in Australia and Thailand (Chapter 9).

Preface

This book was conceived by the editors in 2001 during their conducting of a large management development programme at the Ministry of Finance in Beijing, People's Republic of China. Many discussions carried out during the associated long flights, in airport lounges, hotel restaurants and traffic jams, led to the refinement of the concept towards its present form. The process has been truly inspiring for us, as we have endeavoured with our regional academic colleagues to present the contemporary management trends and transitions in eight Asian nations within an integrated analytical framework.

Asia itself and Asian management in particular, are undergoing dramatic changes. The predominance of family-managed enterprises, the lack of accountability and transparency in corporate governance, the influence of cultural heritage and the role of governments in economic management, are only a few of the challenges faced by countries in the region. Whilst the divergence between countries is at times formidable, a clear regional identity is also evident, as the book's authors illustrate. In particular, one of the most significant features of the last decade has been the emergence of a new form of intra-Asian competitive collaboration in the economic sphere. Two of the region's largest economies and, indeed, the world's (namely, China and India) are in Asia, and the cross-fertilisation of managerial mindsets and practices between these powerful nations will undoubtedly have a lasting impact on both the region and the global marketplace. As a practical example, Infosys, one of the leading software services companies in India recently sponsored one hundred Chinese management trainees, and the Chinese company, Huawei, recruited seven hundred Indian software professionals. In similar vein, Jiangsu Province in China recently announced its plans to recruit four hundred Indian software specialists to manage its provincial information technology centre (*International Herald Tribune* 8 November 2005).

As the chapters in this book illustrate, management theories and practices reflect underlying societal assumptions, values and goals, and the unique contextual settings provide authenticity for such theories and practices. As Asian management is embedded deeply within its socio-cultural contexts, if also influenced by some aspects of Western management, a better understanding of its implications can be achieved by studying its commonalities and differences through the prism of an analytical framework such as is presented in this book. As Asia emerges as the fastest growing region in the world, the demand for innovative management theories, state of the art management practices, and high quality managers and professionals at all organisational levels, is gaining increased momentum.

The chasm between the dominant Western management theories and the needs of the Asian context is likely to widen more rapidly as globalisation intensifies. In our view, the missing element in understanding Asian management is a broad-based and integrated perspective that views Asia from an insider's rather than an outsider's frame of reference. We have chosen our regional authors with considerable care, and have requested them to present their chapters from their own countries' point of view, for greater currency, and to ensure that an insiders' perspective is maintained throughout the book. Whilst all authors have drawn on their past research and publications, each chapter has been written specifically for this volume.

We expect that this book will inspire its readers as much as it has enlivened its editors and authors. It will be helpful to international business scholars and their students, but also to people wishing to do business within Asia, frequent travellers to Asian nations, and to anyone who has an interest in the dynamics of management in the Asian region.

SAMIR RANJAN CHATTERJEE
ALAN R. NANKERVIS

PERTH, AUSTRALIA

Foreword

The global community is experiencing massive change. Technology and trade are accelerating the integration of the international economy. Against this backdrop, each nation faces the enormous challenge of building sustainable approaches to development. Each nation possesses its own unique history, culture and resource base, and must apply these factors when planning for national development in an increasingly complex and interconnected international system.

With the powerful and historical dominance of Western nations in the global economy, academics and commentators frequently counsel that values should be based on the application of western cultural practices, especially in the international business arena. However, across the world, diverse peoples now feel a need to assert and champion their particular belief systems, values and principles. The shifting realities of economic power bring to the fore critical questions about the assumptions behind the universal values of western business practices.

It would not be an overstatement to claim that Asia is now one of the main driving forces of the global economy and will conceivably sustain its growth for the foreseeable future. Traditional powerhouses such as Japan and South Korea, rising giants such as China and India as well as smaller regional economies such as Malaysia, Singapore, Thailand and Indonesia are forging new and evolving development partnerships.

Asia is, of course, also a region of diverse cultures, religions and ethnicity. For example, Malaysia and Indonesia have enormous diversity within their nations. Each national government must address the complex decision-making challenges associated with nation building, and hence apply particular governance and community development strategies that make local cultural sense to their people.

I am very aware of what this challenge means for Malaysia. In our particular response, we are promoting an approach called *Islam Hadhari*, or Civilisational Islam. This is an approach that propagates comprehensive development and stresses that progress and modernity are consistent with the teachings and traditions of Islam. In a wider context, it is also meant to contribute to greater harmony between peoples, cultures and nations. In Malaysia, we consider our diversity to be an asset to be nurtured, and thus, the promotion and preservation of inter-ethnic and inter-faith harmony to be the highest priority in nation building.

This volume, *Asian Management in Transition: Emerging Themes*, addresses the diverse historic and cultural formational aspects of the eight regional nations represented, and explains the way in which this contributes to the diverse and distinct ways in which each country approaches nation building and economic development. The authors, all experts in their fields, provide insightful explanations of the historic and cultural formation of each key nation as it relates to their distinctive approach to management. In so doing, the book makes a valuable contribution to reframe the understandings now required to achieve a harmonious and integrated global economy. The book applies an approach, which promotes understanding of the deeply embedded nature of the unique character of national heritage and cultural values and how these variously guide each nation's particular managerial approach.

In a pluralistic, dynamic and interdependent global environment, doing business in a 'culturally appropriate' way based on the appreciation of and respect for differences is essential to achieve both local development and stable international relations. Put simply, the rise of diverse cultures participating in the global economy is bringing with it the need to adapt and respond to diverse traditional and emergent management practices, and to understand and respect the cultures within which such practices have evolved. Ultimately, we must all work towards building a more enlightened and tolerant world.

ABDULLAH AHMAD BADAWI
PRIME MINISTER OF MALAYSIA
MAY 2006

Acknowledgements

Undertaking a commitment in putting together a volume such as this which draws on contributions from a diverse range of scholars, and framing it within an integrated perspective generates a great deal of debt. We are grateful to a number of people for their intellectual, professional and collegial support for this project. Their expertise as teachers, researchers and consultants in Asian management has assisted us in interpreting this volume into a consistent framework.

Of our colleagues within the School of Management at Curtin University of Technology, who have particularly supported us, two names stand out – Dr Cecil Pearson, Senior Research Fellow and Dr Helen Singleton, Research Associate – who have so generously provided ideas and feedback on a continuing basis throughout the project. We are indebted to them for their intellectual and personal generosity.

We wish to acknowledge the regional scholars, Professor Lee Ngok, Executive Director of the Vocational Training Council Hong Kong, Professor Juhari Ali of the Universiti Utara Malaysia, Professor Anup Sinha, Dean, Indian Institute of Management, Calcutta, Professor Hock Hwa Chia of INSEAD, Singapore and Professor C. Jayachandran, Director, Centre for International Business, Montclair State University for sharing their insights and encouragement. A special gratitude is due to Ms Ursula Gavin of Palgrave Macmillan. Her confidence in commissioning this book and her encouragement throughout the publishing process has been most productive and rewarding to us.

We express our gratitude to the following copyright owners for granting us permission to use their material in the text:

Department of Foreign Affairs and Trade (DFAT), Australia
Department of National Accounts, ESRI, Japan
Elsevier, UK
Greenwood Publishing Group, USA
Heldref Publications, USA
International Institute for Management Development (IMD),
  Switzerland
National Economic Action Council (NEAC), Malaysia
Tata Sons Limited, India
Transparency International, Germany

Abbreviations

ADB	Asian Development Bank
AOF	Allied Occupational Forces
ASEAN	Association of South East Asian Nations
BAPPENAS	The Indonesian Government Planning Agency
BPO	business process outsourcing
BUMN	government–owned companies Indonesia (*Badan Usaha Milik Negara*)
CBD	central business district
CCP	Chinese Communist Party
CEO	chief executive officer
CII	Confederation of Indian Industries
CPF	Central Provident Fund (Singapore)
CPI	corruption perception index
CPM	Communist Party of Malaya
CPPCC	Chinese Peoples Consultative Congress
CSR	corporate social responsibility
DAP	Democratic Action Party (Malaysia)
DBS	Development Bank of Singapore
DRAM	dynamic random access memory
FDI	foreign direct investment
FECL	Foreign Economic Contract Law (China)
FIEs	foreign invested enterprises
FKTU	Federation of Korean Trade Unions
FTAs	free trade agreements
FTZs	Free-Trade Zones
GDP	gross domestic product
GEM	Global Entrepreneurship Monitor
GLCs	government-linked companies
GNP	gross national product
GOEs	government-owned enterprises
EDB	Economic Development Board (Singapore)
HDI	human development index
HQ	head quarters
HR	human resources
HRD	human resource development
HRM	human resource management
ICA	Industrial Coordination Act (Malaysia)
ICOR	incremental capital-output ratio
ICT	information and communication technology

ILO	International Labour Organisation
IMF	International Monetary Fund
IMP	Industrial Master Plan (numbered) (Malaysia)
IOS	International Organisation for Standardisation
IT	information technology
JVs	joint ventures
KADIN	Indonesian Chamber of Commerce and Industry
KBE	knowledge-based economy
KDP	Community (*Kecamatan*) Development Project (Indonesia)
K-economy	knowledge-based economy
KKN	corruption, collusion and nepotism (*korupsi, kolusi, dan nepotisme*)
KPI	key performance index
LCD	liquid crystal display
KPI	key performance index
LNG	liquefied natural gas
M & A	mergers and alliances
MBAs	Masters of Business Administration
MBO	management-by-objectives
MIC	Malaya Indian Congress
MIDA	Malaysia Industrial Development Authority
MITI	Ministry of International Trade and Industry (Japan)
MNCs	multinational corporations
MOF	Ministry of Finance
MOU	Memorandum of Understanding
NDP	New Development Policy (Malaysia)
NEET	not in employment, educations or training (Japan)
NEP	New Economic Policy (Malaysia)
NERP	National Economic Recovery Plan (Malaysia)
NGOs	non-government organisations
NIE	newly industrialising economy
NOL	Neptune Orient Lines (Singapore)
NPC	National Peoples Congress (China)
NPLs	non-performance loans
NTU	Nanyang Technological University (Singapore)
NU	Nahdlatul Ulama (Indonesia)
NUS	National University of Singapore
ODI	overseas direct investment
OECD	Organisation for Economic Cooperation and Development
OPEC	Organisation of Petroleum Exporting Countries
PAP	People's Action Party (Singapore)
PAS	Pan-Malaysian Islamic Party (*Parti Islam Se-Malaysia*)
PCs	personal computers
PDI	People's Democratic Party (*Parti Democrasi Indonesia*)
PKI	Indonesian Communist Party (*Parti Komunism Indonesia*)

PM	Prime Minister
PNI	*Partai Nasional Indonesia*
PRC	People's Republic of China
R & D	research and development
SAMC	State Asset Management Commission
SARS	severe acute respiratory syndrome
SET	Stock Exchange of Thailand
SEZs	special economic zones
SOEs	state owned enterprises
SOIs	state owned industries
SMEs	small-to-medium enterprises
SPSI	All Indonesia Union of Workers
TFP	total factor productivity
TNCs	transnational corporations
TQM	total quality management
UMNO	United Malays National Organisation
VOC	*Vereeniggde Oost-Indische Compagnie*, formerly Dutch East India Company
VRS	voluntary redundancy scheme
WTO	World Trade Organisation

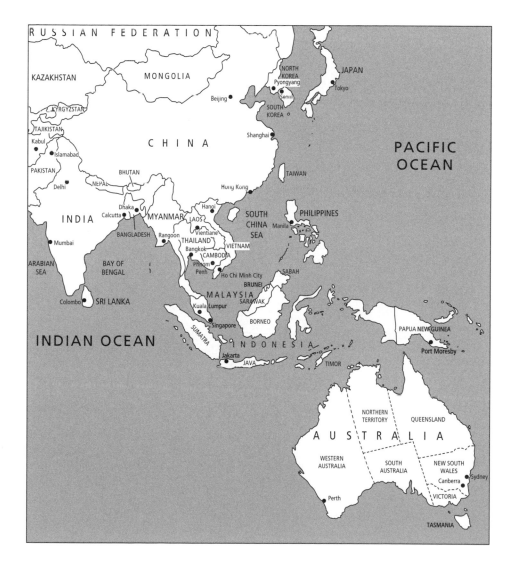

Overview

Asian management in a changing world

Introduction

The major difficulties involved in any study of Asian management include definitional and associative issues such as economic size, capabilities, strategic framework and sub-regional diversities, as well as the varied perspectives of its observers. The apparent heterogeneity of 'Asia' and the cause–effect linkages between its cultural, societal and historical characteristics, and particular management styles and approaches, provide significant challenges for the identification of a differentiated Asian management paradigm. As Lithgow (2000, p. xiv) cautions, 'perhaps the single biggest mistake that commentators make (is to) lump this diverse mass of human souls and geography into a convenient but essentially inaccurate word. Such treatment belies the most outstanding characteristics of Asia: its diversity'. A vast region encompassing sub-continental India and Pakistan, the various countries of Central Asia, as well as China, Japan, Korea and the disparate nation states of Southeast Asia, with 'vast plains, icy mountain ranges, volcanoes, deserts, and thick tropical jungles' (Dobbs-Higginson 1993, p. 5); together with an enormous diversity of ethnic groups, political systems, languages and dialects, religious traditions and different stages of industrial development, defies simple classifications. In spite of such geographic, cultural, linguistic and religious diversities, there are a number of trends contributing to their unique Asian identity and destiny.

Among the top ten countries with the highest populations in the world, six countries are in Asia (China, India, Indonesia, Bangladesh, Japan and Vietnam). Two Asian countries (Japan and South Korea) have met the defined standards of individual wealth and economic size in order to be qualified as members of the Organisation for Economic Cooperation and Development (OECD), and China and India enjoy the highest Gross Domestic Product (GDP) growth in Asia as well as in the world. Table 1.1 shows the population sizes, total and per capita GDP in eight Asian countries, and also indicates that the key sectors in all these countries are moving away from agriculture and industry towards services. Understanding the shift towards service and consequently knowledge economies will inevitably lead to the creation of new managerial imperatives not only in structures, systems, cultures and strategies,

Table 1.1 GDP and population of the eight Asian countries

Countries	Population (Million)	GDP ($Billion)	GDP/Capita ($)	GDP in Key Sectors (%)		
				Agriculture	Industry	Services
China	1,281.00	1,237.10	7.262 trillion	13.80	52.90	33.30
Japan	127.10	3,978.80	3.745 trillion	1.30	24.70	74.10
India	1,043.30	515.00	3.319 trillion	23.60	28.40	48.00
Korea	47.60	476.70	925.1 billion	3.20	40.00	56.30
Indonesia	211.70	172.90	827.4 billion	14.60	45.00	40.60
Thailand	61.60	126.40	524.8 billion	9.00	44.30	46.70
Malaysia	24.30	95.20	229.3 billion	7.20	33.60	59.10
Singapore	4.20	87.00	120.9 billion	0	32.60	67.40

Source: *CIA World Factbook* (http://www.cia.gov/cia/publications/factbook).

but also a renewed pressure for the localisation of innovation, quality and intra-Asian synergies.

The changing world of Asia is witnessing increasing intra-Asian interactions of immense potential. The rise of the business activities of Chinese and Indian diasporas and ethnic families living in various Asian countries have significantly contributed to this development. Over the past two decades, Asian students have been educated in significant numbers by regional countries like Australia and New Zealand. Not only have student numbers from Asian countries increased exponentially, but also universities from Australia and New Zealand had been setting up collaborative educational partnerships in many Asian countries.

Despite the region's inherent diversities and associated contradictions, it is generally accepted that the countries comprising the Asian region have sufficiently similar geographic, historic and cultural characteristics to consider them as parts of a cohesive geopolitical entity differentiated from their Western counterparts. Consequently, it is possible to build a case that these similarities have led to the development of differences and particularities in Asian management systems and processes to those of the West. In the major traditional societies of Asia, it is the extended family system that not only preserves social cohesion and solidarity, but in many cases provides the backbone of business and industry. The host of Chinese and Indian family-owned and operated companies in all Asian countries, the infamous Korean *chaebols* and Japanese cartels and indigenous family businesses in Indonesia and Malaysia, are all examples of this characteristic. It can be argued that the historic internal migration of Chinese and Indian family entrepreneurs throughout the region, coupled with the effects of and reactions to European colonisation, have contributed significantly to the economic resurgence of Asia in the post–Second World War era.

A brief overview of Asian management

Asia had a great tradition of global trading links in the pre-industrial period. This became more systematic during the colonial period, and in the aftermath of the Second World War Japan showed the way by breaking ranks with the rest of Asia by joining the West in global economic competitiveness. Centuries before the Industrial Revolution, trade and commerce in rare silk, pottery, paper, silver, tea, spices and many other items were booming across Asia, including Malacca (Malaysia); Ujung Pandang (Indonesia); Goa; Calicut and Cochin (India); and in Macau, Shanghai and Canton (China). As examples, in the seventeenth century, Indonesian traders from Ujung Pandang (now called Macassar) harvested sea cucumbers (trepary) from the northern coastline of Australia and benefited by selling them in China (Marr and Miller 1986, Shaffer 1996). Chinese General Zheng He had a fleet of 300 ships and 30,000 men with whom he went as far as Africa on several trading voyages in the 1420s (Lombard and Aubin 2000, Menzies 2003, UCLA 2005). Table 1.2 shows the strength of the maritime commercial activities of Zheng He as compared to the more well-known European explorers. The general assumption that the practices of modern management were imported from the West could not be entirely true, given the highly sophisticated strategic planning, logistical management, recruitment, training as well as team leadership in the breathtaking managerial practices needed for such sea voyages.

These managerial strengths of the merchant class, and the emergence of global trade may have been eroded in subsequent centuries with the ascendancy of power by Confucian scholars in China, Brahmanical Hinduism in India and the spread of Islam in South Asia (Moddie 1968, Pye 1986, Redding 1990). In his reform platform in the People's Republic of China, Deng Xiaoping acknowledged a profound debt to Confucian tradition while rejecting some of his ideas. He emphasised that China's economic advances would be critically dependent on managerial expertise (Taylor 2005). In the case of India, the presence of managerial know-how is also illustrated through the work over 22 years by 22,000 skilled workers in building the Taj Mahal about 300 years ago. The recruitment and training of exceptionally talented workers, global procurement systems and logistical sophistication were all essentially indigenous innovations. Insightful knowledge and the wisdom of Asian managerial traditions still have forceful

Table 1.2 Maritime managerial strength in Asia

Navigator	Number of Ships	Number of Crews
Zheng He (1405–33)	48 to 317	28,000
Columbus (1492)	3	90
Da Gama (1498)	4	Ca. 160
Magellan (1521)	5	265

Source: UCLA, Asia Institute 2005.

relevance in the contemporary context (Low 2001). For example, Sun Tze's philosophies on strategy development in China and Kautilya's principles of governance in India underpinned the ideas of institutional management for thousands of years in their respective countries. Chinese philosopher, Mencius (372–289 BC) may have been the father of modern production management (Cauquelin, Lim, and Mayer-Konig 2000, Low 2001).

Until the sudden 'meltdown' of Asia's unprecedented economic success in 1997, four economies – Singapore, Hong Kong, Taiwan and South Korea – were hailed by business commentators around the world as models for the rest of Asia. Their success was mainly based on the development of export-oriented industry sectors, government participation in corporate strategic development, entrepreneurial risk-taking and diligence of the human capital. Besides these four 'tiger' economies, Malaysia, Thailand and Indonesia were also gripped by the euphoria of economic optimism. The specific trigger that initiated the crisis was the collapse of financial institutions in Thailand. The catastrophic effect of Thailand's financial crisis generated a domino effect on the region leading to massive economic shock. Countries that were affected severely included Thailand, Indonesia, South Korea, Malaysia and Singapore. China, Japan and India escaped this meltdown relatively lightly perhaps due their internal market size and reasonable 'economic distance' from the affected countries.

The crisis, however, had a dramatic positive effect in many Asian countries where indigenous corporate governance began to receive renewed attention. Of course the aftermath of the Asian Financial Crisis has increased scrutiny on the 'Asian values' concept. The concept has lost some of its currency following the Asian financial crisis, but the concept of Asian values as a unique set of values grounded in the Asian tradition was a popular concept until then. Essentially, Asian values encompassed Confucian elements in terms of foregoing personal democratic freedom to ensure social stability and progress. The pursuit of hard work, thrift, academic excellence and long-term orientation are also seminal characteristics. Critics have pointed out that it was not possible to have a single unified concept of 'Asian values' because of the diversity of national priorities. Cracks in the concept began with the 'bursting of the bubble economy' in Japan in 1989, and more recently, with the collapse of the Thai, Malaysian and South Korean currencies and economies in 1997. The issues of corporate transparency and ethical and social responsibility gained increased public attention, and managers at all levels had to pay enhanced interest to these imperatives. Large scale corporate collapses through corruption, nepotism, cronyism and fraud in Japan, China, Korea and India over the past decade, make this issue perhaps the most significant area of attention for managers in Asia. Table 1.3 indicates the variations in the perception of business corruption in the eight countries of this book. While Singapore leads the table as the least corrupt business context (9.3, and a global ranking of 5), Indonesia is far behind with a score of 2.0 and a global ranking of 133. Legal and managerial weaknesses in this area need to be addressed seriously for Asian managers to become fully accepted.

Table 1.3 Corruption perception index for eight Asian countries (2004)

Countries	Score (1)	World Rank (2)	Surveys used
Singapore	9.3	5	13
Japan	6.9	24	15
Malaysia	5.0	39	15
China	3.4	71	16
Thailand	3.6	64	14
India	2.8	90	15
Indonesia	2.0	133	14
Korea	4.5	47	14

Source: Transparency International 2004 http://www.transparency.org/cpi/2004/cpi2004.en.html#cpi2004).

Note: (1) A score of 10 indicates the least corrupt country.
(2) Ranking based on eight countries.

Asian values and economic development

More recent developments (e.g. Singapore's employment problems and Hong Kong's economic decline) further question the significance of the relationships between 'Asian values' and economic development. That is, valuing family relationships became nepotism, preferring personal relationships to legalism was cronyism, the overbalance of consensus over autocracy led to corruption and the value of conservatism and respect for authority over individualistic behaviours translated into rigidity and the inability to innovate. Educational achievements become rote learning and a refusal to question those in authority.

Henderson (1998) noted that simultaneous with rapid economic growth was a rise in Asian self-confidence, which was partly a natural consequence of the deeply felt bitterness, humiliation and injustice which resulted from the past subjugation of Asia by the West. Asians sought to explain Asian success by examining Asian society and philosophy, and further, began to claim that the relative decline of the West was because of the decadence of Western societies and the inadequacies of Western individualistic philosophical approaches. Asian values and the Asian interpretation of human rights issues were touted as the driving causes of the Asian 'economic miracle'. This sense of euphoria meant that there while there was pointed criticism of Western institutions, there was very limited attention paid to any Asian social or economic shortcomings. This unbalanced coverage created a climate in which institutional and retail investors continued to channel money into the emerging markets, despite disappointing results in some cases.

Backman (1999) also linked the concept of Asian values with the Asian economic collapse, but in a more fundamentalist way. Noting the centrality of

Confucianist ideas to the Asian values concept, he pointed out that Confucian orthodoxy had a crucial inadequacy – the relationship between individuals and outsiders. As a result, many modern Asian corporations treat deals with outsiders via stratagems and subterfuge. An Asian corporation is like a kingdom, autocratically run with a ruling family. The use of rules and guidelines for the use of power in the organisation, and any form of built-in checks and balances, accountability, transparency or adequate corporate governance, is regarded as acceding authority to outsiders. In a similar vein, formal, legally binding contracts to govern relationships between corporations are not favoured (Backman 1999). Whatever the actual link between Asian values, transparency and economic outcomes, it seems clear that regional interests have attempted to manipulate the perceived relationships for political benefit. The intensification of globalisation has highlighted the convergence–divergence debate in Asia and the recent literature has indicated a trend towards the evolving cross-verging synergies (Haley, Tan, and Haley 1998; Lau, Wong, Law, and Tse 2000).

For Mahbubani (2004), within the context of the ongoing modernisation and globalisation of Asian nations, a key question is whether Asian managers will be able to preserve the traditional strengths of Asian values (the importance of the family institution, deference to societal interests, thrift, conservatism in social mores and respect for authority) with the strengths of Western values (an emphasis on individual achievement, political and economic freedom and respect for the rule of law and key national institutions). It is important for non-Asians to comprehend that Asians do not see their values in narrow political terms, but rather in a much broader sense, which includes a desire to reconnect with their historical and cultural past after the disruption by Western colonisation and economic domination. It is about establishing self-esteem as an essential ingredient in the transformation of societies. The great challenge for Asian societies is to simultaneously integrate with the modern world and to rejoin with their past. This runs counter to the commonly held Western view that without Western systems, which are held to be universal, no society can successfully enter the global era.

A key question for the Asian societies is the extent to which modern management concepts from the West will prevail over the indigenous traditions and wisdom. The adoption of a broader and more encompassing social perspective of management goes beyond the imperatives of profitability, efficiency or competitiveness. A holistic perspective of the Asian managerial challenge may be evident through the United Nation's Human Development Index (HDI) shown in Table 1.4. The statistics in the Human Development report are drawn from expert agencies compiling specialist and specific indicators of social and human development. The data is created by including items such as life expectancy at birth, adult literacy rate, enrolment in primary, secondary and tertiary education, GDP per capita and a number of other items. The pillars of the human development strategy are measured in terms of democracy, pro-poor growth, and the equitable expansion of social opportunities, cultural policies and the wide ranging issues of social sustainability.

Table 1.4 Human development index for eight Asian countries

Countries	HDI Value	Ranking
Japan	0.938	9
China	0.745	94
India	0.595	127
Korea	0.888	28
Singapore	0.902	25
Malaysia	0.793	59
Indonesia	0.692	111
Thailand	0.768	76

Source: *United Nations Human Development Report* 2004 (http://www.un.hdi.org).

A number of commentators on Asia have emphasised the multi-directional learning for Western managers working in Asia, as Asia is certainly the most diverse of the world's continents and the opportunities for learning for managers from outside are enormous (Dobbs-Higginson 1993; Mahbubani 2004). Learning at individual, organisational and community levels can be gained and this can guide the generation of a wholesome process of inquiry for managers around the world. As has been inferred, 'the world will be a much richer place when Western minds stop assuming that Western civilization represents the only universal civilization. The only way that the western mind can break out of its mental box is to first conceive of this possibility that the western mind may also be limited in its own way' (Mahbubani 2004, p. 10). An example of this 'dual learning loop' is the Anglo-Dutch consumer company Unilever. Most of the four hundred brands of Unilever were originally locally innovative successes and were ingeniously converted to global products. Unilever's learning ability made it a success story in India long before most Western companies began to consider India as a location for their strategic business platforms.

As discussed, it is possible to build a credible argument for the concept of an 'Asian' region with a series of diverse countries sharing many common historical, political, economic, social and cultural characteristics, even if its colonially-imposed descriptors (e.g., 'Far East', 'East Asia', 'Southeast Asia') are less defensible. However it is more problematic to suggest that, as a consequence of their shared and disparate heritages, management patterns and processes in Asian countries are either transforming towards a global universalistic framework (convergence), maintaining their unique characteristics (divergence), or gradually creating an amalgam of both (cross-vergence). Rowley and Benson (2002, pp. 90–91) suggest that their empirical research in Japan, Korea, China, and Thailand indicates the latter:

> While several common patterns were emerging across advanced industrial states, at the same time cross-national variations existed … local customs, institutions, and labour forces do, however provide serious constraints on the degree of convergence, and may well lead to increased levels of divergence.

Convergent and divergent paradigms

The staggering diversity in Asia in terms of wealth, economic momentum, ethical assumptions, corporate governance models, and thus managerial systems, defy a simplistic and facile normative model. Diversity is often under-emphasised in the search for a convenient, yet elusive, Asian frame. The 'competitiveness' scores of eight countries included in this book are illustrated in Table 1.5. It shows the achievement of Singapore as the second most competitive country in global ranking and Japan's slide from one of the top three competitive countries to a relatively low rank of 23 in 2004. During the past ten years China has climbed up the competitive ladder from a very low ranking to score a rank just behind Japan in 2004. Interestingly, this scoring measure includes a wide range of variables from the degree of government proactivity to the level of managerial sophistication. This model of competitive drive has been characterised as a 'flying geese' model of competitiveness where each country moved from the manufacturing and exporting of simple products to more capital and 'know-how'.

> As one country moved on to the next level of value added, another developing country would take its place as at the lower-value ends. Japan led the flock, followed by Hong Kong, Singapore, South Korea and Taiwan. Then come Malaysia, Thailand, the Philippines, Indonesia and Vietnam in the tail. Albeit somewhat simplistic, this concept of national geese flying in formation underlay many a government policy and corporate strategy. (Williamson 2005, p. 38)

The flying geese paradigm allows managers in Asia to revisit their mutual strengths and weaknesses and to seek to leverage their competitive positioning through integrated strategic perspectives.

   In spite of the evident divergence among the Asian countries in terms of their competitive strengths, there is a noticeable convergence occurring in terms of an increasing enthusiasm for business, unique work ethics, willingness to learn and the acceptance of global managerial values (Chatterjee and Pearson 2002). The most important point of convergence lies in the sea change in the competitive environment in Asia. The rapid economic development in China and India coupled with the global openness of every economy are creating dual convergence and divergence. However, the converging forces may appear complex and confusing because of the different levels of managerial challenges in different

Table 1.5 2004 World competitiveness scores for the eight Asian countries

Countries	2004 World Competitiveness Score	Global Ranking
China	70.725	24
India	62.971	34
Japan	71.915	23
Korea	62.201	35
Malaysia	75.919	16
Indonesia	38.095	58
Singapore	89.008	2
Thailand	68.235	29

Source: IMD, *World Competitiveness Yearbook* 2004 (http://www.www02.imd.ch).

contexts brought about not only by different levels of economic and human development, but also by the degree of global forces experienced by them. Four major themes in understanding this phenomenon are the professionalisation of the managerial cadre; managerial 'catch-up' with the West not by copying, but by intelligent adaptation; managing the global challenge; and achieving a sustainable and ethical governance culture.

The emergent literature

A number of major books about managerial systems in Asia have been written in the recent years and, in particular, over the past several decades, books on the Japanese management system have been widely popular. The interest in alternative managerial assumptions and practices generated by the widespread discussion of the Japanese management system have now been broadened by the appearance of significant numbers of influential books on the management systems in Chinese, Indian, Korean and other cultural contexts. Except in the case of Japan, where the in-depth micro-level analysis of managerial practices has been explored, most contributions on other Asian countries have generally focussed on broad societal and macro-level perspectives. The genre of micro-level books has generally been addressed to the needs of Western businessmen in their dealings with specific countries and written in the style of 'How to Do Business' in a specific country.

Recent contributions exploring the strategic perspectives of Asian managerial systems have confirmed the emerging sub-discipline of 'Asian management'. Lasserre's and Schutte's (1999) contribution to a strategic analysis of the

Asia-Pacific region has been of seminal influence, Yip's *Asian advantage: Strategic management in the Asia-Pacific* (1998), Williamson's *Winning in Asia* (2004) and the edited volume by Haley (2000) titled *Strategic management in the Asia Pacific*, provide major integrative perspectives for strategy making by multinational companies in Asia. Naisbitt's *Megatrends Asia* (1996), Andrews et al., *The Changing face of multinationals in Southeast Asia* (2003), Lau et al., *Asian management matters* (2000), and Chien et al. (2005) *Business growth strategies for Asia Pacific*, are examples of recent explorations in this area.

Books written with theoretical perspectives include Chen's (2004) analysis of Confucian East-Asia highlighting the managerial cultures of China, Japan and Korea. Though limited in scope, the book enhances the sub-discipline by concentrating on the East Asian countries. A number of similar books have focussed on the contributions of overseas Chinese and Indians, alliance management, Asian legal issues, political and family power in Asian business, and similar topics (Ohmae 1995, Kamm 1996, Haley et al. 1998, Backman and Butler 2003).

These recent publications signal that as Asian countries like China and India improve their managerial capacity, the economic well-being of the people of those countries will improve more rapidly than others. Like the technological catch up after the Second World War that enabled Western Europe to narrow the economic gap with the United States, managerial catch up cannot only power the economic reform and global liberalisation in most Asian countries, but also make it sustainable. As has been pointed out:

> Countries throughout Asia are working hard to overcome past strategic animosities in order to create increasingly integrated flows of merchandise, finance and technology. On the basis of current trends, and a very rough estimate, this integrated Asian economy could reach about half of world GNP (up from a current one-third), with about 60% of the world's population. (Sachs 2004)

These challenges make the sub-discipline of Asian management relevant, and indeed crucial to a diverse range of stakeholders.

About the book

This book explores the managerial trends in Asia by integrating the macro-variables of globalism and national cultures with the evaluation of a range of meso- and micro-level management processes and practices in eight countries of diverse economic, social, cultural and political settings. It provides a special resource to Asian readers by developing an integrated view of the multiple managerial heritages and contemporary responses to the global challenges. It is primarily concerned neither with socio-economic analysis of the countries included nor a recipe for management techniques for readers. The book aims to develop a thoughtful practical framework for interested students, scholars, managers and policy makers in synthesising the divergent as well as convergent forces guiding managerial transitions in Asia. The model adopted for this book outlined in the following chapter highlights the various forces shaping the managerial culture and practices in Asia. The key elements of the macro-societal heritage and institutional driving forces are evaluated in the micro-level managerial contexts. The model aims to explain the close intertwining of cultural forces, economic systems and emerging values as well as the learning orientations in these countries. National cultural, social and economic environments are shown as the platform where global and local managerial ideas and practices are being shaped for the creation of an unique and appropriate variation in managerial mindset.

It is not the purpose of this book to explore all countries that could generally be called Asia. The eight countries included in this book have been chosen to be representative, comprising three major Asian economies (namely Japan, China and India) and three critically important small countries (Singapore, South Korea and Malaysia). In addition, one large and one small country where the effects of the 1997 Asian crisis were very severe have also been included (Thailand and Indonesia). The choice of these eight countries has not only been influenced by their separate economic and managerial heritages, but also by their cultural diversity and the uniqueness of their corporate governance systems. Over the past ten years, a number of significant industries in the United States and Europe have chosen to shift some of their key operational and strategic bases to Asia. It has not been restricted to the conventional areas of manufacturing, sourcing, joint design, OEM facilitation and similar areas where cost advantages have been the traditional attraction. The basic structural forces driving global integration and convergence have largely been in the areas of technology intensity, economics of scale, scope, branding and related factors whereas the structural forces that drive the Asian context are geographical proximity, national cultural colours, different consumption patterns and the intensity of distribution.

As the world changes increasingly from an agriculture and industry-dominated context to services and knowledge-driven societies, managers in Asia have been presented with unique challenges. Asian managers of the next generation will need the skills, values and intellectual depth necessary to harness the global mindset of optimising the forces of convergence as well as those of local heritage. The richness of our current understanding of Asian management can be enhanced by considering the dynamics of managerial engagement in Asia not only in terms of the dichotomy of convergence and divergence, but also through a creative cross-verging prism that emerges at the 'corporate-societal' interface.

Questions

1. Discuss the notion of 'Asian Values', and consider how they manifest themselves in 'Asian' managerial styles.
2. Explain the similar and different historical legacies and cultural traditions in two or three Asian nations.

3. What have been the most significant effects of the 1997 Asian 'economic crisis' on contemporary Asian management?

References

Andrews, T, Chompusri, N & Baldwin, B, 2003, *The changing face of multinationals in Southeast Asia*, Routledge, London.

Backman, M, 1999, *Asian eclipse: Exploring the dark side of business in Asia*, John Wiley and Sons, Singapore.

Backman, M & Butler, C, 2003, *Big in Asia: 25 Strategies for business success*, Palgrave Macmillan, London & New York.

Cauquelin, J, Lim, P & Mayer-Konig, B (eds), 2000, *Asian values: Encounter with diversity*, Routledge/Curzon Publishing, UK.

Chatterjee, SR & Pearson, CAL, 2002, 'Work goals of Asian managers: Field evidence from Singapore, Malaysia, India, Thailand, Brunei and Mongolia', *International Journal of Cross-Cultural Management*, vol. 2 no. 2, pp. 251–68.

Chen, M, 2004, *Asian management systems* (2nd ed.), Thomson, London.

Chien, W, Shih, S & Chu, P, 2005, *Business growth strategies for Asia Pacific*, John Wiley & Sons (Asia), Singapore.

Dobbs-Higginson, M, 1993, *Asia Pacific: Its role in the new world disorder*, William Heinemann Australia, Melbourne.

Haley, G, Tan, C & Haley, U, 1998, *The new Asian emperors: The overseas Chinese, their strategies and competitive advantages*, Butterworth-Heineman, Oxford.

Haley, U (ed.), 2000, *Strategic management in the Asia Pacific*, Butterworth-Heinemann, MA.

Henderson, C, 1998, *Asia Falling? Making sense of the Asian currency crisis and its aftermath*, Mc-Graw Hill, Singapore.

Kamm, H, 1996, *Dragon ascending*, Little Brown, Boston.

Lau, C, Wong, C, Law, K & Tse, D, (eds), 2000 *Asian management matters: Regional relevance and global impact*, Quantum Books, Cambridge, MA.

Lithgow L, 2000, *Special blend: Fusion management from Asia and the West*, John Wiley & Sons, Singapore.

Lasserre, P & Schutte, H, 1999, *Strategies for Asia Pacific: Beyond the crisis*, Macmillan-Business, London.

Lomabard, D & Aubin, J (eds), 2000 *Asian merchants and businessmen in the Indian Ocean and the China Sea*, Oxford University Press, New York.

Low, S, 2001, *Asian wisdom for effective management*, Pleanduk Publication, Singapore.

Mahbubani, K, 2004, *Can Asians think?* Times Books International, Singapore.

Marr, D & Miller, A (eds), 1986, *Southeast Asia in the 9th to the 14th centuries*, Institute of Southeast Asian Studies, Singapore.

Menzies, G, 2003, *1421 the year China discovered the world*, Bantam Books, New York.

Moddie, A, 1968, *The Brahmanical culture and modernity*, Asia Publishing House, Bombay.

Naisbitt, J, 1996, *Megatrends Asia*, Nicholas Brealey Publishing, London.

Ohmae, K, 1995, *The end of the nation state*, Harper Collins, London.

Pye, L, 1986, 'The new Asian capitalism: A political portrait', in P Berger & H Hsien-Huang (eds) In *Search of an East Asian development model*. Transaction Books, Oxford.

Redding, G, 1990, *The spirit of Chinese capitalism*, Walter de Gruxtes, Berlin.

Rowley, C & Benson J, 2002, 'Convergence and divergence in Asian human resource management', *California Management Review*, vol. 44, no. 2, pp. 90–109.

Sachs, J, 2004, 'Welcome to the Asian century', *Fortune*, 26 January, pp. 38–9.

Shaffer, N, 1996, Maritime *South East Asia to 1500*, M.E. Sharpe, New York.

Williamson, P, 2004, *Winning in Asia: Strategies for the new millennium*, Harvard Business School Press, Boston.

Williamson, P, 2005, Strategies for Asia's new competitive game, *Journal of Business Strategy*, vol. 26, no. 2, pp. 37–43.

Yip, G, 1998, *Asian advantage: Key strategies for winning in the Asia–Pacific region*, Perseus Publishing, Cambridge, MA.

UCLA, Asia Institute 2005, 'Zheng He's Voyages of Discovery' [on-line] URL available: http://www.international.ucla.edu/asia/article.asp?parentid=10387 [5 July 2005]

Additional readings

Chen, M, 2004, *Asian management systems: Chinese, Japanese and Korean styles of business*, Thomson Learning, London.

Henderson, C, 1998, *Asia falling? Making sense of the Asian currency crisis and its aftermath*, McGraw-Hill, Singapore.

Hofstede, G, 1980, *Culture's consequences: International differences in work-related values*, Beverly Hills, Singapore.

Hofstede, G, 1991, *Cultures and organisations*, McGraw-Hill, London.

Joynt, P & Warner, M, 1996, *Managing across cultures: Issues and perspectives*, International Thomson Business Press, London.

Lasserre, P & Schutte, H, 1999, *Strategy and management in Asia Pacific*, McGraw-Hill, London.

Porter M, 1980, *Competitive strategy*, The Free Press, New York.

———, 1990, *The competitive advantage of nations*, The Free Press, New York.

Taylor, R, 2005, 'China's human resource management strategies: The role of enterprise and government', *Asian Business and Management*, vol. 4, no.1, pp. 5–21.

Convergence and divergence – a heritage, transition and transformation model of management in Asia

DIVERGING

Introduction

Chapter 1 argues that Asian economic and managerial strategies have an identifiable cultural foundation, but that these traditional influences are being transformed by contemporary global and local influences. This chapter examines the unique and distinguishing characteristics of the Asian region which arguably have led to divergent managerial styles, processes and practices, despite the convergent pressures brought on by increasing global and transnational influences and forces. This contextual approach explains the evolution of Asian managerial cultures through colonial and 'Asian values' periods, towards their more recent 'cross–vergence'. Whilst this discussion explores the homogeneity of the Asian region in historical, social, cultural, geopolitical and economic terms, it also addresses its heterogeneity, as expressed in diverse linguistic, ideological, ethnic and socio-cultural value forms. Thus, countries such as Japan, China and Korea, share some geographic and historic similarities, and others, such as Indonesia, Malaysia and Singapore demonstrate some common ethnic, linguistic and socio-cultural characteristics. Nevertheless, significant differences exist with respect to the stages of economic development, political ideologies, government structures and influences, and religions of these nations.

The primary objective of this book is to examine the ways in which global, regional, and national factors have impacted on the development of esoteric managerial cultures and styles in the Asian countries represented. This chapter builds on the foregoing discussion by presenting an interpretative conceptual model (Asian Management Model) which will illuminate the subsequent country-specific chapters, and encourage a deeper understanding of the management processes and practices employed in the region, and their underpinning heritages. As each chapter has been contributed either by an author from the particular country or one with significant local knowledge and experience, and as they have been written from its national perspective, both the heterogeneity and the homogeneity of the chosen countries are represented in their application of the model. As Rowley and Benson (2002) note, the development of all countries is dynamic rather than static, and Asian management systems and styles reflect diverse historical, cultural and national characteristics, and thus '... divergent and contradictory practices may well exist within one society'(p. 94).

The convergent/and divergent process model for management, (Figure 2.1) attempts to address all of the above complexities by incorporating macro-, meso-,

Figure 2.1 The convergent–divergent process model for management in Asia

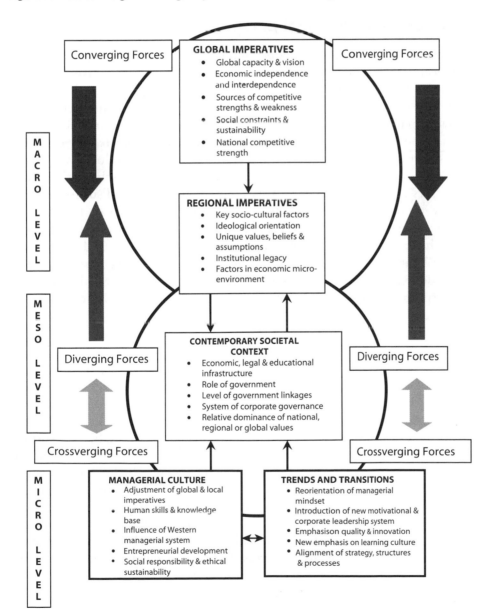

and micro-level perspectives within an overall analytical framework for the understanding of management patterns and processes in eight Asian countries – namely, China, India, Japan, Singapore, South Korea, Malaysia, Thailand and Indonesia. It emphasises how the 'push' and 'pull' influences of prevailing and countervailing influences and forces contribute to the convergent and divergent dimensions implicit in regional, national and local dynamism. The next section discusses the factors implicated for management at macro-regional, meso-societal, and micro-organisational levels.

Macro (or regional)-level perspectives

At the macro-level, *global imperatives* and the *forces of heritage* are positioned in a dialectical relationship. *Global imperatives* represent the convergent management paradigm, whilst the *forces of heritage* (regional, national and local) provide divergent influences. Thus, globalisation encourages universalistic and normative managerial approaches for the purposes of greater efficiency, productivity and competitiveness, through global business strategies, organisational structures and cultures in order to standardise production systems, ensure economies of scale, and staffing flexibilities. Conversely, regional and local factors constrain these imperatives, both consciously and subconsciously, and may in some situations modify the impact and nature of these global imperatives, as indicated by the arrows in the model. Examples of the latter include the cross-transference of total quality management (TQM) techniques from the United States to Japan, and vice versa; the growing significance of Asian-style business networking systems to Europe and the United States; and the incorporation of Sun Tze's 'Art of War' techniques in Western strategic management repertoires.

As illustrated, *global imperatives* (the 'push' factor) encompass a number of interrelated elements, including: 'global capability and vision' (which encompass *both* the perspectives of global businesses *and* the ability of Asian countries to understand, accept and implement them); 'economic dependence and interdependence' (the capability and willingness of Asian countries to conform with or to resist global forces); 'sources of competitive strengths and weaknesses'; 'social constraints and sustainability'; and 'national competitive strength'. Not surprisingly, the elements of the *forces of heritage* (the 'pull' factor) represent the parallel but converse regional or national characteristics, including 'key socio-cultural factors'; 'ideological orientation'; 'unique values, benefits and assumptions'; 'institutional legacy', and 'factors in the economic micro-environment', which enable (or disable) them in the adoption of global managerial philosophies and practices. These 'forces' form the basis of all the subsequent chapters which explore the dynamic environments for business and management in the eight Asian countries.

Salamon (1997) suggests that the overall limitations on convergence in management philosophies and practices include the following divergence aspects:

- countries with different stages of industrial and economic development;

- distinctive political and economic frameworks;

- unique value systems, cultural features and institutions;

- intra-national heterogeneity;

- different choices at macro-(societal) and micro-(organisational) levels on the nature, content, and process of employment relations;

- divergence between stated institutional frameworks and practice;

- variations in the spread, take-up, and operation of technology; and

- alternative solutions to common problems.

This book argues that in varying degrees all of these aspects apply in the Asian nations discussed. However diverse these countries may be, the region contains sufficient homogeneity to permit their grouping as a separate geopolitical entity which has developed and continues to share a distinctive managerial identity.

Meso (or societal)-level perspectives

As the model illustrates, the dynamic tension between global imperatives and the forces of heritage in the region influences, and is influenced by, the *contemporary societal context* in the Asian region as a whole, and in all constituent countries. Whilst factors such as: 'economic, legal, and educational infrastructure'; the 'role of government'; 'levels of global linkages'; the 'system of corporate governance'; and the 'relative dominance of national, regional or global values' are usually established progressively as societies develop, global imperatives exert continuous pressure to modify them to reflect transnational and regional business goals and objectives. Thus, China's educational, administrative and economic infrastructure derives from its Confucian and socialist heritages; India's administrative bureaucracy and adversarial industrial relations system are largely the legacy of British colonialism; the pragmatic and interventionist style of Singapore's government is a consequence of history and ideology; the Malaysian and Indonesian legal frameworks are, respectively, based on English and Dutch law, together with traditional cultural influences. Whilst colonialism can be seen as an earlier form of globalisation, the more recent global forces have transformed many of these societal features with a consequential 'domino' effect on managerial philosophies and processes. However, this change process involves appropriation and assimilation resulting in an amalgam of traditional and global influences rather than the replacement of one by the other.

Thus, while China is currently undertaking significant industrial and economic change in its movement towards global competitiveness that involves: the restructuring of its economically inefficient state owned enterprises (SOEs); enhanced mechanisms for corporate governance; and increasing flexibilities in its regulatory frameworks, it aims to retain its guiding socialist ideology – a market economy with 'Chinese characteristics'. Similarly, Indonesia's recovery from the combination of the 1997 'Asian economic crisis', significant political disruption, the terrorist incidents in Bali and Jakarta, and a catastrophic tsunami in Aceh in 2004, will require support from global finance and corporate investment institutions, the application of global corporate governance standards, and the reduction of corrupt practices. However, these development actions will be implemented within a system dominated by Islamic values, widespread illiteracy, poor infrastructure, and geographic fragmentation. With no colonial history, Thailand has developed its own esoteric societal context, but its economic competitiveness was threatened seriously by its lack of corporate governance, which resulted in the collapse of its currency in 1997. Recovery will be dependent on the development of more transparent accounting systems, in compliance with global imperatives. In line with global trends which now emphasise the economic role of services and the competitive advantages associated with research and innovation capacities, the modernisation of educational infrastructure, in terms of provision, course content, and pedagogical methods, is crucial for all the above Asian countries.

Micro- (or organisational) level

The micro-level reflects the global, regional and national forces described above, and the divergence-convergence dichotomy, as expressed in the design and structure of organisations; their business strategies; their relationships with competitors, suppliers, employees and their associations, and especially with their local communities. At the micro-level this divergence–convergence dichotomy is expressed principally in the *managerial culture(s)* which have developed as a consequence of the nations' particular geographical, historical, political, social, cultural, and industrial legacies. However, as earlier suggested, '… divergent and contradictory practices may well exist within one society' (Rowley and Benson 2002, p. 94) and, arguably, these are most likely to be displayed at the micro-level.

Thus, the 'adjustment of global and local imperatives' for individual organisations might (and do) vary considerably with regard to:

● product or service quality control, marketing strategies and consumers, managerial styles, human resources (HR) and employment conditions;

● dependence on factors such as ownership (for example, multinational versus local corporations, Korean 'chaebol' family-based conglomerates versus small Chinese family companies, state-owned enterprises (SOE) in China, and corporations such as Temasek Holdings associated with the Singapore government);

- location (for example, urban versus rural organisations in Indonesia, Thailand and Malaysia; companies in China's Special Economic Zones); ideological influences (Beijing versus Shanghai in China, Islamic values and Sharia laws in Malaysia and Indonesia, Kerala's socialist state in India); and

- the nature of products and services (for example, information technology and telecommunications versus traditional handicraft organisations).

'The human skills and knowledge base' also differ between and within regional countries, although all, except perhaps Japan and Korea, have significant skills shortages in the managerial, professional and technical disciplines. By contrast, China and India have massive surpluses of unskilled and semi-skilled workers, while Singapore has labour scarcities in these areas for entirely different reasons. The latter has been importing migrant workers for many years from Thailand, Indonesia, Sri Lanka, and more recently China, to fill its vacancies in lower level jobs in the construction and hospitality industries, as well as domestic support positions. Similarly, the knowledge bases of all countries differ according to their stage of economic development, the buoyancy of their financial situation, or their degree of exposure to western management models and technological innovation.

The latter issue, with its associated 'Western managerial system' influence, is perhaps the crux of the convergence–divergence conundrum, and certainly different Asian countries have diverse experiences in their adaptation or incorporation of Western influences in the development of their managerial cultures and practices. The colonial histories and legacies of countries such as Malaysia, Indonesia, Singapore and India have been much longer and more pervasive than those of Thailand, Japan, Korea and even China, although all have been exposed to these influences to some degree. More recently, a surge in the activity of multinational corporations throughout the region, the acceptance of English as the international business language, and the dynamic and potentially destabilising community effects of media such as television, mobile telephony and the Internet, together with the modernisation of educational systems, have ensured that all regional countries are aware of Western social and managerial values and functions.

In the last decade, the 'Asian Values' movement throughout the region was an obvious attempt to resist some of these pressures and influences, and to replace them with more traditional values. Nevertheless, the impact of the 'Asian economic crisis' was largely to neutralise it, or at least to put this resistive approach on hold. The Asian economic crisis spelt a temporary end of the rise of the regionally-prized 'Asian tigers', and emphasised the need for more accountable and transparent Western-style financial systems to remove risk and rebuild investor confidence. In addition, the level of dependence on Western institutions such as the World Bank and the World Trade Organisation increased. China, Indonesia, Malaysia, Thailand, Korea, Singapore and even India and Japan have become more globally dependent as a consequence of these developments.

Despite this, many organisations remain firmly attached to more traditional social and managerial values, and it is arguable that the growing 'entrepreneurial development' in countries such as China, Korea, Malaysia, Indonesia and Thailand, amongst others, is based upon and derives its potency from such values and systems as *guanxi*, *mianxi*, national and regional networking, the flexibility of formal and informal regulations and communication systems, shared languages and cultural traditions. There is also considerable evidence that foreign companies wishing to do business in regional countries increasingly need to understand and apply local approaches in order to penetrate these markets, and so need to adapt their management styles and processes accordingly.

'Social responsibility and ethical sustainability' are constructs derived from global, regional, national, and local sources. Thus, all Asian countries have strong familial values, respect for their elders, avowed responsibilities to their nations, communities and kin, and commitment to the sustainability of their physical environments and traditional cultures to different degrees, based upon moral, religious, ideological and political systems and beliefs. The influence of Western value systems and, in particular, the need to ally these with economic imperatives has been to enshrine them as necessities for global competitiveness. Recovery from the 1997 economic crisis, and China's requirements for its recent admission to the World Trade Organisation, have ensured that regional managers will factor these elements into their strategic business plans as well as their managerial cultures. Conceivably, this will contribute to the gradual reduction or elimination of such aberrations as nepotism, cronyism, and corruption, which arguably in some cases, actually reflected the positive Asian values discussed earlier.

Trends and transitions

Earlier sections of this chapter have explained the elements of the Asian Management Model, presented as an analytical and interpretive lens through which the similarities and differences of Asian societal and business contexts, and consequent managerial cultures may be explored, within an overarching global convergence–divergence dichotomy. Having examined the complex series of factors which apply through the region, as a whole and in each country, the following chapters develop the similar and diverse applications of some common themes of Asian management philosophies and systems. These include the 'reorientation of managerial mindset', the 'introduction of new motivational and corporate leadership systems', an increasing emphasis on 'quality and innovation', a 'new emphasis on a culture of learning', and closer alignments of 'strategy, structure and processes'. These issues have been addressed earlier in the chapter, and will be explored in considerable detail in the following country-specific chapters. However, the Asian Management Model is intended to be used as a framework to promote holistic understanding of the characteristics of Asian management within its global, regional, and local contexts. Overall, the theme of the book encompasses the combined influences of tradition, transition and transformation on management in the Asian region.

Plan of the book

The book consists of four parts, divided into eleven chapters. Part I contains the opening chapter and this one, which together provide a conceptual overview of the dynamic nature of Asian management, a rationale for the differentiation of Asian from Western management styles through the application of the convergence-divergence debate. More particularly, these concepts are integrated into Figure 2.1: The convergence/divergence process model for management as an explanation for management in the Asian region.

Part II, entitled *The management challenges in large Asian nations*, explores the societal contexts, managerial cultures, trends and transitions in three large countries, namely China, India and Japan. The chapter on China examines the managerial implications consequent on its transition from a socialist to a market economy, and from an isolationist to a global mindset, whilst the chapter on India traces the positive and negative aspects of its traditional and colonial heritages, together with more modern influences in the information technology and telecommunications industries. In the context of increasingly closer governmental and business alliances between China and India, these chapters provide understanding of the similarities and differences in their respective development of management processes and practices. As the former pre-eminent Asian economy, Japan's challenges include its recovery from a decade-long decline, and the restructuring of its industries and management approaches to meet the needs of a modern workforce and global competitiveness.

Part III, entitled *The management challenges in small and dynamic Asian nations*, discusses similar management issues in relation to Korea, Singapore and Malaysia. Whilst these countries share some common traditional and heritage aspects with the larger Asian nations, their different challenges are dependent on their particular histories and stages of economic development. Singapore and Korea are both examples of the former 'Asian tigers', but since the 1997 Asian economic crisis both have been confronted with reformist pressures and the need to incorporate both global and more traditional management systems. Of the two, Singapore arguably suffered the most from the crisis, is the least resource-rich, and has most constrained local entrepreneurialism due to the prevailing influence of its government. Malaysia, in contrast, is resource-rich and is strongly influenced by Islamic values, but has been somewhat limited by an internationally antagonistic style of leadership, now replaced by a more collaborative and modernising Islamic leadership approach.

Part IV, entitled *The management challenges in complex Asian Nations*, explores the societal contexts and managerial cultures in Thailand and Indonesia. Their histories, and their recent economic and political difficulties, have been quite dissimilar from those of many of their regional neighbours, and consequently their management styles and processes display common and disparate characteristics. The final chapter concludes the book by elucidating the significant themes which underlie each of the country chapters in relation to the factors included in the Asian Management Model.

Each chapter is loosely based on the following structure, but as the book seeks to promote broad-based understanding of the evolving and interdependent relationships between national discourse, community identity and local organisational and behavioural approaches to management, there may be some differences in the application of the structure in particular chapters. Section 1 of each chapter focuses on the macro-regional level perspectives and identifies how the key local influences and external forces that derive from the specific geography and history of each country have together shaped the prevailing socio-cultural values of the society. The discussion following this section identifies how the community ideology derived from the prevailing socio-cultural values plays a pivotal role in shaping the key political and economic institutions and macro-level strategic approaches applied to national discourse, leadership, community governance and corporate management as embodied in each nation's development vision. Thus, this macro-level discussion, in turn, provides insights into the various kinds of community, institutional and organisational-based strategies each nation applies to manage the nation's political, economic and societal spheres, in order to respond to the increasingly competitive and interdependent pressures brought to bear by the global economy and the sustainable development imperative.

The second section focuses more closely on the meso-societal level to examine the key societal and industrial infrastructure of each nation and more specifically the various institutional and organisational systemic governance and management approaches applied to mobilise its national development vision. Thus key issues, such as: the role of the government; the industry structure, logistics and system of corporate governance; the economic, legal and educational infrastructure; the prevailing corporate mindset; and those associated with international and inter-regional business relationships are explored. Generally, this section identifies the duplicitous tensions often associated with national transitional governance and management strategies that attempt to reconcile political, economic and community issues and productively respond to divergent and convergent local, national and global values and imperatives.

The third section explores how the issues presented in the first two sections manifest in the management patterns and processes at the micro-organisational level. Hence, the focus is on issues that relate to the specific managerial culture of each nation, that is how the prevailing and countervailing culture-based patterns and processes impact on leadership, organisational structure, decision-making, the human resource capacity, development and management system, entrepreneurial approach, the influence of external management systems (western and regional), and how each nation is adjusting to global and local imperatives at the micro-level. Discussion on the nature and quality of these adjustments include the reformist and the new direction initiatives associated with transformation such as: a reorientation of the managerial mindset; the introduction of new approaches to motivational and corporate leadership; commitment to quality and innovation, and how commitment in this direction links with commitment to the requisite 'learning culture-based' pedagogical transformation, along with the facilitation of the managerial alignment of strategy, structure and processes as conceived to build and sustain competitive organisational performance.

Finally, the discussion in each of the three sections identifies and explains how the dynamic and evolving convergent and divergent forces as manifest in prevailing and countervailing global, national and local societal values and national visions variously refract through the governance and management strategies and practices of the eight Asian countries included in the book. Hence, both shared and divergent values, and similar and distinctive societal and managerial characteristics can be identified. Nevertheless, each of the following chapters aims to promote more complex understanding of the diversity that derives from the unique national societal and managerial characteristics found in the dynamic Asian region.

Questions

1. Explain the differences in management issues and practices at macro- and micro-levels in a chosen Asian nation.
2. Discuss the relative importance of global and national influences on Asian management.
3. Argue the cases for *and* against the 'convergence' of management paradigms in Asia.

References

Rowley C & Benson J, 2002, Convergence and divergence in Asian human resource management, *California Management Review*, vol. 44, no. 2 Winter, pp. 90–109.

Salamon M, 1997, *Industrial relations: Theory and practice*, Prentice-Hall, London.

Additional readings

Bartlett, C & Ghoshal, S, 2000, 'Going global: Lessons from late movers', *Harvard Business Review*, vol. 78, no. 2 March–April, pp. 132–42.

Chow, I, Holbert, N, Kelly, L & Yu, J, 2004, *Business strategy: An Asia-Pacific focus*, Pearson Prentice Hall, UK.

Deresky, H, 2006, *International management: Managing across borders and cultures*, 5th edn, Pearson Prentice Hall, New Jersey.

Joynt, P & Warner, M, 1996, *Managing across cultures: Issues and perspectives*, International Thomson Business Press, London.

Trompenaars, F, 1994, *Riding the waves of culture*, Nicholas Brealey, London.

Yip, GS, 2001, *Asian advantage: Key strategies for winning in the Asia-Pacific region*, Perseus Publishing, Cambridge MA.

The management challenges of large Asian nations

Three major Asian economies: China, India and Japan

The three large Asian nations included in this first section of the book are all of immense importance not only to the region, but increasingly to the rest of the world. Whilst on the one hand, Japan has been in economic decline for more than a decade, there are encouraging signs that it is gradually beginning to recover from its malaise and to maintain its global significance. China and India, on the other hand, currently display the highest growth in Gross Domestic Product (GDP) in the region, with China's manufacturing strength and India's information technology dominance. The three countries have been influenced by similar and different philosophical and ideological influences, variously including Confucianism, Hinduism, Communism, colonialism, and more recently, capitalism, and they are all at different stages of industrial development.

Whilst Japan is, of course, a highly developed nation, with comprehensive legal, economic, political and industrial infrastructures, both China and India are rapidly establishing similar industry support structures. However, both India and China have significant agricultural sectors, and compared to Japan's primary focus on the growing global services sector (74 per cent of the economy), both are somewhat behind in this area (India – 48 per cent, China – 33 per cent) if growing. Both similarities and differences can be observed in the Chinese and Indian large family-owned companies, and the Japanese cartels. These are explained in the following chapters.

The relative 'quality of life' of each of the countries can be observed in their Human Development Index (HDI) ratings (see Chapter 1). The HDI shows that individuals' quality of life is lowest in India (127), better in China (94), but by far the best (9) in Japan. It is inevitable that these ratings will change in the future as China's move towards a modern market economy increases its pace, and as India's relative political stability and economic growth lead to the broader spread of prosperity across its population. The associated relative levels of corruption, as measured by the Corruption Transparency Index (CDI), are highest in India (90), medium in China (71), and less but by no means completely absent in Japan (24).

All three countries espouse shared community values, derived from both similar and different philosophical origins, including the importance of the family, collectivism, thrift, social conservatism and a respect for authority. Consequently, management styles and processes reflect these values, albeit in somewhat different ways, and with different reflections in their employer–employee relationships at macro-, meso-, and micro-societal levels. These issues, and many others, are discussed in the following three chapters.

Managing global integration, national values and local development in China

To describe the historical and philosophical 3.1
context of the People's Republic of China (PRC).

To explain the major political, socio-cultural and 3.2
economic influences on management in the PRC.

To outline how regional and local influences, and 3.3
global forces impact on Chinese management.

To explore the linkages between macro-, meso-, and 3.4
micro-level factors in Chinese management, and

To explain the major features of Chinese 3.5
managerial values, systems and practices.

Introduction

China's economy is evolving from a planned socialist economy, with centralist government-based administrative, legislative and institutional frameworks and structures, to a more market-based economy undergoing significant administrative, regulatory and institutional reform. This dramatic reform relates to China's strategic approach to integrate its national economy into the global economy. This integration strategy, along with subsequent high rates of economic growth and its growing importance in the global marketplace, means that both international business and academics now focus attention on understanding the changing management practices of China. However, the dynamic and rapid nature of this macro-level economic transformation contributes to mixed, complex and evolving corporate and community management systems at the macro-, meso- and micro management levels.

Thus, management approaches based on traditional Confucian values operate side-by-side with collectivist and institutionalised bureaucratic management approaches, together with more recently introduced and pragmatic international management approaches. Consequently, pluralistic human resource management practices varying from traditional hierarchical and collectivist administrative and supportive roles and functions coexist with those based on merit-based recruitment and reward systems. With increasing competition, brought about by globalisation and China's membership of the World Trade Organisation (WTO), production has become more technologically-geared, market-oriented and quality-driven. The state-owned enterprises (SOEs) are undergoing fundamental changes and state control components are losing their significance in the gross national product (GNP). The current Chinese leadership now faces critical management and institutional reform challenges associated with maintaining sustainable levels of economic growth, and the facilitation of a more even distribution of economic development across the country. Addressing economic disparity will be crucial to maintain broad-based community support for the significant transformation processes underway, and the social and political stability that is essential in a dynamic and potentially volatile national context.

The macro-regional level: Local issues and external forces influencing the management context of China

The title of this chapter indicates that China faces considerable corporate and community management challenges which are associated with its various responses to global imperatives, the forces of heritage and the diverse nature of local issues associated with the vast nature of the territory of China. The enormity of China's recent economic success in the global marketplace means that China has now become the new global macro-level force destabilising existing global and regional economic power relations. This power shift means that a dialectical process is taking place between China and its particular economic development and managerial approach, and the prevailing 'universalist' approach to international management. This section discusses how the recent dramatic corporate, institutional and societal transformational processes relate to complex macro-level management strategies which attempt to reconcile deeply entrenched local influences with the powerful external forces associated with global economic market integration. This next section discusses the macro-level implications for management of key local heritage influences and global imperatives.

The forces of heritage: A brief history of Chinese management concepts

During the last two decades of the twentieth century, one of the greatest economic revolutions took place in the People's Republic of China (PRC). In that time, under the leadership of Deng Xiaoping (1977–97), the Chinese economy underwent a dramatic but pragmatic reform process to achieve the goals of the Four Modernisations – the modernisation of industry, agriculture, defence, science and technology. An open door and market reform policy approach was introduced in 1978. Since these broad ranging strategic reform policies were introduced understanding Chinese management practices has become crucial to foreign investors who intend to set up manufacturing, or trading activities in the 'land of the dragon'. China has a long history and the longevity of the 'Middle Kingdom' heritage means that the Chinese purview on change is extensively long-term oriented. This longevity also means that the socio-cultural legacy associated with the Middle Kingdom heritage is deeply embedded in the Chinese world view. Hence, important historical notions that were laid down a long time ago are still culturally significant today:

> China took shape as a political entity in the first millennium BC, and until the 20th century largely remained a coherent empire governed by scholar officials after the Confucian vision of a meritocratic, ordered society. Even foreign conquerors like the Mongols (1279) and Manchus (1644) did not change the essential character of Chinese society, and became partly Sinicised themselves. The attitude towards outsiders was primarily one of condescension. (The Economist, 29 January 2004)

China's long history means that the cultural logic of Confucian and other important cultural influences buried deep within Chinese world views play a pivotal role in guiding Chinese thinking and behaviour. Moreover, the longevity of Confucianism in framing the guiding principles for social organisation indicates its success in sustaining the Chinese empire through its dynamic history within a changing global context. Thus, the cultural assumptions that derive from early history still have a significant effect on how businesses and people are managed in the contemporary corporate and community context. More recently, these early socio-cultural and political concepts were reinterpreted and interwoven with Marxist/Leninist ideas to frame the collectivist socio-political logic that in the second half of the twentieth century and under the powerful leadership role of Mao Zedong, shaped the PRC. Subsequently, as a strategic response to the economic impact of globalisation, more liberalised and open market-oriented corporate and community management policies have been implemented. Thus, the 'modus operandi' of China's management practices is based on foundations that range from Confucianism to the economic thoughts of Presidents Mao Zedong, Deng Xiaoping, Jiang Zemin and Hu Jintao. The modern Chinese approach to management can be divided into four stages: traditional thoughts, Mao Zedong's thoughts, Deng Xiaoping's thoughts and post-Deng thoughts. These stages emphasise the crucial role of the leadership in shaping the evolving nature of Chinese management.

Traditional thoughts

The frequently quoted historical 'great sages' that have had significant effects on Chinese value systems are: Confucius (551–479 BC), Mencius (372–289 BC), Xunzi (297–238 BC), Sunzi (551–470 BC), Hanfeizi (280–233 BC) (Lui, 1996), and even the 'First Emperor' Qin Shihuang (Fukuda, 1998). Table 3.1 summarises some of the key historical ideas that have distinctively shaped the culture of Chinese management and the corresponding twentieth-century notions in Western management. The great differential in the development timeframe between these Chinese and Western management notions is of great significance to the Chinese

Table 3.1 Key traditional management ideas and corresponding Western management ideas

Chinese philosophers	Main Chinese management thoughts	Corresponding Western management thoughts
Confucius	◆ Rules of etiquette ◆ Rules of virtue	◆ Business ethics & managerial controls
Mencius	◆ Harmony ◆ Rules of benevolence & righteousness ◆ Virtuous human nature	◆ Division of labour ◆ Education & training ◆ Theory Y
Xunzi	◆ Evil human nature ◆ Importance of human needs, sense of responsibility & human relations	◆ Theory X ◆ Hierarchy of needs & ◆ Social Science school
Sunzi	◆ The Art of War ◆ The importance of planning, organising and directing ◆ The importance of positive motivation	◆ Strategic management ◆ Organisation theory ◆ Motivational theories: Expectancy and equity
Hanfeizi	◆ Rule by law ◆ The importance of the relationship between the leader & the group ◆ Rewards and punishment	◆ School of legalists ◆ Chain of command ◆ Behavioural theory
Qin Shihuang	◆ Centralised government ◆ Bureaucratic organisation ◆ Standardisation & strict application of laws	◆ Centralisation versus decentralisation ◆ Theory of bureaucracy (Weber) ◆ Legalism

who place great pride on this ancient intellectual heritage along with their capacity to adapt and apply these historical ideas to a modern global economic context. The value of any attempt to study the history of this early Chinese thinking cannot be underestimated by anyone wishing to be involved in business with China and to gain a deeper understanding of Chinese approaches to management.

Historical Pre-Reforms

Mao Zedong's thoughts

Chairman Mao was the supreme leader of the Chinese Communist Party who, in 1949 successfully led the political party to the proclamation of the foundation of the PRC. He held the powerful role of 'supreme leader' of China until his death in 1978. His charismatic style of leadership, a centrally planned economic development model and a collectivist political governance strategy, brought to an end the ongoing internal factional fighting and external international interference associated with historical western and more recently Japanese imperial activity. Chairman Mao's collectivist community governance concepts and dedicated struggle to win the leadership have had significant effects on the current population of 1,284.3 million (Economist.com, 2004), in general, and on management practices, in particular, in modern China (Yun, 1998). He had a grand national

Table 3.2 Mao's management thoughts

Management and leadership system: Democratic centralism & party rule	Quality of managers: Political awareness, sacrifice, independence, & consciousness	Managerial methodology Pragmatism, people-oriented, & convergence
Appointment of staff: By ability & coaching	Democratic management: Collective leadership & participative management	Ideological work: Very important, using persuasion & education to uphold Marxism & Leninism

policy vision for the successes of agricultural and industrial collectives. Many of his philosophical sayings have been used as guiding principles especially in the management of the SOEs, and literal interpretations of Mao's philosophy were consistently applied. The planned social economy meant that the state powerfully engaged with all aspects of people's lives. The management implications of Mao's thoughts are summarised in Table 3.2.

In the leadership tradition of a powerful Chinese emperor, Mao ruled supreme. However, his didactically managed and often coercively applied collectivist agricultural policies resulted in famine, and the subsequent austerity experienced during the Cultural Revolution contributed to both political and social turmoil.

Deng Xiaoping's ideas

After Chairman Mao died the Chinese Communist Party (CCP) was open to a new reformist governance and management approach. As 'paramount leader', Chairman Deng Xiaoping adopted a pragmatic reformist approach to economic management, concentrating in particular on this strategic area rather than on political reform. The maintenance of a centralist and collectivist socio-political approach to governance indicates the leadership's strong belief in China's need for this national political governance approach so as to be able to manage social cohesion across the extensive Chinese territory and across rural and urban economic community disparity. The increased importance of the global market economy presented new manufacturing opportunities for economic development in China.

Through the successful promotion and adoption of a pragmatic approach to economic reform Deng Xiaoping has extensively contributed to the development of more internationalised management practices in China. Deng adopted a Confucian-based management doctrine and provided more autonomy to the local governments and local enterprises (Fukuda, 1998). Confucianism teaches that one should be loyal to one's family, friends and rulers and treat others as one would like to be treated. Moreover, it teaches that people are not equal, that they play different roles in society and hence, the behaviour of people is regulated by special relationships that dictate their obligations to each other (Lewis, 2003).

Figure 3.1 Economic growth levels of the Chinese economy (1992–2004)

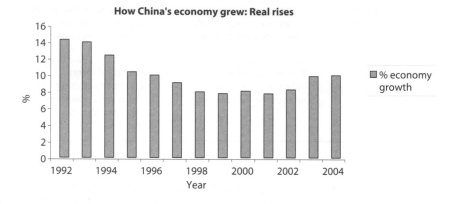

Source: IMF, cited in Shanahan, *The Weekend Australian*. April 16–17, 2005, p. 32.

The pragmatic approach which underpins Deng's new economic development guidelines included the following management strategies:

- Manage by taking into account the actual situation in China and through the application of management approaches that incorporate Chinese cultural assumptions;

- Be scientific and practical;

- Focus more on 'responsibility' systems and rewards for increases in productivity;

- Open China's doors selectively to private and joint venture enterprises; and

- Advocate socialist marketing concepts, which in essence directed Chinese enterprises towards modern marketing management.

Recognising that China needed Western technology and investment, the transformation process was initiated in 1978 when Deng Xiaoping announced a new 'open door' policy. This strategy was linked to considerable agricultural reform and the establishment of four special economic zones (SEZs) in the south of China offering tax incentives to attract foreign investment and business. The majority of early activity came from overseas Chinese investors. The adoption of Deng Xiaoping's economic reformist approach over two decades meant that China's engagement with Western capitalist economies grew significantly. Figure 3.1 indicates the dramatic and sustained high levels of economic growth achieved through the latter part of Deng's leadership and the subsequent period up to now.

Post-Deng reformist ideas

After the death of Deng in 1997, a range of national and international events and issues meant that the leadership recognised that additional reform to Chinese management approaches was required if the nation was to continue to flourish under a market-orientation. In particular, the following events have together been catalysts in shaping the pragmatic directions of the economic reform process:

- the return of the sovereignty of Hong Kong (1997) and Macao (1999) to China;

- the Asian financial turmoil in 1977–1999, the admission of China into the WTO in 2001;

- the nomination of Beijing for the Olympics in 2008; followed by

- the SARS crisis; and more recently
- the significant geo-political shifts in regional power.

Just catalysts

With the Chinese economy increasingly interconnected to the global economy, the new CCP leadership (President Jiang Zemin, 1997–2002; and President Hu Jintao 2002–07 five-year terms) has responded to the new and interrelated global, national and local economic management challenges by proposing a range of reform measures to indicate that there will be:

- a greater emphasis on market mechanisms and pragmatism (i.e., profit seeking motives will continue to dominate management practices);

- an acceleration of market openness and the establishment of more global and multinational businesses in China that will result in greater convergence of Chinese management styles and some Western practices; and hence,

- management issues associated with institutional strengthening, human resource management (HRM) and capacity development, and business ethics are expected to take on more significance for both Chinese and international management.

The political system

While the economic system has undergone significant reform over the last thirty years and the Chinese economy has increasingly opened up and become more integrated into the global market economy, there has been considerable resistance to direct political reform as an approach to the governance of China. Indicating the momentum for economic reform over political reform Deng Xiaoping is widely quoted as having said that: 'To get rich is glorious'. The implication of this saying in a Chinese cultural context is that it is everyone's collective responsibility to pursue this glorious economic goal. Nevertheless, the CCP remains all-powerful in both the appointment of the nation's leaders and the determination of the nation's strategic direction. Moreover, it is crucial that those engaging in business relations in China understand the powerful influence of the CCP:

> The CCP is a secretive, selective organisation of about sixty-five million members who have positions of influence in all sectors of Chinese society, whether as village leaders, university officials, factory managers, newspaper editors or bureaucrats in change of everything from public health to police intelligence. The Party's national congress consists of about two thousand persons divided into provincial delegations, elected by Party members throughout the country. It meets once every five years to elect a Central Committee, currently of about 370 persons. (Nathan and Gilley, 2003, p. 7)

Hence, the Chinese political system is described as a national version of the classical Leninist party-state and, more particularly, one that has applied a form of personal authoritarianism in which one leader holds the highest authority in all systems of power – Party, state, and military (Nathan and Gilley, 2003). This all encompassing leadership role has its roots in the longstanding cultural heritage of the all wise and all powerful Chinese emperor. The country's potentially more democratic institutions include the National People's Congress (NPC) who are mostly Party members, while the Chinese People's Political Consultative Conference (CPPCC) includes respected representatives of academia, business and the professions, who 'are invited to show their support for CCP rule and offer suggestions for improving government' (Nathan and Gilley, 2003, p. 10).

The new Politburo, elected in 2002 under President Hu Jintao and Premier Wen Jiabao both replicates many of the characteristics of the Jiang Zemin leadership, but at the same time is strikingly distinct from the generation of revolutionary leaders, such as Mao Zedong and Deng Xiaoping (Lyman Miller, 2003). The distinctive characteristics of the new leadership include:

● A younger leadership with an average of 60 years of age, in contrast to the 72 years of age in 1982;

● The best educated in PRC history, with 22 of the 25 members of the new Politburo being university educated;

● The new leadership is strongly technical in background, with 16 of the 22 being trained as engineers (including President Hu Jintao), one in military engineering, one geology (Premier Wen Jiabao), two in economics, or management, one military academy and one in humanities (philosophy);

● Most of the new Politburo only saw their careers take off with the onset of reforms inaugurated by Deng Xiaoping in the later 1970s;

● Many have no military experience; and

● Greater plurality with the leadership – 11 of 25 come from coastal provinces, 4 trace their origins to Manchurian provinces, 5 to north China (Hebei, Shanxi and Shaanxi) and 4 to the central-south (Jiangxi, Hubei and Hunan) (Lyman Miller, 2003, pp. 60–61).

Nevertheless, others view President Hu Jintao as 'the ultimate product of the system ... He never studied overseas or had much contact with the outside world. He was educated by the system, spent his entire career in the system, and his values are the same as the system's' (Pan, 2005, p. A01).

Under this new leadership it is predicted that ongoing pragmatic-based economic reform will continue to promote growth and development through further integration into the international economy. The logic underpinning this pragmatic economic reform approach, when coupled with the deeply embedded collectivist socio-cultural values, is that the fruits of economic success will negate the needs for political reform. 'If anything, the Communist Party in China is tightening its grip ... There is a new emphasis on the strength of the party'. In a recent speech President Hu Jintao focused on 'a campaign to maintain the "advanced nature" of the party to "strengthen the building of the party's ruling capabilities" and to maintain the "advanced nature of party members" '. 'In a recent development, senior bureaucrats are reportedly required to engage in time-consuming "political study" ' (Ryan, 2005, p. 23). Instead of pursuing restructuring and reform of economic institutions (i.e., restructuring the banking system or reform of stock markets) President Hu has:

> Focused the economic policy of shifting resources to the country's poorer interior and promoting what he calls a 'scientific development concept,' which officials have described as an attempt to balance economic growth with concerns about the environment, the welfare of rural farmers and workers, and a widening income gap. (Pan, 2005, p. A01)

The evolving Chinese characteristic cultural, political and economic thinking of the leaders during these four distinct modern historical periods have variously shaped the special characteristics and features of contemporary management in China. While the process of economic reform has occurred in an extremely short timeframe, in practice the very strong residual cultural influences of many earlier characteristics included in Chinese management approaches prevail. As a result, Chinese management in practice embodies the following particular characteristics, or features that can be summarised to include:

- A unique form of management with a long history and cultural flavour;

- An holistic concern for workers' home and working lives; lifetime employment; non-standardised and slow evaluation and promotion procedures; horizontal career paths; and semi participative decision-making (Lindsay and Dempsey, 1985);

- Strong and explicit political and ideological influences and government intervention;

- Diversity, idiosyncrasy, paternalism and egalitarianism; and

- Dual operational tracks of rigid formal systems and flexible informal structures.

During the past twenty-five years of economic reform in China and with the increasing levels of foreign business involvement, investors in China have advocated that common sense is the best guide available (Epner, 1991) in order to cope with the very different Chinese cultural norms and codes of practice. The unique ways in which Chinese institutions, world views and practices have been shaped by history, culture, economics and politics means that foreign investors often complain about the unexpected behaviours of their fellow Chinese managers, and conclude that a Chinese management is essentially an evolving model (Lockett, 1988). Nevertheless, understanding the ways in which the long history of traditional Chinese socio-cultural approaches to societal management, the socially planned economic system that derived from the Communist Revolution, and the more recent economic reform-based and free-market oriented developments in the PRC interweave together, provides a basis on which to comprehend how these have variously influenced the evolving approaches to management in China.

The impact of global imperatives

The key macro-environmental issues in China today relate to the ongoing reform process associated with continuing economic liberalisation and the management challenges associated with maintaining sustainable levels of economic growth. The international community widely promotes the idea that ongoing policy, fiscal and institutional reform is critical for China to fully gain and sustain the benefits of increasing integration into the global economy.

> Reform of loss-making state-owned industry and the indebted financial sector is essential, but here is the risk of generating social-unrest. It is also giving more room to private interest, which may now compete more effectively with state-owned enterprises for markets and resources. (Economist.com, 2004)

In addition, there is both internal Chinese and international concern that the uneven impact of development across the diverse regions of China and, in particular the disparity between rural and urban communities, must be addressed in order to maintain internal political stability. Moreover, addressing important business and community issues, such as environmental management and unemployment will become increasingly important. Recognising the importance of these, the government maintains that sustaining economic growth will provide the best strategy to secure investment in infrastructure, growing employment opportunities, capacity building and performance improvement. Furthermore, the government is applying regional development strategies that attempt to address this economic development disparity between rural and urban communities.

The logic behind the new leadership's strategy to maintain the focus on economic reform pursuing the benefits of development while rejecting direct political reform is that this approach will provide the more stable national environment that is essential to attract investment and sustainable levels of growth. Despite becoming the world's largest recipient of total foreign direct investment (FDI) in 2002, China needs to attract higher levels of foreign investment to underwrite the required investment in human resource capacity development, and new technology to support and improve the performance of industry and institutional administration. This national economic reality creates the paradoxical dilemma of finding ways to balance China's need for US markets, investment and technology, in particular, against the power of the US dominant strategic global position (Lyman Miller, 2003). In addition, there are calls (from the United States in particular) for monetary reform as the Chinese currency (yuan) is pegged to the US dollar at an undervalued fix rate in order to make Chinese exports more competitive. These concerns also raise the issue of attracting diverse forms of FDI:

> In the 25 years since China opened the door to foreign investment, much of the spending has been concentrated in low-technology, labour-intensive manufacturing projects ... China's challenge now is to develop a more transparent business environment with a clear legal and regulatory framework. That should help to attract higher-quality investments that are focused on the long-term, high technology, capital intensive-projects. (OECD, 2003)

For the more ambitious Chinese companies wishing to expand in off-shore markets, there is the challenge of being unknown. Not being prepared to wait to build off-shore customer support ambitious Chinese companies are now taking ownership of well-known foreign companies (Chong, 2005). 'The Chinese government supports 22 companies with global potential ... more Chinese companies will try to buy American companies for distribution, marketing and visibility' (Straszheim, cited in Chong 2005, p. 20). Economic analysts warn of the dark side of the highly competitive cheap pricing strategy of Chinese companies:

> They won market shares by undercutting their foreign rivals with ever low prices. But now they find themselves trapped in hyper-competitive low-margin businesses at home. Their razor thin margins make it almost impossible to accumulate funds to invest in research and development that would enable them to move up the value-added ladder to higher-profit businesses. (Chi Lo, cited in Chong 2005, p. 20)

By the end of 2003 Chinese companies had invested $US33 billion in almost 7500 companies in more than 160 countries (Chong, 2005). At the same time as China is making these market expansion initiatives there are those who believe that China is on the verge of making the sudden transformation from being a global production base to becoming an enormous consumer market (Dossin, cited in Armitage 2005). Nevertheless, with changes in the welfare net the new burgeoning middle class prefer to save rather than spend their money resulting in one of the highest savings rates in the world, with comparatively low consumption (Armitage, 2005).

Nevertheless, despite these various international management perspectives on Chinese reform there is considerable international agreement of the continuing importance of China in the expansion of the global economy. The following facts indicate the colossal importance of China to the global economy: In the past two years China has accounted for one-quarter of the growth in the world economy and in global trade; China is the largest importer of iron ore, accounting for a 34 per cent of the global market and is the second largest importer of oil; It commands international reserves of $US500 billion; by some estimates China accounts for 90 per cent of marginal growth for Japanese and European companies; and Chinese manufacturing is revolutionising global consumer culture: Eighty per cent of US retailer Wal-mart's supplier factories are in China, with the United States now having a SUS164billion trade deficit with China (Sheridan, 2005). Figure 3.2 indicates the predicted expansion of China's output and that this will overtake that of the United States by 2020. This power shift in the global economy has enormous political and economic implications for the Asian region as well as the international community. These facts indicate China's enormous and rapid success in integrating into the global economy and the complexity of international interdependencies with China in sustaining growth in the global economy.

China's economic success has meant that it has already taken on an increasingly important global and regional role. The new leadership has used the term 'the peaceful rise of China' to counter international concern for the potential

Figure 3.2 The projected international shares of global output (2005; 2020)

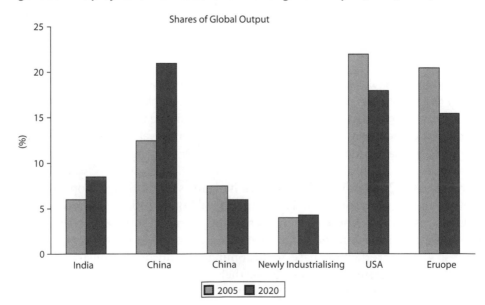

Source: Westpac cited in Shanahan, *The Weekend Australian.* April 16–17, 2005, p. 32.

'clash of powers' model for strategic international relations (He, 2004, p. 4):

> [The new leadership] holds the view that China's path towards becoming a greater power will not follow the logic of conflict as seen in 20th century Europe and Asia. Instead, China's foreign policy focuses on maintaining stability and peace as a basis for economic development. Especially, in the wake of the SARS crisis, Beijing has embraced the concept of being a responsible state and a good international citizen.

Furthermore, the next few years will see an increasing international spotlight on China's corporate and community governance and management approaches, as Beijing moves towards the international scrutiny that will inevitably follow hosting the Olympic Games in 2008.

The meso-societal level: The management of Chinese institutional infrastructure

The complexity of contemporary management structures, systems and styles at the meso-societal level reflects the evolving institutional nature of Chinese infrastructure. The dynamic nature and scale of the evolution at the meso-level means that residual collectivist and centrally controlled structures, systems and styles coexist with radically different and emergent new competitive market-based structures, systems and styles.

The dominant management paradigms and concepts

In light of the complexities and evolving nature of Chinese business approaches, when international organisations conduct business in China, flexibility is recommended as being the key to successful management. Flexibility is required because Chinese managers may employ several management strategies based on the various models made up of a range of principles, systems and approaches (Ye, 1993). These various principles, systems and approaches are indicated in Table 3.3. Some of the five approaches may be unique in the context of the socialist market-oriented economy, while others are derived from Western management principles. The following sections discuss each of these approaches.

Materialistic motivational approach (economic, or market mechanism)

The underlying principle in Deng Xiaoping's reform was that business management should follow the goal of economic development. A study of the 30 different types of enterprises in the Zhejiang province confirmed that material rewards and remuneration (including bonuses) had had significant effects on the performance

Table 3.3 Summary of the basic principles, systems and approaches of Chinese management

Basic principles	Systems	Approaches
Combination of political and economic leadership	Relationship between enterprise owners and managers	● Materialistic motivation (economic) or market mechanism approach.
Combination of centralised leadership and democratic management	Full managerial responsibility of factory managers/general managers	● Administrative approach
Consensus of authority and responsibility	Staff representatives council to monitor enterprise and protect labour welfare	● Legislative approach
Management by effective planning Appropriate staff motivation	Economic responsibility system to enhance productivity	● Social and psychological approach
Acceptable financial management and accounting systems		● Mathematical approach

of enterprises (Cheng et al., 1998). In the materialistic motivational approach to Chinese business management the following practices are applied:

● Economic responsibility system with contracted jobs;

● Wages and bonuses;

● Commodities price;

● Penalties for failure to discharge economic contracts;

● Fixed charges imposed on profits; and

● Material rewards or punishments (Ye, 1993).

These motivational management practices take into consideration the humanitarian and benevolent characteristics inherent in Confucian principles, as well as the psychological value of using rewards to motivate the workers. The average income level of the Chinese workers is still very low, and hence a very small amount of extrinsic rewards enhance their satisfaction. Therefore, the use of tangible, materialistic motivational methods has been considered a very effective tool in maintaining or developing productivity, efficiency, quality and loyalty. However, following the increase in income and foreign investments, talented local PRC managers are now emphasising career development, relationships with superiors and overseas expenses rather than monetary incentives alone (Cheng, 1999).

The special characteristics of using the materialistic motivation approach (or an economic approach) are:

● Indirect effect, non-mandatory to the staff concerned;

● Flexibility in using differential measures for different target groups; and

● Strong economic signals to those affected (Yun, 1998).

However, the following example indicates that this approach may need to be modified in response to changing economic or political circumstances. During the late 1990s Communist Party officials suspended an initiative among 20 SOEs in Shanghai to reward staff with stock options. The initiative, designed to motivate managers and to persuade them to remain in state industries, was stopped because of opposition within the Communist Party which argued that heads of SOEs should not have such high incomes. According to a report in the *South China Morning Post* (May, 1999), a government economist explained that 20 SOEs in Shanghai were giving managers stock options, but that it has been 'frozen now. It is off the agenda for 1999'. This year, he said, is too sensitive due to the significant anniversaries being marked, and the rising social unrest. 'The Shanghai media are not allowed to report for fear of attracting Beijing's attention,' he added. The first State firms to give executive stock options were in Shunde in Guangdong in 1994. Firms in Wenzhou, Zhejiang province and Shanghai followed.

Administrative approach

During the first 50 years of a planned economy, Chinese managers, especially those working in SOEs, or more recently, those having intimate trading activities with them, relied on the guidelines given by senior bureaucrats. Within the context of economic reform and market-oriented business attitudes, this administrative approach, which allows public administrative institutions (such as the State Assets Administrative Commission), or officials to give directives to SOEs, is still widely used. In contrast to the less interventionist approaches of the Western economies, in the PRC the public bureaucratic administrative system has a strong influence over the both private and public sector business management. The maintenance of this top-down and centralist bureaucratic administrative approach is counter to reformist market-based management mechanisms and whilst it may have been effective in dealing with previous turbulent incidents in the short term, in the long term, it should only be used to supplement the economic management approach so that optimum market functioning can be achieved (Yun, 1998).

In summary, the administrative approach is characteristically authoritarian, mandatory, discriminatory, direct, consistent and time-specific. The following example from the *South China Morning Post* (October, 1999) illustrates some of these administrative features together with the legislative approach discussed below. In an effort to promote equal job opportunities for the disabled, Guangzhou passed legislation that obliged enterprises to employ a certain proportion of disabled people in their workforce. Employers that did not comply faced a fine. The legislation, entitled *The Municipality, Arranging the Proportional Employment of Disabled People Procedures*, promulgated on 10 June 1999, stipulated that disabled people should make up not less than 1.5 per cent of the average number of staff, including contractual and temporary workers. It applied to non-Guangzhou-based work units or enterprises operating in the province. Companies not meeting the set figure were required to contribute an amount equivalent to 80 per cent of the average wage of all the staff and workers in the municipality for the previous year, to the employment security fund for disabled people.

Legislative approach

Although Chinese management has a long history of being influenced by legalism (e.g., Hanfeizi), there are frequent complaints about the complexity, illogical interpretation, and the inconsistent execution of the laws. The Chinese Business Laws volumes consist of over 1750 complex legal requirements and the coverage ranges from central government ordinances to citywide by-laws. Hence, local expertise is required to interpret this. The most significant problems lie in the failure of officials and managers to abide by the statutory rules, and the lack of respect for the principle of the 'rule of law'. The characteristics of the Legislative Approach are very much similar to those of the Administrative Approach as they are imbued with paternalistic, supervisory and directional values. Their common characteristics include:

● A regulatory framework;

● Consistent application;

● Preventive measures; and

● Equality before the law.

Social and psychological approaches

The social and psychological approach has unique interpretations and applications in Chinese business management. The most significant example relates to the extensive use of *guanxi*, which refers to a reciprocal connection between two independent individuals to enable some bilateral flow of personal or social transactions. Both parties derive benefits from the transaction so as to ensure the continuation of such a relationship (Yeung and Tung, 1996). The reciprocal nature of benefits maybe derived in the short-term or very long-term. *Guanxi* relationships may vertically or horizontally connect individuals across various societal spheres to create complex *guanxi* networks. *Guanxi* has an undeniable effect in facilitating business transactions in the PRC. A recent survey reported that more than 70 per cent of Chinese respondents preferred to use *guanxi* rather than normal bureaucratic procedures (Wood et al., 2002).

In recruiting local managers to manage their businesses in the PRC, foreign investors have come to understand the value of an incumbent manager's possession of, or the ability to secure, *guanxi* networks. Some SOEs or public sector positions are still appointed by the government, or based on university credentials with formal job interviews not yet being a common feature, People who have better *guanxi* will be advantaged. Even when an interview is conducted, the nature of questions asked will relate to family background, kinship, clan membership and relationships with teachers, alumni and even various kinds of friendship. Interviewees demonstrate their *guanxi* background by producing testimonials or references from their relatives, particularly those who occupy high party or public office posts. *Guanxi* management is considered to be an art and building up better *guanxi* needs multiple and complex strategic, or tactical efforts. Four strategies are suggested for maintaining *guanxi* relationships: tendering favours, nurturing long-term mutual benefits, cultivating personal relationships and breeding trust correlations (Yeung and Tung, 1996).

Mianzi (or saving 'face') is another crucial social element of business relationships in China and concerns the need to avoid pubic embarrassment by not directly criticising, ridiculing or insulting superiors, or subordinates. To the Chinese, and to most of their Asian counterparts, face is serious business and no less so for its lack of tangibility. Those who wish to live, work or do business in China ignore it at their peril. The following list outlines the characteristic nature of *mianzi*.

   Together with money and power *mianzi* is one of three key motivators that govern behaviour in China today;

   A public insult, chastisement, or similar affront to personal dignity results in loss of face;

   Losing personal control in any way always constitutes serious damage to *mianzi*;

   Rescinding an order can also be construed as a loss of face;

   Losing face is justification for retaliation;

   Organisations have face too;

   Chinese spend far more time thinking about face, and see its relevance in far more situations, than foreigners do;

● Things that make others look up to you, or envy you, also confer face on you; and

   Face is so important that it is justification for spending money, even if a Chinese person has little of it (Seligman, 1999).

Mathematical approaches

The Chinese equivalent of the European abacus, the *suan* (meaning to calculate) *pan*, has a long history as an effective mathematical tool in China. Nevertheless, conventionally, Chinese management applied very simple mathematical approaches to business transactions and most of their business decisions were based on qualitative rather than quantitative assessments. Following a greater exposure to Western management and the prevalent use of information technology, Chinese managers are now using quantitative methods to guide decisions in marketing research, planning, work-related studies and auditing. However, the availability of computer hardware, rather than the software and skills, impacts on the application of this approach in some contexts. Accessing reliable sources of information is another factor determining the value of this approach.

Moving towards a computer technology supported quantified approach to management, is a new area of development in Chinese management, illustrated in the following example (Hu, 1999): Wuhan Plaza was a very successful case of a joint venture (Hong Kong capital and Chinese capital) shopping mall that served as a window for China's retail operations, promoting understanding of the Chinese market. The General Manager successfully developed a new business model called 'Department Store Plus Shopping Centre' which turned Wuhan Plaza into the nation's best shopping mall. Writing about the shopping plaza success in her book – *Striving for First Place* – the manager identified mathematics and a personal computer as being the two keys to her successful managerial approach.

The micro-organisation level: Critical traditional, transitional and transformational issues in Chinese management

Intermixed traditional, planned and market-based management patterns

The development of a deeper cultural understanding of particular contexts is critical to the success of managing others in the global environment. Nowhere is this truism more apparent than in China. China has one of the oldest continuous civilisations in the world and is the oldest centralised bureaucratic state. As indicated previously, a number of historical factors interweave to influence the values and behaviour of current organisational or enterprise activities in China. The founding of the Communist-based planned social economy in the PRC in 1949 augmented the traditional Confucian-based culture of China, while more recently Confucian values have been interwoven with western free-market assumptions to pragmatically frame the macro- and micro-reformist economic management approaches required to promote economic development and to integrate the Chinese economy into the global economy. The following discussion presents some of the key cultural assumptions that shape contemporary

Chinese worldviews, and hence, underpin the cultural logic that frame contemporary Chinese micro-organisational management systems.

The current structure of most Chinese companies can be traced back to Qin Shihuang, the 'First Emperor' in the year 221 BC. He was responsible for the standardisation of China's legal system and for the establishment of a centralised government which was the administrative basis for China's imperial system. The Qin dynasty was overturned after just 15 years mainly because the Emperor rejected Confucian values. However, afterwards emperors adapted their beliefs and incorporated Confucian values while having strong convictions about additional scholarly and spiritual teachings. Thus over time, Confucian values were influenced by other beliefs such as Legalism, Buddhism, and other religions.

The socio-cultural notion of *Dyads* is fundamental to Chinese society. The five specific *Dyads* (social relationships) indicate the various types of relationships necessary to maintain the harmony of society. *Dyads* include the relationships between the king and civil servants, father and son, husband and wife, elder and younger children, and among friends. The pursuit of social harmony is an important part of the Chinese cultural heritage, and the collective assumption is that if everyone plays their proper role, overall harmony will be created and maintained. For individuals, self discipline and moderation are considered essential elements to achieve social harmony. The Chinese place a high cultural value on the loyalty of citizens. For example, from a historical perspective, it is a Chinese cultural belief that to commit suicide under the instruction of the Emperor or similarly, to sacrifice yourself for the country as the historical hero 'Lei Feng' did, are noble acts of loyalty. The same self-sacrificing attitude of loyalty is symbolically reflected when the son takes instruction from his father.

The administrative structure and the role of bureaucracy are derived from Confucian cultural notions of the ranked nature of social order. These hierarchical cultural notions of the social order mean that everyone fits into a very complex system of superiors and subordinates. Hence, people are accorded respect in relationship to their place in the hierarchical social order. For example, a former senior representative of government or business will be highly respected because of the ascriptive status associated with the seniority of their previous position.

The Chinese concept of a family is very different from the predominant Western concept of a nuclear family. The respect for superiors, or seniors in a family is a basic requirement within a Chinese family. The Chinese notion of a 'family' can be extended to include members of different families with the same surname in the overseas-Chinese communities throughout the world. Confucian beliefs imply that all Chinese are brothers and sisters with the same blood from the same ancestors. Respect for the superiors of different families gives individuals the required recognition of their social standing and position, and is also associated with the concept of *mianzi* discussed previously. The defined social obligations, tight social framework, and the concept of the collectivism, enable minor members of the family to be protected by other members in the same family. In exchange, the minor ranked family members owe absolute loyalty to the family. Along with the hierarchical, interdependent and collectivist view of the social order, the ideological features of Communism have been embedded into social phenomenon, especially, for example in the SOEs. However, the strength of these cultural notions about the social order has important implications for the support and resistance for the ongoing reform of management systems in China, and in the SOEs in particular.

The word 'China' literally means 'Middle Kingdom', and the Chinese cultural interpretation of this implies that foreigners are inferior, barbarous and lack manners. This implies that the Chinese take great pride in the long history of their civilisation. While Chinese may admire and respect foreign innovative capacity, achievements and cutting edge technology, Confucian-based patriotic beliefs mean that the Chinese do not tolerate irreverent criticism of their national or local leaders, policies or laws. This patriotism, when coupled with a high value for social harmony, accounts for example for the Beijing government's labelling of pro-democracy political activists in Hong Kong as being 'anti-patriotic' and 'selfishly disruptive of social cohesion'.

Over the last 50 years, Chinese have experienced many *Yun Dong*, or government or self-imposed migratory movements, in response to famine or industrial and agricultural development policies. The various revolutionary Communist armies' 'Long March', particularly the one that commenced in 1934 with some 90,000 people crossing in one year some 8000 kilometres of inhospitable terrain with only 20,000 surviving, provides an important cultural symbol for the shared nature of suffering in the search of security experienced by the Chinese people. Thus, the idea of economic security is important in China. Hence, in the bureaucracy and the SOEs lifetime employment and ongoing support into retirement was provided by the centrally planned economy. Under the collectivist organisational logic of the SOEs, in exchange for lifetime employment, all behaviour was guided by formal rules with no tolerance for non-conformist ideas and behaviours.

There is significant debate about the management issue of business ethics in the context of a global economy. The ethics of business can be identified through particular values, attitudes and behaviours. However, the interpretations of ethics will vary according to the prevailing cultural assumptions of a particular national context. It is essential to understand how contemporary Chinese cultural values shape the ethical assumptions in decision-making, and hence, to be able to recognise the ethical issues considered to be important in China. Confucianism frames key cultural notions of ethics in China and, more particularly, guides how ethical decisions are made.

Confucian societies operate on the basis of tight, close knit networks among people in business. These networks have been an essential vehicle for doing business in China. Thus, popular saying amongst the Chinese is: 'Who you know is more important than what you know'. The issue of connections with the right people are often a very important consideration in business decision-making. This 'know-who' networked relationship approach is in stark contrast to the Western (usually US) 'know-how' task and performance approach where reputation stands on the basis of most recent achievements, and decision-making is more conventionally based on outcomes. The Chinese argue that the very strength and longevity of particular *guanxi* networks are based on the ethical practice of Confucian values.

Managerial attitudes

China's dominant management style has been moulded by the Communist Party's beliefs – a blend of 40 years of socialism, Confucian values and a labour intensive economy. Together these elements place managers into low positions of power. However, Chinese managers tend to develop good 'family' styles of managing relationships with their workers, often offering rewards and advantages, and loosening the guidelines and regulations. *Guanxi* relationships provide the basis for starting a business. Managers seldom separate their private interests from their business dealings, and gift-giving and taking is an accepted way of building and maintaining relationships and, hence, of doing business.

Communication

Communication refers to the transmission of information and the interactive sharing of messages and their meanings. The closed, hierarchical, and top-down approaches to communication of the conservative and centralised political system, and the more open and participatory approaches of a reformist and liberalising market economy, present paradoxes in the area of communication management in China. This paradoxical communication reality raises additional ethical management concerns for business. In general, the meanings derived from Chinese communication styles are highly context-dependent. Hence, the kinds of interactions that take place between Chinese senior bureaucrats, civil servants, business managers and workers will vary according to the context and the ascriptive status of the participants. Moreover, the particular interpretations of and responses to various bureaucratic and business interpersonal communications and information materials made by Chinese managers, workers and other community organisations' representatives will be highly context dependent. This means that the Chinese have developed sophisticated understandings of the behaviour and values required to effectively perform in particular institutional and community contexts.

Hence, this high context approach to communications means that an effective communicator has a high capacity to switch between, for example, the kinds of interpretations made of business and political information, and of official and private communications. By contrast, international business communications, in general are low context dependent assuming that all the required information to enable shared or 'universal' interpretations is included in the communication strategy. These highly contrasted communication styles and contextual approaches mean that all areas of communication in international business relationships are potentially problematic when seeking to build cross-cultural understanding. This communication reality contributes further to complex cross-cultural ethics issues. This high context characteristic links with the characteristics of *guanxi* and *mianzi* culture to complexly shape the behavioural nature of Chinese communications and interpretations.

The complex ways in which the traditional Chinese cultural values, the political values of the centrally planned economy and the more recent liberalising values of economic reform frame complex Chinese worldviews, means that understanding the Chinese interpretation of ethics is not an easy task. The determination of whether a manager's action can be described as ethical or unethical in China depends on the interaction between social values, culture, the issue itself and the guidelines given by the government. In other words, it is highly context dependent: 'Chinese communication style is more subtle and higher–context than the Western focus … Each communication is inclusive and conveys more meaning than its literal forms' (Hempel and Ching-Yen, 2002, p. 84).

Decision-making systems

Conventionally, Chinese managers demonstrate two key distinguishing decision making characteristics from other national managers:

● The influence of historical Chinese culture;

● The influence of the reform process that is transforming China from a centrally planned model to one based on market mechanisms.

The historical cultural influence

The traditional Chinese cultural model for authority was patriarchal and feudalistic. Under the influence of this historical culture the authority to make decisions is based on an individual's social status (party leader/ landlord), gender (male) or family seniority (father or eldest son), rather than expertise. This paternalistic and feudalistic-based culture means that there is a gap between the authority and decision-making responsibilities of superiors and subordinates. Subordinates are obliged to pay due respect to their superiors and as a result, Chinese superiors tend to be authoritarian in decision-making. Any consultation in decision-making is often bypassed as subordinates are expected to obey the wishes of their superior. Hence, subordinates will behave submissively. The individual responsibilities of employees are often unclear, ambiguous and unspecified, and they are expected to follow the decisions and instructions from the organisational leaders who may give little consideration to individual workers' performance. Hence, Chinese decision-making process is more centralised, and few invitations are made for comments from subordinates (Hollows & Lewis, 1995).

The influence of reform – from planned to market economy

In accordance with Marxist/Leninist socialist theory, the essence of the Communist approach to economic management (the 'command' or 'planned' economy) entailed the twin pillars of centralised economic planning and the public ownership of all enterprises. Whilst there has been some political fluctuation between centralised and decentralised planning since 1949 (Zhu, C, 2006), the 'basic characteristic of Chinese enterprises [was] their integral incorporation in the government administrative system' (Riskin 1987, p. 159 cited in Zhu, 2006). Public and collective ownership was regarded as the cornerstone of Chinese political ideology, and state institutions 'controlled managers through hiring, firing and compensation, and had the right to allocate residual surpluses, losses or risks' (2006, p. 15). In 1978, almost 78 per cent of China's production came from the SOEs, with the remainder attributed to peoples' collectives (*China Statistical Yearbook*, 1993).

SOEs (*guoyou*) served as a feudalistic local social unit (*danwei*), or a 'mini-society' (2005, p. 5), which provided its employees with low basic wages, but substantial additional benefits including, for example, 'housing, cultural and gymnastic facilities ... barber shops and bathhouses' (Isihara, 1993, p. 28, cited in Zhu, 2005, p. 8), and also had a paternalistic political role, for example, 'providing permission to travel or get married and handling residency permits' (p. 8). This system imposed significant constraints on managerial autonomy and responsibilities, but assured employees of lifetime employment in an organisational community based on strong incentives for compliance and cooperation.

As discussed previously, during the 1980s and 1990s, under the leadership of Deng Xiaoping, a series of reforms were introduced to transform the economy from a centrally planned economy to a market economy. This transformation involved the decentralisation and deregulation of responsibilities and the 'gradual separation of enterprises from government administration' (Zhu, 2005, p. 5). The liberalising reforms began with the *Provisional Regulations on Further Extending the Decision-Making Power of the State Industrial Enterprises* (1984), and expanded during the 1990s to develop into more modern and competitive market-based organisational forms. The extensive restructuring of SOEs then commenced, and this organisational reform is an ongoing process. However, the restructuring process has not been without economic and social costs that include numerous corporate failures and high numbers of employee redundancies.

More recently, propelled by China's admission to the WTO and as a part of the Chinese government's ongoing strategic approach for integration into the global economy, foreign investment has been encouraged and formerly restrictive trade, licensing, and monetary repatriation regulations have been relaxed (e.g., work visas have been extended) along with the introduction of a series of new organisational forms (e.g., Foreign Invested Enterprises, Wholly Owned Foreign Enterprises, International Joint Ventures). Notwithstanding, as China is a collective and high context-oriented society, the deeply rooted factors shaping social relationships (*guanxi* and *mianzi*) and the conventional paternalistic and authoritarian approach to command and management, the development of pragmatic and utilitarian Western style decision-making has been significantly hampered. With little experience in autonomous decision-making Chinese managers are unwilling to give explicit orders, and are reluctant to criticise those senior to them. The maintenance of social harmony, or the status quo, is considered to be more important.

The implications for transforming management

As the above discussions indicate, China's distinct historical, social and cultural traditions frame the management styles applied in both the public and private sectors, and the deeply embedded and pervasive nature of these cultural influences mean that they will undoubtedly continue to influence management decisions, despite the internationalisation of the economy. The three most important underlying Chinese socio-cultural principles are: the central importance of humans, 'morality above all' (derived from Confucianism) and the belief that human nature 'can be moulded' (Dongsui, Yang & Hulpke, 1998). While arguably these socio-cultural principles have universal relevance, they are fundamental principles guiding the governance of China and in its particular approach to business management.

Together, Confucianism Communism and many other Chinese ideologies emphasise the importance of social cohesion based on the ideas that 'the people are the foundation of the country, and the country will be strong only after the people are stable' (Shangshu); 'the people are the most important, the country is less important, and the emperor is least important' (Xunzi cited in Dongsui et al., 1998, p. 136). This social cohesion-oriented principle has had both positive and negative consequences for management that include; a strong collective commitment to organisational outcomes, on the one hand, and unquestioning conformity and a lack of creativity on the other. This human focus is demonstrated through such managerial qualities as 'courtesy, magnanimity, good faith, diligence, and kindness' (Shih, 2001, p. 79). Modern Chinese managers may be able to harness its advantages, and minimise its drawbacks, through the design of innovative leadership styles that promote appropriate consultative and participatory mechanisms. It also provides a powerful cultural basis for the implementation of contemporary HRM strategies such as change-management, teamwork, multi-rated performance feedback, 'employer of choice' attraction and retention techniques and customised remuneration programmes.

The second principle, of 'morality above all', which compares with Western notions of 'organisational citizenship' (Dongsui et al., 1998, p. 137), is illustrated by the paternalistic leadership and concern with employee welfare demonstrated by many Chinese SOE managers and their private sector colleagues. Many former SOEs, for example, provide financial assistance to the widows and the families of deceased employees and hold regular social occasions for retired employees (rather like the 'alumni' trend in some Western organisations). The 1995 Labour Law, which included wider social responsibility considerations, was designed to create greater flexibility in employment conditions while excluding several specific employee categories (e.g., divorced or separated workers, workers with dependent children under 19 years, 'model' employees, direct family members of PRC 'martyrs', and disabled employees), from its redundancy provisions (Nankervis, 2003). Whilst such practices may in some cases restrict the flexibility demanded by pragmatic and competitive Western human resource management (HRM) approaches, they address reform requirements in ways that incorporate more culturally acceptable methods to employee commitment and productivity.

The cultural assumption that human nature can be 'moulded' or modified has been a fundamental socio-cultural community design principle throughout China's long history. Various positive motivational and more negative coercive 'social engineering' strategies have historically been applied to achieve this. Hence, there are both positive and adverse consequences to historical top-down social engineering, but despite this history the Chinese people are extremely resilient and optimistic (Clissold, 2004), which suggests that if Chinese employees are managed astutely significant organisational and national outcomes can be achieved in the long term. It is noteworthy that the Chinese character for 'crisis' is identical to that for 'opportunity' (Liu and Mackinnon, 2002, p. 123). Thus, the Chinese character is a potent linguistic and social symbol that indicates both Chinese resilience and optimism, which is in contrast to the traditional reductive and binary Western cultural approach that conventionally views something as either a crisis, or an opportunity, but not both.

However, the potential (and actual) strengths of Chinese management culture need to be reflectively balanced against its more limiting cultural features such as: its nepotic leadership styles; the lack of transparency and accountability associated with ideology, familism and *guanxi*; ambiguous organisational structures; ideologically-driven rewards systems, and paternalistic decision-making (Shih, 2001, p. 82). These characteristic cultural features are of particular concern in the government regulatory agencies, where 'Chinese officials are capable of stonewalling when it suits, and ... the government might prefer to cover up problems rather than to be embarrassed by them' (Brownrigg, Senior Vice President, Vest Inc., cited in Wonacott et al., 2003, p. 2). This bureaucratic 'cover up' response was clearly demonstrated recently when the SARS crisis first emerged in Guangdong Province and Hong Kong. Yet at the same time international concern and support during the crisis provided an opportunity for the government to publicly demonstrate commitment to strengthen the institutional capacity and to increase the transparency of the government departments responsible for managing the issue.

Human resource management
(*Renzhi Zlyuan Guanli*)

While organisations in the West place a high value on HRM as a key factor to determine corporate success, the development of HRM in China remains primarily as 'personnel administration' (*renshi guanli*). Before 1978, HRM problems in China were conceived as political management issues, in the sense that the central government and its labour bureaus strictly governed all HR planning and policies. Under the centrally planned administrative system

Chinese enterprises had no say in HR plans and had no formal personnel or HRM departments. Employees were provided with a 'cradle-to-grave' welfare-based system of coverage that included lifetime employment, a guaranteed wage and seniority system – the so called iron rice bowl. HRM in China was mainly a bureaucratic function involving the administration of supported benefits, and developing a relationship with the relevant government labour bureaux (McComb, 1999). Strategic aspects of the HR function, such as performance appraisal, employee motivation and career planning and development, were not taken into consideration. Conventional HR practice and thinking in China are shaped by the influence of the application of Chinese cultural values, socio-economic influences and China's legal framework.

The impact of cultural values and socio-economic influences on HRM

HRM practice is affected heavily by the traditional Chinese cultural values such as *guanxi*, *mianzi* and social harmony. These three cultural values underpin the high emphasis on the importance and quality of relationships in China. The cultural value placed on the management of relationships explains why the Chinese prefer to work in groups or work units and view them as an extended family. In this cultural context it is wise for HR professionals to build relationships that closely link individual interests to those of the group, or organisational goals, in order to achieve higher workplace commitment and better individual performance (Satow and Wang, 1994). In applying HRM strategies it is important to save face, and to deal with the right people in a group in order to maintain social harmony and hence, a smooth organisational operation. Under the egalitarian cultural influence of the Marxist/Leninist political logic of the socially planned economy Chinese organisations have also applied the philosophy of 'absolute egalitarianism' in dealing with human resources and discouraging people from competing for jobs, pay and promotions (Sudhir, 1993). However, with the increasing internationalisation of business this is now changing to some degree.

Contemporary liberalising economic reforms have relaxed state control over economic planning and the planning of HR deployment to some extent. These deregulating institutional reforms are also transforming SOEs and collectively owned enterprises from being government production units into independent and more market-oriented economic entities. These enterprises have been given greater autonomous power and so may set their own production plans, including HR plans, to meet their specific production needs.

HRM and China's legal framework

China has a socialist system of law, in which the legal framework is based upon a civil law model. This legal system has been shaped by various evolving historical influences that include: the historical Chinese legal tradition, which was modified since the 1949 Communist Revolution by Marxist-Leninist and Maoist concepts, Soviet legal theories and structures and more recently, some

Western influences, especially with respect to international trade as required by its membership of the WTO. In essence, Chinese legislative authority and statutes derive from its Constitution, with which all laws must comply.

International treaties agreed to by the Standing Committee of the National People's Congress do not require legislation and override contradictory domestic laws. Thus the Chinese government is a member of the World Bank, the Asian Development Bank (ADB), the International Monetary Fund (IMF), the International Labour Organisation (ILO), and the WTO. With respect to the ILO, China has been active in participating in its labour law programme, including legislation for trade union occupational safety inspectors, employment contracts in state-run enterprises, unemployment insurance, and the recruitment of workers in state-run entities. China's Foreign Economic Contract Law (FECL) is an important piece of legislation which applies to economic contracts between Chinese and foreign entities, including contracts between Foreign Invested Enterprises (FIEs) and Chinese partners. It specifies three types of contract, and allows the parties to choose either arbitration, or litigation options:

- Cooperative exploration and development of PRC natural resources;

- Establishment of an equity joint venture; and

- Establishment of a contractual joint venture

From an HRM perspective, the most important recent piece of legislation is the 1995 Labour Law which was designed to increase flexibility in employer–employee relationships, shifting emphasis away from the traditional welfare focus and the low productivity that resulted from the 'iron rice bowl' administrative philosophy. The implementation of the new Labour Law in 1995 introduced the employment contract system, which grants enterprises the power to hire and terminate their employees in response to their specific operational needs. Moreover, this Labour Law encouraged the incorporation of efficiency and competitive values in the workplace. New HR policies for cultivating labour loyalty, productivity and retention schemes, such as work incentives and career development, have to be implemented to retain qualified and experienced staff. After the introduction of liberalising economic reforms, the setting up of the SEZs was a key strategic role to attract foreign investors to China. The influx of FIEs into China has brought new management knowledge and skills along with modern technology and new products. Thus the strategy to integrate the Chinese economy into the global market place means that engagement with the international corporate and community management and governance sector now plays an important role in the evolution of HRM practices in China.

Evolving human resource management processes

Staffing

For decades, the recruitment of personnel for SOEs was under the strict control of the government labour bureaux. This administrative strategy was designed to restrict the migration of China's huge population, as well as to satisfy the needs of central planning. Jobs were assigned to fresh graduates who would work in individual enterprises according to set production quota. The list below illustrates the priorities of the former centralised approach to the management of employees, and identifies its underlying ideological elements. It is important to note the hierarchical distinction between 'cadres' (administrative and technical staff), who had special conditions and benefits, and 'workers', whose entitlements were less:

● Classification of cadres and workers;

● Iron rice bowl (*tie fanwan*) – life time employment;

● Iron wages (*tie gongzi*) – centrally fixed wage scale;

● Government-conducted planning;

● Centralised labour allocation;

● Seniority-based and egalitarian compensation and welfare;

● Political/ideological selections, promotion, performance assessment and training; and

● Cooperative labour relations (adapted from Zhu, 2006).

Labour relations within this highly centralised personnel management system are described in the following way:

> Theoretically, the interests of an enterprise became the same as the employees. As a result, disputes in an enterprise should not theoretically involve confrontation between managers and employees, and should be solved peacefully with the help of trade unions. In practice, enterprises were controlled by the state, and managers held no power in human resource activities such as hiring, firing and compensation; employees were allocated by the state and offered tenured positions with their wages and welfare centrally controlled and adjusted. Therefore, the employment relationship was actually between the state and the employees. (Zhu 2006, p. 15)

In recent years, graduates have been allowed to find their own jobs. Western recruitment and selection procedures, such as vacancy advertising and job hunting, application forms, testing, interviewing, reference checking and medical examinations, may now be found in Chinese organisations (Sudhir, 1993). Since 1986, FIEs have enjoyed more freedom in recruiting local staff. A FIE can recruit workers from the local area after the completion of some administrative procedures with the local labour bureau. The most common forms of recruiting local staff by FIEs are through more traditional networking and referral, or advertisements, on-campus recruitment, private or official employment agencies and more modern recruiting media such as the Internet.

FIEs face two concerns in recruiting local staff. The first is the difficulty in finding the right candidates, as China's rapid economic development has resulted in a shortage of skilled local management, especially those with English speaking capabilities, and profit and market oriented business experience. The additional issue concerns the lack of flexibility in recruiting workers from state organisations. Bureaucratic procedures mean that it is necessary to obtain an administrative authorisation for the transfer of individual personnel files. Compensation payments to the original work unit for the economic loss that results from the departure of an employee may be needed to promote an expedient employee release (Tsang, 1998).

Remuneration and benefits

Under the egalitarian political logic of the centrally planned economy, local employees were paid at the same rate, with the pay scales being determined by length of service rather than on performance or actual skill level. A salary could be divided into four different components – basic pay, incentives, allowances and benefits. Pay differentials were usually small and material incentives strictly limited.

The dramatic influences of Western management ideas, labour reform and labour shortages in the Chinese market have produced rapid changes in the salary structures of local employees. The new Labour Law introduced a new wages and welfare system based on enterprise productivity and individual performance. Non-monetary incentives to improve worker motivation are also required under this system. However, remuneration policies and practices vary among different organisations, and in different sectors. Some subscribe to the policy of paying according to production, while many others still pay an equal bonus regardless of individual productivity (Sudhir, 1993). Nevertheless, there is a growing disparity with regard to the remuneration of employees between wealthy urban contexts of the Special Economic Zones and the poorer rural provinces. FIEs offer significantly higher levels of remuneration for both expatriates and local labour that includes benefits such as accommodation, company vehicles, incentive trips, cost of living adjustments and hardship allowances. Strategies will have to be set in place that address this growing disparity in order to maintain political stability.

Retention

The rapid increase in foreign enterprises has resulted in a high demand for competent Chinese employees, and 'job hopping' among these employees in this sector is common. Most local staff decide to change jobs not on the basis of salary levels, but rather because of dissatisfaction with their current position, the attraction of new positions and other collateral factors such as job development opportunities and interpersonal relationships (Goodall, 1998). Motivating workers by monetary methods alone is not likely to work in a context where a high value is placed on interpersonal relationships in the workplace. There is a need for Chinese organisations to consider structural and policy changes in the areas of rules and procedures, reward systems, corporate identity and career planning (Jackson and Bak, 1998). To retain local staff, businesses need to provide attractive salary and benefits, as well as additional incentives in the form of performance based bonuses and housing. In light of the high social value placed on the workplace in China, the provision of quality and safe working environments, career planning and staff development programmes (particularly high status overseas training and job rotation), are very useful ways to foster staff retention. In addition, keeping staff informed of specific succession plans within prescribed timeframes can further contribute to organisational loyalty.

Training and development

As mentioned previously, the recent reforms have contributed to the new strategic decision-making role of managers. However, managers with experienced knowledge in the areas of HR development, market and organisational analysis are urgently required. In light of a critical shortage of capable local managers, high staff turnover and a low level of managerial skills, the professional development and expansion of management training in China is now crucial. This capacity development need has resulted in the recent increased numbers of university-based management education and training offered by either on- or off-shore programmes. FIEs are seen by the Chinese as valuable training facilities for gaining new management knowledge and skills for local employees. Hence, they are able to attract the best Chinese graduates and develop the leading examples of modern managers in China.

Nevertheless, China still faces the significant HRM problems of limited resources, inadequate processes, and ideological restrictions in providing staff training and development programmes. Moreover foreign investors face difficulties in understanding Chinese managers' conventional approach to learning and decisions around what capacity development approach and skills are relevant to China (Branine, 1996). To increase the desirability of staff training and management development, increasing top management's understanding and support is essential. Western training programmes need to be responsively modified in light of Chinese learning styles, cognitive frameworks and the current knowledge and skills base (Branine, 1996). At the same time the goal of elevating reflective cross-cultural management competencies in management training will give managers the capacity to adapt leadership and decision-making to the diverse organisational contexts in China.

The changing role of HRM

Managing HR in China today means managing dramatic change. The role of HRM has become increasingly significant with the dynamic changes that follow the influx of FIEs and labour reform. The demand for strategic recruitment programmes, effective staff retention and incentive schemes, together with adequate training and development programmes, make the HRM function increasingly important. HRM in China is also facing uncertainties such as the rapidly changing labour legislation in different business structures (e.g., SOEs, collectively owned enterprises and FIEs), and the challenge of clarifying HR practice through standardisation. All these issues make HRM a particularly complex and challenging task, as HR practitioners not only have to keep abreast of the current changes, but to develop a vision for future change based on reconciling diverse international and Chinese organisational and employee needs.

Some of the specific HRM changes which have taken place following the move towards a more market-oriented economy include: the replacement of the former centralised labour allocation system with more localised and flexible staffing options (e.g., labour bureaux, collective enterprises, self-employment); the linking of collective and individual wages and benefits with enterprise performance, and organisational autonomy in determining wage distribution; greater opportunities for training and career development, based on identified employee potential; and (albeit patchily) the gradual adoption of modern HRM theories and concepts. These developments have been inspired by the government's liberalising reform imperatives, but they have also been facilitated by '... a new generation of bright and confident Chinese professionals ... The cohort is comfortable with international industry and commerce and eager to make it work' (Martinsons, 1999, p. 125).

Production, technology and quality

This section discusses the problems associated with the application of technology in production systems in China and how the Chinese government formulates policies to encourage enterprises to use more such technology. Government policy and figures indicate increasing support for investment in science and technology. In 2002, the total amount expended on science and technology activities increased by 15.5 per cent over the previous year, with state investment in scientific institutions increased by 14.4 per cent, and investment in institutions of higher learning by 23.1 per cent (National Bureau of Statistics, 2003). During 2002, the following increases in expenditure on particular types of research were achieved: fundamental research increased by 32.7 per cent, applied research by 33.4 per cent and experimental development by 20.6 per cent.

According to statistics from the State Administration for Industry and Commerce, the number of small and medium size enterprises (SMEs) accounts for a substantial proportion of the total registered enterprises in China, and their total production comprises more than half of China's GDP (Wu, 1998). As a result, SMEs now comprise a major element of the Chinese economy and this sector is crucial for sustaining Chinese economic development.

In comparison to larger established corporations, SMEs are characterised by small production scales, disorganised entrepreneurial experience, low financing, risk avoidance and low market penetration. These SME characteristics lead to difficulties in the application of high technology to production systems in the pursuit of greater efficiencies and quality improvement. The government has identified that the following factors have hindered the implementation of new technology:

● Insufficient resources to support research and development;

● Insufficient resources to transform the developed technology into the production stage;

● Lack of motivational policies for scientists to continue research;

● Weak linkages between research institutes and enterprises; and

● Unwillingness of scientists to use their researched technology for business uses (Wu, 1998).

In light of this the Chinese government is applying a variety of strategies to improve this capability. Specific new technology development policies that relate to the investment in research institutes, scientists and enterprises include:

● offering preferential advantages to enterprises which are developing new technology;

● establishing a sound intellectual property protection system;

● establishing technological zones and preferential policies, to attract technological innovation;

● developing broadcasting and communication systems to publicise the importance of technological innovation;

● establishing productivity centres, business centres and state engineering centres in order to provide consolidated business services and technical support to enterprises;

● increasing the provision of research and development resources to research institutes and universities; and

● designing policies to bring together the cooperation between research institutes and enterprises.

The government has introduced a range of initiatives to address these innovation and new technology related deficiencies. In the 1998, the State Council decided to establish a RMB 10 billion Small and Medium Enterprise Innovative Fund and the banks made available an RMB 20 billion research and development loan to assist small and medium enterprises to implement their technological innovation projects. In addition, the development of a Regulation to Accelerate Innovative Technology, Research and Development was announced, to provide research institutes and research scientists with directives on how to incorporate innovative technologies to further develop their businesses. The regulation specifically aims to:

1. Encourage research institutes to make use of their innovative technologies as capital to set up their own businesses.

2. Increase the bonus for scientists by not less than 50 per cent of the total bonus.

3. Permit scientists to leave their work temporarily to set up their own businesses, provided that these businesses are technologically innovative in nature.

4. Support R & D scientists to work in paid amateur innovative technology projects.

In addition, the Government Regulation for New Product Development Initiative was also established to:

1. Encourage new product development by redeeming 15 per cent of actual product development costs as a tax payment if the firm's new product development cost account for at least 10 per cent of the total company cost.

2. Allow companies to treat any joint development cost used with other corporations for joint technological invention as capital expenditure.

3. Encourage the production of newly invented items with market potential by providing financial subsidies, low interest loans, or "National brand" awards.

E-commerce in China

According to the general manager of China.com, Internet usage has recently been rapidly increasing. As most of the registered users are government and company users, each registration account will be used by more than one user (e.g., many Internet Cafés & Bars have been established). Changing internet usage is illustrated below (Table 3.4).

Table 3.4 Internet usage patterns in China (2000–05)

Population (2005 Est)	Internet users, (Year 2000)	Internet users, (Year 2005)	Use Growth (2000–05) (%)	Penetration (% population)	(%) Users in Asia
1,282,198,289	22,500,000	94.000,000	317.8	7.3	31.1

Source: The China Internet Network Information Centre (CNNIC), cited http://www.internetworldstats.com/stats3.htm.

Students and technicians still make up the main body of the Internet community respectively accounting for 29.2 per cent and 13.7 per cent (Argaez 2005). As the 'Internet' is not yet classified officially as 'media' by the PRC government, PRC companies can use this communication technology to advertise products that are now restricted in the international media (e.g., cigarette advertising.). Apart from Internet advertising, more and more Chinese organisations are gearing up for electronic commerce (e.g., the Bank of China now offers a full internet banking system). Shopping online or doing other e-businesses account for only 0.4 per cent of Internet usage (Argaez, 2005). The current characteristics of e-commerce in the PRC include a shortage of the following:

● PRC managers with good management and technological expertise;

● traditional management reliance on cheap labour rather than technology; and

● available training

In addition, there is a lack of government data to confirm information on levels of usage levels. While PRC management needs to improve its e-commerce knowledge, it also needs to further implement such technologies as Internet marketing and sales. The growth in e-commerce usage signals the increasing role of this important information and communication technology for all levels of PRC management dealing with internal management issues and external stakeholder and customer relations.

Changing industry structures and policies

This section discusses the specific challenges and opportunities faced by the former SOEs and private enterprises in the PRC. It illustrates the major problems of the SOEs in the context of the dramatic forces for change at both political and economic levels and identifies the policies governing these changes. In China, the centrally planned government system was based on the concept that the entire national economic system was run as a large enterprise (Ma, 1994). As discussed previously, the emphasis was placed on the roles of government, cadres and workers in SOEs, and the SOE economic and social functions. The government used SOEs to minimise social instability by absorbing unemployed workers into the SOEs, which provided all basic life necessities to workers. Management functions were delegated to cadres by the government, although actual management functions were decided under the centralised government plan. Cadres were subordinated to central government administration, and the very extensive functions of government included not only the design and implementation of macro economic policy, but also the direct command of SOEs (Zhu, 1995).

Intrinsic central command-related problems in formulating plans created an imbalance between supply and demand for products, and huge losses of revenue.

Government intervention and other de-motivating factors that existed among the employment-guaranteed cadres created inefficient systems of production and various behaviours resistant to change. The consequences of this command system were a failure to manage economic activities at both macro- and micro-levels (Zhu, 1995). The overwhelming majority of SOE cadres and workers were permanently employed, and cadres did not have the authority to hire, allocate, transfer or dismiss any workers unless with the official approval of the government (Korzec, 1992).

The major cause of the problems with SOEs arose from government intervention and control. Central and local governments controlled almost every aspect of the enterprises, including traditional management functions, such as planning, leading, organising and control. The second cause was the policy to position the role of SOEs as welfare units rather than market economy-based business enterprises. The non-competitive nature of SOEs, and the intrinsic nature of lifelong employment, created an inefficient system of production and very limited opportunity to pursue excellence. Before the introduction of liberalising market reform, the SOEs accounted for almost China's entire industrial sector. Thus, evolving systemic change is occurring that includes:

● The reduction of government control of SOEs, and the granting of greater autonomy to SOE managers;

● The transformation of SOE ownership from public to private ownership;

● The elimination of the lifelong employment system, and its replacement by contract systems; and

● The development of a new social welfare, or insurance system, to replace the SOEs as the institutional vehicle for the social welfare system.

SOE reform policies

The central task of reform was to replace direct government intervention with enterprise autonomy based on market mechanisms. In order to support reformist transition the government focussed attention on macroeconomic adjustment and development planning that could be invoked when the market failed to deliver results. In addition, the pattern of government economic management has evolved from a centralist emphasis on administrative decrees to the adoption of macroeconomic indirect management strategies, such as managing interest rates, taxation, exchange rates, and legislation (Korzec, 1992). The core challenge has been to convert an inefficient and inflexible production system into a competitive and profitable one. Many large- and medium-sized SOEs have set in place a contract management system, and small SOEs have started to use a leasing management system. Recently, SOEs all over the country have been transformed into shareholding firms, and the result is a greater diversity in enterprise types. Besides the dramatic changes in the characteristics of domestic firms, foreign investment has also increased significantly, and joint ventures and wholly foreign-owned firms have become increasingly economically important (Korzec, 1992).

Individual firms have now gained autonomous decision-making on management concerns such as the number of workers hired, the terms of employment and the termination of employees under the 1995 Labour Law. An employment contract system has replaced traditional lifelong employment. In addition, since the implementation of the Regulation on Discharging Employees, enterprises have acquired the power to dismiss workers. Under the new wages and welfare system benefits vary according to the type of employment. The idea behind these reforms is to link wages with enterprise productivity, or individual performance. The new wage system – 'the structural wage system' – has been in existence since 1985. This system incorporates a distinct mix of basic wages (traditional standard wages), functional wages (by status or seniority), and 'floating' wages (such as bonuses, which link enterprise and individual performance (Korzec, 1992). The welfare system obligations have been a financial burden for enterprises, and so management now pursues ways of minimising costs. The commonest way is to use the insurance system to cover the payment of retirement pensions, unemployment benefits and medical costs. Arguably, this approach represents an amalgam between the 'soft' and 'hard' characteristics of contemporary Western HRM theory, to develop a model of 'HRM with Chinese Characteristics' (Nankervis, 2003).

Unemployment insurance was first introduced in 1986, and the unemployment insurance fund was based initially on the total sum of standard wages, with the enterprise contributing the equivalence of 1 per cent of that sum. Eligibility for unemployment benefits was conditional on having been employed for over five years, and the benefit amounted to between 50–70 per cent of the standard wage and was payable for 24 months, for those employed for less than five years (Geng, 1992).

Joint venture management structures

In the West, the creation of a management post is generally based on an operational need. In China, the creation of such posts in a Joint Venture (JV) may be due to: the perceived need to balance power in the management board, the influence of the PRC labour movement or a wide range of political and business motives. The appointed 'unqualified' managers may not play a significant role in day-to-day operations, but may play a valuable *guanxi* and ascriptive status role for external publicity. However, in the long term, foreign partners will require their counterparts to have professional capacity (or *guanxi*) to develop their local businesses.

China's entry into the WTO has inspired a new wave of foreign multinationals to enter the China market. However, the complex and cross-cultural nature of relationships and realities on the ground when developing and managing a JV operation are significant. For example, when a Western company sets up a joint-venture factory to manufacture its product for the domestic market, all may seem to be proceeding satisfactorily until it notices that its local partner has stolen its technology and set up an identical factory next door. The multinational may find that not only has its corporate brand's reputation been compromised by an inferior product marketed next door, but that these inferior products are flooding the market. Further investigations may reveal that the venture's bank account has been stripped, and the local workers turned against them. Legal recourse is impossible because the former partner, now competitor, has strong *guanxi* relationships with the mayor, police chief and district court judge. The next recourse for a larger foreign company may be to seek diplomatic help from their embassy. However, on the formidable basis of local complexities smaller companies may have no alternative but to walk away from their loss.

The following example illustrates some of the additional problems which Joint Ventures may face in China, and highlights that WTO membership is no substitute for the rule of law (*Cautionary tales undermine China's eastern promise*, August, 2003). Pepsi has invested $US500 million ($A918 million) in China over the past 20 years, but is still to make a profit and so is applying a 'long-term investment' approach. In 1994, when the government provided joint-venture partners for big projects, Pepsi set up its Sichuan JV. However, under the political logic of the centralist government Pepsi was partnered with the local bureau of the State Administration of Film, Radio and Television, the ministry that regulates China's media. This highly unlikely business partnership presented Pepsi with considerable management concerns. Pepsi has since alleged that without approval the venture's Chinese chairman provided himself with luxury cars and European vacations and suspects that additional funds were sidelined for private gain by inflating the costs associated with marketing campaigns. Naturally, in light of the cultural importance of *mianzi* the Chinese Chairman denied the accusations. But the dispute has become so bitter that local company employees threatened Pepsi officials trying to visit the plant and inspect its financial records. By Western standards China's courts are often corrupt and so to manage risk most Western companies insist that their contracts with Chinese partners and clients include a provision for international arbitration. Pepsi has applied this international arbitration approach and has now taken the Sichuan case to a panel in Stockholm. Nevertheless, if the arbitrators favour the American company, enforcement of the decision will still be dependent on the action of the local courts and the ruling of a local judge.

In response to these joint venture complexities, some multinationals investing in China are now setting up wholly owned foreign enterprises. However, there are, for example, the additional difficulties associated with obtaining land for operations and the complexities associated with further obtaining bureaucratic approval. In the case of Pepsi, after its Sichuan dispute is resolved, the company hopes to find a new partnership based on 'observing law and order, mutual trust and transparent decision making'. In a national context, such as China, where partnerships are based on significant long-term and interpersonal investment in building quality and trusting relationships, and where there is limited institutional capacity to support the rule of law and transparent decision-making, finding such a partner will not be an easy task. Without thorough reform of the judiciary and the required capacity development, it is predictable that in three of four years' time there will be many similar stories of corporate grievances by multinationals who invested in haste in China, with limited awareness of the risks and management complexities involved.

Traditional Chinese Communist management styles do not distinguish between the business entity, the government, and the society. Hence, JVs are also expected to serve all these stakeholders. On the one hand, China wants to introduce new technology and attract foreign capital but on the other, the JVs are required to fit with traditional Chinese organisational structures, and to interface with governmental goals, with the view to minimise unnecessary displacement of the Chinese management system. Many foreign partners find it easier to comply, as they prefer to pay attention to the organisational structure of the JV and the roles of each parent company, as well as the functions of managers. Therefore, management issues such as equality, independence, the importance of the hierarchy and the desired amount of flexibility should be clarified before the establishment of a JV.

The two decades of FDI in China have provided international training opportunities for a new generation of Chinese managers who, because of this international experience, have more market-oriented management perspectives. Multinational employers realise that, apart from monetary rewards, local managers attach a high value to jobs with promotional prospects and propitious working relationships. Hence, multinational employers would do well to design and implement rotation programmes to facilitate international experience for top local managers and hence, to provide them with internationalised career path opportunities.

China's entry into the WTO

The previous discussion indicates that there are significant management implications associated with China's entry into the WTO. The following section identifies some of the key implications:

● *Collapse of non-competitive SOEs* – For many years, the Chinese government protected its SOEs by restricting overseas competitors in the Chinese market. Consequently, most SOEs are highly vulnerable to international competition. It is estimated that more than 12 million SOE workers will lose their jobs due to the collapse of the non-competitive SOEs. For those surviving SOEs, the management will have to face large-scale lay-offs to reduce costs. But this will take time. According to the Sino-US trade agreements, signed on 15 November 1999, most of the Chinese concessions are related to the services sectors. China has to ensure that its SOEs (mostly in the industrial sectors) will be refurbished. This required change includes a radical change of SOE management styles.

● *PRC financial system reform* – With the increase in trade transactions, entities in Mainland China have to be ready to meet situations with a much higher degree of agility. More financial and accounting information will be provided globally. All these will introduce new ideas and practices in China, as many companies demand modern styles of scientific management with clearer systems and greater accuracy.

● *Direct trade between Taiwan and China* – Direct trade between China and Taiwan has been prohibited for more than 30 years for political reasons. Since the WTO encourages its members to conduct direct and free trade amongst its members, antagonistic political historical relationships could be diluted and direct trade between China and Taiwan encouraged. Moreover, PRC management will have to adjust the current practice of using Hong Kong as a middleman and actively seek direct business relationships with Taiwan investors.

● *Strengthened international position* – As a full member of the WTO, its potential trade volume will enable China to gain significant international and regional influence. A strengthened international position will place China in a position to negotiate future long term benefits and so create a more attractive business context for Chinese managers in future enterprise negotiations.

● *Establishment of a stable business environment* – Year after year, the PRC human rights issue was always been linked with the Sino-US 'Most Favoured Nations' negotiations. This practice largely discourages US corporations from placing long-term import orders or setting up production facilities in China. Such barriers will be eliminated with WTO membership, and the resultant more stable business environment will allow PRC management to pursue longer-term planning strategies.

● *Increase in import and export trade* – For those PRC industries with internationally competitive manufactured products, such as electrical goods, the reduction of import duty rates among the WTO members will significantly increase the demand, but adversely, it will also encourage the import of overseas products into the Chinese market. This competition will challenge PRC management to pursue international quality production standards.

● *Import of technology and expertise* – Apart from importing general commodities, overseas investors will also import high technology, working skills and other expertise into China. These will all benefit the PRC managers.

● *Competition and capacity development* – Overseas competitors will force PRC enterprises to rapidly improve themselves. To survive, PRC managers have to improve management systems to ensure greater effectiveness and efficiency.

China's four principal cultural characteristics that affect management have been previously discussed. They are the respect for age and hierarchy, group orientation, *mianzi* and *guanxi*. It is apparent that the powerful cultural influence of these characteristics meant that they were variously incorporated into the administrative features of the historical imperial and centrally planned political systems. The speed with which the Chinese economy has been opened, and liberalising market reform introduced over the past twenty years, has been impressive. The design of responsive and innovative management systems that address and incorporate these deeply held cultural community characteristics, along with the PRC Government's ongoing political commitment to integrate into the global economy, will be critical to build both political stability and sustainable economic growth. This reality presents many macro- and micro-cultural, economic and political management challenges ahead for the Chinese administration, Chinese managers and foreign investment companies engaging in business in China.

At the 15th National People's Congress (1997), one of the core objectives was changed from economic reform to economic development. This shift moves the strategic management emphasis away from the uncertainties, social costs, and trauma associated with the complex and ongoing reform process, towards the more positive and beneficial outcome of economic development. This crisis-to-opportunity reframing management strategy also incorporates the Chinese long-term cultural perspective. Maintaining a shared community belief in the fundamental benefits of economic development will be a key challenge for the administration.

The Chinese government has begun to depend less on collective ownership and more on corporations and shares. The traditional government welfare provision role is disappearing, and the growing disparity between sectors of the community mean that the previous 'harmony' between the government and the citizens is, in some contexts, being replaced by tension. One solution to this potentially destabilising issue is for the government to pass a number of social security laws in the near future to build an institutional safety net so as to maintain community support for the ongoing reform process.

Law makers in China need to develop a regulatory framework that creates greater bureaucratic transparency and professionalism. Civil service reform and capacity development should be one of the main targets of the Chinese government to achieve this. The traditional gift taking practices that prevail in the public sector need to be addressed through improved HRM. These practices are not just a matter of personal ethics, but are systemic. Recognition by the administration of the high incidence and impact of this has to be part of the political reforms that are now underway. The success of these reforms in changing practice will depend on the determination of China's leaders, and their ability to guide the implementation of reform and to co-opt corporate and community management support in this task.

Within a relatively short time frame China has reformed its economic approach from a centrally planned social economy to a market-based economy. As a result of the opening up of the economy and the introduction of liberalising management processes, internationalised management skills have been introduced by foreign investors. At the same time as international business investment and management influence has increased, the Chinese government has allowed and encouraged domestic enterprises to adopt a market-based approach without government intervention. With both these internal and external transformation strategies it is predictable that in the long run, market forces will come to dominate the business decision making process in China. Nevertheless, the ongoing transition will not be without trauma for Chinese businesses, their management and human resources, as they transform their traditional decision-making approaches into more market-oriented styles.

For foreign companies, the crucial factor to achieve long-term success in China is localisation. A responsive and expedient management approach could reduce expatriate costs, break the language barrier, penetrate the intricate network of personal and business contacts and motivate and retain local staff who are familiar with local conditions and can manage local operations more effectively. However, the lack of qualified staff, and the damage that unqualified staff may cause to a business indicates that the pace for implementing localisation will depend on individual companies and specific positions (Lasserre and Ching, 1997; McComb, 1999). Diverse experience in the global business environment, reflective knowledge of the corporate culture, and a high level of professionalism are as important as the understanding of local culture. Effective management requires the integration of these capacity dimensions. China is in the early stage of marketisation and this means that the localisation of HR functions will only be possible when local staff have gained appropriate experience and training in the years ahead (Pang, 1999).

The Chinese government is now focusing on the role of technology, and the implementation of technology in industry requires considerable government effort. The common problems which enterprises face are inadequate funds for the development of technology, an absence of entrepreneurialism and limited human resource capacity. This reality means that the government needs to introduce further policy initiatives, which encourage investment in technology, strengthen entrepreneurialism within the business community, and build the nation's innovative, professional and technical HR capabilities.

Another major administrative issue is how to manage state assets efficiently. The political leadership is committed to maintain state dominance in some industry sectors. However, the establishment of intermediary institutions to represent the State Asset Management Commission (SAMC) by holding shares in SOEs is one recommendation for the implementation of more efficient management of State assets. Such intermediaries could include state financial institutions, such as commercial banks, asset management firms and investment firms. The objective of these financial institutions would be to maximise the value of State assets. However, the notion of maximising the value of state assets could result in new problems, as these players might have a vested interest in the success of non-performing SOEs. For example, if a financial institution has a vested interest in a SOE, which turns out to be failing, the institution might push the firm to merge with another SOE in which it holds shares, even though a private firm may be more efficient, and thus a more rational choice for a merger partner. It might also prove difficult to close down a financially troubled SOE in which state financial institutions hold majority shares (Zhu, 1995).

The types of incentive and monitoring systems the SAMC would adopt to hold these financial institutions accountable for their investment decisions is still to be determined. If these state financial institutions set up their local branches to hold shares in local SOEs, or the local subsidiary of a parent SOE, strong local political influence will be likely to persist over decisions such as lending, mergers and asset transfers across firms. Another concern is that local financial institutions might monopolise local financial markets, thus diverting credit away from the non-SOE sectors and leaving SOEs no closer to full accountability for their profits and losses. Yet another issue is that the institutional mechanisms are not in place to resolve potential conflicts amongst an SOE's managers, workers and institutional shareholders.

In order to strengthen strategic international links around the world and build greater foreign understanding of China, its culture and society, the Chinese government has announced that it would establish 100 Confucius Institutes around the world. These institutes are being set up in off-shore locations where key political and economic relationships are being established. Institutes were already being established at Maryland in the United States, Oslo, Seoul, New Zealand and Western Australia. The recently launched Confucius Institute in Western Australia (WA) will 'facilitate WA's economic development, deepen Australia's knowledge of China, and provide the opportunity for Chinese people to work in Australia and visa versa' (Porter, cited in McNamara, 2005). Closely linked to this Western Australia-based initiative, a Business and Trade Foundation has also been established involving the Australia–China Business Council, BHPBilliton, Woodside Petroleum, and local universities. These organisations will play a key role in breaking barriers and building mutual trust and cooperation (Singam, 2005). This collaborative strategy highlights the ways in which heritage and transformation interlink and the pivotal importance of understanding Chinese culture and how longstanding and deeply held cultural values operate in political, economic and community relationship building and maintenance across all Chinese organisations.

Contemporary micro-level managerial approaches for Chinese national development and global integration

As a consequence of the deeply-embedded 'forces of heritage' in China, contemporary Chinese management represents an esoteric blend of tradition and more recent global imperatives, in transition from centralisation and authoritarianism to newly-found opportunities for entrepreneurialism, intrapreneurialism and individual accountability. Modern management practices are evident in many private sector companies, joint ventures, wholly-owned foreign organisations and some of the more innovative former state-owned enterprises (SOEs). However, hierarchical and autocratic managerial styles persist, especially amongst older or more senior managers in many SOEs and government ministries.

Overall, the salient characteristics of the Chinese management paradigm include an eclectic blend of Confucian and socialist philosophical elements with a pragmatism borne from its long and often troubled history with its regional neighbours and foreign invaders. The paradigm is reflected in such principles as an ongoing concern for the maintenance of face (*mianzi*) between all layers of management and their employees, between managers and overseas business partners and of course, within families and their social or business networks (*guanxi*). Its applications in the workplace have been reinforced by the socialist notions of egalitarianism between managers and their employees' (albeit often more in theory than practice), but are being challenged by the competitive career and salary opportunities being offered to younger and better educated managers, especially in the burgeoning private sector and in the omnipresent foreign multinational corporations throughout China.

However, Chinese managers generally still place high value on the maintenance of harmony in the workplace, and pay considerably more attention to the development of personal relationships with their colleagues and subordinates than do their Western counterparts. It is not unusual for senior managers to mentor, counsel and to provide financial and career assistance to their employees and their families, and most government ministries have retained many of the welfare benefits (for example, subsidised housing, children's educational assistance, medical care, social activities for retired employees) that were mandated prior to the market economy era.

The current Chinese government policy of 'scientific development' illustrates the dominant managerial view of a balance between planned economic and business growth and concerns for employee welfare and equity, and the environment, reflecting global 'balanced scorecard' and 'triple bottom line' imperatives but derived from different foundations. Thus, incipient Chinese entrepreneurialism, stifled during the period of the command economy, is again emerging to take advantage of the opportunities of capitalism, buoyed by access to increased educational options (especially local and overseas MBAs) and international business exposure in multinational corporations. Whilst these developments have begun to replace former seniority-based rewards and promotions systems with performance-based pay and careers on merit, most Chinese organisations (of whatever kind) build employee support and mutual loyalty programmes into their overall management prerogatives. Following the restructuring and dismantling of many SOEs, the central government has urged employers, including foreign multinationals and joint ventures, to allow their employees to join appropriate unions to protect their interests which have been eroded since the 1995 Labour Law. Whilst some MNCs such as Wal-Mart have ignored such requests, at their peril, many Chinese managers choose to adopt a more holistic approach to their employees.

Like some other regional countries, and culturally derivative, Chinese managers usually include collective participation within their decision-making processes, although final decisions are the province of the most senior organisational manager. Innovation amongst employees is sometimes encouraged, although more commonly in the private sector, joint ventures, wholly-owned foreign enterprises and the restructured SOEs and government ministries. Communication is usually formal and hierarchical, except in the smaller and more modern companies, and networking within and between organisations is an essential component of business in all parts of China.

Due to China's long history and complex socio-cultural traditions, Chinese managers are especially skilled in business negotiations and change management, although their approaches to both issues share similarities and differences with both their regional neighbours and with the West. Characteristically Asian components of relationship-building, networking, the exchange of gifts and attendance at frequent banquets, are usually combined with tough, prolonged and sometimes surprisingly frank exchanges; bargaining; and redefinition (and further definition) of terms, conditions, and prices. Change occurs more slowly than may be expected in other Asian or Western countries, but the Chinese government and Chinese organisations are notoriously resilient, and can make radical changes over time, as indicated by the emergence of the market economy 'with Chinese characteristics', the entry to the WTO and the dramatic restructuring of the SOEs in recent decades.

Similarly, at the micro-level, many Chinese managers have proven adaptable to the operational restructuring:

- financial, marketing, and HRM challenges posed by global business, including the establishment of state of the art production facilities;
- the development of transparent and accountable accounting systems;
- internet and mass marketing strategies; and
- modern staffing plans, recruitment and selection techniques, reward and retention strategies, and performance-based promotion systems.

Conclusion

The development of Chinese civilisation over thousands of years lay down strong and deeply entrenched traditions and values. Confucian ideas have been the core elements shaping the Chinese society, the world view of its citizens, and the political framework of most government administrations. After 1949, Marxism and Maoism values were institutionally and often coercively laid over deeply-held Confucian cultural values. Since 1979, the Chinese government has gradually become more liberal and adopted reformist market mechanisms. The highly adaptive nature and long-term orientation of Chinese culture indicates that it has the potential capacity to positively assimilate external influences, especially when these influences are pragmatically linked to increased individual and community economic opportunity.

The government recognises the need to maintain even levels of economic growth, and the importance of achieving more even rural and urban levels of economic development to prevent an ongoing workforce drift towards regional urban centres which will increase unemployment levels and political unrest. At the macroeconomic level, the government is implementing monitory strategies to prevent the economy from over-heating and to maintain steady levels of growth. In addition, the government is decreasing the significance of the state contribution to GNP. SOEs are being restructured and their employees retrenched. The government is changing from direct involvement and control over the economy, to the provision of a supportive environment with fine tuning tools such as interest rates, taxation, exchange rates and legislative measures.

At the micro-level, the Chinese people are becoming more pragmatic and utilitarian, and the political–ideological motivation is being replaced by consumerist material incentives. A centralist government approach to job allocation is being replaced by a market-oriented recruitment approach. Lifelong employment is disappearing with contract and temporary staff appointment systems becoming more prevalent, especially in the more liberal SEZs. Salary and income levels are evolving to become more performance-based and, on the whole, resources are increasingly allocated by market force rationales.

As the Chinese Communist Party has adopted a market mechanism on which to frame its economy, it is predictable that the cultural values linked to this economic shift will become increasingly important in China. However, it is also predictable that in light of the strength and longevity of Chinese cultural systems in assimilating the logic of international market-based culture, a new and evolving culture will emerge in response to the changing corporate and community context. In order for international market-based culture to be accepted it, in turn, will be modified by longstanding Chinese Confucian-based logic as that the emergent culture evolves to makes local sense to the Chinese people.

China's membership of the WTO will force Chinese enterprises, both state- and privately-owned, to compete with the Foreign Invested Enterprises (FIEs) in China and the world market. The FIEs and private ownership will play a more active role in the Chinese economy. Furthermore, under the logic of international market economics important synergies between the off-shore Chinese business community and business in China are occurring. Thus, in light of the binding connection between the convergent and divergent forces of heritage and the global forces for transformation, it is predictable that Chinese management systems will inevitably be modified by international management systems. Nevertheless, it is also predictable that in the long term Chinese cultural values will conversely influence international management systems, especially within the region with significant implications for local and international management at macro-, meso- and micro-managerial levels.

Questions

1. Discuss the macro-level influences of the local and regional 'forces of heritage' on the development of the Chinese managerial context.
2. Discuss the distinctive Chinese elements in Chinese management.
3. Discuss how contemporary global imperatives impact on local Chinese managerial systems and styles.

URL linkages

Government and related information

State Council of PRC	http://www.cei.gov.cn/homepage/gov/gwy.htm
Ministry of Foreign Trade of Economic Cooperation, PRC	http://www.moftec.gov.cn
State Administration for Industry and and Commerce	http://www.saic.gov.cn
State Economic & Trade Commission, PRC	http://www.setc.gov.cn
China Quality Information Network	http://www.cqi.gov.cn
China Law	http://www.chinalaw.net/
China Statistical Information Network	http://www.stats.gov.cn/
China Taxation Consultancy Information Network	http://www.zszx.com/
China Reform Website	http://chinareform.com/

Economy, trading, technology

China Economic Information Network	http://www.cei.gov.cn/
China Finance Information	http://cfi.net.cn/
Made in China	http://www.chinamarket.com.cn/
China Commodity Market Information Network	http://www.ccmnet.com
China Overseas Capital Information Network	http://www.itc.com.cn/CompanyHome/cocin/index.shtml
China Science and Technology Network	http://www.cstnet.net.cn/
Wanfang Data (Chinainfo)	http://www.chinainfo.gov.cn/

News and information

Xinhua News Agency	http://www.xinhua.org/
China Internet Information Centre	http://www.china.org.cn/
China Today	http://www.chinatoday.com/
China Infobank	http://www.chinainfobank.com/
Chinavista	http://www.chinavista.com/
Chinasite	http://www.chinasite.com/
News Era's Web Site for Managers	http://www2.he.cninfo.net/newera/
China Business Centre, The Hong Kong Polytechnic University	http://www.cbc.polyu.edu.hk/
Chinese Management Research Centre, City University of Hong Kong	http://www.cityu.edu.hk/rccm
Hong Kong Trade Development Council, TDC-Link Internet~SOE Database	http://tdc-link.tdc.org.hk/soe/

Search engine

Yahoo! Chinese	http://chinese.yahoo.com/
China.com	http://www.china.com/
Netease	http://netease.com/
Robot	http://www.robot.com.cn/
Infonavi	http://infonavi.cei.gov.cn/
Sohu	http://www.sohoo.com.cn/

References

Argaez, E, 2005, 'China ends 2004 with 94 million internet users'. Retrieved May 17, 2005 from http://www.internetworldstats.com/articles/art045.htm.

Armitage, C, 2005, 'Retailers eye untapped market, The Weekend Inquirer' *The Weekend Australian* April16–17, p. 21.

Branine, M, 1996, 'Observations on training and management development in People's Republic of China', *Personnel Review*, vol. 25, no. 1, pp. 25–38

'Cautionary tales undermine China's eastern promise', 2003, August. Retrieved from: http://www.theage.com.au/articles/2002/08/22/1029114163318.html.

Cheng, BS, Huan, KL & Kuo, CC, 1998, 'A Sinyi cultural series: The management in Taiwan and China', *Human resources management in Taiwan and China* (Volume 3), Yuan-Liou Publishing: Beijing (Chinese Version).

Cheng, G, 1999, 'Money isn't everything – what makes local managers tick?' *China Staff*, September, pp. 7–9.

China Staff, 1999, 'New legislation to encourage private enterprise', October, p. 3.

China Staff, 1999, 'Cultural barriers to training', October, p. 16.

Chong, F, 2005, 'New brand of expansion, The Weekend Inquirer,' *The Weekend Australian*, April 16–17, p. 20.

Clissold, T, 2004, 'Feature interview: Tim Clissold and the myth of Mr China', *Life matters*, ABC Radio National, 12 October. Retrieved October 13, 2004 from: http://www.abc.net.au.rn/talks/lm/stories/s1217577.htm.

Dongsui, S, Yang, Z & Hulpke, J, 1998, 'A management cultural revolution for the new century?' *Journal of Applied Management Studies*, vol. 7, no.1, pp. 135–38.

Economist.com 2004, 'Factsheet', *Country briefing: China* 9 January, The Economist Intelligence Unit. Retrieved October 8, 2004 from: http://www.economist.com/countries/China/PrinterFriendly.cfm?Story_ID=2329952.

Economist.com 2004, 'History in brief, *Country briefing: China*. 29th January, The Economist Intelligence Unit. Retrieved 8 October 8, 2004 from: http://www.economist.com/countries/China/PrinterFriendly.cfm?Story_ID+2384083.

Epner, P, 1991, 'Managing Chinese employees', *The China Business Review*, vol. 18, no. 4, pp. 24–30.

Fukuda, K, 1998, *Japan and China: The meeting of Asia's economic giants*, International Business Press, New York.

Geng, L, 1992, 'Promoting the reform of the social security system', *China enterprises management and training centre: Changing the function of enterprise management – theory and practice*, China People's University Press, Beijing (in Chinese).

Goodall, K, 1998, 'Frequent fliers', *China Business Review*, vol. 25, no. 3, pp. 50–2.

He, B, 2004, 'China: China's 'peaceful rise' doctrine', *Asian Focus Group – Asian analysis*, ANU, October, p. 4. Retrieved October 18, 2004 from http://www.aseanfocus.com/asiananlysis/articles.cfm?Issue=01–Oct-2004.

Hempel, P & Ching-Yen, DC, 2002, 'Reconciling traditional Chinese management with high-tech Taiwan' *Human Resource Management Journal*, vol. 12, no. 1, pp. 77–95.

Hollows, J & Lewis, J, 1995, 'Managing human resources in the Chinese context: The experience of a major multinational', *China Business, Context & Issues*, Longman, Hong Kong.

Hu, BX, 1999, *Striving for First Place*, Hang Ming Publishing: Beijing (Chinese Version).

Jackson, T & Bak, M, 1998, 'Foreign companies and Chinese workers: Employee motivation in the People's Republic of China', *Journal of Organisational Change Management*, vol.11, no. 4, pp. 282–300.

Korzec, M, 1992, *Labour and the failure of reform in China*, St Martin's Press: New York.

Lasserre, P & Ching, PS, 1997, 'Human resources management in China and the localisation challenge, *Journal of Asian Business*, vol.13, no. 4, pp. 85–99.

Lewis, R, 2003, *The cultural imperative: Global trends in the 21st century*, Intercultural Press: Yarmouth, Maine, USA.

Lindsay, CP & Demsey, BL, 1985, 'Experiences in training Chinese business people to use U.S. management techniques', *The Journal of Applied Behavioural Science*, vol. 21, no. 1, pp. 65–78.

Liu, J & Mackinnon, A, 2002, 'Comparative management practices and training: China and Europe', *The Journal of Management Development*, vol. 21, no. 2, pp. 118–32.

Lockett, M, 1988, Culture and the problems of Chinese management, *Organization Studies*, vol. 9, no. 4, pp. 475–96.

Lyman Miller, H, 2003, 'China's leadership transition: The first stage', *China Leadership Monitor*, vol. 5, winter. Retrieved October 11, 2004 from: www.chinaleadershipmonitor.org/20031/1m.pdf.

Ma, H, 1994, *What is the socialist market economy?* China Development Press: Beijing. (in Chinese).

Martinsons, M, 1999, 'The 1999 PRISM Pacific new leadership summit: Management in China after two decades of an open door', *Journal of Applied Management Studies*, vol. 8, no. 1, pp. 119–26.

McComb, R, 1999, '2009: China's human resources odyssey' *The China Business Review*, vol. 8, no. 3, pp. 215–34.

McNamara, J, 2005, 'Chinese learning centre opens, *WA Business News* [on line] May 23. Retrieved May 23, 2005 from: http://www.wabusinessnews.com.au/printstory/php?nid=27233.

National Bureau of Statistics, 1993, *China Statistical Year book*, Beijing.

National Bureau of Statistics, 2003, *Statistical bulletin on the input of science and technology*, 2002. Retrieved October 18, 2004 from: http://www.stats.gov.cn/English/newrelease/statisticalreports/t20031111_119097.htm.

Nankervis, A, 2003, 'HRM with Chinese characteristics: The Ministry of Finance, Beijing', *7th International Conference on HRM*, Limerick, Ireland, April.

Nathan A & Gilley, B, 2002, *China's new rulers: The secret files*, Granta Books, London.

OECD, 2003, *Reforms could boost China's ability to attract foreign investment* 03/0703., Retrieved November 1, 2004 from: http://www.oecd.org/documentprint/0,2744,en_2649_201185_3240968_1_1_1_1,00.ht.

Pan, P, 2005, 'Hu tightens party's grip on power: Chinese leader seen as limiting freedoms' *Washington Post Foreign Services*, April 24, p. A01. Retrieved May 18, 2005 from: http://www.washintonpost.com/as2/wp-dyn/A12427–2005April23?language=printer.

Pang, L, 1999,' Human resistance or human remains: How HR management in China must change', *China Staff*, July/Aug, pp. 8–11.

Ryan, C, 2005, 'Can John Howard conquer China? Perspective' *The Weekend Australian Financial Review*, April 16–17, pp 21–2.

Satow, T & Wang, ZM, 1994, 'Cultural and organisational factors in human resource management in China and Japan: A cross-cultural and socio-economic perspective', *Journal of Managerial Psychology*, vol. 9, no. 4, pp. 3–11.

Seligman, SD, 1999, '*Guanxi*: Grease for the wheels of China', *The China Business Review*, vol. 26, no. 5, pp. 34–9.

Shanahan, D, 2005, 'PM trades on optimism, China Rush', *The Weekend Australian*, April 16–17, p. 32.

Sheridan, G, 2005, 'The China rush, Weekend Inquirer', *The Weekend Australian* April 16–17, p. 19, p. 22.

Shih, SW, 2001, 'Chinese cultural values and their implications to Chinese management', *Singapore Management Review*, vol. 23, no. 2, pp. 75–83.

Singam, PT, 2005, 'WA shows East way to open gates' *The West Australian*, May 21, p. 40.

Sudhir, KS, 1993, 'Managing human resources: China vs. the West', *Canadian Journal of Administrative Sciences*, vol. 10, no. 2, pp.167–77.

Tsang, WK, 1998, 'Can *guanxi* be a source of sustained competitive advantage for doing business in China', *Academy of Management Executive*, vol.12, no.2, pp. 64–73.

Wood, E, Whiteley, A & Zhang, S, 2002, 'The cross model of *guanxi* usage in Chinese leadership, *The Journal of Management Development*, vol. 21, no. 3–4, pp. 263–71.

Wonacott, P, Chang, L & Dolven, B, 2003, 'China's handling of SARS virus concerns investors – new leadership's image suffers amid signs Beijing failed in crisis management', *Wall Street Journal*, A. no.10.

Wu, AD, 1998, 'The threats and development of China's retail businesses', *Commercial and Trading Economy*, May, Renda Social Sciences Information Centre, China.

Wu, JJ, 1998, 'The development of e-commerce in China', *Management of Commercial Enterprises*, Renda Social Sciences Information Centre, China.

Ye, CS, 1993, *China business organization and management*, Commercial Press, Beijing (in Chinese).

Yeung, IYM & Tung, RL, 1996, 'Achieving business success in Confucian societies: The importance of *guanxi* (connections)', *Organizational Dynamics*, vol. 25, no. 2, pp. 54–65.

Yun, GP, Hu, J & Huang, HP, 1998, *Management*, Jinan University Publisher, (Chinese Version).

Zhu, C, 2006, 'HRM in China', in A Nankervis, SR Chatterjee & J Coffey (eds) *Perspectives of Human Resource Management in the Asia Pacific*, Pearson Educational, Sydney (2006).

Zhu, Y, 1995, 'Major changes underway in China's industrial relations', *International Labour Review*, vol.134, no.1, pp. 37–50.

Additional reading

Brown, D & MacLean, A (eds.) 2005, *Challenges for China's development*, Routledge, UK.

Chen, M, 2004, *Asian management systems: Chinese, Japanese and Korean styles of business*, Thomson Learning, London.

Child, J, 1994, *Management in China during the age of reform*, Cambridge University Press, Cambridge, UK.

Hofstede, G & Bond, MH, 1988, The Confucius connection: From cultural roots to economic growth, *Organisational Dynamics*, Spring, pp.5–21.

Warner, M, 1995, *The management of human resources in Chinese industry*, Macmillan, London.

Whitley, RD, 1992, *Business systems in East Asia: Firms, markets and societies*, Sage, London.

Bridging the gap between potential and performance: The challenges of Indian management

4.1   To describe the contemporary context for work organisations in India.

4.2   To explain the major political, socio-cultural and economic influences on management in India.

4.3   To outline a model highlighting how various socio-cultural and economic forces are impacting on Indian management as global linkages develop.

4.4   To explore the linkages between macro-, meso-, and micro-level factors in Indian management and to highlight an Indian approach.

4.5   To explain the major features of Indian managerial values, systems and practices.

Introduction

India is a country of considerable contradictions. On the one hand, it is emerging as one of the very small number of nations willing and able to play a leading role in the global economy. On the other hand, in spite of courageous reforms in the economic sphere since the 1990s, India is still a closed economy in terms of labour, capital and knowledge. In 2004, India's share of global GDP was 1.62 per cent, but it accounted for only 1.07 per cent of world trade (IMF 2005). Contradictions are also evident in the country's national and managerial mindset. The national mindset in India is fast becoming highly confident of its abilities and future. The euphoria surrounding the business mood in the country has been compared to that of Japan in the 1950s and 1960s, South Korea in the 1970s, Singapore in the 1980s and China in the 1990s.

A recent study by *McKinsey Quarterly* on confidence in the future, which elicited responses from 9,300 global executives including 537 Indian managers, showed Indian managerial leaders to be more optimistic about the future than the rest of the respondents (Bever et al., 2005). However, in contrast to this optimism, the entrepreneurial confidence in India's corporate sector has been limited to only a small number of sectors and companies. Hence, as the title of this chapter suggests, the challenge for management is to bridge the gap between India's potential and performance. Many 'traditional' characteristics of management in India remain in place. The domination of family, highly bureaucratic government systems, a lack of professionalisation in management 'know-how', quality, ethical probity, labour laws and human resource practices are some of the areas where managerial gaps need to be addressed. Since the country's independence from the British rule in 1947, for five decades the government-controlled and inward-looking business culture has shielded companies in India against domestic and foreign competition. This protectionist culture, often referred to as the 'License Raj', not only bred inefficiencies and status-quo at the national level, but also contributed to a system of corruption and poor governance (Davis et al., 2005).

Nevertheless, there is a clear indication of a breaking out of the vicious circle of inefficiency and bureaucratic stagnation, and the momentum of transformation is being facilitated by the significant global leadership of sunrise sectors such as software services, automobiles, bio-technology and pharmaceuticals. Companies in these sectors are demonstrating that Indian managers can compete effectively on the world stage and, that when challenged, they can overcome the formidable obstacles of systemic inefficiencies and mindsets.

The macro cultural context: Local issues and forces of tradition influencing the management heritage of India

'India's cultural life bears the mark of the past, but the mark is that of its inter-active and multi-religious history' (Sen, 2005, p. 57). Sen argues that 'rationality' in Indian thinking is much stronger than widely acknowledged. The traditions of the secular and wisdom-seeking practices of the Buddhist Emperor Asoka in 300 BC and the Muslim Emperor Akhbar in AD 1500s characterise the deep human and intellectual pluralism of the Indian socio-cultural heritage. Ideas and practices to build and sustain institutions have been in Indian society over thousands of years. A handbook of public administration called 'Arthashastra', written by the legendary royal minister Kautilya around the Fourth Century BC, recorded detailed theories and practices of the management of government affairs. One of the key features of this text was its emphasis on the creation of a secular administrative cadre based entirely on merit. Arthashastra contains 150 chapters categorised into fifteen sections and three themes, namely, public policy, administration of the state and people, and administration of the financial management (Rangarajan, 1992; Sihag, 2004; Sen, 2005).

Key traditional socio-cultural influences on the Indian mindset

Over the centuries, cultural and spiritual forces have left a very strong residual influence on the Indian mindset. It has been argued that Indians can maintain a duality of essence by accepting one type of behaviour in the organisational context and a completely different type of behaviour at a very personal level (Lannoy, 1971). This duality is guided by three culturally defined behavioural variables. These variables are *Desh* (the site or location), *Kaal* (the timing) and *Patra* (the specificities of the context) (Sinha and Kanungo, 1997). The dynamics of these three variables create a mixture of horizontal and vertical collectivism within a work-related organisational context. Another significant element contributing to dissonance in the Indian social construct is the concept of the caste system. The earliest reference to the system can be noted in diaries of the Greek ambassador to India, Megasthenes, who visited the court of Emperor Chandragupta Maurya in the Third Century BC. He recorded occupational groupings in the kingdom as being priests and teachers, agricultural workers, craftsmen, traders, soldiers and government councillors (Saha, 1993). Even though Megasthenes did not specifically use 'caste' as a phrase, it can be considered to be the earliest outsider's record of such occupation groupings.

Gradually, four major caste groups emerged and in order of social esteem, they are:

- *Brahmins* occupying supreme status as priests, intellectuals and teachers;

- *Kshatriyas* maintaining social order as warriors and aristocrats;

- *Vaishyas* which originated from agricultural workers, merchants and include managers in business and commerce. This caste dominated the indigenous entrepreneurial activities in the country during the British rule; and

- *Shudra* was considered to be people whose main purpose was to serve others.

Outside these broad occupational groupings, were the untouchables who were listed in the schedules of the Indian constitution for their social deprivation and needing affirmative action, and, therefore, often referred to as 'scheduled castes'.

The Indian Constitution and a large number of national and state level regulations address the issues of socio-economic injustice suffered by the lower castes through what is called the 'reservation' system. There is a strict quota system of affirmative performance for the lower castes in vogue in the areas of education, employment, and a number of other areas.

A traditional influence of considerable significance in workplace motivation is the concept of 'Guna Dynamics'. There have been interesting applications of this framework in employee training, team building and performance evaluation (Sharma, 1999). 'Guna' is a personality attribute guiding individual, group or institutional behaviour. The *Sattava* guna (or virtue orientation) is the idealisation of higher values in individuals, organisations or society. The *Tamasik* (or negative value orientation) guna demonstrates darker aspects, ignorance and corrupt forces. The third guna, *Rajas* (or action orientation) emphasises strong purpose focus in human action (Chakraborty, 1998; Sharma, 1999).

In spite of the apparent acceptance of Western paradigms of managerial practices, Indian values temper such practices more in invisible domains than in a very obvious manner. For example, one needs to have a deeper historical knowledge to understand the motivation of the House of Tatas and their managers. This century-old legendary business house, discussed in more detail later in this chapter, grew out of the strong ethical and work values of its founding father Jamsedji Tata. As a Parsee entrepreneur, his patriotism and religious values shaped this company's far sighted contributions to India. The embedded core values drawn from a nationalistic commitment during the colonial rule and the Zoroastrian belief system of its founder Jamshedji Tata still dominate its ethos after a century of achievements (Worden, 2003).

In a recent interview, the Indian-born former CEO of McKinsey, Rajat Gupta, indicated that his managerial worldview derived from the deep spiritual Indian idea of '*Nishkama Karma*'. *Nishkama Karma* is the central concept of the ancient Hindu source of human endeavour, the *Bhagavad Gita*. Gupta contended, 'I think if we judge ourselves by results too much, we're always out of balance. Whether we are far happier than we should be, or sadder' (Singh, 2001, p. 39). This view is widely shared by senior managers in India and is drawn from the famous Sanskrit *Sloka* (verse), '*Karmanye vadikaras te ma phaleshu kadachana. Ma karma-phala-hetur bhur. Ma te sangu stva karmani*'. (Your role in the working world is to focus on your full commitment, not on your outcome. Attachment to the outcome spoils the right intentions of your commitment to the duty.)

One of the main sources of the ancient and deep rooted ethos guiding human actions can be found in a set of philosophical discourses called Vedantic philosophy. The 'holistic' interpretation of Vedantic philosophies is being widely applied in management literature as well as executive training programs in India (Chakraborty, 1998). Well-known ancient Hindu scriptures emphasise *Dharma* (principled and ethical core), *Artha* (practical challenges), *Kama* (worldly motivation) and *Moksha* (self-actualisation) as the four main pillars which sustain individuals, organisations and societies. Theories of managerial leadership, the development of organisational culture, and the formulation of general strategic approaches, are domains where such indigenously derived values are becoming dominant in a large number of organisations in India. The largest Business House, Tata, for example, identifies *Dharma*, (or principled action), as the primary touchstone for appraising managerial performance. In the longer term, these socio-cultural developments may even allow India to make its own contribution to the broader global paradigms of management theory. Chakraborty (1998) calls for India to act as a mature civilisation in its response to the complex waves of change, and, in fact, argues that India has the potential to make an original theoretical contribution to the world of management (Chakraborty, 1998).

It has to be noted that the emergence of India as a software superpower may not only be due to its cost and language advantage. No other developing country has ever taken on the developed world in a craft needing a complex intellectual and pedagogical heritage. Commentators have suggested that:

> Indian software aptitude rests on both the emphasis on learning by rote in Indian schools, and a facility and reverence for abstract thought. These biases of Indian education are usually considered mutually exclusive in the West, where a capacity for abstraction is associated with creativity. In India, rote learning is seen by most conventional teachers as essential grounding for speculation. (Barron, 2004, p. 5)

The ancient tradition of India emphasised 'exactitude' to be the most important virtue as the Ashramic (forest abode) civilisation and depended on the pupil being 'the effective data storage medium'. It is often contended that rote learning has been enriched by intuition and logic for thousands of years. Atomic theories were developed in India before the Greeks, based not on experimentation, but on logic. This learning towards abstraction in India may have resulted in its poor record in the practical sciences, compared with the emphasis on practicality inherent in the Chinese intellectual tradition. This strength has allowed China to emerge as the global leader in manufacturing whereas India's dominance in software can be attributed to its special pedagogical heritage (Barron, 2004; Sen, 2005).

A significant cultural bonding that can be observed widely across all types of work organisations in India involves the dynamics of 'Sradha' and 'Sneha'. Sradha is the upward loyalty to someone senior, and Sneha is the reciprocal affection and acceptance of the mentoring role. Within a family this would be visible between parents and children, elder siblings and younger siblings. But these dynamics go beyond the family to broader networks, workgroups and other relations. In a private interview, one of India's most celebrated management thinkers and practitioners, Narayan Murthy of Infosys, considered family bonding and social links at the workplace as one of the most positive cultural practices that sustains Indian organisations (Narayan Murthy, pers. comm., 27th August 2005, Perth, WA).

Differences in the perceptions of governance have also been attributed to cultural dimensions unique to India. Hofstede's study categorised India as having high power distance, collectivism and masculinity with low uncertainty avoidance (Hofstede, 2001). However, the collective culture has not been transferred to the work organisations in the way that this was applied by the Japanese. Indeed, it is argued that Indians demonstrate contrasting cultural dimensions in work and non-work contexts.

> A typical Japanese, Indian or Iranian person is very loyal to his or her own group or team, and places the interest of the group before his or her own interests. On the face of it, one would expect to see this characteristic–collectivism–to have been carried over into their

work organisations; in the form of, for instance, hard work and high degree of commitment, dedication and emotional attachment to the company ... it is only in Japan that the collectivism of Japanese culture has been carried over into its companies. The Iranians and Indians as employees are as detached from their work organisations and have as individualistic a relationship with their work places as any individualistic nation. (Tayeb, 1996, pp. 434–5)

Furthermore, the governance culture has also been negatively affected by lack of empowerment, giving rise to a widespread dependency on hierarchy that often artificially exaggerates the 'power distance' and reinforces a bureaucratic structure.

Managerial context and global competitiveness

One of the significant features of the managerial context in India is the stability of its institutions. In spite of weaknesses in terms of slowness, bureaucracy and rigidity, the rule of law and an independent judiciary give the country a major strength. A free and quality media of about six thousand daily newspapers with a combined circulation of 70 million provide strength to the democratic processes. India has a well-developed financial market infrastructure. Political and economic risks for foreign investors are also increasingly being lowered with the strengthening of the democratic political system, and a broad socio-political consensus on the managerial reform needed for the global integration of the Indian economy is slowly emerging in the country.

In the early 1950s, soon after India's independence from Britain, India was one of the two most industrialised nations in Asia with per capita productivity much higher than Japan. In the decades after the country's independence in 1947, India pursued a development policy based around the promotion of a highly planned, state-interventionist 'command' economy. For five decades, the experimental era of a 'mixed economy', where large-scale efforts in building a 'socialistic pattern' of society, dominated Indian economic life. This era came to be known as 'License Raj' where bureaucratic control of the private sector through licenses, permits, taxes and tariffs exasperated enterprise, quality, global competitiveness and managerial imagination.

India's share of world trade fell from 2.4 per cent in 1947 to 0.4 per cent in 1990, with the economy growing around 3 per cent annually over this period. 'In 1991 Singapore's per capita energy consumption was over 6,000 kg of oil equivalent. Hong Kong's just over 1,400, South Korea's over 1,900, Malaysia's over 1,000 and India's was 337' (Tayeb, 1996, p. 427). In spite of recent spectacular economic achievements, India's share in the US$33 trillion global economy is less than 2 per cent. Although there were many notable successes during this period, criticisms of this approach increased, which by 1991 led to the implementation of a series of economic reforms. These reforms led to the opening of the corporate sector to the global arena, and a range of macro-level economic changes.

The privatisation and deregulation of government enterprises stimulated new energy by boosting productivity, economic growth and the 'new economy' of the services sector in areas such as information technology, telecommunications and financial services. Over the past fifteen years, the corporate sector in India has undergone a radical paradigm shift. The comprehensive changes in the mindset of political and corporate leaders have been fundamental and irreversible. From an economy of chronic food shortage, it has been transformed into a service-oriented one. Growth in the knowledge-based new economy has been breathtaking. With the emergence of a host of globally competitive local firms, evidence of world class management is abundant.

Table 4.1 India's global strengths and weaknesses

	Indicators	2005 Position
1.	International growth competitiveness index	Rank of 50 and score 4.04
2.	Availability of scientists and engineers	No. 1 among 117 countries
3.	Quality of management schools	No. 6 among 117 countries
4.	Effects of privatisation on competition and the environment	No. 9 among 117 countries
5.	Business competitiveness	Rank of 31 out of 117
6.	Average time to export goods	36 days in India compared to 20 days in China
7.	Hiring and firing practices	No. 111 among 117 countries
8.	Average time needed to start a business	71 days compared to 48 days in China
9.	Market capitalisation of listed companies	$ 387 billion in India against $ 640 billion in China
10.	Percentage of population living on less than $ 1 a day (in 2004)	31 per cent in India compared to 13 per cent in China
11.	Literacy rate age 15 plus (in 2004)	India 61 per cent compared to China 91 per cent
12.	Perception of business corruption	CPI index of 2.9 (ranking 88 out of 159 countries. China's CPI index is 3.2, ranking 78)
13.	Info-tech and service firms	Combined sales of $28 billion. 130 per cent increase since 2000.
14.	Cell phone subscribers	55 million in 2005
15.	Internet users	33 million in 2005

Source: Adapted from Chandler (2005); Lopez et al. (2005); and Transparency International (2005).

India's global image in terms of its economic success has been boosted considerably. In recent years, India's GDP grew an unprecedented eight per cent in the fiscal year ending in March 2005. Demographically, 70 per cent of India's population is less than 35 years old and interestingly 20 per cent of the worlds' population under the age of 25 live in India. In spite of a staggering quarter of its population of 1.1 billion people living in poverty, the signs of economic improvement are visible everywhere (Sinha, 2005). In the past five years, the quality of locally made products has improved considerably in response to global challenges. 'The first time that any Indian company got the Coveted Deming Award for Product Quality was in 1998. But after that the flood gates opened – there was one award in 2001, two in 2002 and five in 2003' (Nadkarni, 2004). Over the past decade, India has emerged as a leading provider of IT-enabled services to the world. This demonstrable brain power can be seen in the context of producing half a million engineers, a quarter million doctors and more than one hundred thousand MBAs per year. Table 4.1 highlights some of the indicators of economic competitiveness, as compared to other countries and specifically China.

There has been a massive growth of management schools and a new impetus for knowledge-based industries. In many ways, this is not a new phenomenon, as traditionally India has always had a strong emphasis on the importance of education. For example, over many years engineering schools in the country have produced around 250,000 world class graduates annually. However, it is fair to say that there has been a strategic redirection in India today. The image of the country is slowly being transformed from a land of spiritual *swamis* and impoverished rural 'masses' to a modern intellect-leveraged corporate society. This change in the economic and mental landscape away from the traditional agrarian base to a knowledge-driven society has seen leading MNCs relocate major research and development facilities in India in recent years. Microsoft, Motorola and General Electric are just some of the knowledge-based corporations that have invested in India's long-term potential to become a leading agent in the global information revolution (Chandler, 2005).

Indian competitive advantages and constraints

India's competitive advantage lies, firstly, in a large pool of English-speaking and knowledge-intensive human resources. Second, India offers a very attractive cost structure. Attention to quality and logistics has also improved significantly over the past five years. Nevertheless, an entrenched bureaucratic culture, corruption at all levels of society and general organisational inefficiency still characterise the broad managerial canvas in India. The broad vision of economic and managerial reform over the past decade has undoubtedly been a step in the right direction, but the concrete implementation of reformist policy measures has remained slow. Perhaps these difficulties are inevitable, given the sheer complexity and diversity of India's economic, political and social systems. Moreover,

India has 15 recognised major languages, 2,378 castes, 7 religious categories and 70 per cent of the population are non-urban (Chandler, 2005).

India has a unique advantage in terms of the quality of its knowledge-intensive workforce in contrast to the major disadvantage of aging populations in most western countries. It is estimated that in 25 years, the United States will have more than quarter of its population above 60 years. India is expected to have only one-tenth of population above 60 years in the next 25 years. This scenario suggests that India may become a source of supply of young professionals to the aging Western economies in the decades to come (Chatterjee, 2006). In a recent survey of the top performing companies, *Asia Business Week* ranked seven Indian companies within the first fifty companies. Ranking highly are companies such as Oil and Natural Gas Corporation, Tata Steel, Reliance Industries, Tata Motors, Larsen and Toubro, Infosys Technologies and ICICI Bank (*Asia Business Week*, 2005).

Transparency International ranked India in the 90th position amongst 163 countries in the 2004 Corruption Perception Index (CPI) (Transparency International, 2005). However, within the country the state of Kerala ranks as the least corrupt state, while Bihar ranks as the most corruption ridden state. Regional diversity is another very important managerial concern. The level of competitiveness is significantly divergent in different states. Even the perception of corruption widely differs in different parts of the country. For example, in spite of India and China being predominantly agriculture-based economics with per capita income of about US$300, China's economy is now more than twice as large as India's and per capita income in China more than double that of India. The slowness of the political process in India is certainly a contributor to this.

Explanation of why a country like India with its abundance of natural, human and knowledge resources has not been able to bridge the gap between potential and performances may be found in the inconsistencies in economic ideology, governance, managerial mindset and a very slow-moving political process. The democratic process gives India in many ways an inner strength, while less productively, this process has often stalled necessary key reform initiatives.

An ideology of nationalisation, regulatory control and bureaucratic hurdles have not served India's interests well over the past five decades, widening the gap between potential and performance. The 'red tape' culture still persists in most governmental roles and regulations. An example given by the former national Minister for disinvestment may be instructive:

A tree fell on the residence of the Indian High Commissioner in Singapore, a prize property, nine years ago. Today, it is a *bhoot bangla* (meaning ghost house) next to Singapore's Foreign Ministry, as bureaucracy has overtaken simple common sense. Files are doing the rounds as the architect has drawn a repair plan for a 780 sqm wall while there is a government rule saying that a High Commissioner's residence must not exceed the height of 760 sqm. (Shourie, 2004)

A mindless bureaucracy and the lack of innovative solutions to social, educational, corporate and other affairs of national life have been sapping managerial initiatives in India for decades. Though the reforms of the recent years have eased this to a considerable extent, there are still areas of major rigidities that corporate India needs to overcome. For both local and international companies, obtaining and maintaining power connections, energy input, compliance with labour regulations, access to infrastructure and logistical support are still areas of considerable exasperation.

The meso-societal level: The management of Indian institutional infrastructure

The corporate context

The meso-societal level of India illustrates the country's mixed and evolving traditional, transitional and transformational institutional and industrial infrastructure. From a managerial point of view, the Indian corporate sector can be broadly categorised into five groups:

1. Family conglomerates.

2. Born-global.

3. Multinational firms.

4. Government-owned and controlled large entities.

5. Small and medium entrepreneurial enterprises.

Family conglomerates

The first *family conglomerates* group dominates the Indian corporate scene in all sectors of the economy and wields enormous socio-political power. Many of these business houses now aspire to become truly global corporations within the coming decade. India's leading family conglomerate is the House of Tata which is led by a dynamic and visionary CEO, Mr Ratan Tata. Tata's managerial culture is a hybrid mixture of indigenous and highly sophisticated global approaches. The recent acquisition by Tata Tea of the large British Tetley tea company and Tata Steel's acquisition of a leading Asian steel company, Natsteel of Singapore, are examples of courageous and bold attempts by Indian companies to emerge as global corporate players of considerable sophistication.

The Tata Empire is more than a business house as it has represented the business culture in India for more than a century (see Figure 4.1). Established in 1886 as a cotton mill, Tata's history is intertwined with the political history of India over the past century. The big three companies in the Tata Group are Tata

Figure 4.1 The Tata Group sectorial portfolio

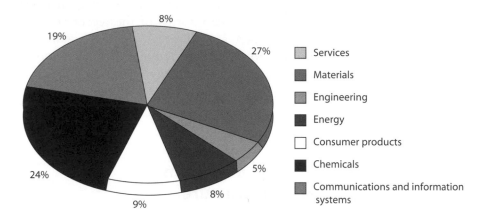

Source: Tata Sons Limited 2005, 'Group financial performance and sector-wise operations', available http://www.tata.com/0_investor_desk/business_sectors.htm.

Consultancy Services, Telco and Tata Steel, which account for more than half its revenue.

Family-controlled conglomerates, such as Birlas, Reliance, Tata, Bajaj, Mahindra, Godrej, and Thapar, are still the backbone of Indian economic and managerial life.

> The affiliates of family business groups play a leading role in nearly every industrial sector, including petrochemicals (Ambani), Steel (Tata), auto manufacturing (Tata, Mahindra, Birla), telecommunications (Tata, Ambani) and consumer products (Godrej). Even the nation's relatively new software industry counts family led concerns (TCS, a Tata Affiliate and Wipro, 85 per cent owned by cooking oil scion Azim Premji) among its top performers. (Chandler 2005, pp. 56–7)

Born-global

The *born-global* corporations are found within the knowledge industry sector. The managerial culture within this sector enshrines 'world class' quality, flat and empowered work teams with a strategic managerial vision, and global scope never before seen in the country. Examples of leading corporations in this group are Infosys, led by a charismatic CEO, Narayan Murthy, and Wipro, led by the visionary leader Azim Premji, and Bio-Con led by the indomitable CEO, Kiran Mazumdar-Shaw.

Multinational firms

The *multinational firms* are large MNCs, or the local entities of large global corporations. They employ the best of global management practices even though only a few of their employees are expatriates. However, the senior managerial cohort in this group is essentially western educated. The leading corporations within this group are Hindustan Lever (the local entity of the MNC Unilever), Coca Cola and IBM, as well as consulting services firms like McKinsey and PriceWaterhouseCoopers.

The government-owned and controlled large entities

The *government-owned and controlled large entities* remain extremely significant and encompass a wide range of industry sectors, particularly in essential infrastructure such as airlines, shipping, railways, postal services, major steel plants, machine tools, mineral exploration, power, oil and gas. In fact, a majority of those employed in major industries in India still fall within this group. For example, the government controlled 'Indian Railways' alone employs an astounding 1.8 million people. Within this segment the management culture varies from world class, as in the case of Hindustan Machine Tools (HMT), to the pre-modern and exceedingly bureaucratic, as in the example of the postal services. Overall, the economy is still strongly reliant upon the SOEs, which employ more than 25 million people throughout the country.

But a lack of performance focus and managerial skill still dominates this sector. An observation from a respected management guru may be revealing.

> I was stupefied to read in March 2002 that the railways plan to bottle water. In that case, I thought, why don't they also grow tea (and meat and rice) for their catering department? And cotton for their drivers while they are at it? Perhaps then we can get someone to run the trains safely. The issue is not bottled water, but the astounding mindset of the Railway Board that is ignorant of the basic managerial concept of core competence and things that the railways, which are inefficient, high cost labour, and can do it cheaper. (Das, 2002, p. 63)

The small to medium entrepreneurial enterprises

The *small to medium entrepreneurial enterprises* have variable managerial approaches and standards. Some of these enterprises are run by motivated and highly educated managers who employ global benchmarks, while others barely keep their organisations afloat. The overwhelming mindset of the managers in this group can be described as a 'trading mindset'. This mindset has evolved as, until recently, the government had reserved about 800 industries and products for the small-scale industry sector. Simple products like garments, toys, and shoes are some of the examples of sectors in which only small-scale businesses were allowed to operate. Government regulations did not allow this sector to develop strategic export oriented enterprises as was the case in most Asian countries, including China. They were unable to use scale economies, as that would make them ineligible to be in the industries they were in.

In general, it is important to note that the Indian corporate sector is undergoing a period of unprecedented change. Well-established corporate champions of the

past have sometimes found it difficult to adapt to the much more ruthless competitive business climate, while a select group of companies particularly within
the 'knowledge' sector have recorded phenomenal rates of growth.

Towards an Indian managerial model

The work of Sumantra Ghosal has made a comprehensive contribution to the
development of Indian managerial models. His meticulous research provided
evidence of world class management in India through a range of corporate case
studies and his intellectual insights offer conceptual underpinnings to the emerging
agenda for the realisation of the potential of Indian business.

The 'brain drain' of trained professionals out of India during the 1960s to the
1980s was considered to be a staggering economic loss to the nation at that
time. Interestingly, this particular phenomenon of a large professional Indian
diaspora has been of invaluable advantage in recent years. Besides the 'reverse
swing effect' of returning entrepreneurial and managerial talent, capital and
'know-how', considerable credit may be due to this group for the success of
Indian corporations in the international business arena.

As indicated in the previous section on the impact of culture on management
approaches in India, a number of trends appear to be emerging. The integration of
these trends is leading to a unique and observable 'Indian style' managerial
approach. The contributory influences leading to this trend have four clear sources:

1. A strong nationalistic pride.

2. The traditional cultural forces originating from the desire of achieving a
    robust global identity.

3. The unavoidable prevalence of the bureaucratic institutional structure, and

4. A new local confidence in innovation, enterprise and global reach (Sinha,
    2005; Chatterjee, 2006).

Table 4.2 illustrates the contributing influences and their impact on managerial
mindset. Ghoshal and colleagues introduced the term *satisfactory under performance* to characterise the complacency surrounding Indian managerial
pathology. They argued that:

> ttlenecks tend to be at the top of the bottle. Here too the most critical barrier to
> ange lies at the level of top managers – in their lack of belief in and passion for change.
> ey all say the right words, publish them in the annual reports and in in-house journals,
> ut deep in their hearts, they do not believe what they say. This is why companies find it
> hard to manage change. Surely, there are many other barriers and obstacles, but none
> f them is as debilitating as the mindset of senior managers. (Ghoshal et al. 2000, p. 13)

Table 4.2 Sources of managerial mindset in India

Contributing threads of influence	Impact on managerial mindset
Nationalistic pride as a counterpoint to colonial rule	Integration of science, technology and related global ideas to indigenous educational and social norm with strong patriotic zeal.
Presence of all pervasive bureaucratic culture in institutional life	Colonial legacy in the work culture and managerial practice in government, public sector and other spheres of life.
Cultural tradition and heritage as a stream of influence	Strong cultural frames such as family bonding, mutuality of obligations and conformity to tradition.
Recent impact of global forces in managerial mindset	Emergence of successful global sectors such as 'information services', BPO, Pharmaceuticals, Optical and Magnetic data storage, Bio-Technology generating a 'Brand India mind'.

Source: Adapted and developed from Sinha (2000).

The contention that the 'enemy is inside', and simply having visionary dreams were not sufficient admonitions to the managerial elite in India. To focus on the central role of innovation and global thinking, managers in India need these characteristics ingrained in the educational, economic and, most importantly, political culture of the nation.

The model presented in Figure 4.2 summarises the changing dynamics in the managerial mindset in India. The model highlights four key areas of managerial mindset reorientation. The first sphere is the 'competitive' sphere where the disappearing regulatory regime of governmental protection and control has led managers to the realities of internal and global competition, and the logic of strategy now dominates managerial mindset more than ever before. The second sphere is the sphere of 'performance'. The complacency of the 'satisfactory under performance' is being overcome by a new urgency of desire in bridging the 'promise' and 'performance'. The third sphere is the new area of the 'balance of global-local' conflicts and cohesions. This is a sphere of considerable untapped potential for India, as many of the elements that can bring managerial success of Indian companies in the Asian region, as well as in the broader global arena, are only being explored in a small number of sectors and companies. The fourth area of managerial attention is the development of an Indian way of managing where the cultural forces of the national heritage and the contemporary imperatives of performance can build a symbiotic relationship.

The purpose of the model is to highlight the new trends and transformations of managerial thinking in India. The four spheres of interaction have provided four stable anchors of 'managerial mindset' thrust. These anchors are the pillars

Figure 4.2 Changing dynamics of management in India

on which the new managerial landscape is being designed. The overwhelming force of 'stretch' is rapidly dominating the cognitive domains of managerial leaders in India. The culturally appropriate idea of paternalistic 'compliance', observable at every level in public sector, educational and governmental department management, needs to be replaced by a sense of discipline and innovation. The managerial emphasis on 'control' instead of 'support' is still not common, and the instrumental and contractual mindsets tend to dominate work culture instead of empowerment and 'trust' in most organisations. The cultural predispositions of hierarchy transcend quite easily in the managerial setting and are often set as an antidote to innovation and creativity.

The market, strategy and purpose – For fifty years, Indian thinking focussed around the thesis that market leadership inevitably led to monopoly. The idea of scale, scope and global depth has only been recognised since the national economic reform was initiated in the 1990s. The shift away from an 'opportunistic' to a 'strategic' orientation is a new anchor for managers. The culture of a 'constraint' orientation epitomised by the bureaucratic heritage is giving way to a 'stretch' orientation. In particular, there is a sense of purpose creating this 'stretch' in organisations led by transformational leaders.

Global threat and opportunity – This is a focus that has transformed managerial thinking in India in the areas of quality, innovation, entrepreneurial thinking and the cultural synergy of joint venture management. The opportunities and threats presented by the entry of global companies in India have brought about shifts in internal management processes, union-management relations and human resource practices.

Strength of cultural heritage – The unique feature of the Indian cultural tradition has been its capacity to absorb and refine other traditions into its own. The traditional belief that there is a link between the dynamics of human energy and action and the universal wholeness of a purpose much greater than individual or organisational life. The ancient Indian concept of 'Nishkama Karma', or devotion to work discussed in this chapter, unifies the diversity of cultural threads.

> But there are always individuals in every culture and in every organisation who are able to transform their risk into a sort of game which requires skill, challenge, clear objectives and immediate feedback. Since they are absorbed, they have no time to worry about themselves, their promotions, or feel envy towards the person sitting next door. (Das, 2002, p. 107)

The reliance of the culture of 'Nishkama Karma' is evident amongst the leaders of global companies emerging in India.

Competency in leveraging and bridging the performance potential – This is the anchor of a new radical shift in micro-level managerial innovations. With the demographic shift of more young workers at the workplace, some flexibility in labour laws and a new compensation system in practice, it has become possible to recruit, retain, train and develop and generate synergy not in terms of 'leveraging cheap workers' but in leveraging 'cheap brain power'.

Managerial emphasis at the micro-level

Motivational dynamics

Characterised by contradictions where both intrinsic (e.g., *Nishkama Karma*) as well as extrinsic (i.e., pay, promotion) motivations may be observed. Motivational patterns differ at various levels and industries, as well as in private and public sectors. For example, while motivational dynamics among call-centre workers are centred on instrumental and transactional lines, employees in other sectors are motivated more by a variety of factors. Recent empirical study indicates a distinct convergence of managerial work goals in India where the priority of 'learning' as a motivation replaces the economic and security motives (Chatterjee and Pearson, 2000a, 2000b). Ghoshal et al. (2000) attributed the motivational deficiencies in Indian organisations to the behavioural contexts characterised by constraint, control, contract and compliance as opposed to the process of motivational challenge provided by support, discipline, trust and stretch.

Decision-making patterns

Decision-making patterns are characterised by a 'top-down' approach, with the exception of non-traditional economic sectors. In most family-run conglomerates, professional and expert advice may be obtained, but participatory synergy in such organisations is not common. Bureaucratic rule orientation dominates the public sector, enterprises, departments and a major segment of the private sector. The paradox may be highlighted with an example. To generate a new vigour to the economic life of West Bengal (population 100 million), the Chief Minister had decided to visit Singapore and Indonesia to speak to CEOs of leading companies in September 2005. In spite of a number of direct flights from the state capital Calcutta to Singapore (three and a half hours) the Chief Minister had to travel backwards to Bombay (three hours) and then to Singapore (five hours), as government rules insist that senior government leaders must travel by the government airline. There was no consideration given for the huge loss of a working day for the Chief Minister.

Communication processes

The day-to-day communication that Indian managers engage in reflects the country's cultural context in a significant way. Assumptions about the 'shared meaning' may be widely divergent depending on the nature of an organisation, relationships and exchanges as well as the demographic profiles of the communications. For example, the sharing of expectations about 'time' may be very different in different industries. While managers in leading global companies in India may emphasise a 'future' orientation in their communication, most government departments, educational institutions or political organisation do not.

Excellence in English language communication skills has been of advantage to a number of economic sectors and the increasing use of information technology creates a more common cultural context for communications. However, Indian managers mostly rely on 'task and role 'oriented communication in their global interfaces. Cross-cultural communications and negotiations are areas where Indian managers need increased attention. Sensitivity to political, religious and social issues is also a significant risk area of communication. The socio-political example of the Cadbury company's promotional advertisement in 2003, which compared product 'temptations' with the disputed state of Kashmir, created an enormous national backlash.

Management of change innovation

In recent years, there has been wider acceptance that the lack of competition and professionalisation were two serious weaknesses hindering managerial change and innovation. Internal competition of more than 100 machine tool manufacturers, nine auto makers, fifteen camera companies and about twenty electronic, and entertainment producers have led India's transformation into the global inno-vation and quality club. Acceptance of change and innovation for managers is becoming more common with the reform movement.

Managerial and leadership culture

Patriarchal leadership dominates Indian managerial and leadership culture, with reverence for elders being a universal assumption; an emphasis on the 'status quo' and a lack of performance focus is viewed in the acceptance of 'satisfactory under performance'. There is also strong organisational discouragement of critical feedback. Sinha's (2000) 'nurturant–task' (NT) model emphasises the conditionality of employee task accomplishment for a manager's benevolence towards subordinates. However, a broader interpretation of this NT model may be found in the 'self-learning' model where humility, faith and total quality con-sciousness are drawn from the cultural tradition of organisational leadership (Chatterjee, 1998).

Industrial relations (IR) and human resource management (HRM) in India

Unlike elsewhere, HRM functions in Indian organisations are generally not treated as a special professional role. HRM is often considered to be an aspect of generalist management, including financial and technical competencies. This approach leads HRM professionals to have a much broader set of skills and experiences than usually called for in a typical Western organisation. This may be one of the reasons why the relationship between HR practices and organisa-tional outcomes is not commonly linked. Over the past decade, the economic reform agenda has kept the HRM focus mostly around rationalisation of work-force in the public sector, the voluntary redundancy scheme (VRS), restructur-ing, and implementing 'reservation' schemes for scheduled castes. It may be noted that until recently the retirement age in the country was 55 years in the private sector and 58 in the public sector. This practice has had a dramatic effect on the demographic profiles of the working population in India. Two-thirds of the working population in India are under 35 years of age.

This shift has affected the long-standing practice of seniority-based promo-tion in a disruptive way. It is now common to see young professionals being recruited with salaries ten times higher than their senior counterparts. As exam-ples, prestigious Indian technology and management institutes place graduating students at ten times the salary of the most senior professors. The ethical and social disruption generated by the importance of youth in a traditional cultural context heavily skewed towards age and seniority has not yet been fully explored. Particularly paradoxical is the shortage of well-trained professionals in a mindset of a plentiful pool of human resources (Chatterjee, 2006). As has been pointed out,

> People are something India has plenty of. But ask any business leader what the biggest problem is today and the chances are he or she will say it is finding the right people and getting them to work productively. That may sound paradoxical. But the fact is that due to its late start on the road to development and a strong history of union activity, Indian has traditionally lagged in the systematic development of high productive talent. (Bucknall and Ontaki, 2005, p. 141)

A study of eleven Indian organisations in nine different industries over a period of five years (1998–2003) indicated the adoption of innovative HRM practices in these industries. These innovative HRM applications have been observed in the recruitment practices, performance appraisals, wages and salary administration, training and development and other related areas (Som, 2006). In a similar study conducted previously, the impact of economic reform on HRM was investigated in 22 companies with employee numbers of between 34,000 and 70,000 to reveal that 13 of the 22 companies were affected significantly by the recent economic reform programme. The imperatives of this change came from foreign equity participation, global competition, productivity improvement and other issues (Monappa and Engineer, 1999).

The business process outsourcing (BPO) industry has not only outsourced global jobs, but also been able to achieve significant changes in the labour laws and union attitudes. However, it should be remembered that in spite of being a world leader, the information technology industry employs only about one million people. It may be noted that the leading technology companies are also recruiting from the global labour market, especially from the United States, United Kingdom, France and Russia.

The trade union movement in India had its origins in the independence struggle over British rule and the deep politicisation of the movement was viewed as contributing to social stability. Each of the major political parties has sponsored its own labour unions at the national or state levels. Union leadership in India is seen not only as the training ground for 'external' politicians, but also an arena for senior leaders to consolidate their holding onto power. This socio-political connection contrasts to the Japanese union experience at the enterprise levels, where micro-issues dominate and direct to political influences rarely filter to the political affiliation of the trade union movement. This disaffiliated model led to unproductive industrial conflicts, inter-union rivalries as well as serious road blocks to the national unemployment scene. The three leading national level unions are:

1. All India Trade Union Congress (AITUC) led by the Communist Party of India has been the leading platform of union voice over the past century.

2. The Indian National Trade Union Congress (INTUC) was the most influential union sponsored by The Congress Party which ruled the country with a massive legislative majority for the first three decades after independence.

3. The most powerful union is the breakaway Communist Party (Marxist)-controlled Centre of Indian Trade Unions (CITU).

Union formation in India is relatively simple as the legal requirement for registering a union only needs a handful of people. In 2005, India had approximately 47,000 registered unions with six million members who are about two two per cent of the total national workforce (Chatterjee, 2006). However, mere registration of a union does not lead to any employer reorganisation under Indian laws.

The legislative infrastructure for industrial relations is guided by a set of laws enacted during the early period of the previous century. The Trade Union Act, 1926 (TWA), Industrial Employment (standing orders) Act 1946 (IEA), Industrial Disputes Act 1947 (IDA) and Indian Factories Act 1948 (IFA) are some of the important legislation guiding workers and employers. The Factories Act of 1948 is considered as the most advanced in the world with its positions on maternity leave, childcare, health regulations and industrial safety. During 2005 a new law called the Employment Guarantee Act (EGA) was passed in the National Parliament. This law guarantees a minimum of 100 days employment for at least one member of every hundred in 200 identified poor districts of the country. The law, enacted under the pressure of the coalition partners, was led by the Communist Party, and means an estimated cost of two per cent of the GDP for its implementation.

A new government emphasis on infrastructure

Compared with China, the weaknesses of India's infrastructure are regularly commented on as being its Achilles heel to ambitions to establish a vibrant corporate sector. Roads, ports, airports and electricity supply are some of the infrastructure areas that need comprehensive attention. It is in this context that the 85 per cent completion of an ambitious highway stretching for 3625 miles and connecting the national capital Delhi with the commercial hub Mumbai in the West, Chennai in the South, and Calcutta in the East may be considered a miracle. The infrastructure project is called the 'Golden Quadrilateral' highway with a budget of $6.26 billion from an outlay of $60 billion Master Plan that will revolutionise the conceptualisation of the supply chain and logistical backbone of management in a few years time. Delhi's new $2.4 billion subway system is another example of a successful infrastructure project management, where a retired engineer was drafted to manage the project. The project was completed three years ahead of schedule, well within budget and with a reputation of unprecedented integrity and transparency of financial dealings.

Government assistance in the development of infrastructure through the establishment of 'state of the art' software technology parks has also been significant.

Bangalore's 'Electronic City' and Hyderabad's 'Cyber City' are not only comparable to global benchmarks, but also link directly to leading educational institutions. A number of leading global IT companies, such as Microsoft and IBM, have also invested in these regions because of proactive policies at a state level. The process of building capacity in knowledge-based services in IT has now extended to other areas, such as basic chemistry, polymer science, mechanical engineering, ceramics, metallurgy, biotechnology and other advanced nitro devices. MNCs in the pharmaceutical industry, such as Bayer, Unilever, Pfizer, Glaxo and SmithKline, consider factors such as India's diversity of population and the availability of cost-effective scientific research staff as being attractive incentives for conducting clinical trials of new drugs in India. Domestic pharmaceutical companies, such as Ranbaxy Laboratories are also emerging as powerful competitors, and the growth of this sector is expected to generate new areas of joint ventures and global and regional strategic alliances (Aiyar, 2003).

Another example of radical managerial success is the emergence of 'Moser Baer' as a leading global competitor in the highly competitive recordable computer hardware industry. In fact, this innovative company is now challenging the three top global players in this industry from Taiwan (Ritek, CMC and Princo) on the two competitive fronts of price and quality. In doing so, it has had to overcome formidable local-level obstacles. As one correspondent has noted:

> Since India's electricity supply is notoriously unreliable, Moser Baer produces all of its own power with on-site generators. Water is pumped from wells on the property. Obliged to rely on the government telecommunications provider, Moser Baer also uses radio links between its facilities as back-up. (Slater, 2001, p. 44)

In this way, only delays in the transport logistics of moving the finished products from its plant in Delhi to Mumbai's port are still affected by national infrastructural weakness. It is notable that the leading global player in this industry, Ritek Corporation of Taiwan, has taken the emergence of this Indian competitor so seriously that it has opened a plant in China in order to regain price competitiveness. In 2004, Mosser spent about US$135 million to expand its capacity to 2.4 billion units, up from 2 billion.

Business process outsourcing is another area that has attracted often controversial global attention. Twelve Indian firms were included amongst the fifty best-managed BPO companies in 2005 by the *Black Book of Outsourcing*. This list was prepared by two of the most well-known outsourcing management training organisations – namely the Outsourcing Management Institute and the CRO (Chief Resource Officer) Institute. In 2005, IBM Global/Daksh – the BPO Company IBM acquired in India in 2004 has been ranked as the number one outsourcer. Other Indian companies on the list are Mphasis as number four, Wipra Spectra third, and 'ICICI One Source' as number six and seven. Satyam Computers and Infosys Technologies are ranked much below at 19 and 25, respectively. The list also includes I-Flex at 32 and Patni Computers at 45 (Brown and Wilson, 2005).

India's vast potential in media and entertainment is also on the threshold of global extension. Besides the recent successes of the Bombay film industry, a synergy between software and media is being established in the area of animation. As the world's largest producer of movies, and, increasingly, with a global presence, this industry may also provide new opportunities for Indian managers to link up with global collaborators. Sony Corporation is the first major MNC to invest in production for the Indian entertainment industry. Even the much-maligned government sector has become more strategic in this area, as is evident in the efforts of the Andhra Pradesh Government to create an advanced studio city complex with facilities for filming, editing and other support services. This new concept of incorporating 'value innovation' to an established home-grown industry signals another solid shift in the reconceptualisation of the role of provincial governments in India.

Nevertheless, Indian managers have gradually been overcoming a perception of 'inferiority' and a psychology of stagnation through recent global challenges and a 'transformation' of this previous perception. Indian organisations like Infosys, Reliance, and Wipro Corporation have become formidable global companies over the past 25 years. For the first time five Indian companies were included in the world's top 500 companies in 2005, and these corporate transformations have had a 'pebble in the pond' effect on influencing the Indian managerial mindset.

Foreign investment is now flowing into the country: Australian steelmaker 'Bluescope Steel' has spent US$77 million in 2004 on building three plants in India to supply carmakers and builders. Nokia has had a dominating presence of $160 million in the handset manufacture. LG, the Korean rival of Nokia, is planning to invest US$ 60 million to make 20 million GSM and CDMA phones in India annually by 2010. Overall, India has the potential to boost its manufacturing exports to US$300 billion by 2015 up from US$44 billion in 2004 (Vellor, 2004, p. 10).

Contemporary micro-level managerial approaches that frame the gap between Indian potential and performance

The micro-level influence of culture remains significant. Managers in India retain a strong orientation towards the cultural legacy of an ancient but continuously evolving civilisation, which is superimposed by changing technology and systems. Tayeb (1989) has argued that cultural factors impact more on the underlying processes and relationships of the formal dimensions of corporate designs and strategies. She claims that the dichotomy between tradition and modernity is perpetuated at several levels. Cultural factors deeply influence many aspects of organisational, social, family and religious life at the micro level, while at the macro level they adjust to the realities of economic reform, communication technology and globalisation. The capacity of Indian managers to tolerate high levels of uncertainty and ambiguity is also indicated by research that shows that India is one of five countries with the lowest scores of 'uncertainty avoidance' of an extensive sample of nations (Hofstede, 2001). Table 4.3 highlights a number of key cultural issues characterising micro-level managerial interfaces in India.

Writers on business culture have been debating theories of 'convergence' and 'divergence' as the influence of globalisation takes hold. The convergence theorists argue that the emergence of a Western market-oriented economy inevitably leads to the adoption of values and culture associated with it (Webber, 1969; Child, 1981; Bond and King, 1985). In contrast, the divergence theorists argue that if the culture of the indigenous location is sufficiently powerful, it will retain its uniqueness in spite of the impact of broader factors of homogenisation (England and Lee, 1974). However, anthropological 'acculturation' theorists suggest that such influences allow for the emergence of 'hybrid' forms of culture (Beals, 1953).

Societal values of self development are still evident amongst elite managerial and entrepreneurial leaders, including the idea that humans can only achieve glorious heights if they can develop both their wings like a bird. The first wing is *Budhi*, which encompasses *Dharma* (virtue) and *Gyana* (knowledge), and the second wing is *Sadhana*, or training and dedication. Moral and technical efficiencies need to operate in harmony in achieving self-mastery.

However, the essence of a business culture is often not what is visible at the overt level of interaction, but the shared ways in which the category or people conceptualise and operationalise their world. In several research surveys of business leaders in Asia, it has been contended that they are able to maintain a duality of values, with one field of value formation drawn from their own cultural heritage, while the other impacts on them through the wider forces of internationalisation (Bedi, 1991). In the Indian context, it can be suggested that a hybrid blending of values is creating neither convergence, nor divergence, but a unique Indian managerial value system. Individual Indian managers have two, almost opposing, forces

Table 4.3 Business culture at micro-organisational level

1	High paternalism with frequent overlap in ownership and professional management
2	More focus on short term than strategic orientation.
3	Emphasis on security and stability by the strong union movement rather than accepting change and risk.
4	Strong masculine values in managerial practices and organisational culture
5	Hierarchy used as the coordinating mechanism with very limited scope of empowerment.
6	Authority and power based on a complex set of organisational and non-organisational variables.
7	Ascription emphasised more than work performance
8	Highly affective behavioural norms with bureaucratic dominance

acting on them. The first stems from phenomena such as the extended family and the social group or community of which the manager is a part. These traditional social and cultural forces tend to push the manager towards acceptance of authority, sticking to established norms and practices, seeking guidance from superiors or elders and limited willingness to delegate authority.

The other set of forces arise from more recent developments such as an intensified sense of international inter-connectedness and a gradual, if frequently interrupted, trend towards greater homogenisation within Indian society, particularly in urban areas. An Indian manager under the influence of this second set of more current forces would tend to behave in a much more individualistic and independent manner. In general, Indian managers deal with these forces by clearly separating their work and personal lives, creating a very low diffused work culture, which is almost diametrically opposite to Japanese business culture with its total overlap of work and personal life. In this regard, it is quite common to witness Indian managers being traditional in personal and social spheres of their lives, and relatively 'modern' and globally oriented in work-related matters. Perhaps, because Indians have always possessed a relatively high level of tolerance for ambiguity, they are able to deal with this apparent dichotomy without too much difficulty (Chatterjee and Nankervis, 2003).

Conclusion: Developing cross-verging solutions

Indian business is in a state of transition, as indeed is Indian society as a whole. However, in a society as old, diverse and complex as India, the pace of change is of necessity slow. The average Indian business is also subject to reasonably similar sets of forces. Traditional social and cultural forces that act on a business stem from expected loyalties to the larger family and community and the traditional acceptance and expectation of hierarchy. The 'modern' forces that act on Indian businesses emanate from economic reforms; global development and change, and the gradual homogenisation of Indian society. The combination of these forces is reshaping Indian business culture, which has been forced to adapt rapidly to these structural imperatives. Presently, Indian business and managerial culture appear to be in the midst of a fundamental transition.

In spite of the euphoria as to the transformative nature of globalisation, Indian managers are less inclined to adopt long-term strategic approaches, preferring to adopt piecemeal and intuitive action-frames. What is interesting to note is that the variables outlined in the paragraph above do not appear to have changed in equal degree during a general period of transition from 'tradition' to globalisation. Indeed, as another study has concluded,

[V]alues must be viewed individually and not as a bundled entity. Some values may change while others do not. Some values may change more rapidly than other values. Other unique values may evolve from a combination of influences. (Ralston et al., 1993, p. 270)

Following recent deregulation and expected lifting of restrictions on foreign investment in the airline industry in India, it is expected that the entry of imaginative new competitors will demand more competitive and innovative responses from the stagnant and bureaucratic traditional players in this sector. For example, a Bangalore-based successful brewery (United Breweries) has thrown a challenge to India's powerful aviation bureaucracy by coopting them as partners (ground handling and maintenance activities) in their bid to make Kingfisher Airline (named after UB's best selling brand name in beer) find a completely new market segment in the domestic air travel. 'India's domestic airlines carry fewer than 20M passengers a year, whilst over 15M people travel by train everyday' (*The Economist*, 2005, p. 64).

Some elements of business culture in India are changing across the board, while others are changing only in internationally-oriented large business houses. While market orientation is perhaps one of those trends that have touched every business entity, Western concepts of 'brand image' and 'value-adding' through differentiation and closer segmentation of the market are still in their infancy. The associative success indicator of market culture, through the adoption of international service standards, is limited only to exclusive tourism and hotel chains. For example, Singapore Airlines came from nowhere in the seventies to become the brand leader in Asia in less than two decades. Yet, Air India and Indian Airlines have been bounded by the managerial inefficiencies of governmental rules, regulations and lack of vision. Interestingly, after 50 years of such poor managerial example, the airline industry in India has suddenly woken up with energy, enterprise and service quality with the entry of a number of private airline companies such as Jet Airways, Sahara and Kingfisher Airlines.

With the increasing dominance of market ideology in all spheres of economic life in India, there is a need for managers to find new ways of conceptualising their work, organisational processes and general approaches. One group of management scholars has noted recently that Indian management systems have a historical tendency to fit structural anatomy to the strategy and lock both in place with separate supporting systems. As a consequence of changed circumstances, they argue the need for a radical shift in the managerial mindset of Indian managers. They further suggest that this predominantly Western managerial worldview is considered to be the key doctrine by most professional managers and leading management schools. They contend that:

> In a highly restrictive and regulated economy characterised by widespread shortages of most products, the key management task was to allocate the company's limited financial resources among the competing opportunities in different divisions and then monitor the performance of divisional managers against their plans through a tight control system. By providing discipline, focus and control, the strategy – structure – systems management doctrine suited the context very well. (Ghoshal et al., 2000, p. 311)

However, in light of the broad economic transformations under way in India today, these same scholars go on to deconstruct this widely held managerial view by advocating, with almost evangelical fervour, a radical mind-scape shift in India. In the new managerial context:

> An internet portal constructed by twenty people at a total cost of Rs. 30 lakh (US$ 80,000) has a market value greater than all the tea gardens of Assam; in which swirling competition outdates established industry structures overnight; and in which hiring an excellent manager or scientist can often be a far bigger triumph than bagging a big bank loan – the strategy – structure – systems model has become obsolete. (Ghosal et al., 2000, p. 312)

Blue-collar jobs comprised 88 per cent of the workforce in India in the 1960s, and have declined to 17 per cent in the 1990s, and are likely to be about two per cent by 2025. Predictably, the composition of the workforce in future will divide into 20 per cent knowledge workers and eight per cent service workers and they will essentially need to be well educated. The idea of job security will inevitably be replaced by a 'performance for survival' mindset.

Other prominent scholars of Indian management strongly advocate that a paradigm shift in managerial values and assumptions can only be possible by adhering to the traditional wisdom of the country (Chakraborty, 1998). These scholars suggest that, like the Japanese, Indian managerial values and goals need to arise out of deeply-rooted social and ethical traditions. While 'tradition' is unmistakably observable in the daily lives of managers and employees across the country, work organisations appear to be at the crossroads. At least amongst senior level Indian managers, there appears to be a parallel emergence of 'global' value paradigms. (Chatterjee and Pearson, 2000a, 2000b).

Questions

1. Explain the influences of the Indian political and economic system on Indian managerial styles
2. What are the similarities and differences between Indian and Western management paradigms? How are the differences displayed?
3. Explain the major opportunities and constraints in the development of Indian management into the twenty first century

References

Aiyar, S, 2003, Made in India, *India Today*, December 1, pp. 20–8.

Asia Business Week 2005, 'The Best Asian Performers', October 24 (Special Report), pp. 55–82.

Barron, C, 2004, 'Gurus of a spectral art', *The Australian Financial Review*, Friday, April 16, Review, p. 5.

Beals, R, 1953, 'Acculturation', In Krober AL, (ed.), *Anthropology Today*, University of Chicago Press, Chicago.

Bedi, H, 1991, *Understanding Asian managers*, Allen & Unwin, Sydney.

Bever, E, Stephenson, E & Tanner, D, 2005, 'How India's executives see the world', *McKinsey Quarterly*, Special Edition, pp. 35–41.

Bond, M & King, YC, 1985, 'Coping with the threat of westernisation in Hong Kong', *International Journal of Inter Cultural Relations*, vol. 9, no. 4, pp. 351–64.

Brown, D & Wilson S, 2005, *The black book of outsourcing*, Wiley Publishing, Indianapolis, IN.

Bucknell, H & Ontaki, R, 2005, *Mastering business in Asia: Human resource management*. John Wiley, Singapore.

Chandler, C, 2005, Dealing with dynasties. *Fortune*, October 31, pp. 56–62.

Chakraborty, S, 1998, *Values and ethics for organizations: Theory and practice*, Oxford University Press, New Delhi.

Chatterjee, D, 1998, *Leading consciously*. Butterworth-Heinemann, Boston.

Chatterjee, SR, 2006, 'Human resource management in India', in A Nankervis, SR Chatterjee & J Coffey (eds), *Perspectives of human resource management in the Asia Pacific* Pearson Education, Melbourne (2006).

Chatterjee, SR & Pearson, CAL, 2000a, 'Indian managers in transition: Orientations, work goals, values and ethics, *Management International Review*, vol. 40, no. 1, pp. 81–95.

—— 2000b, 'Work goals and societal value orientations of senior Indian managers: An empirical analysis', *Journal of Management Development*, vol. 19, no. 7, pp. 643–53.

Chatterjee, SR & Nankervis, A, 2003, *Understanding Asian management: Transition and transformations*. Vineyard Publisher, Perth.

Child, JD, 1981, 'Culture, contingency and capitalism in the cross-national study of organisations', In LL Cummings & GM Staw (eds), *Research in Organisational Behaviour* (vol. 3), JAI Publications, Greenwich pp. 303–56.

Das, C, 2002, *The elephant paradigm*, Penguin Books, New Delhi.

Davis, H, Chatterjee, S & Heuer, M, 2005, *Management in India: Trends and Transition*. Sage Publishers. New Delhi.

England, GW & Lee, R, 1974, 'The relationship between managerial values and managerial success in the United States, Japan, India and Australia', *Journal of Applied Psychology*, vol. 59, no. 4, pp. 411–19.

Ghoshal, S, Piramal, G & Bartlett, CA, 2000, *Managing radical change: What Indian companies must do to become world-class*, Viking, India.

Hofstede, G, 2001, *Culture's consequences*, (2nd edn.), Sage, London.

IMF, 2005, 'World Economic Outlook', September, INF Publications, Washington.

Lannoy, R, 1971, *The speaking tree: A study of Indian culture and society*, Oxford University Press, Oxford, UK.

Lopez, CA, Porter, M & Schwab, K, 2005, *The Global competitiveness report 2005–06*, Palgrave-Macmillan, Basingstock, Hampshire.

Nadkarni, S, 2004, 'The rise of the tiger', *Big Quotient*, September–October, p. 14.

Monappa, A & Engineer, M, 1999, *Liberalisation and human resource management* Response Books, New Delhi.

Ralston, DA, Gustafson, DJ, Cheung, FM & Terpstra, RH, 1993, 'Difference in managerial values: A study of U.S., Hong Kong and PRC managers', *Journal of International Business Studies*, vol.10, no.1, pp. 249–75.

Rangarajan, LN, 1992, *The Arthashastra*, Penguin Books, New Delhi.

Saha, A, 1993, 'The caste system in India and its consequence', *The International Journal of Sociology and Social Policy*, vol 13, no. 3/4, pp. 1–76.

Sen, A, 2005, *The Argumentative Indian*, Penguin Books, London.

Sharma, S, 1999, *Management in new age: Western windows, Eastern doors*, New Age International, New Delhi.

Shourie, A, 2004, 'From red tape to red carpet', *India Today International*, March 29.

Sihag, B, 2004, 'Kautilya on the scope and methodology of accounting, organisational design and the role of ethics in Ancient India', *The Accounting Historians Journal*, vol. 31, no.2, pp. 125–48.

Singh, JP, 1990, 'Managerial culture and work-related values in India', *Organizational Studies*, vol.11, no. 1, pp. 5–101.

Singh, JV, 2001, 'McKinsey's managing director Rajat Gupta on leading a knowledge-based Global Consulting organization', *The Academy of Management Executive*, vol.12, no.2, pp. 34–44.

Sinha, J, 2005, 'Checking India's vital signs', *McKinsey Quarterly, Special Edition*, pp. 17–25.

Sinha, J & Kanungo, R, 1997, 'Context sensitivity and balancing in organisational behaviour', *International Journal of Psychology*, vol. 32, no. 2, pp. 93–105.

Sinha, JBP, 1991, *Work culture in the Indian context* Sage, New Delhi.

Slater, J, 2001, 'Delhi's disc dreams', *Far East Economic Review*, Nov.1, pp. 42–4.

Som, A, 2006, 'Bracing MNC competition through innovative HRM practices: The way forward for Indian firms', *Thunderbird International Business Review*.

Tata Sons Limited, 2005, 'Group financial performance and sector-wise operations', available [online] http://www.tata.com/0_investor_desk/business_sectors.htm.

Tayeb, M, 1989, *Organisations and national culture: A Comparative analysis*, Sage, London.

Tayeb, M, 1996, 'India: A non-tiger of Asia', *International Business Review*, vol.5, no. 5, pp. 425–45.

The Economist, 2005, India's high-flying liquor king, July 16, p. 64.

Transparency International, 2005, 'Corruption Perception Index', available [on-line] at http://transparency.org

Vellor, R, 2004, 'Indian producers set to take off globally', *The Straits Times*, Singapore, December 17, p. 10.

Webber, RH, 1969, 'Convergence or divergence', *Columbia Journal of World Business*, vol. 4, no. 3, pp. 75–83.

Worden, S, 2003, 'The role of religious and nationalist ethics in strategic leadership: The case of JN Tata', *Journal of Business Ethics*, vol. 47, no. 2, pp. 147–61.

Additional readings

Chakraborty, SK & Bhattacharya, P, (eds) 2001, *Leadership and power: Ethical explorations*, Oxford University Press, New Delhi.

Das G, 2002, *The elephant paradigm: India wrestles with change*, Penguin, New Delhi.

Davis, H, Chatterjee, S & Heuer, M, (eds) 2005, *Management in India: Trends and transition*, Sage, New Delhi.

Ghoshal, S, Piramal, G & Bartlett CA, 2000, *Managing radical change: What Indian companies must do to become world class*, Viking Press, India.

Lannoy, R, 1971, *The speaking tree: A study of Indian culture and society*, Oxford University Press, London.

Mason, P, 1985, *The men who ruled India*, W.A Norton Publications, New York.

Sinha JBP, 1991, *Work culture in the Indian context*, Sage, New Delhi.

Managing long traditions and innovation to sustain development in Japan

5.1 To describe the historical and philosophical context of modern Japan.

5.2. To explain the major political, socio-cultural and economic influences on management in Japan.

5.3 To outline how regional and local influences, and global forces impact on Japanese management.

5.4 To explore the linkages between macro-, meso- and micro-level factors in Japanese management.

5.5 To explain the major challenges for Japanese managerial values, systems and practices.

Introduction

Japan is renowned for its economic superpower status and global car and electric appliances manufacturers, such as Toyota, Nissan, Honda, Mitsubishi, Mazda, Sony, Panasonic, Canon, Toshiba, Fujitsu, NEC and Sanyo. The nation's long and independent history and the unique features of its heritage are less understood. Important international, regional and local heritage forces have played a key role in shaping Japan's socio-cultural, political and economic development and insights from this provide a valuable framework for understanding Japanese society and its characteristic approach to business management. Essentially, Japanese heritage has collectively endowed its people with a highly disciplined capacity for learning and the application of this to innovate in times of need. Over time, and forming a pattern response to crisis, a historical series of orchestrated development strategies (i.e., the *Taika* Reforms (645), the Meiji Restoration (1867), and Post War reconstruction (1945)) applied by Japanese leaders have strengthened nationalism and facilitated the 'Japanisation' of foreign expertise. These factors, together with the unique and powerful features of Japanese cultural heritage, mobilised the successive phases of industrial development that ultimately led to the world-wide implementation of the worker empowered and quality-based Japanese management model. This remarkable Japanese success has attracted significant international interest, in particular qualitative socio-cultural, structural and operational dimensions of Japanese management as applied at the meso-societal and micro-organisational levels. However, contemporary Japan faces new external and internal destabilising issues brought on by the ever intensifying forces of globalisation. The country is now closely considering the next crisis response required to achieve a more sustainable approach to development. As the most developed nation of the Asian region, this current review process and its outcome will continue to be of high regional and international interest.

The macro-regional level: Local issues and external forces influencing the management context of Japan

The miraculous transformation of Japan from an insulated, small and island-based agrarian state to a highly industrialised nation, and subsequently from a war-torn state to a country with super power status has captured great attention. This transformation process is the story of how Japanese leaders and people responded to external threats in times of state crisis. In essence, their development approach has involved a historical and crisis-based response pattern guided by a conscientious Japanese approach to learning applied to gain advanced international expertise interpreted through unique Japanese socio-cultural values and institutionalised practices. The story of Japan offers insights into the paradoxical nature of the relationship between the two wheels of a nation's development (i.e., one being inherently quantitative, or economic, and the other being qualitative, or socio-cultural) and into the challenges now presented to the super power nation by the forces of global imperatives. In the early 1990s, Japan went into a decade-long period of economic downturn and currently faces the complex transition challenges associated with repositioning itself in a competitive and dynamic global market context.

The unfolding story of Japanese development highlights the key interactive processes between macro-regional level and meso-societal level influences and the way that these have shaped Japanese management. The chronological review of Japanese transformation adopted in this chapter reveals the essential Japanese cultural logic underpinning the development of Japanese management strategies, structures, systems and styles, and insights gained from this explain the complex and interdependent nature of organisational and societal issues now faced by management in Japan. The aim of this approach is to present the reader with frameworks with which to appreciate the characteristic underlying management principles in contemporary Japanese response patterns at macro-, meso- and micro-managerial levels. The next section discusses the macro-regional impact of geography, religion and culture in shaping of the early development of Japan.

The forces of heritage

Stretching from the north to the south and surrounded by the sea off the eastern coast of the Eurasian continent the four main islands of Hokkaido, Honshu, Shikoku and Kyushu of the Japanese archipelago lie on the western rim of the Pacific 'Ring of Fire'. The land is characteristically mountainous with limited natural resources. This geography meant that the ancient Japanese had to develop systems of agricultural production through the modification of the environment while being regularly subjected to destructive natural forces, such as, typhoons, flood, earthquakes, tsunamis and volcanic eruptions. As a response to this unpredictable environment, a deep appreciation and reverence for both the majestic 'life-giving' and 'life-taking' power of nature grew. Thus, the external environment was viewed as something to 'co-exist' with in 'harmony'. Hence, a degree of 'fatalism' is included in ancient sense-making in this context (Reischauer, 1977).

The pre-modernisation era: The foundation of Japanese socio-cultural heritage

Indigenous accounts of early Japanese history, the *Kojiki*, (Record of Ancient Things, 712 AD) and the *Nihon Shoki* (Chronicles of Japan, 720 AD), offer vital clues to Japanese foundational socio-cultural traditions. These two complementary early chronicles present mythological accounts of the 'Age of Gods and Goddesses' similarly to polytheistic Greek mythology, and so form an important basis for understanding the influence of early Japanese society in the modern Japanese worldview. In Japanese mythology, accounts of gods and goddesses are described as being good, bad, innovative and reckless to reflect the social norms and customs of early Japanese communities (Miura, 2003). Absent in the myths is a concept of ethics. The basis of the cultural rationale embedded in these ancient narratives is contextual, rather than the application of universal moral principles. This rationale is indicative of the relativistic nature of early Japanese socio-cultural systems. The chronicles also date the establishment of the Yamato State in 660 BC, in the present day Prefecture of *Nara*, by the first Emperor *Jimmu* ('divine warrior'). *Jimmu* was represented as the direct descendant of the Sun Goddess *Amaterasu* (the supreme god in the mythology), as well as the first in line of the unbroken imperial lineage to the current 125th Emperor *Akihito*. Although modern historians discard these early accounts as legend, ancient Chinese records support early archaeological evidence of the Japanese '*Yamato*' state (ibid).

The cultural logic underpinning the ancient explanation for the divine rule of the Emperor, together with early animist and polytheistic values, provides a unique foundation for Japanese socio-cultural heritage (Reischauer, 1977). While debate continues about the exact establishment date, Japan has one of the longest independent state histories which accounts in part for the strength of

Japanese national socio-cultural identity built around the ancient indigenous religion *Shintō* the direct descendents of the supreme God, the emperor. However, these complementary traditional socio-cultural institutions did not emerge in isolation, or as a matter of chance. Rather, they are the result of particular strategic responses by early political leaders to external (religious and political) pressures (Morishima, 1982). For instance, the early customs of animist and ancestor worship were transformed into the national religion *Shintō* in response to the external influence of Buddhism brought from China via Korea (Hiro, 1987). Later, the *Taika* Reform (645 AD), political reform based around *Shintō* beliefs, fundamental to future Japan, took place. According to the *Nihon Shoki*, the reform was triggered by a political coup led by Prince *Naka no Ōe* (later Emperor *Tenji*) and his supporters who pursued a political doctrine built on a political aspiration to:

1. Transform the state into a sophisticated sovereign state under the emperor, equivalent to an advanced neighbouring state in China (i.e., the Sui, 581–618) through the institutionalisation of civil bureaucracy, *ritsuryo* (a code of laws), centralised administration systems, and

2. Legitimise the imperial lineage as the rightful ruler of the country or state loyalty to the emperor. The Japanese emperor became known as '*Tennō*' (Heavenly Emperor) where previously the title had been '*Ō-kimi*' (Great King) (Morishima, 1982).

Morishima (1982) describes the underpinning of this utmost important political reform in Japan as follows:

> The change had far-reaching results; it implied that the Emperor was no longer a king, but was a Manifest God (*ara-hito gami*) and was thus identified with God. There could consequently be no possibility of conflict between God and Emperor ... The imperial throne was thus provided with divine right ... the political axiom that in their country, as opposed to China, the claim to the throne could be made only with the authority of descent. (pp. 23–4)

Although in contemporary Japan the emperors' political influence has declined to a nominal role, these early religious and political perspectives underpin the unique foundational elements of the Japanese socio-cultural developmental path.

The regional influence of China

The Japanese did not originate in Japan. 'The Japanese, like all other peoples, are the product of long and largely unrecorded mixtures' (Reischauer, 1977, p. 34) of successive patterns of regional migration. This early settlement pattern underscores the importance of the ancient civilisation of early migrants. Japan lies within the powerful sphere of influence of China. Chinese institutions, such as administrative systems, religions and philosophies, writing and education systems, were instrumental in the early political, socio-cultural and economic development of Japan. Furthermore, when China was not the cultural originator (as is the case of Buddhism), it served as an important conduit. According to *Nihon Shoki*, Chinese institutions were originally imported via Korea and, later, the result of direct contact. As these cultural influences were not preceded, or accompanied by foreign political control, they established themselves in Japan by virtue of their utility, or prestige (Beasley, 1999). Moreover, the 'Japanisation' assimilation process meant that the imported values and practices were adapted to incorporate the rationale of local values, and the conditions. The ongoing cultural 'indigenisation' process led to the development of the distinctive character of Japanese practices and institutions; For example, the unique Japanese writing system was developed by adopting the script of the 'monosyllabic' Chinese language to write the 'polysyllabic' Japanese; another important example is Confucianism, Taoism and Mahayana Buddhism, which had arrived successively during the fifth and sixth centuries and their later variants (i.e., Zen Buddhism and Neo-Confucianism) (Morishima, 1982).

The 'Japanisation' of Chinese religious and philosophical influences

In the course of Japanese history, Chinese religions and philosophies have been adapted to fit with the circumstances and agendas of Japanese political leaders. For instance, Confucianism was adopted as a socio-political code for its disciplinary, rather than religious values, so as to institutionalise a system of ethics into *Shintō* (Morishima, 1982). Additional selective dimensions are noteworthy. The superordinate value of Confucianism – benevolence – was replaced by loyalty, and this value shift set Confucianism on a different philosophical course in Japanese Confucianism; similarly, Taoism, with its practical 'way of life' focus on a philosophical understanding of the universal nature of the order of things and the importance of attaining inner spiritual harmony was easily assimilated with early *Shintō* animist and ancestor worship and customs, which came to underscore the harmony of the earth and spiritual features of the national *Shintō* religion (Morishima, 1982). Buddhism introduced individualist-oriented beliefs which neither *Shintō* nor Confucianism included. Despite earlier state resistance, Buddhism won state support in the seventh century and began to symbiotically co-exist with *Shintō* (Hiro, 1987) to evolve into various Japanese Buddhist denominations. Later, during the *Kamakura* era (1191–1333), Japanese Confucianism and *Shintō* ideas were infused with the self-discipline of the newly imported religion from China, Zen Buddhism, which stresses emptying the mind through meditation as the means to enlightenment and these spiritual concepts were to become the foundation of *Bushidō*, or the Way of the Warriors (Nitobe, 1905).

The ideological foundations for a nation: The feudal era and *Bushidō*

The *Kamakura era* (1192–1867) marked the dawn of a feudal era where successive military governments controlled the state and the political influence of the imperial court government declined. Whilst the feudal era shared common characteristics with the Western medieval world, it also had distinctive features which indicate that 'literature, art, and learning showed remarkable continuity and the high culture that once was largely limited to the capital region spread widely throughout the nation' (Reischauer, 1977, p. 59). Unlike their European counterparts, who often drew on Roman law to adopt a contractual lord-vassal feudal relationship, Japan's military retainers, or *samurai*, pledged loyalty to their lords (i.e., clan leaders) as an 'ethical absolute' and possessed a high respect for intellectual activities in line with the *Bushidō* code (Reischauer and Craig, 1979). A distinct different between the Chinese and Japanese Confucian socio-cultural concept of loyalty can be made:

> Loyalty to the ruler was important in the Chinese Confucian system, but it was usually overshadowed by loyalty to the family. In fact, three of the five basic Confucian ethical relationships had to do with filial piety and other family loyalties. In Japan, loyalty to the lord was more central to the whole system and, despite the importance of the family, took precedence over loyalty to it. Thus, in Japan, the supra-family group early became established as more fundamental than the family itself, and this made easier the transition in modern times to loyalty to the nation and other non-kinship groupings. (Reischauer, 1977, p. 57)

The *Bushidō* code prescribed the moral framework to guide the *samurai* in the pursuit of lifelong commitment to enrich human values and master the martial arts. The *samurai* strove to develop highly refined personal characteristics based on seven principles: *chūgi* (the duty of loyalty), *gi* (the righteousness), *yū* (the spirit of daring and bearing), *jin* (benevolence), *meiyo* (honour), *rei* (politeness) and *sei* (veracity and sincerity). Of these *Chūgi* was regarded as the superordinate principle, and the *gi* and *yū* were regarded as instrumental in its righteous pursuit (Nitobe, 1905). The notion of serving public interests by repressing self interests and through self-sacrifice (*messhi hōkō*) was the prescriptive assumption guiding loyalty (Ueda, 1998). 'Thus, the code demanded that its followers pursue both physical and spiritual training of the highest order and thus resulted in the development of a class of people who were extraordinarily disciplined and accomplished' (De Menthe, 1995, p. 65).

A centralised feudal system: Tokugawa Shogunate

The powerful Tokugawa Shogunate (military leaders) and *Bakufu* (military-based government) (1603–1867) finally brought peace and stability to the state ending some 150 years of power struggle among the feudal lords. 'Despite its old-fashioned feudal pattern, Japan in the seventeenth and eighteenth centuries was certainly more orderly and in many ways more uniformly and efficiently ruled than any country in Europe at that time' (Reischauer, 1977, pp. 69–70). Various innovations in the *Bakufu*'s administrative systems and trade policies were instrumental to the subsequent two hundred fifty years of political and social stability. Four particular innovations were notably influential on Japanese development:

1. The '*baku-han* system' wherein the land was divided into two categories: the land ruled directly by the central government *Bakufu* and that ruled by the *han-shu*, or feudal lords, who ruled the centrally assigned lands (i.e., the *han*) on the appointment or approval of the *Bakufu*. The *Bakufu* retained absolute authority over promotion, demotion and even the existence of the *hanshu* clan, but generally allowed autonomy in the management of the *han*. Associated with the *han* as a power base for the feudal lords, the subject of the *samurai's* duty of loyalty, or *kō* in *messhi hōkō*, logically shifted from the family and clan, to the *han* (Ueda, 1998).

2. The '*terauke* system' institutionalised Buddhist temples within a local community by law. Though originally introduced as a measure to eliminate Christians, this system enabled the temples to establish a firm foundation as local community centers by making education one of their central institutional functions (i.e., the '*terakoya*' – the temple school) through opportunities offered to under-privileged commoners' children. While teaching commoner children was largely limited to elementary levels of writing, reading and calculation, this community-driven education system was a critical ingredient for Japan's later economic development (Takahashi, 1969). This widespread grass-roots learning, together with the formal child education of the court noble and samurai classes helps to explain how that at the end of this historical period, despite being economically underdeveloped, Japan had a higher rate of literacy than Europe (Sen, 2004).

3. The *Bakufu*'s administrative model, as institutionalised over many *han*s, was built around a hierarchical group council, shared authority and consensual decision-making (Reischauer, 1977). These administrative characteristics remained intact among modern Japanese organisations until recently.

4. The seclusion policy (1639–1858) banned all foreign trades but those with China, Korea, and Holland in order to stop inflows of Christian influences from Western countries, such as Portugal, Spain and England. This deliberate inward-looking policy was the prime driver behind renewed national enthusiasm for history and *Shintō*, as well as Neo-Confucian learning. A consequential reflective question arose as to who should be the subject of the duty of loyalty of the people – the *han* and the *Tokugawa Shogun* or the land nostalgically called '*Yamato*' and the emperor? (Morishima, 1982). Towards

the end of the feudal era, this debate instigated division of the *samurai* class along with court nobles and, thus, the state. Additional growing frustration with the submissive *Bakufu*'s dealings with ever increasing Western (i.e., the United States, Britain, France and Russia) dominance over state sovereignty fuelled strong nationalism and concern for foreign involvement in the state's demise (Henshall, 1999). The seclusion policy was designed to ensure the maintenance of the 'status-quo' power of the state, but ironically the policy created an environment for an alternative pro-imperialist reformer political force to the *Bakufu* to emerge and so their growing support ended the long period of *Bakufu* rule.

During this lengthy and stable period, *Bushidō* values were further refined and embedded in wider Japanese society. In a peaceful context, as part of the self-discipline associated with the martial arts, the samurai actively engaged in wide-ranging intellectual activities. Rather than the pursuit of knowledge for the sake of scholarship, the *samurai* regarded learning as a way to strengthen their calibre. Hence, the focus on learning was directed at the practical application – building the embedded nature of knowledge through practice; 'knowledge becomes really such only when it is assimilated in the mind of the learner and shows in his character' (Nitobe, 1905, p. 17). This *samurai* epistemology still prevails, and can be identified in the emphasis on 'tacit' or 'embedded' nature of knowledge over the 'explicit' or 'abstracted' form in the contemporary Japanese approach to the field of knowledge management (Nonaka and Takeuchi, 1995; Fruin, 1997; Cohen, 1998). By the middle of the Tokugawa era, the values and practices of *Bushidō* were increasingly being transferred to commoners, and so became the moral ideal of the Japanese, or *Yamato Damashii* (Nitobe, 1905) or, a 'secularisation of bushidō' (Morishima, 1982, p. 50).

New leadership, political and administrative systems: *Meiji* Restoration

The *Meiji* Restoration (1867) brought the end of the feudal era and introduced a second critical period in Japan's history. As had been the case with earlier state reform, this second period was triggered by growing external pressure and driven by strong nationalism built around *Shintō* and the Emperor. However, this time the source of external pressure was the Western countries that had established their dominance in the Asia Pacific region. Japanese national security consciousness arose in 1853 when US Navy Commodore Matthew Perry forced his way ashore near the present day *Yokosuka* and demanded a bilateral trade relationship between the two countries. The demise of state sovereignty became predictable in 1858 when the protector of the state, the *Tokugawa Bakufu*, was forced to sign the excessively unfair commercial treaties with Western countries (United States, Britain, France, Russia and Holland) which afforded Japan semi-colonial status (Reischauer and Craig, 1979). In this context, military conflict began between the *Satsuma* and *Chōshō han* driven by their political slogan, *sonnō-jōi* (i.e., honouring the Emperor and expelling the Westerners) and the Western countries (England, United States, France and Holland). With advantageous Western technological weaponry, the conflict did not last long. The demoralising experience of the military might of the Western countries, together with rising nationalism, led to an anti-*Bakufu* political ideology with preference for the pursuit of the state security and independence through rapid state modernisation under the leadership of the Emperor (Reischauer and Craig, 1979).

Following this pervasive national humiliation, Japan then achieved in only thirty years what had taken Britain some one hundred and fifty (Beaseley, 1999). A range of revolutionary meso-societal level modernisation and industrialisation strategies were set in place. The young Meiji Emperor was moved to Tokyo from Kyoto, where his predecessors had resided for over a millennium; direct ruling power was restored to the Emperor with the support of the Grand Council; *Shintō* was elevated to the state religion; and the feudal system was abolished. Administrative power was handed to leaders of a new government who were drawn from the former *samurai* of *Chōshū* and the *Satsuma hans* and anti-*Bakufu* nobles who had fought against the *Tokugawa Bakufu* and pledged loyalty to the state and the Emperor. This administrative strategy was adopted because the young Meiji Emperor and the Imperial Court had neither sufficient hands-on military and political knowledge, nor necessary leadership skills, to reengineer and modernise the state. Financial reforms were introduced to improve the government's economic position, restrictions of the class system were introduced, a Charter Oath declared the need to 'seek knowledge widely throughout the world' (Cummings, 1980, p. 17 cited in Sen, 2004), and in 1872 a compulsory education law was passed (Takahashi, 1969).

New infrastructure systems

New institutional structures were required to implement these visionary political and economic reforms, symbolised in the two following development slogans – *fukoku-kyōhei* (i.e., rich country, strong military) and *oitsuke, oikose* (i.e., catch-up and overtake) (Takahashi, 1969):

> Westernisation would make Japan stronger, better able to compete with western powers, and perhaps even match, or surpass them ... A westernised Japan would be taken more seriously by the west, and Japan very much wanted to be taken seriously. It did not like the humiliation of 'unequal treaties' signed during the death those of the shogunate, and was very keen to have them revised. (Henshall, 1999, p. 75)

Western institutions were actively sought as models for modernisation and industrialisation. For example, British systems for the telegraph, the railways and the Imperial Japanese Navy; the French highly centralised education model, the Imperial Japanese Army, and the Criminal Code; the US tertiary education system for universities; and German systems for the *Meiji* Constitution, the military and the Civil Code (Morishima, 1982). A German model for the constitution was chosen because this enabled considerable power to be retained by the Emperor, or those advising him, and limited the political involvement of the cabinet (Henshall, 1999). These imported institutions were localised to incorporate traditional Japanese socio-cultural values applied through the assimilation principle of *wakon yōsai* (i.e., Western capabilities under Japanese spirit). Human resources for state development were recruited on a 'meritocracy' principle rather than the traditional hereditary-profession system. Young elite Japanese were sent to the West for education and Western engineers and technicians were invited to Japan to educate and train the Japanese (Takahashi, 1969; Fürstenberg, 1974). Through the assimilation of western science, the Japanese became increasingly technologically capable by innovatively combining this Western knowledge with traditional Japanese technologies (Debin, 2004).

Education: The key strategic value for the national development

The following statement by an influential leader at the time indicates the key modernisation role attributed to education by the new administration: 'Our people are no different from the Americans or Europeans of today; it is all a matter of education or lack of education' (Kido Takayoshi cited in Sen, 2004, p. 51). Strong political commitment to education as a meso-level development strategy, coupled with a disciplined approach to learn from foreign education and training systems, are recognised as the key factors that rapidly accelerated the modernisation of Japan. Between 1906 and 1911, education consumed as much as 43 per cent of the budgets of the towns and villages, for Japan as a whole (Gluck, 1985, cited in Sen, 2004, p. 51).

> By 1913, even though Japan was still economically very poor and underdeveloped, it had become one of the largest producers of books in the world–publishing more books than Britain and indeed more than twice as many as the united States. Indeed, Japan's entire experience of economic development was, to a greater extent, driven by human capability formation, which included the role of education and training, and this was promoted *both* by public policy and by a supportive cultural climate. (interacting with each other).
> (Sen, 2004, p. 51)

However, in reactive response to the destabilising influence of Western values a nationalist approach was adopted that included Confucian and Shinto moral education, morally uplifting songs, flag raising ceremonies and other nationalist symbols. This 'supportive' cultural climate for education was linked to the high scholarship and disciplined ideals of the *Bushidō* code. By the 1890s the more cohesive nationalist ideology was promoted to the society at large: 'The Meiji government had relearned from the nation's ancient leaders the value of indoctrination' (Henshall, 1999, p. 82).

Changing the commercial ethos:
State-based to private enterprises

Japan was determined to build the economy through its own resources (Takahashi, 1969, p. vi). In the absent of market capital, management talents and entrepreneurs, the government initially adopted a 'state' capitalism approach making active investments in strategic industries while sponsoring other industries, through technical assistance, favourable credit and/or subsidies, to build the requisite infrastructure required for rapid industrialisation. Social elites, who were commonly former samurai, predominantly managed state-owned enterprises (SOEs). However, many were financially unsuccessful as management decisions were based not on economic rationality, but on the ethical ideals of *Bushidō* which traditionally despises money-making activities (Nitobe, 1905; Takahashi, 1969). This early mindset, together with the high wages paid to the former military retainers, led to a growing accumulation of financial losses and government burden. Facing this reality, in 1879 the government abandoned this state-based administrative system and progressively transferred the management of state enterprises to trustworthy and capable entrepreneurs (Takahashi, 1969; Morishima, 1982).

Those entrusted to run businesses in key industries received early state assistance, while accepting their national obligations and social responsibilities (Reischauer and Craig, 1979). Embracing these they were endowed with the cultural attributes of being 'gentleman businessman' as associated with the noble loyalty ideal of *Bushidō* – putting the nation's interests before their own – the self-sacrificing ethos of *messhi hōkō* (Takahashi, 1969, p. 28). The performance rationale for these early modern Japanese companies was for individuals to pursue success for collective Japanese national development, rather than for the personal benefit of individuals and companies; i.e., the holistic co-existence and co-prosperity idea of *kyōzon kyōei*. A collective national development responsibility underpinning key modern corporate activities was often characterised by a pragmatic mix of national and social obligations, alongside the pursuit of profitability (Dore, 1973). An emergent pattern of close working relationships between politicians, bureaucrats and industry became coupled to this characteristic Japanese corporate culture. In the West, this characteristic cross-sectoral relationship was later referred to as *Japan, Inc.* Nevertheless, this arrangement incorporated 'the Japanese tradition of private acceptance of government leadership and the wide-spread recognition that government officials have knowledge, experience, and information superior to that available to the ordinary firm' (Ackley and Ishi, 1976, pp. 236–7). By the end of the nineteenth century, with these various meso-level development strategies set in place, Japan began to mobilise rapid industrialisation processes.

The meso-societal level: The management
of Japanese institutional infrastructure

This section discusses how the vision for national development based on: appropriated western knowledge, institutional systems and technologies; a

Bushidō-based community culture, and a range of mutually supportive strategies enabled a rapid industrialisation process across Japanese institutions and organisations. The comprehensive and systematic nature of the meso-level industrial revolution is still relevant today.

Industrial infrastructure: Powerful industrial conglomerates

The Japanese Industrial Revolution began towards the end of the nineteenth century. Successful regional military campaigns provided the impetus for rapid commercial development (i.e., the Sino-Japanese War: 1894–1905, the Russo-Japanese War: 1904–5, and the First World War: 1914–18). Some enterprises (e.g., Mitsui, Mitsubishi, Sumitomo and Yasuda) developed to form huge family-controlled financial and industrial conglomerates (*zaibatsu*) with the exclusive ownership of holding companies across banking and insurance, trading, shipping and shipping services, manufacturing, chemical and heavy industrial production, construction and mining companies (Morikawa, 1992).

At the core of the *zaibatsu* groups were the banking and trading companies, which were instrumental to further group expansion. For instance, Mitsui & Co., the largest trading company before the Second World War, began its own operations in Europe as early as 1878 through its Paris branch, and then opened offices in London (1880), Milan (1880) and Hamburg (1899). This led other Japanese international business interests (i.e., banking, shipping and insurance) to establish themselves in Europe (Mason, 1992) and in the United States in 1879 (Wilkins, 1990). The *zaibatsu* group activities facilitated the import to Japan of advanced Western manufacturing machinery and capital goods, and the export of silk products. Since 1920s, rapid industrial growth led to the creation of a unique Japanese dual industry structure with highly modernised large companies and traditional labour-intensive medium and small companies coexisting (Nakamura, 1981). By the 1940s, under the military government's patronage six influential *zaibatsu* groups rapidly developed – Asano, Furukawa, Nakajima, Nissan, Nomura and Okura. They came to be referred to as 'new' *zaibatsu* in relation to the four long established groups which developed rapidly under the Meiji government's foster care (Morishima, 1982).

Development of Japanese human resource management (HRM) models

While prototype paternalistic and long-term approaches to business management existed even in the seventeenth century, (e.g., merchant houses like *Mitsui* and *Sumitomo*), the Japanese socio-cultural managerial conventions of the 'Three Sacred Treasures' (*shūshin koyō* or lifetime employment, *nenkō joretsu chingin* or seniority based wage, and *kigyōbetsu kumiai* or enterprise based unionism) derive from Japan's industrialisation period prior to the end of Pacific War (1941–45) (Nakamura, 1981). Labour was originally sourced from rural agricultural towns and villages. Whole village groups, with clan and hierarchical relationships intact, migrated to industrial centres in search of work, bringing their community culture. As large numbers of re-located workers grew in the urbanising industrial centres, management was challenged to provide better working conditions. In response, business leaders began to search for a management idea which incorporates humanity into economic rationality. At least two inspirational sources have had a lasting influence: The first source was the philosophy of *Baigan Ishida*, Father of *Shōnindo* (the Way of the Merchants) who advocated the virtue of building commerce onto a commoner-oriented (especially merchants) moral philosophy, *kyōzon kyōei*, which drawing on early eighteenth century *Shintō*, Confucianism and Buddhism values (Yui, 1991); The other source was *Ei'ichi Shibusawa* (1840–1931), Father of Japanese Capitalism, who promoted the altruistic Confucian values of 'the harmony of morality and economy' integrating *Bushidō* ethics into Commerce (Yamamoto, 1987).

Labour requirements changed as the focus of the state industry shifted from light to heavy industries, with specialisations such as chemical manufacturing. During early industrialisation, as typified by the textile industry, labour was provided by relatively unskilled workers from the rural districts, but as technology advanced, so did the demand for more skilled technical and administrative staff. In response to the ever-growing demand for and limited supply of highly skilled labour, large organisations found it necessary to offer long-term job guarantees to attract and retain scarce skilled labour (Taira, 1970). Instead of relying on an uncertain labour market, large companies in the chemical and heavy industries recruited those who had just finished school on a permanent basis with the aim to provide standardised in-house training (the '*Kogai*' system) (Watanabe, 2000). Gradually, this extensive in-house training practice became the conventional Japanese recruitment and development model. As early as the beginning of the twentieth century, Mitsui Mining and Mitsubishi Shipyard took the HRM strategy one step further, building and running their own schools (Morishima, 1982). Notably, the long-term employment policy necessitated a new wage system. Companies in favour of long-term employment began to introduce a wage system where the wage progressively increased in accordance with the length of employee service as an incentive for employee's long-term commitment to the company. During war time, under the 1940–41 government's wage controls, long-term employment and seniority-based wage system spread widely across industries (Nakamura, 1981).

Japan's labour movement evolved in parallel with these employment systems. However, under a growing fascist influence its development was restricted after reaching the peak of its power during the Taisho Democracy period (i.e., 1912–26). For instance, the 1925 Peace Preservation Law was introduced to restrict public comment by confining radical and subversive individuals whose socialist and communist values challenged national policies, with the result that 'independent labour unions were not permitted ... and only the labour-front organizations with pro-capital and/or pro-military orientation were allowed' (Tsuru, 1993, p. 23). During the 1940s, when Japan's war efforts intensified, these remaining labour unions were disbanded. Instead, each company organised a 'Patriotic Industrial Association' involving labour and management and 'an industrial safety program, guidance for living, the rationing of materials' (Nakamura, 1981, p. 18) was set in place.

The Postwar period: Demilitarised and democratising reform for re-development

Japan's aggressive imperial vision drove the country into the second Sino-Japanese War (1937–45) and the Pacific War (1941–45) with the eventual humiliating defeat. The war left Japan in tatters and brought an end to Japan's imperial rule of Taiwan, Korea and Manchuria and Japanese war-time control of Burma, Cambodia, Malaya, the Philippines, Thailand, Vietnam and most of the then Dutch East Indies.

Under the US led Allied Occupation Forces (AOF) (1945–52) a campaign to rebuild the nation began. In association with the AOF's structural political reform 'demilitarisation' and 'democratisation' principle, the Japanese Constitution was rewritten to establish a parliamentary state with the Emperor as a constitutional monarch (i.e., a symbolic head of the state); the industrial, land and labour systems were democratised; and the education system and curriculum overhauled replacing the *Bushidō* values with the imported democratic values – equity, freedom and individualism – providing a new framework for Japan's state ideology (Morishima, 1982). The following statement captures the demilitarisation and democratisation rationale of *zaibatsu* dissolution:

> They are the greatest war potential of Japan. ... They profited immensely. ... Unless the Zaibatsu are broken up, the Japanese have little prospect of ever being able to govern themselves as free men. As long as the Zaibatsu survive, Japan will be their Japan. ... The concentration of industrial control stimulated the existence of semi-feudal relations between labour and capital, depressed wages, and obstructed the development of labour unions. Moreover, it interfered with the creation of new enterprises by independent businessmen and prevented the rise of a middle class in Japan. ... Furthermore, low wages and the accumulation of profits under the exclusive control of the zaibatsu choked off domestic markets, increased the importance of exports, and thus spurred Japan forward into an imperialistic war. (Chief of the Zaibatsu Mission 1946, cited in Kosai, 1986, pp. 23–4)

Hence, in 1947, the Anti-Monopoly Law, which prohibits the possession and operation of holding companies, was enacted to dismantle the *zaibatsu*.

Initially, the law produced positive signs of shareholder democracy with 70 per cent share dispersion of the former *zaibatsu*'s holding companies amongst ordinary citizen in 1949 (Nakamura, 1981). Nevertheless, against the AOF directors' vision, the trend was not sustained. The citizen share ownership was replaced by institutional share holders such as the company's banks and affiliates (Maswood, 2002). The issues behind this emergent

found difficulty raising investment capital from the Tokyo
early postwar years.

ar of hostile takeover from foreign companies of Japanese com-
the liberalisation of foreign direct capital investment.

the Anti-Monopoly Law in 1949 and then in 1953 after the
introduction of the Peace Treaty in 1952 (Nakamura, 1981).

Keiretsu: A modern industry structure

Following a relaxation of the Anti-Monopoly Law, a new type of enterprise
group (*keiretsu*) emerged, with large banks and general trading companies at the
core, as with the *zaibatsu*. Though this structural duplication did not conform
to conventional economic theory, the inter-*keiretsu* group competition and the
shared capacity within the *keiretsu* network played an instrumental role in
Japanese economic recovery, and from the 1950s onwards. Various terms have
been applied to characterise this Japanese economic model – 'corporate' capitalism (Okumura, 1975), 'group-enterprise' capitalism (Chandler, 1984), and
'alliance' capitalism (Gerlach, 1992). Six *keiretsu* groups significantly influenced
the postwar economy: those developed by the original zaibatsu group around its
bank (i.e., Mitsui, Sumitomo and Mitsubishi) and those formed by groups of
zaibatsu around banks (e.g., Itsukan, Fuyo & Sanwa) (Kikkawa, 1996).

Two additional differences between the *zaibatsu* and *keiretsu* grouping are
noteworthy. In the zaibatsu governance structure the family controlled the holding,
or head company which, in turn, controlled group companies (Kikkawa, 1996).
In contrast, the companies drawn to the *keiretsu* group motivated by tradition
and/or a survival instinct (i.e., access to investment capital through debt loan)
established and maintained their association through mutual cross-share holding.
The absence of a hierarchical ownership structure within the enterprise group
facilitated inter-group democracy where each member company assumed more
or less an equal status in the group (Gerlach, 1992).

A vertical ownership structure was replaced with a unique Japanese financial
system – the main bank system. This system is often contrasted with the market
financial system of the United States, and is characterised by the company's
heavy reliance on loans from the main bank and the main bank's shareholding
of the company. The resultant long-term and stable working relationship between
the debt company and the bank, as a lender and shareholder, is attributed to the
unique corporate behaviour of Japanese companies – i.e., characteristically long-
term investment behaviour immune from pressure for short-term performance
from the market (Aoki et al., 1986). Although the company may have to forgo
its full autonomy and accept managerial intervention by the main bank,

especially in cases of financial difficulty, the commitment of the main bank could be counted on along with support from all group member companies (Aoki, 1994).

Typically, the *keiretsu* were as diversified as the *zaibatsu*, having at their core, a major bank and 'a trading company' coupled together under a 'one-set principle' where each group encompasses all major industries (Itoh, 1990, p. 158). In addition to this networked form, another type of keiretsu existed – a *vertical keiretsu* – where multiple-tiers of sub-contractors along a supply chain are closely linked to large automobile and electric appliance manufacturers like Toyota and Canon (for a discussion on its strategic application see Rexha and Miyamoto, 2001).

Corporate management and HRM system reform

After the war, the purging of thousands of senior war-time managers and executives (including *zaibatsu* family members) of large companies (i.e., capital exceeding 100 million yen) was another important reform initiative (Morikawa, 1992). As a result the average age of top management dropped from 60 down to 50 and the elevation of younger middle managers into senior positions resulted in a rejuvenation of management practice (Takahashi, 1969; Morikawa, 1997). New corporate leaders, together with the postwar entrepreneurs, who founded Japan's present corporate giants such as Sony, Honda, Yamaha and Sanyo, devoted their energy to building a foundation for Japan's later industrial success and actively extended their energy and leadership beyond their company and *keiretsu* groups. Associations of corporate leaders were established to promote learning and amass their collective power as a specific corporate business lobbies, e.g., *Keidanren* (the Federation of Economic Organisations in 1946) and *Nikkeiren* (the Japan Federation of Employers' Associations in 1948) (Nippon Keidanren n.d.). For the rebuilding of the state, they chose to work together with Japan's policy-makers and continued to shape Japan's later economic and social developments along their due diligence of social responsibility based on the pre-existing cultural principle of *messhi hōkō*.

Under the pro-democratisation labour/human rights sentiments of the Allied Occupational Forces (AOF), three Labour Laws (i.e., the Trade Union Law of 1945, the Labour Relations Adjustment Law of 1946 and the Labour Standards Law of 1947) were successively enacted (Morishima, 1982). In the context of a critical shortage of food and a hyper-inflationary economy, workers quickly organised company unions around the war-time Patriotic Industrial Associations and fought for better wages (Nakamura, 1981). Nonetheless, in this struggling economy context, industrial harmony was by no means guaranteed. In fact, the scale and violence of the labour disputes followed mass lay-offs in 1949 and 1953 to 1954 are still remembered. Between two waves of large-scale labour disputes was the Korean War (1950–1953) which brought about US$4 billion worth of emergency military procurement orders from the United States and a temporary manufacturing boom to the depressed economy, but subsequently left the legacy of excessive capacity and labour (Reischauer and Craig, 1979).

Innovative management and manufacturing systems

The Japanese actively sought new US management theory and practice in order to catch up with the industrialised world, and acquired foreign technology licenses, advanced manufacturing machinery and capital goods. The successive visits of two US industrial scientists in the 1950s – W. Edwards Deming and Joseph M. Juran – had a catalytic influence on Japan's later industrial success. The former taught them how to use statistical quality control methods, while the latter educated managers on quality control implementation (Ishikawa, 1985). Although the introduction of the notion of quality control to dates back to the AOF influences in 1946, over time the Japanese progressively applied the notion of quality control to develop a unique management paradigm – a 'company-wide', or 'total quality management approach' – built on the local cultural logic of *kaizen* (Mizuno, 1988).

Kaizen describes a continuous improvement in products and business processes achieved through 'grass-root' company-wide and 'collective' efforts. This managerial approach contrasts to the US approach which typically focusses on the design of radical improvement or innovation as conceived by specialists. The application of Japanese quality concepts, such as market-in product design, target costing, quality function deployment, quality control circles, as well as the subcontracting system, subsequently revolutionised manufacturing industries across the world (Ishikawa, 1985; Imai, 1986; Mizuno, 1988; Womack et al., 1991; Fruin, 1997).

In further pursuit of the notion of quality, Japanese manufacturers continued to acquire technology licensing and advanced capital equipment from the West. For instance, in the early 1950s the founder of Honda, spent 450 million yen (70 times more than the company's capital) (Kajiwara, 1992) on advanced Western manufacturing equipment as a basis for company development. In parallel with this company-based technology acquisition, Japanese engineers sought insights into Western technologies through the process of reverse engineering (i.e., dissembling sophisticated Western products and analysing the technologies embedded in the products) to acquire the implicit knowledge and associated technical capacity) (Porter, 1985).

High economic growth (1955–73)

During this period, the economy achieved an average growth rate exceeding 10 per cent. The workforce increasingly shifted from the agricultural sector to the expanding industrial sector, especially heavy industries, and this shift led to phenomenal urban growth. This strong economic growth was driven by domestic demand, which was supported by favourable terms of trade – stable, cheap price of imported oil and raw materials; all critical ingredients of Japan's economic development (Itoh, 1990). Between the 1950s and 1960s, with a rapidly expanding domestic economy and limited natural resources, Japan applied a FDI strategy in natural resource-based investment. By the 1970s in order to move

Figure 5.1 Japan's GDP annual growth rate between 1956 and 2000

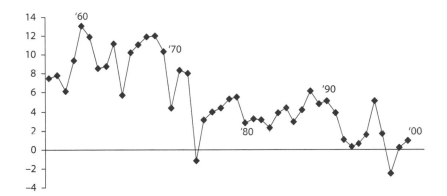

Source: Department of National Accounts, ESRI, Japan.

beyond the demands of the domestic market the country's FDI strategy shifted to a market-expansion investment strategy (Park, 2003). The development of this market expansion FDI management strategy over the next decade facilitated the industrialisation of a number of economies in the East Asian region.

Although the rate of wage increase was substantial, it did not fully reflect the gains in labour productivity and company profit. Instead, financial gains were recycled back for further business expansion (Morishima, 1982). In 1968, Japan became the third largest GNP country under the US and the former Soviet Union. By the 1980s offshore manufacturing driven further by the market-expansion FDI strategy increased and this in turn was further expanded by a combination of cost-reducing (low-cost labour-seeking FDI and market-penetrating FDI in the 1990s (Park, 2003). This macro-regional FDI strategy was of critical impetus to the 'Asian miracle' and the rise of the Southeast Asian tiger economies. Figure 5.1 presents a time series data of Japan's GDP annual growth rate between 1956 and 2000.

A paternalistic and collaborative labour relations management paradigm

Essentially, the collaborative efforts and cross-sectoral relationships based on the *kyōzon kyōei* (i.e., co-existence and co-prosperity) socio-cultural principle (i.e., the collaboration between labour and management, in addition to the aforementioned partnerships between manufacturers and their suppliers, and between policy makers and corporate Japan) were instrumental to Japan's spectacular economic development. Having experienced antagonistic, large-scale labour disputes (e.g., the Nohon Steel Company's *Muroran* Plant in 1953 and the Mitsui Mining Company in 1959 and 1960 (Hanami, 1984)), management became receptive to a more altruistic Confucian-based management philosophy and so unions were willing to trade-off their loyalty to the company for long-term job security in an improving economy.

In an improving economy, unions were willing to trade-off their loyalty to the company for long-term job security. Against this, the lifetime employment and seniority-based wage systems were firmly institutionalised by large companies and extended to blue-collar workers (Cole, 1971). A remuneration system, linked to the cost of living, age and length of service, was extended. Various kinds of allowances were introduced to supplement the low-base income. This evolution of the remuneration system meant that payment levels were determined by a combination of educational background, age, length of service, position held in the organisation and performance appraisal (Watanabe, 2000). In addition, many companies began to institutionalise a company-wide wage supplement system or semi-annual bonuses (usually July and December) as a profit-sharing scheme, rewarding the employee's achievement and loyalty in accordance with the company's profitability (Dore, 1973).

An implication of the paternalistic 'welfare corporatism' labour relations paradigm was a view of a company as a social institution, or an 'enterprise community' (Nakane, 1972; Dore, 1973), or *Gemeinschaft* (community organisation) (Kono, 1982). Thus, the labour was democratised through organisation-oriented employment systems that replaced:

> The spot contract – easy-hire-fire assumption – on which much writing about labour markets is based, by the long-term – indeed career-perspective – relation. The contract is seen, in fact, less as any kind of bilateral bargain, than as an act of admission to an enterprise community wherein benevolence, goodwill and sincerity are explicitly expected to temper the pursuit of self-interest. (Dore, 1987, p. 183)

The following remark of a Toyota employee captures this shared sense of community and its embedded cultural spirit of 'coexistence and co-prosperity':

> 'Our unions fight management,' a young Toyota engineer, an avowed leftist and socialist with strong pro-union leanings, recently told me. 'But yours [unions in the U.S.] fight the company. How can they not know that for anything to be good for the company's employees, it has to be good for the company? Where this is not taken for granted – and it's completely obvious to every one of us – no Japanese could be a manager; but no Japanese could be an employee or a subordinate either.' (Drucker, 1981, p. 88)

In the unique socio-cultural context of Japan's industrialisation, humanistic managerial concern for the welfare of employees framed the emerging paternalistic employment system. Likewise, criticism of the short-term driven, mechanistic-orientation and impersonal Western interaction styles of management emerged. Japanese humanism is more likely to be expressed in terms of the welfare of the group, and the maintenance of harmonious human relations (Alston, 1985), whereas Western humanism focuses on individual human rights.

The term *wa* expresses harmony and peace in Japanese group relations. This social concept derives from the Japanese's collectivist ideal of harmonious co-existence among group members which encourages the containment of conflicts (i.e., incompatible self interests) through stressing common interests. The Japanese commonly use expressions of *uchi* and *soto*, equivalent to 'we' and 'they' or 'in-group' and 'out-group', in defining a boundary for the concerned domain of *wa*. In many respects, the concentric structure of layers of an *uchi-soto* boundary, unique to Japan's traditional agrarian society (i.e., the family → the extended family → the halmet → the village → the *han* → the state), is relatively intact in modern-day Japan (Ishida, 1984). In the industrialised context, the concentric structure transposes as: the family → the workplace (section and department or union and management) → the company → the *keiretsu* group → Japan and even beyond Japan. The Japanese applied the *uchi-soto* cultural notion on a macro-regional basis beyond its national boundary; in the *Greater East Asia Co-Prosperity Sphere* – the 'Asia for Asians' ideology, applied as a philosophical ideal, but also used to justify Japan's Pacific War aggression (Ishida, 1984). The high humanistic Japanese managerial emphasis is evident when compared to that of US managers. Table 5.1 shows the differences identified in the perceived relative importance of '71 Strategic Factors in Business Success' between Japanese and US managers.

Behavioural manifestations of this 'community enterprise ethos' were: active company-wide employee participation to decision-making, knowledge sharing, and collective learning (e.g., quality control circles) for enhanced productivity (Cole, 1994; Koike, 1994). Although the Toyota Production System, which has become a macro-global manufacturing model, is commonly known for Just-in-Time, *Kaizen* and automation principles, full optimisation of the system is not achieved without the commitment and empowerment of line workers under a paternalistic and collaborative labour relations management paradigm (Womack et al., 1991). The same principle applies to the business relationships between manufacturers and their key suppliers (i.e., suppliers of a high valued added component items sourced in large volume or high value items), or within a supplier network (i.e., a vertical *keiretsu*) (Miyamoto and Rexha, 2004).

Table 5.1 Comparative importance of strategic factors in the area of personnel in ordinary rankings

	Japan (N = 721)	U.S. (N = 711)
Establishing better personnel relations with employees	1	10
Ability to get along with labour unions	2	18
Ability to level peaks and valleys of employment	4	20
Ability to optimise employee turnover (not too much and not too little)	10	52
Ability to stimulate creativity in employees	12	48

Source: Elsevier.

The role of the government's industry policy

The role of government administrative and industrial policy in Japan's rapid economic revival is noteworthy. Customarily, Japanese government–business relationships are based on co-operation and guidance rather than direct intervention, or coercion. The bureaucracy, in particular the Ministry of International Trade and Industry (MITI) and the Ministry of Finance (MOF), developed a high profile, and until the early 1990s enjoyed an enviable national and international reputation for their economic planning expertise (Johnson, 1982). For instance, during the 1950s, MITI's foreign trade policies were pivotal in the post-war industrial development (Edwards and Samimi, 1997). Such arrangements, which were subsequently characterised as 'Japan Inc.', included the triangular relationship between the political and bureaucratic arms of government, and the *keiretsu* via the peak private sector economic body (*zaikai*). Japan Inc. was attributed with steering the economy through change and growth in a series of well-orchestrated phases (Gerlach, 1992). During this high growth period, Japan's unique financial banking system further strengthened its foothold in corporate Japan. In the mid-1960s, a sharp decline in stock prices, and the fear of hostile takeovers prompted many large Japanese companies to increase the shareholdings of their financial institutions and other *keiretsu* member companies in order to stabilise stock prices. This, in turn, entailed a further stabilisation of their relationship with the main banks, or the increased authority of the banks (Miyajima, 1999).

Maturity for international economic superpower status (1974–90)

The oil crises of 1973 and 1979 had a severe effect on the Japanese economy (see the drop in GDP annual growth rates after the two years in Figure 5.1). The crises led to double-digit inflation and brought extreme pressure on corporate business costs. To counter the cost-pressure, a series of stringent cost-cutting measures was adopted through rationalisation and restructuring (Nakamura, 1981). Many companies pursued leaner organisations by selling off excess buildings and properties, eliminating many managerial positions, and implementing *shukkō* (i.e., inter-firm employee transfer within the corporate and/or *keiretsu* group). Grading systems, based on performance and multiple career paths, were progressively introduced to provide appropriate status and salary to staff that had lost their managerial positions (Mroczkowski and Hanaoka, 1989). In particular, large companies mindful of ethical obligations to maintain employee security found the *shukkō* system a useful employment adjustment measure to eliminate the surplus of middle-aged and older white-collar employees. Under the seniority-weighted wage system, these older employees commanded higher wages irrespective of their real productivity. The application of this strategy was also an effective means of transferring managerial competence and culture between group companies (Grainger and Miyamoto, 2003a).

During this uncertain time of national adjustment an influential book, *Japan as Number One: lessons for America* (Vogel, 1979), reached Japan and in a context of declining national confidence, the overt international praise for Japan's institutional arrangements as the basis for the nation's powerful economic achievements, was reassuring.

The macro-global level influence of Japan

By the 1980s, a decade began when Japanese industrial growth was driving the world economy, and with quality as a strategic management weapon, Japanese manufacturers had widespread international success (Womack et al., 1991). This success brought a sustained exports boom and economic prosperity, creating a continual unilateral trade deficit. In their major export destinations the typical Japanese strategies overwhelmed local manufacturers, which resulted in growing trade conflicts, especially with Japan's biggest exports market, the United States whose economy was suffering from continued foreign debt-driven government funding, debt-leveraged consumer demand, ever-growing trade deficit, the hollowing-out of the US manufacturing sector and the resultant deterioration of labour markets (Feldstin, 1987).

In August 1985, finance ministers and governors of the reserve banks of five leading economies (the United States, Japan, Germany, Britain and France) – the Group of Five – held a secret meeting at the Plaza Hotel in New York to discuss concerns and agreed to restore order in the international economy through intervention in the foreign exchange market. Their focus on the fact that Japanese policy makers historically had kept the yen undervalued against the US dollar, so as to develop an economy based on demands for local goods and services as well, as to make Japanese exports internationally competitiveness is noteworthy (Itoh, 1990; Tsuru, 1993). The outcome of the Plaza Accord was substantial: the US currency lost almost 9 per cent of its value from 237.1 yen to 216 yen within a month, and in just over two years, it reached a historical low of 122 yen (Bank of Japan, 2004).

The new order in the currency market had profound implications. Firstly, a strong yen meant weakened international competitiveness for Japanese products and this led to high '*yen*' recession. To remain competitive export oriented companies further enhanced their cost-cutting efforts, including FDI, in the form of transfer of productive capacity, such as new plants and equipment, as well as in the retail and services areas (Mroczkowski and Hanaoka, 1989). Simultaneously, the strong yen meant a greater purchasing power. In addition to benefitting import-related businesses, in 1986 the stronger yen elevated Japan's position in the world as the largest net creditor nation and the second largest gross creditor nation in 1988 (Kawai, 1998). The strong yen promoted active FDIs among cash-rich Japanese companies. For instance, Japanese FDIs, which sometimes involved acquisitions of some American icons (e.g., Rockefeller Centre by Mitsubishi Jisho, the Exxon building by Mitsui Fudosan, Citicorp Centre by Dai-Ichi Real Estate, the record business of CBS Inc. and Columbia Pictures by Sony and MCA/Universal by

Matsushita), fuelled a fear among the Americans and triggered a series of so-called 'Japan bashing' from the US politicians and media (Wilkins, 1990).

In the latter half of the 1980s, low domestic and international interest rates, and a strong domestic economy led to an unprecedented stock and property boom in Japan and financial speculation kept feeding stock and property market prices. *Zaitech* (i.e., financial techniques) and money-games became a widespread social phenomenon. Japanese companies were drawn to this nation-wide money-game 'frenzy' actively investing idle capital in the ever-growing stock and property markets, driven by a gaming psyche – to be a winner in the game. For instance, even Toyota, which is reported to have retained its focus on the core business, made the earnings equivalent to 43 per cent of the company profit from its core business of car production in 1986 through *zaitech* (Itoh, 1990). The economic prosperity and confidence of corporate Japan during this period of a so-called 'bubble economy' was also evident in their aggressive investments into productive capacity. In 1989, Japan's total capital investments reached US$549 billion, or on a per capita basis, Japanese capital investment amounted to almost twice as much as the US (*Japan Statistical Yearbook*, cited in Maswood, 2002, pp. 18–19). After financial deregulation in the early 1980s, there was a dramatic shift in corporate financing from bank financing to equity financing (Miyajima, 1999). While weakening the existing long-term stable relationship between the company and the main bank as the principal monitor of corporate governance, the deregulation also enabled corporations to raise money to pump into increasingly speculative stock and property markets.

While the 1980s marked Japan's golden age as an economic superpower, some sectors, such as textile, steel and shipbuilding, continued to struggle from intensifying competition from developing countries. Later, it became evident that these sectors were the front-runners for the reform which corporate Japan came to face in the following decade. More specifically, they were the first to address the issue of excessive aged workers under the long-term employment system through voluntary early retirement and *shukkō* practice, or by creating spin-off subsidiaries for the exclusive purpose of out-placing workers (Befu and Cernosia, 1999).

The lost decade and economic recovery: The 1990s and beyond

In the early 1990s, Japan's buoyant economy faltered with the collapse of the 'bubble economy' (Yoshikawa, 2002). The collapse was triggered by a sharp decline in the stock market price (1989), and land prices (1990); over the 1989 to 1992 period more than half of value of the stock market was lost (Bank of Japan, 2003). Japan then entered a sustained economic recession. In the mid-1990s, the economy began to recover, but then went into a deeper recession through a series of domestic and regional events that included: misjudged fiscal policy under the Hashimoto Administration (i.e., tax increase to reduce the accumulated government debts), the Asian financial crisis in 1997, a series of large scale corporate bankruptcies, which then triggered a chain of bankruptcies among their small and medium sized creditor companies, and a systemic banking crisis in 1997–98 (Grainger and Miyamoto, 2002; Yoshikawa, 2002; Miyamoto and Grainger, 2004).

To counter mounting problems and to facilitate economic recovery, the government and its agencies introduced a series of policies and rescue packages. For example, in late 1997, the Anti-Monopoly Law was finally revised by lifting the ban on holding (or head) companies, which were banned since 1947 due to their *zaibatsu* group association, so as to give the same flexibility to Japan's corporate system as in Western countries. While relaxation of the law allows Japanese companies to spin-off their operations as wholly owned subsidiaries and implement a HRM system which reflects the performance and operations of each division, it also assists them to address corporate governance issues with the company replacing the main bank, which previously performed a monitoring role (Ichiyanagi and Hosoya, 1998). With regard to the financial system, the government poured trillions of yen of public funds into failed and troubled financial institutions to stabilise the financial market and retain public confidence in the financial system. The Financial Reconstruction Commission was created in 1998 to monitor and ensure stability in the financial institutions and market through necessary injection of public funds (Kawai, 2003).

In a desperate attempt to rekindle corporate and consumer confidence, since 'the collapse of the bubble economy, the Japanese government spent Y120 trillion in economic stimulus packages to little real effect' (Maswood, 2002, p. 93). However, even the government efforts failed to rejuvenate troubled economy (see Figure 5.1). On average, Japan's annual GDP growth rate during the post-bubble decade (1992–2002) was only 1.1 per cent. This figure contrasts with 4 per cent between 1981 and 1991 and 5 per cent between 1970 and 1980. Furthermore, the average annual growth rate of private capital spending during the 1991 and 2000 was near zero, compared to the 8.4 per cent of the 1981 to 1990 period and 4.5 per cent of the 1971 to 1980 period (Bank of Japan, 2003). Indicative of the seriousness of the prolonged economic problems (e.g., poor private capital investments, increasing deflationary pressure, ever-growing unemployment rate, and a near zero interest rate), the decade came to be referred to as a 'lost decade' (Yoshikawa, 2002). The subsequent consensus was that the economic problem was not cyclical, but structural, and the problem is more commonly attributed to interconnected and multiple causal factors ranging from rapid globalisation, the IT revolution, poor political leadership, inadequate economic and industrial structures, outdated financial system, company's overemphasis on *Kaizen* over innovation, inflexible employment systems, the aging of employees and society, a pension system crisis and cultural change (Porter et al., 2000).

At the meso-level then, it appears that Japanese policy makers have been continuing to struggle with overdue structural (i.e., economic, financial and regulatory) reforms to address the ever intensifying erosion of the economic, political, technological, socio-cultural and legal sovereignty of the country, as well as with other demographic issues, such as the aging of the population and a low birth rate. While the policy-makers may have been aware of the anticipated tidal wave of changes, in hindsight, they misjudged the scale and ferocity of actual changes brought forward by globalisation and the IT revolution, as well as the extended time required for the implementation of necessary reform policies. The fundamental policy initiative problem appears to lie in their naïve approach to 'liberalisation' as a countermeasure for the tidal wave of globalisation, that is that they attempted to reform within the existing regulatory framework (i.e., de-regulation), rather than to create a new framework (re-regulation).

Unfortunately, in the present crisis the government and political leaders have failed to demonstrate the required leadership qualities and determination to stimulate Japanese capacity for dynamism and innovation which was previously displayed by their earlier counterparts. They have been unable to build consensus among influential interest groups (including ministries) of the need for radical meso-level change. As a consequence, existing problems have not been dealt with and new economic and social problems are emerging. It is noteworthy that in 1997, in response to growing public scrutiny of government bureaucratic inefficiency and poor political leadership, the government restructured the cabinet structure to 1 cabinet office and 12 ministries, down from 22 (Prime Minister of Japan & His Cabinet n.d.).

The micro-organisational level: Critical traditional, transitional and transformational issues in Japanese management

At a micro level corporate Japan is confronted with unprecedentedly complex challenges. The unique building blocs of the Japanese business and managerial model, which were attributed to the very global success of corporate Japan are now critically viewed as a hindrance to Japan's survival and future prosperity in a more competitive global context. For instance, a recent government report identified the following key shortcomings of the Japanese corporate system: '(1) low labour force mobility, (2) a lack of active participation by foreign-affiliated companies and new start-ups and (3) weak corporate governance by shareholders' (Bank of Japan, 2003, p. 7). The report identifies the very foundation of the postwar Japanese management and industrial systems – lifetime employment, *keiretsu* and main bank systems – as being the key management problems.

As a result of their overly opportunistic expansion and diversification strategies, and irrational investment in stock and property markets during the previous boom, the economic collapse left many companies in financial distress. Against this background, corporate leaders began to pursue a self-renewal strategy of *hongyō kaiki* (refocus on the foundation of their business) as if they had been awakened by the spirit of *Baigan Ishida* and *Ei'ichi Shibusawa* or 'the spirit of capitalism' (i.e., the attitude of righteous, rational and systematic profit-seeking as fulfilling 'of the obligations imposed upon the individual by his position in the world' (Weber, 1976, p. 80). Under the strategy companies began to shed their non-core businesses and excess properties, including production facilities and focussed their corporate resources on core businesses. Through this, companies returned to the fundamental purpose of business – the creation of authentic customer value – as opposed to increasing sales volume. The corporate reform strategy of manufacturing companies included the aggressive transfer of production capacity to more favourable overseas locations, especially China, based on proximity, cheap labour and a vast market size; between 1990 and 2002 the proportion of overseas production of Japan's manufacturing production almost tripled to 17 per cent (Ministry of Health, Labour and Welfare, 2003). Moreover, as a result of increased company dependence on capital markets through the globalisation of financial markets, many companies also had to address management accountability and short-term performance expectations of overseas equity holders in their reform pursuits. Following the collapse and deregulation of the financial system in the years 1997 and 1998, increasing reform pressure meant that corporate Japan was more or less ready to remodel on United States management principles built for the market financial system. Support grew for the views of the early reform advocates (e.g., Nonaka, 1988), who questioned the validity of traditional Japanese business and management models for the globalisation era.

Ongoing convergent micro-level structural and systemic corporate reform

Despite all the pressure to change, Japanese companies have found reform of the conventional lifetime employment and seniority-based, wage-based HRM system a significant challenge (Mroczkowski and Hanaoka, 1998). In principle, a system which makes employment a fixed cost contradicts the underlying reform principle to become lean and flexible in an increasingly unpredictable environment. In addition to the prolonged economic setback and intensifying competitive pressure from foreign competitors for whom labour costs are, in a large part, variable costs, there are two other important management challenges: the adoption of International Accounting Standards and the aging of workforce (Watanabe, 2000). The new accounting system now requires Japanese companies to report their expected costs for future employee retirement bonuses and pension payments explicitly as a 'liability'. This financial system reveals the long-term employment system as a very expensive option. Another important issue is the substantial increase in employment costs due to the high numbers of workers taken on during high economic growth. These workers are currently reaching the highest level in the wage scale under the seniority-based wage system (Watanabe, 2000). This time around the strategic weapon in employment adjustment, the *shukkō* system, is proving to be of little help as corporate Japan literally has too many redundant aged workers for the internal labour market to absorb in the nationwide economic depression. As a result, Japanese companies have been forced to take drastic measures to curb regular employees and the associated fixed costs, and to become more flexible. While cutting back intake numbers of new graduate recruits, they have been actively promoting voluntary early retirement among mature employees (Ministry of Health, Labour and Welfare, 2003).

Notably, not all companies had the privilege to survive independently. Some companies were forced to secure their survival only through a merger and acquisition (M&A) strategy. According to the Bank of Japan (2003), the number of M&A activities involving Japanese companies has continued to rise since 1993. The previously discussed six prominent *keiretsu* groups have not escaped from this M&A corporate phenomenon. Over the past decade, *keiretsu* groups have been undergoing previously unthinkable dynamic re-structuring. To date, the re-structuring has resulted in the emergence of a four keiretsu structure: Mitsui-Sumitomo (a merger between Mitsui and Sumitomo), Mizuho (from Itskan, Fuyo and Kōginn), Mitsubishi UFJ (between Mitsubishi and United Financial of Japan which emerged through the early merger between Sanwa and other financial groups) and a newcomer, Risona.

Those Japanese companies that have failed to secure additional necessary bank credits from increasingly conservative banks in a tightening monetary context, and have failed to find M&A partners, have literally been left to go bankrupt. Table 5.2 presents historical summary statistics of corporate bankruptcies in Japan and it provides some insights into the turbulent nature of economic and management problems over the past two decades. For instance, more than half of all corporate bankruptcies reported during the post-bubble economy period are accounted for by 'stagnation of sales'. Here it should be noted that these bankruptcies have not only resulted in retrenched employees, but have also left creditors in financial distress. In the case of 2000 alone, corporate bankruptcies led to creditor losses of 23,987 billion yen in total (*Japan Statistical Yearbook*, 2004) and with Japan's 2000 GDP being 511,462 billion yen (Department of National Accounts, Economics and Social Research Institute) the loss equated to fully 4.7 per cent of the second largest world GDP.

Since the end of the bubble economy, these corporate upheavals have manifested in Japan's unprecedentedly high level of unemployment rate. Figure 5.2 presents time series data of Japan's unemployment rate from 1972 and 2004.

Figure 5.2 indicates that the upward unemployment trend since 1991 finally ended in 2003 and continued to decline into 2004. This positive economic sign is also found in other statistical sources. For instance, according to OECD data (OECD, 2005), the Japanese economy grew at the annual GDP growth rate of 2.7 per cent during the 2003–04. The figure is certainly positive, but this growth rate is still below that of the G7 average growth rate of 3.3 per cent. Underlying this macro-economic performance is Japan's ever-strong export performance which has been robust since 2001 and is expected to exceed the record exports of ¥54,548 billion set in 2003 by a substantial margin in 2004 (Ministry of Internal Affairs and Communications, 2004). This positive macro-economic data is translating into a more confident corporate Japan. Available data collectively suggests a continuing upward economic trend (i.e., declining unemployment

Table 5.2 Summary statistics of corporate bankruptcies in Japan

	Bankruptcies Total (A)	Causes of bankruptcies				Amount of liabilities (billion yen)
		Stagnation of sales (B)	B/A %	Reckless management (C)	C/A %	
1980	17,884	5,230	29.2	5,778	32.3	2,707
1985	18,812	6,416	34.1	5,336	28.4	4,186
1990	6,468	1,613	24.9	2,851	44.1	1,945
1995	15,086	7,745	51.3	3,085	20.4	9,033
1996	14,544	7,546	51.9	2,728	18.8	7,994
1997	16,365	8,716	53.3	2,802	17.1	14,021
1998	19,171	11,229	58.6	2,785	14.5	14,381
1999	15,460	9,632	62.3	1,917	12.4	13,552
2000	19,071	12,446	65.3	2,027	10.6	23,987
2001	19,441	12,811	65.9	1,744	9.0	16,213
2002	19,458	13,068	67.2	1,490	7.7	13,756

Source: Statistics Bureau, Director-General for Policy Planning, Japan.

Figure 5.2 Historical unemployment rate in Japan

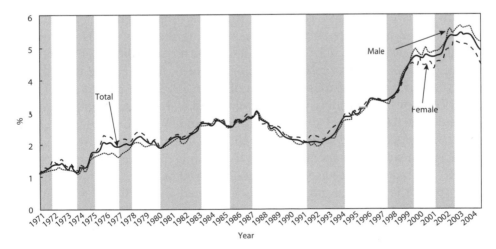

Source: Ministry of Health, Labour and Welfare 2004, *White Paper on the Labour Economy* 2004, Figure 24: Trends in unemployment rates by sex, p.19.

rate and bankruptcies and growing private investments in capital investment) and improving sentiment (i.e., positive Business Confidence Index) (see statistics available from the websites of Bank of Japan, Ministry of Internal Affairs & Communications and Ministry of Health, Labour & Welfare as listed at the end of the chapter).

Contemporary micro-level managerial approaches to sustain Japanese national development

In the past decade, globalising forces have intensified and reshaped international business and the international economic landscape. Intensification of competition is characterised by the rise of China in the manufacturing sector, and India in the services sector. Although recent statistics suggest a turning point for Japan's economy towards recovery, sustainability of this trend depends on corporate Japan's ability to effectively manage both internal and external challenges. The following section discusses three major and interdependent challenges in the areas of:

1. Community socio-cultural values;

2. Corporate behaviour; and

3. Human resource management.

Appropriate micro-level management responses and reform in these areas indicate pathways to a more effective and sustainable corporate future.

Critical managerial challenges: Meso-level socio-cultural dynamism

As with many other mature economies, the work force of Japan is aging. After experiencing a peak in population increase during the early 1970s, population increase has been in a continuous decline pattern. According to the Statistics Bureau (n.d.) as of October 2004, almost one out of five Japanese were the age of 65 years or over, compared to one out of ten in 1985. The percentage of those over 65 and over the productive age population (i.e., between 15 and 64) almost doubled from 15.1 to 28.5 during the same period. With the substantial social impact of delayed marriage and fewer children since 1970, almost one out of five Japanese were 65 years of age or over in 2003, compared to one out of ten in 1985. With the sustained social impact of delayed marriage and fewer children since 1970, the Japanese population is estimated to reach 127.6 million by January 2005, and is projected to begin a decline after peaking in 2006. In terms of the ratio of the working age population to the country's population, the figures have not changed markedly in the same period (e.g., 68.2 per cent in 1985 and 66.9 per cent in 2003) (http://www.stat.go.jp/english/data/jinsui/ 2004np/ index.htm; http://www.stat.go.jp/english/data/jinsui/wagakuni/zuhyou/15k5-3.xls). While these statistics suggest a constant supply of labour in relation to the country's population, it fails to reflect a fundamental socio-cultural change in the working age group which reflects a transition of work ethos across generations.

As previously discussed in this chapter, the conventional Japanese management model is framed on a humanistic socio-cultural approach derived from Japanese

Confucian and *Shintō* values or *Bushidō* ethics. The following points summarise key manifestations of these cultural influences in Japanese management:

- A long-term business purview and employment relationship;

- A group and communal enterprise orientation which places emphasises on consensus building and maintenance of '*wa*' guided by the ideology of 'co-existence and co-prosperity'; and

- Paternalism, a hierarchical authority structure and vertical cross-firm structures (welfare corporatism and Japanese network capitalism system) built on reciprocal inter-personal, employee-company, and inter-firm relationships.

According to Akio Morita, the former Chairman of Sony Corporation and renowned international advocate of the humanistic Japanese management model, the success of Sony and other major Japanese companies was due largely to an emphasis on the maintenance of positive human relations within the organisation based on the assumption that the most effective way to motivate people is to treat employees like respected members of the family (Morita et al., 1986). His advice to Western managers was that distinctions made between blue- and white-collar workers should be small, and the ideal types for management or supervisory positions were those who gained cooperation from people not via coercion, but through *taiwa* (i.e., dialogue). All those employed in a company, and not just those in senior management positions must have a 'sense of ownership'. Emphasising the benefits of trust between management and staff in the Japanese system, Morita was highly critical of American managers.

> Management doesn't trust its employees, and employees don't trust management. The government doesn't trust business organisations or industry, and industry doesn't trust government. Sometimes at home the husband doesn't trust his wife, and the wife doesn't trust her husband – although that isn't strictly an American characteristic. About the only person you can trust in America, it seems, is your lawyer. The conversation and correspondence between the lawyer and client are protected legally. All other things can be disclosed in court, so how can you trust anybody else? (Morita et al., 1986, p. 175)

Instrumental to the humanistic Japanese management paradigm have been the social concepts of '*on*' (i.e., the reciprocal obligations of the inferior for the benevolence bestowed by the superior) and '*ko*' (i.e., the duty to the superior) developed in the political and social organisation ('*ie*') system during the feudal period (Murakami, 1984). The '*ie*' was the smallest communal unit, consisting of not only the kinship family but also non-blood related adopted heirs and servants, that runs the family's occupation. Its primary purpose was to manage and develop, as a group, both the family's tangible and intangible assets by each member performing the tasks specifically assigned within it. The engines driving this collective effort were '*ko*' and especially '*on*' discerned by the members. These particular socio-cultural concepts help account for a further departure of Japanese Confucianism, in which loyalty resides at the super-ordinate value;

from Chinese Confucianism Confucian 'ko', as is practised in China which means absolute allegiance to the parents, whereas in Japan it encompasses not only the duty to the parents, but also the 'on' and it was the 'ie' family system that made possible expansion and longevity of family businesses by accepting non-blood related heirs, unlike the Chinese family kinship system where hereditary succession is strictly observed (Bahappu, 2000).

Generational value shifts

In the corporate context, this *ie* system has been applied to a company and/or a *keiretsu* network. In the system, management and employees seek effectiveness and productivity guided by the work ethic of *messhi hōkō* (i.e., serving the company and/or *keiretsu* network interests by repressing self interests) from their 'on' and 'ko' sentiments beyond their contractual obligations (Mito, 1994). Their shared vision and goal is the prosperity of the 'ie'. Nonetheless, this traditional Japanese cultural ethos, or the spirit of corporate Japan, which drove Japan's development has been under attack from a new generation of Japanese. Drawing on the work of Miyamoto and Grainger (2004), the following section discusses the current dynamic transition of the dominant work ethic in corporate Japan. Figure 5.3 depicts the dynamic transition and gradual transformation of the dominant ethos and work ethic in corporate Japan with three major cohorts identifiable over the past six decades.

Corporate warriors

The pre-1947 education reform generation or 'the corporate warrior' represents those born prior to 1935, who experienced collective war efforts and were raised by the ethical ideal of *Bushidō* spirit's *messhi hōkō* both at home and throughout the six years of their compulsory education prior. In particular, those middle manager positions that constituted the company's core work group during the high economic development period (1955–73) were referred to as 'corporate warriors' charged with dedicatedly re-building the Japanese economy through a highly disciplined work ethos (Hazama, 1996). Essentially, this corporate attitude derived from an integration of country and company goals. As Figure 5.3 indicates, they were the engine of Japan's rapid economic growth and the commanders of corporate Japan during the country's journey to become an economic superpower.

Company men

The first baby boomers (born 1947–49), or 'the company man', are distinguished from the senior generation on the basis of their democratic cultural assumptions attained through education. While their work ethos was not as devoted as their predecessors (Misumi, 1993), they still held a high regard for the ethical principle of *messhi hōkō* which was inculcated through interactions

Figure 5.3 The transition of ethos and work ethics in post-war corporate Japan

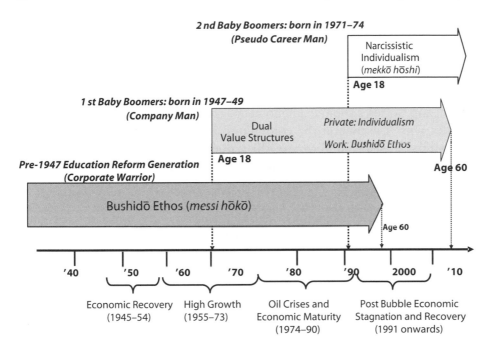

Source: Adaptation of 'Figure 5.4: Shift of Dominant Ethic and Work Ethic in Japan' in Miyamoto and Grainger 2004.

with the senior generation. Nonetheless, their moral obligation and *messhi hōkō* endeavours were primarily directed to achieving the company goals implicitly in return for an agreed lifetime employment. A 'company man' is willing to put the company's interest ahead of himself and his family's and work extended hours for the company (Hazama, 1996) and so this generation was responsible for Japan's stable economic development after 1973 and the lead-up to Japan's achievement as the world largest creditor nation. Their spouses had a support role with almost the sole parenting responsibility. Contrary to this conservative domestic arrangement, this generation holds a more democratic world view. The postwar cultural development is often labelled as an 'Americanisation' of Japanese culture and it was the First Baby Boomers who led the trend towards American democratic values.

Arguably, the democratic cultural shift of the First Baby Boomer generation articulates to the different generational corporate middle-management approaches found in Japanese companies. The Second Baby Boomers born between the years 1971 and 1974 as offspring of the First Baby Boomers represent the emergence of a new generation who are the Japanese-version of the *Generation X* increasingly subject to the macro-influences of global consumer culture. This generation was raised with domestic and educational democratic values in the context of the booming consumer economy of the 1980s, often with absent fathers during their teenage years but facing a depressed socio-economic reality upon their graduation in the 1990s.

Pseudo career man (Second generation baby boomers)

The second generation baby boomer, or 'pseudo career man', who began to enter the labour market in the 1990s, have come to be associated with more destabilising socio-economic phenomena. The upbringing of this generation coincides with a decline in the community inculcation of traditional Japanese moral ideals derived from *Bushidō* ethics, due to a break-down in extended family-relations and intensifying urbanisation. Nishijima (1995, p. 12) described the second baby boomers as follows:

> With the second baby boomers, individualism came close to autism and narcissism. The majority live in crisis and are the products of modern urban cosmopolitanism, conscientious dropouts from the notorious institutions of Japan Inc ... If they are ordered to perform a job they do not like, they do not hesitate to say so; they might even forthrightly refuse an assignment that upsets their private lives ... Reflecting their youthful absorption in solitary video games, they prefer to set personal goals and pursue work they enjoy rather than join in corporate endeavours that involve troublesome human relations ... The second baby boomers are realists; they entertain none of the dreams for the future or for neither progress as their parents did, nor any motivation to change or reform society. They revel in the pleasures of the present, making few sacrifices for the future or for any particular ideas.

Hence, these young adults are culturally classified as 'narcissistic individualist' (Nishijima, 1995). They are characterised as highly cynical about the work ethos and lifestyle of their generational predecessors. Nonetheless, the anti-social sentiment should be viewed as a natural self-defensive response to their cross-generational experiences: Absent father-figures had devoted their life to the company on the assumption of the progressive remuneration of the seniority based wage system, but instead faced unemployment due to the company's bankruptcy, or under an increasing pressure to take a voluntary early retirement option in the struggling economy. Accordingly, a cross-generational absence of loyalty to and distrust of the company as the '*ie*' and opportunistic pursuit of self-interest distinguishes them from the previous two generations.

A survey conducted by the Ministry of Health, Labour & Welfare found that 73 per cent of junior high school graduates, 50.3 per cent of high school graduates and 36.5 per cent of university graduates in 2000 left their hard-won first jobs within three years or sooner (*The Nikkei Weekly*, 2004). In one case, half of the 150 new university graduate recruits of a company left within their first year. High achievers who gain competitive employment opportunities at a high status corporation, like Sony, are no exception, e.g., only one of Sony's 47 elite graduate recruits intended to stay with the company until retirement (*Economist*, 1994). The most frequently cited reason for their departure was that the job that did not suit them (*White Paper on Labour,* 1999; 2000). This individualistic logic for resignation is also prevalent among young adult job seekers. Of 1.54 million young adult (i.e., 15 to 34 age bracket) job seekers in the 2004 January–March period, over sixty percent (0.94 million) attributed their joblessness to similar reasons, such as mismatches between their desired and available job content, work hours and days of work and wages offered in market (Ministry of Health, Labour and Welfare, 2004). Thus, these second 'wave' baby boomers can be regarded as the 'pseudo' career man who are directed only by individualism and only willing to make commitments if a job provides the opportunity for their personal goals without much sacrifice. This attitude means that the traditional ethical ideal of *Yamato Damashi, messhi hōkō* is replaced with '*mekkō hōshi*' – a self-indulgence pursuit with little wider consideration at the expense of others (Miyamoto and Grainger, 2004).

This socio-cultural concept of individualism is traditionally foreign to Japan; however, this generation has more in common with Western employees than their predecessors. Nevertheless, emphasising both socio-cultural convergence and divergence, the current generation is different from Western workers in at least two ways: Despite a strong self-actualisation ambition, few have had a specialised vocational education to support their professional ambitions. Until recently, under the conventional *kogai* system (standardised in-house training), the educational assumption was that this would be provided by the company in a context where corporate Japan preferred the generalist over a specialist graduate. Furthermore, their self-interest values are paradoxical in that the very basis of their individual freedom claims is built on the assumptions of a collectivist socio-cultural support structure, or *amae* (indulgent dependency) (Behrens, 2004). The growing trend of unemployed young adults and their changing work ethos are of great concern to corporate Japan and its policy makers (Miyamoto and Grainger, 2004). With the conventional Japanese business and management models dependent on the traditional socio-cultural values such as *messhi hōkō, kyōzon kyōei* and the *Bushidō* moral ideal, the values of the pseudo career man work ethos no longer serves the efficiency objectives of the system. The first Baby Boomers, or company men, will soon be leaving the workplace along with their *Bushidō* work ethos, to be replaced by younger workers with the distinctive self-serving work ethos. While some leading Japanese companies are eagerly experimenting with new HRM models in part to address the issue, progress appears to be slow. This trend is discussed later in this chapter.

An increasing number of Japanese young adults have been identified as being less motivated to attain independence than their predecessors, preferring instead to remain at home dependent on their parents. According to Japanese sociologist, Yamada, who labels them as *parasito shinguru* (i.e., parasite singles), their numbers were predicted to grow from 10 million in 1995 to 12 million in 2000 (Yamada, 1999). This group has been criticised for their lack of discipline and career ambition, and these characteristics are increasingly associated with growing number of '*freeters*' (*freeter*: a compound of 'free' in English and 'arbeiter' in

German, literally meaning a 'free worker') and more recently NEETs (i.e., English acronym for Not in Employment, Education or Training). *Freeters* are serial part-timers, or job hoppers, with little or no concern for future career development as their typical temporary jobs are low-skill and low-paid; NEET are those unemployed youth without intention to work. Whilst they are not a totally new phenomenon to Japanese society, their numbers have significantly increased over the past decade. The *freeter* numbers have more than doubled from 1.83 million in 1990 to 4.17 million in 2001 and are expected to grow (*Japan Times* [on-line], 2003). Similarly, the number of NEET is rising and currently amount to 760,000 (*The Nihon Keizai Shimbun*, 2004b).

Human resource management reform

Since the collapse of the bubble economy, the conventional Japanese HRM approach is increasingly internally and externally challenged (Mroczkowski and Hanaoka, 1998). Despite criticisms, leading Japanese companies – especially those aiming to build competitive advantage on 'knowledge-seeking and knowledge-exploiting workers' (Fruin, 1997, p. 17) and their firm-specific skills acquired over years of service – have persistently resisted wholesale HRM system change, especially the lifetime employment system. In addition to the logic of maintaining their existing human capital, their attitude stems from concern for the social consequences of laying-off large numbers of long-serving staff members into a social system which is not designed for the long-term unemployed (Grainger and Miyamoto, 2003b) and is also associated with the Japanese *kaizen* tradition of continuous and incremental improvement to solve problems.

Contrary to internal and external media reports of the demise of the system, corporate Japan is still supportive of their HRM tradition of lifelong employment. According to the Ministry of Health, Labour & Welfare, almost 80 per cent of companies with more than 1,000 employees still supported the traditional system (Ministry of Health, Labour and Welfare, 2003). Given the pervasiveness of this view, it is critical to understand what the lifetime employment system really means. Although even in Japan, the practice is referred to as *shūshin koyō* (i.e., permanent or lifetime employment) strictly speaking, this is not what the term implies – all workers' guaranteed lifetime employment at the company (Abegglen, 1958). It is not a legal contract but a psychological contract between the company and employees. The Japanese Ministry of Labour defines *shūshin koyō* as:

> The practice of companies to hire their core employees primarily from among new graduates and other young persons, to plan their continual training and development, to continue their employment within the company group over a long period of time [usually until age 55 or 60], and not to discharge or lay off such employees except in very unusual circumstances. (1995, p. 2)

According to this definition, the practice applies only to 'core' workers, not *all* workers. The question then arises – who are the core workers? Traditionally excluded are temporary, seasonal, part-time, female and foreign workers and this principle still remains more, or less, intact. First, temporary, seasonal and part-time workers are those workers who can be hired and fired at will and used as a buffer against economic volatility. Secondly, although the social status of female workers has improved, and since 1986 has been strengthened through the Equal Employment Opportunity Law and its revision in 1999, evidence suggests that the progress of female workers up the corporate career ladder remains disappointing and falls far behind international standards (Debroux, 2003; Yuasa, 2005). Similarly, foreign nationals are generally excluded from the system and are employed on a contract basis. However, since the 1980s, there has been an upwards trend of the status of foreign workers as regular, full-time employees (Whitehill, 1991), on the basis that these workers are 'specialist' employees with unique skills sets not easily developed through internal training, or a complementary workforce, and hence are not competing with local labour.

For Japanese male workers, lifetime job security is offered to only those elite who won their employment at large companies through academic achievement and demonstrations of loyalty on the basis of company performance criteria. In reward for loyalty and competence acquired through on- and off-the-job learning, this elite is retained within the company, or at least within a corporate group through the *shukkō* system, regardless of business environment. Alternatively, unsatisfactory workers are not fired under the long-term employment system, but instead, induced, or even coerced, to retire voluntarily. Hence, as experienced in the steel-making and shipping industries in the 1980s and more recently across corporate Japan, harsh economic realities have obliged many Japanese companies to confront their non-core workers with a voluntary retirement option (Mroczkowski and Hanaoka, 1998). Prior to the 1990s, approximately 30 per cent of the work force enjoyed the privilege of lifelong employment security (Befu and Cernosi, 1990), but more recently, the figure has dropped to roughly 20 per cent (Hirakubo, 1999). While the lifetime employment system is still at the cultural heart of corporate Japan, companies have become tougher with non-core regular full time male workers. In future, it is clear that companies will be expected to focus more on the identification of their core workers. Since 2003, Sanyo has implemented an innovative HRM practice where a preselected elite handful of new graduate recruits is assigned to a career-track management course as future senior management candidates (*The Nikkei Weekly*, 2004).

It is clear that since the beginning of economic recession, the corporate Japanese system has been under pressure primarily because of the long-term implications of labour costs and inherent inflexibility (Mroczkowski and Hanaoka, 1998; Debroux, 2003). Rethinking lifetime employment necessarily entails rethinking of the traditional seniority-based wage and promotion system. Inherent in the system are wage increases related to the worker's age and length of service, regardless of his, or her, real productivity and contribution. To counter this inherently problematic situation, two types of wage and promotion system have been devised. The first is aimed at managers, and has more emphasis on employee work performance over personal factors (age, education and length of service). Another is for those who have not reached managerial positions and who require skill acquisition and improvement (i.e., on- and off-the-job learning), with an almost equal emphasis on both personal factors and work capabilities (Watanabe, 2000). This approach supports company efforts to reduce labour costs associated with middle-aged and elder employees and to reflect the employee's ability and performance in the remuneration system (Ministry of Health, Labour and Welfare, 2004).

A recent *Nihon Keizai Shimbun* survey (2005) found that 28 percent of all Japanese companies utilise remuneration systems based on employee and company performance. While many companies are still in transition from the old seniority-based system to a new performance or merit-based wage and promotion systems, some leading companies are experimenting with the merit-based pay system in response to global imperatives, while at the same time addressing local issues. For example, Sony introduced a performance-based pay system without the traditional salary-linked allowances to over 6,000 managerial employees in 2000 and was expected to extend the system to some 12,000 non-managerial employees in Japan by April, 2004 (*The Japan Times,* 2004). Similarly, Toyota extended a new merit-based payment system beyond employees in administrative, clerical and engineering positions, to professional factory workers in April 2004, to replace the traditional seniority-based system, (*The Japan Times,* 2004). Despite the magnitude of these changes, initiatives have not led to labour disputes because of the weakening bargaining power of labour unions over the past decade (Debroux, 2003) and the need for both management and unions to collaborate in the revitalisation of corporate Japan.

A recent study found mixed feelings among employees towards newly introduced merit pay systems. Their overall assessment of the new system was negative, and they preferred some systemic indigenisation (*Nihon Keizai Shimbun,* 2004, August 9). There is no doubt that the traditional Japanese HRM model has to change, but it must be sensitively done in the context of unique socio-cultural characteristics and, more recently, the particularised nature of the new generation of young workers and female worker needs, and the ageing of the nation's workforce. In many respects, corporate Japan is entering into unknown territory, and the reform process associated with an HRM paradigm shift has just begun. Again, in the context of an emergent crisis the Japanese need to design uniquely Japanese management solutions to respond to global and local imperatives.

Transforming corporate behaviour

Over the previous decade the terms corporate governance, citizenship and social responsibility have become familiar to Western corporate managers. Whilst in Japan these issues are somewhat more broadly dealt with under the overarching umbrella of 'corporate behaviour', Japanese managers have also become embroiled in this trend (Nakano, 1999). Prior to the collapse of the bubble economy, the issue of corporate behaviour rarely attracted public attention except in the case of corporate scandals involving politicians. Public assumptions of community goodwill and trust in corporate Japan pervaded on the basis that companies, especially the elite ones, would act responsibly under the traditional Japanese moral ideals. Nevertheless, since the economy went into prolonged recession, an increasing number of corporate scandals have come to attract wide media attention and fuelled growing public hostility against corporate Japan. These scandals ranged from individual employee corruption to systemic company-wide cover-ups. In response to public outcry and growing shareholder democracy, leading Japanese companies increasingly promote corporate integrity (i.e., fairness, transparency and accountability) to restore local and external confidence (Nippon Keidanren n.d.).

Organisational culture is acknowledged to be an important organisational control mechanism. Japanese organisations are renowned for the importance of culture in maintaining control mechanisms (Ouchi, 1981). In companies with a strong ethical corporate culture, the core values of the founding philosophy and mission are applied to promote ethical company policy and values on which managers are to base their decision-making (Nakano, 1999). However, what if a company fails to maintain such a culture in the context of the new generational work ethos of young organisational members, and fails to manage employee behaviour?

Leading Japanese companies have been collectively promoting corporate integrity in Corporate Japan through Keidanren and its successor Nippon Keidanren (The Japan Business Federation). The federation is continuously re-evaluating what constitutes appropriate ethical corporate behaviour and revising the member code of corporate conduct. At present, Nippon Keidanren prescribes the fourth version (*Charter of Corporate Behaviour*) of the original code of corporate ethics (*Charter for Good Corporate Behaviour*), which was first prescribed in 1991 under Keidanren, due partly to the sustained emergence of corporate scandals, and partly to the globalisation of Japanese companies, necessitating a redefinition of corporate integrity from a global perspective (Nippon Keidanren n.d.).

Nonetheless, many Japanese companies have a long way to go assimilate a global perspective. For instance, the recent decision by the International Organisation for Standardisation (ISO) to develop a global standard for corporate social responsibility (CSR) will affect, and may determine the future course of corporate Japan's CSR effort. An important implication of this standardisation strategy is that a company, regardless of the country of their operation, will be regarded as a global citizen and expected to comply with the so-called global CSR standard. For this reason, leading companies in the CSR field, such as Sony, Matsushita, Komatsu, NEC and Toyota, are expected to exercise far greater initiative to align corporate Japan's CSR pursuit effort with the global standard (*The Nikkei Business Daily*, 2005). More specifically, the CSR related challenge of leading manufacturers will not end there. As a consequence of their powerful positions in supply chain networks and their strategic positions in the global marketplace, their CSR competence will also relate to their competence in directing the standards of their suppliers beyond Japanese national territory.

As part of corporate integrity management strategy, many companies have also adopted a more decentralised and lean decision-making system so as to increase the efficiency, transparency and accountability behind the decision-making process. Toyota and Matsushita have been trend setters in this paradigm shift (Lincoln and Nakata, 1997; Edwards, 1999). Traditionally, Japanese companies were renowned for their consensus-based group decision-making. The maintenance of harmony within the company and organisation-wide support for decisions are instrumental to the successful implementation of any strategic decision. Many Japanese companies now regard the benefits to be outweighed by the inherit problems of the decision-making system required for operational decisions, that is, the length of time required to build a group consensus and the masked accountability of each individual involved in a group decision making (Porter et al., 2000). These shortcomings are evident in the *ringi* system which has traditionally been used for the decision-making associated with complex operational and strategic issues.

Within the *ringi* system it is noteworthy that decisions are always made around a change: not whether a change should be made. The system is summarised (see Grainger and Miyamoto, 2002) as follows: first, an initiator of a change approaches organisational members who are affected by possible alternative decision outcomes with an idea. The initiator seeks prior unofficial support from those (the *nemawashi* process) process so that those directly or indirectly involved in decision-making issues are consulted and involved before the idea is subjected to official discussion and judgement. After securing informal support through consultation and lobbying and, if necessary making adjustments to the original idea, a formal written proposal, called a *ringi-sho*, is prepared to define the problem and prescribe the proponent's recommended decision together with a justification argument. Then, the proposal is fed into the company's decision-making hierarchy. Finally, a decision is made on the proposal on a personal assessment and in light of the level of support by others.

In many ways the recent shift in the decision-making paradigm reflects a Westernisation of the Japanese system. The current literature cites examples of the westernisation of the Japanese companies' decision making system. For instance Toyota has introduced a 'less-vertical decision-making' system for daily operational issues as part of its new management system since 2003:

> Matters concerning daily operations in specific fields/division will be settled at no higher then the level of senior managing director; senior managing directors, as the highest authorities in their areas of supervision, will participate in overall management of the company while overseeing 'on-site' decision-making related to their fields of operations. (http://www.toyota.co.jp/en/news/03/0328_3.html)

The currently more positive economic environment and outlook offer Japanese policy makers and corporate managers the reflective opportunity to assess the effectiveness of the ongoing reform journey. Drawing on past successes, current Japanese corporate and community leaders need to embrace a more convergent managerial approach that innovatively combines unique Japanese principles (e.g., the *kyōzon kyōei* ideal) with the US management principles to develop a more sustainable corporate model for a new global era.

Conclusion

This chapter has outlined the evolving nature of Japanese responses to a range of macro-level local issues and external forces that have periodically arisen to shape the country's socio-cultural, economic, legal and political landscape. From a base of small islands and limited resources the people of Japan have modernised their country and its economy to leading developed nation status. Moreover, this great achievement has been coupled with the development of unique socio-cultural community, corporate governance and management characteristics established around the traditional Japanese moral ideal, *Yamato Damashi*. At the meso-societal and micro-organisational level the country and its corporate sector now face ever intensifying economic uncertainty and significant strategic regional challenges associated with an increasingly competitive global economy and with a rapidly changing internal socio-cultural community milieu. Nevertheless, as history has illustrated that within the pragmatic, conservative, resourceful and innovative capacity of Japanese leaders and the people, it is predictable that ongoing consistent and incremental levels of community governance and managerial reform will inevitably reveal a unique Japanese response pattern. Japanese management is expected to continue to play an important role in providing solutions to the challenges now faced in the maturing processes of the global economy. Continuing analysis of its developmental path will provide invaluable insights in this overall process.

Questions

1. Discuss the macro-level influences of the local and regional 'forces of heritage' on the development of the Japanese managerial context.
2. Explain the evolving relationship between the political and economic system and meso-societal level development in Japan
3. Discuss how contemporary global imperatives impact on local Japanese managerial systems and styles.

URL linkages

Government and related information

Bank of Japan	http://www.boj.or.jp/en/index.htm
Cabinet Office	http://www.cao.go.jp/index-e.html
Imperial Household Agency	http://www.kunaicho.go.jp/eindex.html
Ministry of Economy, Trade and Industry	http://www.meti.go.jp/english/index.html

Ministry of Education, Culture, Sports, Science & Technology	http://www.mext.go.jp/english/index.htm
Ministry of Finance	http://www.mof.go.jp/english/index.htm
Ministry of Foreign Affairs	http://www.mofa.go.jp/index.html
Ministry of Health, Labour and Welfare	http://www.mhlw.go.jp/english/index.html
Economic and Social Research Institute	http://www.esri.cao.go.jp/index-e.html
Prime Minister of Japan	http://www.kantei.go.jp/foreign/index-e.html
Statistics Bureau & Statistics Centre	http://www.stat.go.jp/english/index.htm

Economy, trading and technology

All Japan Federation of Management Organizations	http://www.zen-noh-ren.or.jp/e/page1.htm
Nippon Keidanren	http://www.keidanren.or.jp/index.html
Keizai Doyukai (Japan Association of Corporate Executives)	http://www.doyukai.or.jp/en/
Japan External Trade Organization (JETRO)	http://www.jetro.go.jp/index.html
Japan Industrial Management Association	http://www.jimanet.jp/english/english.html
Japan Institute for Social and Economic Affairs	http://www.kkc.or.jp/english/
Japan International Cooperation Agency	http://www.jica.go.jp/english/
Japan Management Association (JMA)	http://www.jma.or.jp/indexeng.html
Japan Materials Management Association	http://www.jmma.gr.jp/english/ jmma/jmma_index. english.htm
Japan Productivity Centre for Socio-Economic Development	http://www.jpc-sed.or.jp/eng/index.html
Japan Science and Technology Corporation	http://www.jst.go.jp/EN/
Japan Society for the Promotion of Science	http://www.jsps.go.jp/english/ index.html
National Institute of Advanced Industrial Science & Technology	http://www.aist.go.jp/index_ en.html
National Institute of Informatics	http://www.nii.ac.jp/index.html
The Japan Chamber of Commerce and Industry	http://www.jcci.or.jp/home-e.html

Japan Statistical Yearbook 2005   http://www.stat.go.jp/english/
                                         data/nenkan

News and information

Asahi Shinbun   http://iij.asahi.com/english/
                                         english.html

Kyodo News   httpontrac://home.kyodo.co.jp/
Mainichi Daily News   http://mdn.mainichi.co.jp/
Nihon Keizai Shinbun   http://www.nni.nikkei.co.jp/
The Daily Yomiuri   http://www.yomiuri.co.jp/
                                         index-e.htm

Japan Echo   http://www.japanecho.co.jp
The Japan Times   http://www.japantimes.co.jp/
Japan Information Network   http://jin.jcic.or.jp/
Ancient/Classical History – Japan   http://ancienthistory.about.
                                         com/od/japan/

Internet Sacred Text Archive – Shinto   http://www.sacred-texts.com/shi/
                                         index.htm

National Archives of Japan   http://www.archives.go.jp/
                                         index_e.html

WIKEPEDIA- History of Japan   http://en.wikipedia.org/wiki/
                                         History_of_Japan

Search engine

Excite   http://www.excite.co.jp/
FreshEye   http://www.fresheye.com/
Yahoo Japan: http://www.yahoo.co.jp/
Google Japan: http://www.google.co.jp/

References

Abegglen, JC, 1958, *The Japanese factory*, Glencoe, Ill.

Ackley, G & Ishi, H, 1976, 'Fiscal, monetary and related policies'. In H Patrick & H Rosovsky (eds), *Asia's new giant: How the Japanese economy works*, The Brookings Institute, Washington, DC. pp. 153–247.

Alston, JP, 1985, *The American samurai: Blending American and Japanese managerial practices*, Walter de Gruyter, Germany.

Aoki, K, 1994, 'Monitoring characteristics of the main bank system: An analytical and developmental view'. In M Aoki & H Patrick (eds). *The Japanese main bank system*, Oxford University Press, Oxford, pp. 109–41.

Aoki, M, Koike, K & Nakatasni, I, 1986, *Nihon Kigyo no Keizaigaku* (Economics of Corporate Japan, TBS Britanica, Japan.

Bahappu, AD, 2000, 'The Japanese family: An institutional logic for Japanese corporate networks and Japanese management', *Academy of Management Review*, vol. 25 no. 2, pp. 409–15.

Bank of Japan, 2003, 'Recent trends in business fixed investment and the issues attending to a full recovery: Restoring firms' capacity to generate production capacity', *Quarterly Bulletin*, November, Retrieved 24 November 2004 from: http://www.boj.or.jp/en/ronbun/03/data/ron0309a.pdf.

Bank of Japan, 2004, 'Foreign exchange rate'. Retrieved 9 November 2004 from: http://www.boj.or.jp/en/stat/stat_f.htm.

Beaseley, WG, 1999, *The Japanese experience: A short history of Japan*. Weidenfeld & Nicolson, London.

Befu, H & Cernosia, C,1990, 'Demise of 'permanent employment' in Japan', *Human Resource Management*, vol. 29, no. 3, pp. 231–50.

Behrens, KY, 2004, 'A multifaceted view of the concept of *amae*: Reconsidering the indigenous Japanese concept of relatedness', *Human Development*, vol. 47, no. 1, pp. 1–27.

Chandler, AD, 1984, 'The emergence of managerial capitalism', *Business History Review*, vol. 58, no. 4, pp. 473–503.

Cohen, D, 1998, 'Toward a knowledge context: Report on the first annual U.C. Berkeley Forum on knowledge and the firm,' *California Management Review*, vol. 40 no.3, pp. 22–39.

Cole, RE, 1971, *Japanese blue collar: The changing tradition*, University of California Press, Berkeley.

Cole, RE, 1994, 'Different quality paradigms and their implications for organisational learning'. In M Aoki & R Dore (eds), *The Japanese firm: Sources of competitive strength*, (pp. 66–83) Oxford University Press, New York.

Debin, M, 2004, 'Why Japan, not China, was the first to develop in East Asia: Lessons from sericulture, 1850–1937', *Economic Development and Cultural Change*, vol. 52, no. 2, pp. 369–94.

Debroux, P, 2003, *Human resource management in Japan: Changes and uncertainties*, Ashgate, Hampshire, England.

De Mente, BL, 1995, *Japan encyclopaedia*. Passport Books, Lincolnwood, Illinois.

Department of National Accounts, Economics & Social Research Institute, Cabinet Office, 'Gross domestic product classified by economic activities (1990–2002)', http://www.stat.go.jp/data/nenkan/pdf/y0308000.pdf.

Dore, R, 1973, *British factory, Japanese factory: The origins of diversity in industrial relations*, University of California, Berkeley.

——, 1987, *Taking Japan seriously: A Confucian perspective on leading economic issues*, Stanford University Press, Stanford, California.

Edwards, B, 1999, 'Survey: Business in Japan: From squares to pyramids', *The Economist*, London, Nov 27.

Edwards, CT & Samimi R, 1997, 'Japanese inter-firm networks: Exploring the seminal sources of their success', *Journal of Management Studies*, vol. 34, no. 4, pp. 489–510.

Feldstin, M, 1987, 'Correcting the trade deficit', *Foreign Affairs*, vol. 65, no. 4. pp. 795–806. Retrieved from ABI/INFORM Global.

Fruin, WM, 1997, *Knowledge works: Managing intellectual capital at Toshiba*. Oxford University Press, New York.

Fürstenberg, F, 1974, *Why the Japanese have been so successful in business*. Leviathan House, London.

Gerlach, M, 1992, *Alliance capitalism: The social organisations of Japanese business*, University of California Press, Berkeley.

Grainger, R & Miyamoto, T, 2002, 'Management in Japan: Contemporary Issues'. In S Chatterjee & A, Nankervis (eds), *Asian Values and Management Styles*, Vineyard Publications, Guildford, (pp: 98–127).

Grainger, R & Miyamoto, T, 2003a, 'Shukkō and amakudari: Uniquely Japanese approaches to knowledge management'. In R, Lee (ed.), *Knowledge management in Asia*, Singapore Institute of Materials Management, Singapore.

——, 2003b 'Human values and HRM practice: The Japanese shukkō practice, *Journal of Human Values*, vol. 9, no 2, pp. 105–15.

Hanami, T, 1984, 'Conflict and its resolution in industrial relations and labour law'. In ES Kraus, TP Rohlen & PG Steinhoff (eds), *Conflict in Japan*, University of Hawaii Press, Honolulu, pp. 107–35.

Hazama, H, 1996, *Keizai Taikoku wo Tsukiuriageta Shiso* (*Ideology that built an economic power*), Bunshin do.

Henshall, KG, 1999, *A history of Japan: From stone age to superpower*. MacMillan Press, Hampshire, UK.

Hirakubo, N, 1999, 'The end of lifetime employment in Japan', *Business Horizon*, vol. 42, (November/December), pp. 41–46.

Hiro, S, 1987, *Bukkyo to Shinto: Douchigauka 50 no Q & A (Differences between Buddhism and Shinto Q & As)*, Shinchosha, Tokyo, Japan (Japanese).

Ichiyanagi, Y & Hosoya, Y, 1998, *Keizai Seisaku no Aratana Tenkai* (New Development in Economic Policy), Discussion Paper #98-DOJ-89, retrieved from: http://www.meti.go.jp/topic/mitilab/downloadfiles/m4189–1.pdf (Japanese).

Imai, M, 1986, *Kaizen: The key to Japan's competitive success*, MaGraw-Hill, New York.

Ishida, I, 1984, 'Conflict and its accommodation: Omote-ura and uchi-soto relations'. In ES Krauss, TP Rohlen & PG Steinhoff (eds), *Conflict in Japan*, University of Hawaii Press, Honolulu, pp. 16–38.

Ishikawa, K, 1985, *What is total quality control? The Japanese way*. Prentice-Hall, Inc., Englewood Cliffs, New Jersey.

Itoh, M, 1990, *The world economic crisis and Japanese capitalism*, MacMillan, Houndmills, England.

Japan Statistical Yearbook 2004: '6–15 Cases of suspension of business transactions with banks and bankruptcy'. Retrieved November 15, 2004 from: http://www.stat.go.jp/english/data/nenkan/1431–06.htm.

Johnson, C, 1982, *MITI and the Japanese miracle*, University of California Press, Berkeley.

Kajiwara, K, 1992, *Honda Soichiro: Omou-mama ni ikiro* (A biography of Soichiro Honda: Live with a free spirit. Kodansha, Tokyo (Japanese).

Kawai, M, 1998, 'Japan as a creditor nation: What is happening to its net external assets?' In B, Junji (ed.), *The political economy of Japanese society, Volume 2: Internationalisation and domestic issues*, Oxford University Press, UK, pp. 7–43.

——, 2003, 'Japan's banking system: From the bubble and crisis to reconstruction', PRI Discussion Paper Series, No.03A-28, December 25 http://www.mof.go.jp/jouhou/soken/kenkyu/ron080.pdf

Keegan, WJ, 1975, 'Productivity: Lessons from Japan', *Long Range Planning* vol.8, no.2 pp. 61–71.

Keidanren 1996, *Keidanren charter for good corporate behaviour*, http://www.keidanren.or.jp/english/policy/pol052.html.

Kikkawa, T, 1996, *Nihon no kigyo shudan: Zaibatsu tono renzoku to danzetsu*, Yuhikaku, Tokyo.

Koike, K, 1994, 'Learning and incentive systems in Japanese industry'. In M Aoki & R Dore (eds), *The Japanese firm: Sources of competitive strength* (pp.41–65) Oxford University Press, New York.

Kono, T, 1982, 'Japanese management philosophy: Can it be exported?' *Long Range Planning*, vol.15, no. 3, pp. 90–102.

Kosai, Y, 1986, *The era of high-speed growth: notes on the post-war Japanese economy*, University of Tokyo Press, Japan.

Lincoln, JR & Nakata, Y, 1997, 'The transformation of the Japanese employment system: Nature, depth, and origin', *Work and Occupation*, vol. 24, no.1, pp. 33–55.

Mason, M, 1992, 'The origins and evolution of Japanese direct investment in Europe'. *Business History Review*, vol. 66, no. 3, pp. 435–74.

Maswood, SJ, 2002, *Japan in crisis*, Palgrave MacMillan, Basingstoke, UK.

Ministry of Health, Labour and Welfare 2003, *White Paper on the labour economy*: Summary, http://www.mhlw.go.jp/english/wp/wp-l/2–2-4.html.

——, 2004, *White Paper on the labour economy* 2004 http://www.mhlw.go.jp/

Ministry of Internal Affairs & Communications 2004 'Monthly statistics of Japan: I.1. Exports and imports by region, November 2004, No. 521'. Retrieved November 24, 2004 from: http://www.stat.go.jp/english/data/geppou/zuhyou/i01.xls.

Ministry of Labour, 1995, *Nihon teki toyō seido no genjō to tenbou*, JMOL, Tokyo.

Misumi, J,1993, 'Attitudes to work in Japan and the West', *Long Range Planning*, vol. 26, no. 4, pp. 66–71.

Mito, T, 1994, *Ie toshiteno Nihon shakai*, Yuhikaku, Tokyo.

Miura, S, 2003, *Kojiki Kougi* (transl. 'Seminar on the Record of Ancient Things').Bungei Shunju Ltd., Japan.

Miyajima, H, 1999, 'Presidential turnover and performance in the Japanese firm: The evolution and change of the contingent governance structure under the main bank system'. In Dirks, D, J-F Huchet & Ribault T, (eds), *Japanese management in the low growth era*, Springer, Germany, pp. 121–41.

Miyamoto, T & Grainger R, 2004, 'Changing work ethics and sustainable development in Post War Japan'. In P Šauer, A Nankervis & A Mensik (eds), *Sustainability in global services: Selected essays*, Nakladatelstvi a vydavatelstvi litomyslskeho seminare, Praha, pp. 66–87.

Miyamoto, T & Rexha, N, 2004, 'Determinants of three facets of customer trust: A marketing model of Japanese buyer-supplier relationship', *Journal of Business Research*, vol. 57, no. 3, pp. 312–19.

Mizuno, S, 1988, *Company-wide total quality control*. Asian Productivity Organisation, Nordica International Limited, Hong Kong.

MOL, 1999, *White paper on labour*, Ministry of Labour, Tokyo.

MOL, 2000, *White paper on labour*, Ministry of Labour, Tokyo.

Morikawa, H, 1992, *Zaibatsu: The rise and fall of family enterprise groups in Japan*, Tokyo, University of Tokyo Press.

——, 1997, 'Japan: increasing organizational capabilities of large industrial enterprises, 1880s–1980s'. In AD Chandler, F. Amatori & T. Hikino (eds), *Big business and the wealth of nations*, Cambridge University Press, Cambridge, pp: 307–35.

Morishima, M, 1982, *Why has Japan 'succeeded'? Western technology and the Japanese ethos*, Cambridge University Press, Cambridge, UK.

Morita, A, Reingold, EM & Shimomura, M, 1986, *Made in Japan: Akio Morita and Sony*, Dutton, NewYork.

Mroczkowski, T & Hanaoka, M, 1989, 'Continuity and change in Japanese management', *California Management Review*, vol. 31, no. 2, pp. 39–53.

——, 1998, The end of Japanese management: How soon? *Human Resource Planning*, vol. 21, no. 3, pp. 20–30.

Murakami, Y, 1984 '*Ie* society as a pattern of civilization', *Journal of Japanese Studies*, vol. 10, pp. 281–363.

Nakamura, T, 1981, *The post-war Japanese economy: Its development and structure*, University of Tokyo Press, Japan.

Nakane, C, 1972, *Japanese society*, Penguin Books, Middlesex.

Nakano, C, 1999, 'Attempting to institutionalise ethics: Case studies from Japan', *Journal of Business Ethics*, vol. 18, pp: 335–43.

Nihon Keizai Shimbun, 2005, Annual Environmental Management Survey, Tokyo.

Nippon Keidanren (n.d.) 'Charter of Corporate Behaviour', Retrieved from http://www.keidanren.or.jp/english/policy/cgcb.html.

Nippon Keidanren (n.d.) '*Nippon Keidanren* towa?' (About Nippon Keidanren) (Japanese). Available http://www.keidanren.or.jp/japanese/profile/pro001.html

Nishijima, T, 1995, 'How the baby boomers stirred up society', *Japan Quarterly*, vol. 42, no. 1, pp. 6–13.

Nitobe, 1905, *Bushidō: The soul of Japan–an exposition of Japanese thought*, Putnum, New York.

Nonaka, I, 1988, 'Self-renewal of Japanese firms and human resource strategy', *Human Resource Planning*, vol. 27, no. 3, pp. 20–31.

Nonaka, I & Takeuchi, H, 1995, *The Knowledge-creating company: How Japanese companies create the dynamics of innovation*, Oxford University Press, New York.

OECD, 2005, 'Annual National Accounts, Statistics, Data & Indicators (5), Gross domestic product'. http://www.oecd.org/dataoecd/48/4/33727936.pdf.

Okumura, H, 1975, *Houjin shihonshugi no kouzou*, Nihon Hyoronsha, Tokyo.

Ouchi, WG, 1981, Theory Z: *How American business can meet the Japanese challenge*, Addison-Wesley, New York.

Park, KH, 2003, 'Patterns and strategies of foreign direct investment: The case of Japanese firms'. *Applied Economics*. vol. 35, no. 16, p. 1739.

Prime Minister of Japan and his Cabinet, n.d., retrieved from http://www.kantei.go.jp/foreign/cabinet_asystem/3–2.html

Porter, M, 1985, 'Technology and competitive advantage', *Journal of Business Strategy*, vol.5, no. 3, pp. 60–78.

Porter, M, Takeuchi, H & Sakakibara, M, 2000, *Can Japan compete?* Perseus, Cambridge, MA.

Reischauer, EO 1977, *The Japanese*, Harvard University Press, Boston.

Reischauer, EO & Craig, AM, 1979, *Japan: tradition and transformation*, George Allen and Unwin Australia Pty Ltd, NSW.

Rexha, N & Miyamoto, T, 2001, 'Management of supplier network knowledge for enhanced manufacturing efficiency', *Best Practices in Purchasing and Supply Chain Management, CAPS Research*, vol. 5, no. 1, pp. 10–14. Available from: http://www.capsresearch.org/publications/pdfs-protected/practix092001a.pdf.

Sen, A, 2004, 'How does culture matter?'. In Rao, V & Walton (eds), *Culture and public action*, Stanford University Press, Stanford California, (pp. 37–58).

Statistical data in Japan: *Jyuyō kōmoku betsu jikeiretsu hyou* (Time-series data on demands in national economy). Retrieved 14 November 2004 from http://www.esri.cao.go.jp/jp/sna/qe011–68/ritu-jcy01168.csv.

Statistics Bureau 2004, 'Japan in figures – population and households: 6. Projections of total population, elderly population'. http://www.stat.go.jp/english/data/figures/zuhyou/1606.xls.

Taira, K, 1970, *Economic development and the labour market in Japan*, Columbia University Press, New York.

Takahashi, K, 1969, The rise and development of Japan's modern economy: The basis for 'miraculous' growth, The Jiji Press, Led, Tokyo.

The Economist, 1994, 'Life-time underemployment', July 9, pp. 10–12.

The Japan Times, 2004, 'Toyota to make full shift to performance-based pay', February, 18 2003, 'Sony plans to introduce merit-based pay system', November 30.

The Nihon Keizai Shimbun 2004a, 'FY04 Real growth downgraded to 2.9%: Private-sector think tanks', November, 18, 2004.

——, 2004b, 'New Hope needed for labour market', Tuesday June 1.

The Nikkei Business Daily, 2005, 'Sony No. 1: In corporate social responsibility: Nikkei survey', January 17, http://www.nni.nikkei.co.jp/AC/TNKS/Search/Nni20050116D14JSN09.htm

The Nikkei Weekly, 2004, 'Insight: graduates enrol in hire education', April 12.

Toyota: History of Toyota. Retrieved 17 November 2004 from: http://www.toyota.co.jp/en/about_toyota/history/index.html.

Tsuru, S, 1993, *Japan's capitalism: creative defeat and beyond*, Cambridge University Press, Cambridge.

Udea, A, 1998, 'Neo-Bushido for tomorrow's Japan', *Japan Echo*, vol. 25, no. 3, pp. 55–9.

Vogel, EF, 1979, *Japan as number one: Lessons for America*, Harvard University Press Cambridge, MA.

Watanabe, S, 2000, 'The Japan model and the future of employment and wage systems', *International Labour Review*, vol. 139, no. 3, pp. 307–33.

Weber, M, 1976, The protestant work ethic and the spirit of capitalism, Charles Scribner's Sons, New York.

Whitehill, AM, 1991, Japanese management: Tradition and transition, Routledge, UK.

Wilkins, M, 1990, 'Japanese multinationals in the United States: Continuity and change, 1879–1990', *Business History Review*, vol. 64, no. 4, p. 585.

Womack, JP, Jones, DT & Roos, D, 1991, *The machine that changed the world: The story of lean production*, Harper Perennial, New York.

Yamada, M, 1999, *Parasito Shinguru no Jidai (The Age of the Parasite Singles)*, Chikuma Shinsho, Tokyo.

Yamamoto, S, 1978, *Kindai no sozo: Shibusawa Eiichi noshiso to kodo*, PHP Kenkyujo, Tokyo (in Japanese).

Yoshikawa, H, 2002, *Japan's lost decade*. International House of Japan, Tokyo.

Yuasa, M, 2005, 'Japanese Women in Management: getting closer to 'realities' in Japan', *Asia Pacific Business Review*, vol. 11, no. 2, pp. 195–211.

Yui, T, 1993, *Seiren no keiei: 'Tohi mondo' to gendai (Refining management thinking: Learning from Ishida Baigan)*, Nihon Keizai Shinbunsha, Toykyo (in Japanese).

Additional readings

Debroux, P, 2003, *Human resource management in Japan: Changes and uncertainties*, Ashgate, Hampshire, England.

Fruin, WM, 1997, *Knowledge works: Managing intellectual capital at Toshiba*, Oxford University Press, New York.

Haag, R & Pudelko, M, (eds), 2005, *Japanese management: In search for a new balance between continuity and change*, Palgrave Macmillan, New York.

Nonaka, I, 1988, Self-renewal of Japanese firms and human resource strategy, *Human Resource Planning*, vol. 27, no 3, pp. 20–31.

Nonaka, I & Takeuchi, H, 1995, *The knowledge-creating company: How Japanese companies create the dynamics of innovation*, Oxford University Press, New York.

Morita, A, Reingold, EM & Shimomura, M, 1986, *Made in Japan: Akio Morita and Sony*, Dutton, New York.

Watanabe, S, 2000, The Japan model and the future of employment and wage systems, *International Labour Review*, vol. 139, no. 3, pp. 307–33.

The management challenges of small and dynamic Asian nations

Three critically important small Asian countries: South Korea, Malaysia and Singapore

This section includes three small Asian nations which have significantly different geographic, historical, political and economic characteristics, but which are strategically significant in the region, and which share some common Asian influences. Thus, Singapore is considered to be a developed nation, whilst South Korea and Malaysia, to varying degrees, are still developing. However, until the 1997 economic crisis both Singapore and South Korea were members of the much-vaunted 'Asian tigers' group of nations, ostensibly leading Asia's economic resurgence. All three countries have been influenced heavily by colonialism, particularly the British in Singapore and Malaysia; and Chinese, Japanese and American legacies in South Korea. South Korea and, to a less extent, Singapore, are both ethnically homogeneous nations with strong Confucian and Buddhist traditions, whilst Malaysia is a pluralistic and multiracial state with an influential moderate Islamic heritage.

Malaysia has the broadest range of industry sectors, with around 7 per cent agriculture, 33.6 per cent manufacturing, and 59 per cent services. South Korea has a smaller agricultural base (3–4%), but more manufacturing (40%); especially in information technology, whitegoods and automobiles; and a growing services sector (56%). With no natural resources, Singapore's reliance on the innovation of its human resources, supported by a high level of government intervention in the economy, has resulted in a dominant services sector (67.5%). All the three countries are competitors in the regional and global services marketplace.

The relative 'quality of life' of Singapore and South Korea, reflected in the Human Development Index, is similar (Singapore – 25, South Korea – 28), with Malaysia somewhat lower on the scale (59), yet against the World Competitiveness Scores (see Chapter 1) Singapore rates number 2, with Malaysia (16) well ahead of South Korea (35), due perhaps to the greater geopolitical stability of the former two countries, and the growth potential of Malaysia. With respect to corruption, the Corruption Transparency Index indicates similar rankings, but with Malaysia closer to South Korea (39, compared to 47).

All three nations espouse similar social values to those of the earlier three larger Asian countries, based on their particular 'forces of heritage' (social conservatism, family, conscientiousness, respect for authority), and all have inculcated global managerial imperatives, to varying degrees. However, Singapore and South Korea have arguably absorbed the latter more than Malaysia, due to the mediating influence of Islam and its greater heterogeneity. These similar yet different influences are reflected in these countries' management styles and processes, at macro-, meso- and micro-societal levels, and are further discussed in the following chapters.

Managing industrial development through learning, the family and competition in South Korea

To describe the historical and philosophical context 6.1
of South Korea.

To explain the major political, socio-cultural and economic 6.2
influences on management in South Korea.

To outline how regional and local influences, and global 6.3
forces impact on Korean management.

To explore the linkages between macro-, meso-, and micro- 6.4
level factors in Korean management

To explain the major features of Korean managerial values, 6.5
systems and practices.

Introduction

The story of management in South Korea reflects the complex societal processes that derive from the nation's regional location on the Korean Peninsula and over time the important socio-cultural influences and variably cooperative and coercive interrelationships with important regional neighbours, especially China and Japan. While Chinese, Japanese and more recently American influences have significantly shaped the evolution of Korean society, nevertheless these influences have been appropriated and adapted to build a characteristically unique South Korean national world view and identity. And while Korean society has much in common with its regional neighbours, it has developed a unique approach to management framed around the core Neo-Confucian heritage values of learning and the centrality of family, with the austerities of colonisation and war providing an instinctive national impetus to drive a highly competitive approach to industrial development. Since the end of the Korean War, the government has applied a uniquely Korean approach to industrial development through policy and infrastructure support that encouraged and expanded the country's family-centred Chaebol industrial conglomerates. With the Chaebol as the centrepiece of an industrial development strategy, the remarkable successes of the South Korean economy have not only dramatically improved the standards of living for the South Korean people, but also enabled the country to become a major economic power in the global market. More recently, the country is engaging with ongoing reform and associated transitional strategies to sustain and improve its competitive market approach.

The macro-regional level: Local issues and external forces influencing the management context of South Korea

South Korea includes half of the Korean Peninsula from the Straits of Korea in the south, which separates the country from Japan, to the demilitarisation zone bordering North Korea. The majority of the country is mountainous with only 17 per cent arable land. The lowland territory, located mainly in the south and the west, also includes the main areas of settlement where population density is very high (CIA World Factbook, 2005). The close proximity of China and Japan has meant that at particular times in history both antagonistic and collaborative cross-border interactions have had a significant societal impact, and these neighbouring countries have been a key source of socio-cultural and economic influence. As a result of this proximity, Koreans share a common heritage with their neighbours. Nevertheless, there is significant national pride in the unique characteristics of Korean culture and the particular achievements of the Korean people. The regional distinctiveness of Korea means that in a business setting, Korean managers and workers behave differently from their counterparts in other countries (Chang and Chang, 1994). Hence, understanding Korean society – its heritage, national culture and socio-political and economic institutions – is essential to interpret the particular characteristics, logic and approach applied at macro-, meso- and micro-management organisational levels in contemporary Korea.

This chapter first discusses the relationships between the history and culture of the Korean people and how these factors have shaped Korean society and, more particularly, influenced the development of management in Korea. The history of the Korean people, their religions and national culture all contribute to a Korean heritage which played a crucial role in characteristically shaping the nation's specific political and economic governance and management approaches. In the second half of the twentieth century these specific Korean approaches to governance and management:

● Mobilised the remarkable successes of the post-Korean War industrialisation strategy;

- Shaped the characteristics of the major structural elements of the modern Korean industrial system;

- Underpinned the management patterns and processes which prevail amongst the enormously powerful family-dominated industrial conglomerates, the Chaebol; and

- Guided the various macro-, meso- and micro-strategies set in place to respond to the increasing competitive and integrated nature of the global economy.

Despite limited resources and the adverse geopolitical circumstances of the Korean Peninsula, the Korean people have nurtured a society that has empowered its people through its societal approach to education, the family system, and fierce competition (Chang and Chang, 1994). The next section briefly discusses how the key local influences and external forces implicit in the Korean heritage have contributed to a unique Korean approach to management.

The forces of heritage: A historical process of the localisation of external influences

Although the precise origins of the Korean people are obscure, it is generally believed that Korea was first populated by migrants from the north-western and central parts of Asia, the Lake Baikal region, Mongolia, and the coastal areas of the Yellow Sea. Currently, South Korea has an estimated population of 48.5 million (CIA World Factbook, 2005). Linguistic and ethnographic studies have classified the Korean language within the Altaic language family, which includes Turkic, Mongolic and Tungus-Manchu languages (Korea.net, 2005). Koreans proudly claim a national heritage based around a united state for more than a thousand years. While there are several Korean dialects all Koreans speak and write the same language and this unified linguistic communication vehicle is one factor that is attributed with forging a strong Korean national identity. The Korean language, which has affinities to the Japanese language, contains many Chinese loanwords and written characters, and has a unique phonetic script, known as *Hangul*. With the intensification of globalisation and the pervasive nature of American influence, English is now widely taught. Nevertheless, for Koreans, the longevity of the state administrative system, unified from the seventh century under the rulership of the Silla Kingdom (57 BC to AD 935), contributes to a national homogeneity that has enabled Koreans to be relatively free from ethnic problems and to maintain a firm solidarity with one another (Korea.net, 2005).

Korea is the anglicised version of *Koryo*, the name given to the kingdom in 918 AD. Like neighbouring Japan and other regional countries, the influence of Chinese culture over the past one thousand years has been strong. The legacy of this Chinese influence is identifiable in the evolving Korean political, legal and social systems, along with the arts, and religion (Chen, 2004). More particularly, the Chinese religions of Buddhism, Confucianism, Shamanism and Taoism have been key socio-cultural influences. According to the ancient Korean Shamanist perspective, the world is inhabited by an 'unorganised pantheon of literally millions of gods, spirits, and ghosts, ranging from the "god generals" who rule the different quarters of heaven to mountain spirits (*sansin*) ... These spirits are said to have the power to influence or to change the fortune of men and women' (US Library of Congress – South Korea n.d.(a)). While in modern times the government has discouraged the belief in Shamanism as superstition, and so now its influence is limited, in a context of rising nationalism and cultural self-confidence, the dances, songs and incarnations associated with shamanistic performance rituals (the female shaman, or *mudang*, led *kut)* have come to be recognised as an important aspect of Korean culture (US Library of Congress – South Korea n.d.(b)).

Religious and philosophical influences

Taoism and Buddhism came to Korea from China during the era known as the Three Kingdoms (the fourth to seventh century) along with Confucianism. Under royal patronage many temples and monasteries were built and by the sixth century monks and artisans were going to Japan with scriptures and religious artefacts to form the basis for the early Buddhist culture there. By unification in 668 AD Buddhism had been embraced as the state religion with a period that followed producing great Buddhist artefacts and architecture, while Confucian principles guided the administration. However, over time the state cult of Buddhism began to deteriorate as the nobility indulged in a luxurious lifestyle (Ministry of Culture and Tourism, (a) n.d.). During the early period of the Choson Dynasty (1392–1910), in response followers of Buddhism were persecuted by the ruler Yi Song-gye, who established Neo-Confucian institutions of learning, to institutionalise Korea as a Confucian state. Buddhism then established the *Seon* (Zen) sect focused on finding universal truth through a life of frugality (Ministry of Culture and Tourism, (a) 2001.).

In contrast, the more worldly Neo-Confucian learning institutions produced scholars who were to become the *yangban* class – those then recruited for government administration. Hence, while Taoist and Buddhist cultural values were incorporated into early Korean society, the values of Confucianism were to play a pivotal role in shaping not only the culture of the society, but also the institutional structure of the social and governance systems. Buddhism is a highly disciplined philosophical religion which emphasises personal salvation through rebirth in an endless cycle of reincarnation. Confucianism is a system of ethical precepts – benevolent love, righteousness, decorum and wise leadership – designed to inspire and preserve the good management of family and society (Ministry for Culture and Tourism, (a) 2001).

A Neo-Confucian society

Neo-Confucianism defines the social relations of all societal levels, and in terms of the harmonious integration of individuals into a collective whole that mirrors the harmony of the natural order (US Library of Congress n.d.(a)). Early notions of the harmony in the natural order derive from the Taoist interpretation of the universe as being made up of two – yin and yang – cosmic forces. Implicit in understanding this fundamental dualistic characteristic relationship, for example – positive/negative, masculine/feminine, day/night – is recognition of the complementary and synergistic nature of the seemingly opposite characteristics found in natural world. This difference – complement functional dichotomy emphasises an interdependent relationship, and so when this notion was philosophically applied to interpret the order of the social world, the pursuit of harmony is viewed as the essential goal of community life (US Library of Congress n.d.(a)). Confucianism conceived a hierarchical notion of the social order, with the importance of individual self-control emphasised, and social relations defined in terms of the Five Relationships (*o ryun*), which state that between:

- father and son there should be affection;

- ruler and minister there should be righteousness;

- husband and wife there should be attention to their separate functions;

- the old and the young there should be proper order; and

- friends there should be faithfulness.

Only this last relationship was considered egalitarian, while the other relationships indicate hierarchies with the father elevated to the highest position (US Library of Congress, *Social structure and values* n.d.(a)).

While Confucianism has had considerable impact in China and Japan, unique local interpretations have emerged in Korea. During the Choson Dynasty this foundational Neo-Confucian ideology led to the development of a four level hierarchical social strata: the *yangban* (the scholar-officials); the *chungin* (the middle people) who were the subordinate technicians and administrators; the *sangmin* (the commoners who made up 75 per cent of the population) consisting of farmers, craftsmen, and merchants; and the *ch'ommin* at the bottom of society. This social hierarchy was, however, not rigidly applied, and under Confucian pro-learning logic an individual could rise to any level depending on their talent, capacity and family status (Chang and Chang, 1994). Hence, a high cultural value for education became implicit in this social order, along with a hierarchical and paternalistic administrative approach, and an elite administrative class emerged whose position and lineage was based on merit rather than just birth. The meritocratic and scholarly characteristics of the Korean administrative (*yangban*) literati elite contrasts with the equivalent Samurai warrior class in Japan (Chang and Chang, 1994).

> In Korea educated men or scholars have been highly respected ... many Koreans could enjoy the privileges and status of the higher class ... by passing the rigorous civil service examinations (*kwageo*) to become civil servants. In order to pass the examination, candidates prepared themselves for Confucian literature and politics. This implies that

education was critically important … since it determined success or failure in … career paths. (Chang and Chang, 1994, p. 13)

Another key Confucian derived socio-cultural value which is of pivotal importance in Korean society is that of filial piety, or family loyalty, based around a patrilineal (father-son) genealogy. 'This means that the family system or family prestige has been the primary objective in Korea' (Chang and Chang 1994, p. 13). The fundamental principle underpinning the family system is the obligation of the eldest son to the parent. This traditional duty principle links with the high value of education as the eldest son is able to fulfil obligations to the father through the attainment of education. The foundational strength of these two values in Korean society underpins the family as the core unit of community life. Meticulous records of the family-tree have been a key element for establishing authentic Korean identity.

The influence of Christianity

Christianity came to Korea at the end of the eighteenth century with Roman Catholic missionaries who had arrived earlier in China. By the 1860s there were some 17,500 Roman Catholics in the country, but with the persecution that followed in the next twenty years many fled the country. However, after the 1880s many Protestant missionaries came to Korea. Methodist and Presbyterian missionaries, in particular, converted a high number of locals and their role in establishing schools, universities, hospitals and orphanages played an important part in the modernisation of the country (US Library of Congress n.d.(b)). Christianity became the religion associated with modernisation and social reform.

Christianity, in general, but more specifically Protestantism, is culturally associated with individualistic behaviour. Many Christian South Koreans, such as veteran political opposition leader Kim Dae Jung, a Catholic, have been outspoken advocates of human rights and critics of the government (US Library of Congress n.d.(b)) and through international acknowledgement, President Kim Dae Jung became a Nobel Peace Laureate in 2000. Christian sponsored organisations, such as the Urban Industrial Mission play an important role in promoting labour organisations and the union movement (US Library of Congress n.d.(b)). Nevertheless, it is noteworthy that Korean socio-cultural values have been thoroughly assimilated into Korean Christianity. 'In the church, the Korean Christians behave exactly like real Christians. Outside the church, they transform … into Korean Christians, who unwillingly acknowledge the existence of other religions and the yin-yang concept of different but complementary relations' (Chang and Chang, 1994, p. 17).

A pluralist religious society

Regardless of the religious affiliation of the citizens of contemporary Korea, religious freedom is guaranteed by the Constitution. According to government statistics in 1995 51 per cent of the population claim to follow a specific religious faith with the relative proportions as follows: Buddhist – 47 per cent; Protestants – 39 per cent; Catholics – 13 per cent; and Confucianists 1 per cent (Ministry for Culture and Tourism, (a) 2001). These figures indicate that Korea has the highest Christian affiliated population in Asia after the Philippines. However the cultural assimilation and integration of the diverse values and practices of these various religions into society means that together they have had an important role in shaping the unique characteristics of the Korean world view and identity. This religious context sits comfortably with the high value placed on educational achievement and the family system, previously identified as being key socio-cultural characteristics of contemporary Korean society. These values have had an important impact on shaping the Korean management system and the Korean culture of management.

While the Korean heritage displays many influences from its regional neighbours, the resultant socio-cultural intermix of group-orientation and individualistic behaviour is especially unique (Kim, 1982; Chang, 1989 cited in Chang and Chang, 1994). Research indicates that Korean behaviour patterns exhibit both individualistic and group-oriented activity, with individual interests pursued through informal groups and the informality of formal groups (Chang and Chang, 1994).

> This individualistic behaviour ... can go in any direction. It may have a negative connotation in that the Koreans may not be interested in the well-being of the entire society. However, this behaviour has also many positive features. It will intensify severe competition amongst members of a group to attain personal goals ... [Nevertheless] the concept of compromise in a group ... has to be used strategically to achieve one's goals in a group setting (p. 56).

Regardless, the aspects of the Korean socio-cultural heritage discussed to this point only account in part for the highly competitive nature of Korean society. More recent circumstances of regional history have more obviously shaped this distinctive Korean socio-cultural characteristic.

The intensification of the regional activities of international powers

By the last quarter of the nineteenth century the commercial push and imperial activity of European nations (the British, French, Russians, Prussians and Americans) in the region were intensifying, and this was met by strong Korean resistance. Simultaneously, as a part of an industrialisation and modernisation strategy, Japan initiated the first steps of an aggressive policy towards the Korean Peninsula, which Japan viewed as giving access to the important natural resources and rice production necessary to mobilise Japanese development and increase its regional power. With political support from the Americans, the Japanese began aggressive military activity first on the Korean islands in the

Korean Straits and then on the Korean Peninsula. The outcome was an unequal treaty drafted by Japan which: 'provided a legal basis for Japanese aggression by granting the Japanese such privileges as extraterritoriality, exemption from customs duties, and legal recognition of Japanese currency in the ports to be opened to foreign trade' (Ministry for Culture and Tourism (b) 2001). With Japanese territorial encroachment extending two opposing Korean responses emerged. These responses were:

- A reformist position, which promoted the acceptance of European institutions and technologies as an economic development strategy, coupled with a military collaboration with China, Japan and the United States, to thwart Russia's expansionist ambitions. This conciliatory Confucian-based strategy resulted in a group of elite scholars being sent by the government to Japan to study administrative, military, educational, industrial and technological institutions.

- An oppositionist position, which looked to China to quell the Japanese. However Korea's fate became caught up in international rivalries which resulted in the Japanese making increasingly aggressive resource demands on the Korean people. (Ministry for Culture and Tourism, (b) 2001).

These two Korean responses highlight the inter-relationships between the politics of modernisation and the politics of anti-imperialism (Millet and Mason 1995). During the following years Korea suffered ongoing turmoil associated with aggressive military, economic, diplomatic and territorial interference from China, Japan and Russia, and with competition between the United States, Great Britain, France and Germany bringing additional pressure to bear to win favourable economic concessions. As a result Korea was progressively deprived of its properties by the world powers as it granted unconditional concessions under duress (Ministry for Culture and Tourism, (b) 2001).

The Japanese colonial period

By 1904 Japan claimed military control over the entire Korean peninsula which by 1910 was subject to colonial rule by Japan with the Korean government forced to accept Japan's aggressive policy in the areas of finance, banking, agriculture, forestry, mining, transportation, education, culture, jurisprudence, internal security, local administration and the royal household. Pleas for support from the Korean Emperor to the United States and Europe were unsuccessful. Community resistance, led by Confucian scholars and volunteer soldiers, was gradually driven underground with the members of the resistance movement relocating to Manchuria. In a bid to suppress Korean nationalism the Japanese destroyed Korean libraries and historical material, and the educational system was remodelled to suit a Japanese imperial agenda. A rapid growth of Japanese investment in fundamental industries resulted in a greatly reduced role for

Korean capital investment in the economy. By the 1920s in response to diverse Korean resistance the Japanese authorities implemented a colonial education policy in which the teaching of the Korean language was banned and replaced by Japanese language and history. Korean political exiles established an independence movement-based provisional government located in both Vladivostok and Shanghai (Ministry for Culture and Tourism, (b) 2001).

By the early 1930s increased productivity demands were placed on agricultural producers with some 50 per cent of, for example, rice production going to Japan and farm rents being as high as 50 to 80 per cent of annual income. Destitution amongst farmers drove them off the land to seek work in factories and 19 per cent emigrated to Manchuria, Siberia and Japan (Ministry for Culture and Tourism, (b) 2001). Nearly 80 per cent of urban dwellers lived in conditions of severe poverty with, under Japanese policy, Korean workers being paid half that of their Japanese counterparts. These impoverished worker conditions gave support to the rise of the socialist movement along with a community strengthening of the Christian Churches. Despite significant efforts to suppress Korean nationalism throughout the period of Japanese oppression, a cohort of Korean nationalist groups arose, whose resistance activities were variously based around the Korean language, literature, culture and ideals of Confucian scholarship and the pursuit of economic-self-sufficiency and self-determination. There was deep community resentment in relation to ethnocentric Japanese rewriting of Korean history (Ministry for Culture and Tourism, (b) 2001).

By 1933 the Japanese had annexed Manchuria. The Japanese aggressive expansionist strategy across the Asian continent led to a further tightening of Japanese control with Korea conceived of being utilised as a strategic logistical base (Ministry for Culture and Tourism, (b) 2001).

> Monopolistic capital from Japan flowed into Korea ... Cheap labour was available as a result of Korean impoverishment ... Rapid advances had been made in some manufacturing, but it was 'dependent' industrialisation ... During the 1930s the industrial emphasis of the Japanese gradually shifted from foodstuff manufacturing to such heavy industries such as machines, chemicals and metal. In 1939, heavy industry constituted more than 50 percent of all industrial sectors. (Ministry for Culture and Tourism, 2001 (b))

During the 40 years from 1905 to 1945, the Koreans lost to Japan the opportunity of modernising their country based on their own initiatives and directions. This circumstance emphasised that the only way for independent development to be achieved was through education and industrialisation (Chang and Chang, 1994). The defeat of the Japanese in 1945 left Korea with the legacy of a dire human resource shortage, but in the South the advantageous legacy of light, or consumer goods industries, was more suited for economic restructuring than that of the heavy industry built by the Japanese in the north.

The collapse of Imperial Japan created a regional vacuum of political power (Millet and Mason, 1995). The optimism of the post-Second World War era, symbolically implicated in the democratic election (held only in the South) of a new

National Assembly, was cast aside as the country once again became entangled in regional conflict, this time between the United States, the Soviet Union and the newly established People's Republic of China (PRC). The aggressive military action of the PRC, which sought to create a unified and Communist Korea, was in response to Chinese perceptions of a strengthening strategic regional position of the United States, which was to utilise Korea and Japan as a counterbalance to the growing Communist PRC and Soviet Union imperial threat (Millet and Mason, 1995). From 1950 to 1953 South Korea, supported by the US and the United Nations Allied forces, fought the PRC which was supported by military technology from the Soviet Union, with the resultant division of the country into North and South, with the South under an American military government and a Soviet-style Communist government in the North. With the Korean War, the economy became almost paralysed: 'the war destroyed 26 per cent of heavy industry, 35 per cent of machinery industry, 64 per cent of textile industry, and 75 per cent of the printing industry' (Lee, 1983, cited in Chang and Chang, 1994, p. 22). Only after the war ended were the people of South Korea given the opportunity to reconstruct their war torn economy with the strategic support of aid from the United States. The ignominious and painful nature of these national experiences contributed to a deeply felt survival instinct which underpins the modern competitive Korean drive.

The economic industrialisation development achieved by South Korea in subsequent decades has been truly remarkable. The traumatic history of the first half of the twentieth-century history helps to explain the deeply felt and complex nature of the Korean competitive mindset, as applied at both individual and collective level towards securing a more certain and comfortable future. Moreover, this drive, coupled with deeply ingrained Confucian-based pro-education community values, has contributed both the impetus and the approach required for national economic development. With the family being the core structure on which the society was framed, the *Chaebol*, or family-based industrial conglomerates, was to become the structural basis to build economic wealth. 'Despite the harsh restrictions under Japanese colonialism, several Korean nationalistic entrepreneurs still emerged. They urged the Koreans to educate themselves and to build their own industries' (Chang and Chang, 1994, p. 28).

The political economy

South Korea is a liberal democracy based on a presidential system whereby the president and the national assembly are directly elected with the national assembly elected under a mixed system of first-past-the-post and proportional representation. The president is elected for a single term of five years and the president appoints the State council comprising the president, the prime minister and between 15 and 30 ministers. Cabinet Ministers are not normally members of the National Assembly. The next round of elections is for June 2006 (local), December 2007 (presidential), and April 2008 (parliamentary) (Economist.com, 2005a).

The current President of South Korea, liberal reform leader Roh Moo-hyun, became President in February 2003. His early career began as a human rights lawyer defending pro-democracy and labour rights activists, and then he entered politics in 1988 to pursue an agenda of political and governance reform (Cheong Wa Dae, (Office of the President) 2005).

> He leads a younger generation in facing several major challenges, including how to tackle changes in the economy, the society and the business environment ... All economic decisions are, however, subordinate to a much more pressing issue for Roh – how to predict and manage the challenges to the Republic's security posed by the dangerous drift towards military confrontation between the United States and North Korea. (Broinowski, 2003)

President Roh's approach to leadership, in light of his background and the geopolitical realities, is to actively promote the win-wins to be gained by international economic and political collaboration.

North Korea, on the other hand, is a communist dictatorship with a dynastic iconoclastic leadership. Politically isolated, it retains one of the world's last centrally planned economies, and currently faces desperate economic conditions and is dependent on foreign aid. Much of the nation's industrial capital stock is beyond repair resulting from years of under-investment and neglect, and industrial output has declined consistently (CIA World Factbook, 2005). In contrast to the impoverished North Korean economy, South Korea now has a powerful economy and is a major industrial and trading nation with one of the fastest growing economies in the Asia Pacific region, with an average annual growth rate of more than eight per cent over three decades (CIA World Factbook, 2005). In the 1970s, GDP per capita was comparable with levels in the poorer countries of Africa and Asia. Even after the setback posed by the Asian Financial Crisis of 1997, its GDP per capita is sixteen times North Korea's, seven times India's, and is currently comparable to the smaller nations of the European Union. In 2004 South Korea was the 12th largest economy and a global leader in producing high-tech industrial goods (CIA World Factbook, 2005).

Meso-societal level: The management of South Korean institutional infrastructure

A government-led approach to industrialisation

The South Korean economy has undergone an extraordinarily rapid process of industrialisation. In the aftermath of the Korean War, economic aid from the United States and Japan were instrumental in its transition from one of the world's poorest nations to a contemporary industrial power. With support from the United States, Korean businessmen began to produce plate glass, fertiliser and cement, along with the three 'white' industries (sugar refineries, flour and textile mills) supplied with raw materials from the United States (Chang and

Table 6.1 South Korean five-year economic plan

Five-year economic plans	GNP growth rate(%)
The 1st five year (1962 to 1966) plan	7.8
The 2nd five year (1967 to 1971) plan	9.6
The 3rd five year (1972 to 1976) plan	9.7
The 4th five year (1977 to 1981) plan	5.8
The 5th five year (1982 to 1986) plan	8.6
The 6th five year (1987 to 1991) plan	9.9
The 7th five year (1992 to 1996) plan	7.5[1]

Source: Greenwood Publishing Book.
[1] Estimated real average growth.

Chang, 1994). After 1960, imbalance in the economy emphasised the need to develop heavy industries and recognition of this was to play a key role in the rapid development of the economy especially during the 1970s. On an average, the country's GDP expanded by more than nine per cent annually since the mid-1960s, when the military-dominated government established economic development as its primary goal and mobilised the nation's resources to achieve this goal (Chung et al., 1997). A series of five-year economic plans began in 1962 and Table 6.1 indicates the relatively consistent high levels of growth achieved over more than thirty years.

The plans, framed on Korean 'Guided Capitalism' (Lim, 1975 cited in Chang and Chang, 1994, p. 30) logic, concentrated on the development of export-oriented manufacturing fostered by strong government support in terms of sweeping economic, currency and financial reforms. Applying a strong foreign direct investment (FDI) strategy the country was able to raise the necessary capital for this development. 'According to the Bank of Korea (1992), total foreign loans amounted to $40.18 billion at the end of February 1992' (Chang and Chang, 1994, p. 32). During this high growth era, economists branded South Korea as one of Asia's 'Four Tigers', joining Singapore, Hong Kong and Taiwan, and in 1996 Korea gained membership of the OECD. By 1997, annual national budget figures showed revenues of US$94.5 billion and expenditures of US$83 billion (Chung, Lee and Jung, 1997).

However, Korea was not immune to the Asian Financial Crisis. In November 1997, Korea followed Thailand and Indonesia in suffering a loss of international investor confidence, which resulted in a severe foreign exchange liquidity crisis. The Korean currency (the *won*) lost over fifty per cent of its value against the US dollar by the end of 1997, and foreign currency reserves dropped to dangerously low levels. In December of the same year, Korea signed an enhanced US$58 billion aid package, including loans from the IMF, the World Bank and the ADB (Morden and Bowles, 1998). In recovery from the Asian financial crisis,

Year	2000	2001	2002	2003	2004	2005p/	2006p/
GDP (%change, previous year)	8.5	3.8	7.0	3.1	4.6	4.2	4.8

Source: World Bank, 2005.'East Asia Update Report, South Korea: Key indicators'.

South Korea began an economic reform programme designed to address some of the fundamental conditions which had destabilised its economy. The following key economic indicators for South Korea figures (World Bank, 2005) since 2000 reveal the process of rebuilding confidence in the Korean economy.

During the growth era, observers characterised the close business-government relationship between the Chaebol and the Korean Government as 'Korea Inc.', where the national government set the policy frameworks in which the conglomerates operated and prospered (El Kahal, 2001). 'In this system, government traditionally controlled a firms' access to capital and thereby dictated the strategy and operations of the Chaebols' (Ungson et al. 1997, p. 43). *Chaebol's* past successes meant that wealth had been concentrated in the hands of a few powerful businessmen, with a resultant potentially destabilising economic disparity. As a part of a reform process, the South Korean government began a programme to reduce the general economic influence of the *Chaebol* (large, multi-industry conglomerates), especially in relation to the financial sector, which was weakened by a large number of non-performing loans.

As part of the reform process, the *Chaebol* have been pressed to relinquish their non-core businesses, and to rationalise their corporate structures. In other economic measures, aimed at stimulating domestic demand, the South Korean government enacted a package of tax cuts directed at lower and middle income workers. The government also introduced plans to privatise several large state-owned enterprises, including the State Electric Utility, Korean Electric Power Corporation (KEPCO) and natural gas monopoly Korea Gas Company (KOGAS) (El Kahal, 2001).

Services industries make up approximately 60 per cent of the Korean GDP followed by manufacturing (36.4 per cent), and agriculture (3.6 per cent) (CIA World Factbook, 2005). Korea is currently the world's largest ship builder, the second biggest steel producer, and home to the world's leading semiconductor manufacturers. Exports in 2003 earned US$201 billion with semiconductors, wireless telecommunications equipment, motor vehicles, computers, steel, ships and petrochemicals being the major export commodities. Major export partners were China (18.2 per cent), the United States (17.8 per cent), Japan (nine per cent) and Hong Kong (7.6 per cent). Imports in 2003 totalled US $175 billion with machinery, electronics and electronic equipment, oil, steel, transport equipment, organic chemicals, plastics being the major commodities. Korea's major import partners were Japan (20.3 per cent), the United States (13.9 per cent), China (12.3 per cent) and Saudi Arabia (5.2 per cent) (CIA World Factbook, 2005).

External imperatives: Drivers of globalisation and foreign investment policy

A range of external factors have influenced both the rapid industrialisation of the Korean economy, and its sustained competitiveness. The key strategic macro-management responses have been: a strong FDI policy and an overseas direct investment (ODI) policy; interlinked with the five year plans designed to develop specific industries; and with a global market orientation (Sachwald, 2003).

> Korean state policies toward multinational companies remained restrictive and selective until the 1980s and were hesitant until the late 1990s. The situation has evolved more clearly after the Asian crisis, and Korea now actively tries to stimulate inward investment, which has nevertheless dramatically decreased since the 1999–2000 year peak. Attraction of multinational companies has now become a central component of Korea's business-hub strategy. (Sachwald, 2003, p. 85)

However, early restrictions on foreign ownership slowed technological transfers and restricted Korean opportunities to integrate export networks (Sachwald, 2003). 'The state developed elaborate bureaucratic mechanisms to steer foreign investment in the targeted sectors and to facilitate technology transfer as a basis for the development of domestic enterprises', which meant that foreign control was rare and closely monitored (Mardon, 1990, cited in Sachwald, 2003, p. 85). A more liberal approach to FDI then evolved. Table 6.2 indicates the levels of

Table 6.2 Foreign direct investment (FDI) in Korea in 2003

Country	Amount invested in Korea (000s US$)
USA	1,239,925
Japan	540,661
Germany	370,022
Hong Kong	54,801
Netherlands	161,465
Switzerland	20,883
UK	870,505
France	149,606
China	50,230
Others	3,009,763
TOTAL	**6,467,861**

Source: Korea National Statistics Office 2005.

Table 6.3 Korean overseas direct investment (ODI)

Region	Amount invested (000s US$)
Asia	2,223,011
North America	1,030,913
Middle America	180,401
Europe	208,752
Middle Asia	10,555
Africa	23,591
Oceania	89,388
TOTAL	**3,766,611**

Source: Korea National Statistics Office 2005.

foreign investment by overseas MNCs in the Korean economy. The United States, United Kingdom, Japan and Germany in the IT and services industries are leading investors. Hong Kong and China have expanded their FDI in Korea gradually over the past few years.

Table 6.3 indicates the diversity of foreign investment by Korean MNCs in overseas locations. A number of Korean conglomerates including LG, Samsung, Kia and Daewoo have significant investments in Asia, America and Europe. Table 6.3 indicates the strong Asian nation investment orientation of the Korean off-shore investment strategy. The major forces driving Korea as a leading world economy have been the supportive government policies on foreign investment and efficiencies derived from adjusting to increased competition in a variety of industries within the Asia-Pacific region, technological advancements and infra-structure building, low cost production offering economies of scale and scope, and increases in disposable income and market size in the Korean economy (Kim and Campbell, 1995; Sohal and Ritter, 1995). A closer examination of the various government-led development policies and local and international indus-try responses shows how these have enabled the development of the Korean economy at the meso-level of management. Four strategic management enablers played a key part in Korea's remarkable economic development since the 1960s: government enablers, demand-side enablers, supply-side enablers, and market enablers.

Government enablers

Continuing since the 1960s, South Korean government intervention to facilitate the establishment of an export-oriented and relatively protected domestic econo-my has been a highly successful formula for growth. However, as part of the recovery process from the Asian Financial Crisis, the government is currently steadily changing its longstanding discouragement of foreign participation in the indigenous economy (Whiteley and England, 1977). 'Liberalisation and deregulation is slowly opening the economy to foreign investors, especially in the areas of construction, telecommunications, distribution and finance' (Jun and Yip, 2000 p. 70). The basic policy direction of the Korean government on foreign investment in the post Asian Financial Crisis era has been to facilitate market access and to provide domestic status to foreign firms after their establishment, through a number of initiatives (El Kahal, 2001). Some of the initiatives which have brought about a positive climate for investment in Korea include:

- granting domestic status to foreign investors to encourage free and fair competition between indigenous and foreign companies;

- the replacement of the Foreign Capital Inducement Act of the 1960s with the new Foreign Investment Promotion Act to attract foreign investment; and

- the implementation of the High Tech Industry Cooperation Act of 1995, to provide financing and taxation benefits for FDI.

The government has also directed initiatives towards reducing and eventually dismantling restrictive trade barriers which have protected the indigenous economy against foreign influence. The government has also promoted use of market mechanisms to improve the competitiveness of Korean firms by lowering tariffs and loosening regulations. For example, one of the major trade barriers against Japanese imports was the import diversification regulation which was intended to block Japanese imports that might have had a direct negative impact on Korean products, such as consumer electronics and automobiles. This regulation disallowed Japanese-made Toyotas, or Hondas, from being imported into Korea, while American and German cars were allowed to be freely imported (Jun and Yip, 2000).

Recently, the government has proposed a series of laws related to the protection of intellectual property rights and patent laws, which will be crucial to encourage American, Japanese and German Multinational Companies (MNCs) to invest capital or transfer technology to South Korea (Jun and Yip, 2000). The government hopes to attract foreign investment and to acquire the latest technology by implementing these laws governing intellectual property and patents. In addition, it is now promoting South Korea as a 'welcoming' high technology business-hub for Northeast Asia.

Demand-side enablers

A number of observers have noted South Korea's growing importance as an economic powerhouse not only in the Asian region, but also as a global player. A wide variety of Korean MNCs across the automobile, semiconductor, consumer electronics, steel and ship building industries are now world leaders in their respective fields. For example, Hyundai, Samsung and LG together account for approximately twenty six per cent of the global memory chip industry (Jun and Yip, 2000). Daewoo, Hyundai and Kia have made strong inroads into a number of countries in the Asia-Pacific and across the globe. Furthermore, the information revolution, supplemented by a burgeoning middle class and a rapid expansion of per capita income, has led to an enormous increase in demand for new appliances in the domestic market. The cellular phone market began during 1993 to 1994 and by 1996, expanding demand reached 2.4 million units. More recent estimates show demand in the range of 33 million units in 2003 (CIA World Factbook, 2005). Furthermore, with 29.33 million internet users connecting to the information gateway, the demand for personal computers is rapidly increasing (CIA World Factbook, 2005).

A number of global players have developed a keen interest in the Korean personal computer (PC) market. LG-IBM formed an alliance in South Korea to produce and sell PCs together in the indigenous economy, where IBM provides the key components and design know-how and LG provides the logistics, distribution network and production facilities. Compaq has also been negotiating with South Korean PC Giant Sambo Computers. With continuous innovations in Dynamic Random Access Memory (DRAM) for personal computers and workstations, Liquid Crystal Display (LCDs) for computer monitors, satellite receivers, ultrasound diagnosis technologies, semiconductors, wireless telecommunications equipment, the South Korean economy is being touted as a centre for industrial innovation. Coupled with its growing strategic importance in the world economy, this is encouraging foreign MNCs to enter the South Korean economy in search of competitive advantage, especially in the high-tech and service sectors (Jun and Yip, 2000).

Supply-side enablers

When compared to Japan, Singapore, France, the United States and Germany, South Korea is no longer attractive as a low labour-cost production site owing to increased manufacturing wage rates, higher inflation rates and interest rates, (Jun and Yip, 2000). However, South Korea with its well-educated and highly trained workforce provides operational efficiencies and production improvements for high value-added products, as an offset to high labour costs. The unfavourable increase in labour costs is being offset by the rapid expansion of its domestic market, which makes it easier for companies to achieve economies of scale and scope in production and marketing. This has led to a radical change from labour-intensive to capital and technology-intensive mechanisms whereby production has shifted from multi-stage assembly-type handling with large number of workers involved to a high degree of automation, electronically controlled testing and inspection, and the development of new parts and components. Technology adoption and deployment has given South Korean firms a healthy advantage, especially in DRAM, LCDs, satellite receivers, ultrasound diagnosis technologies, semiconductors, memory chips and wireless telecommunications equipment including pagers and mobile phones (Kim et al., 2004).

The South Korean government has been continuously upgrading its infrastructure to promote the country as an attractive business location as well as to assist indigenous industries to compete in the global arena. The government has initiated a number of large-scale public works to remove bottlenecks and to improve transportation and logistics infrastructure throughout South Korea (Kim, 1996). Government initiatives aimed at improving logistical networks include the construction of Yongjong-do New International Airport, the expansion of port capacity at Kadok-do and Kwangyang, completions of the West Coast Freeway and the Seoul Pusan High Speed Railway. The government is also considering initiatives to strengthen international trade, banking, finance and transportation regulations and to reduce bureaucratic restrictions to business initiatives (Kim, 1996).

Market enablers

With a per capita GDP of US$17,800 as per 2003 estimates (CIA World Factbook, 2005), the level of disposable income in the hands of South Korean consumers has provided a general rise in the standard of living and has altered consumer tastes and preferences. South Koreans are being exposed to foreign cultures as opportunities for higher education, international travel and cross-border business networks and alliances have increased (Morden and Bowles, 1998). Research on changing consumer preferences indicates that younger Koreans are developing internationalised consumer tastes, and correspondingly the demand for Western style goods is increasing. A recent Electronics Industry of South Korea study presented in Jun and Yip (2000) indicated that 29.6 per cent of Korean respondents preferred South Korean products whereas 6.6 per cent purchased foreign products. However, 63.8 per cent of the respondents indicated that they were undecided, suggesting that there were favourable market opportunities for foreign goods to enter the South Korean markets.

Over the past ten years, several foreign MNCs have made inroads into the South Korean economy. These include fast food giants KFC and Pizza Hut and home appliance MNCs including Phillips, General Electric, Siemens, Whirlpool, Westinghouse and Moulinex. With the Korean government's initiatives to deregulate distribution channels from July 1993, more than one hundred distribution-related foreign businesses have commenced operations in South Korea, particularly in areas of retail, wholesale and services. These include Amway and Nuskin in multilayered distribution, Tower Records and Museum Company in specialty distribution, and Sharper Image in catalogue retailing (Jun and Yip, 2000). French hypermarket chain Carrefours, Dutch Makro distribution chain, and American warehouse shopping giant Price Club have all made inroads into the Korean economy. Opening up of the distribution networks has also provided opportunities for Japanese companies to enter the Korean economy. For example, Korean MNC Samsung has entered an equal joint-investment enterprise with Japanese MNC Sony Corporation to start production of the seventh generation amorphous thin-film transistor liquid crystal display (TFL-LCD) panels, which will mean twice the production levels of large LCD TVs and a likely price reduction for consumers (*The Chosun Ilbo*, 2005).

The goal of current South Korean Government policy is to encourage increasing competition in the domestic market place for the indigenous industrial conglomerates, the *Chaebol*, which have been responsible for so much of Korea's export-led growth in the post-Korean War era, and dominated much of the home market. The centrality of the *Chaebol* to the Korean success story warrants closer examination of these organisations at the business management structure and systems management level. Implicit is the notion that understanding this unique South Korean corporate feature is integral to understanding the values and practices of Korean management.

The organisational characteristics of the Chaebol

A *Chaebol* is a Korean business group comprising large companies that are owned and managed by family members and relatives in many diversified business areas (Lee and Lee, 1990; Chung, et al., 1997). The term *Chaebol* means a financial faction linked to various corporate enterprises engaged in diverse businesses that produce and offer a wide variety of products and services. Normally, such a conglomerate is owned, controlled and managed by family group, or perhaps two inter-related family groups (Ungson et al., 1997).

The rise and growth of the *Chaebol*

The first *Chaebol* were formed in South Korea in the 1920s and 1930s when Korea was under Japanese colonial rule. As indicated in the previous discussion, to a large extent it was to meet Japanese economic interests that they planned and shaped Korea's development. The Japanese set up a series of companies in Korea that were privately-owned and managed but under strict control of the central Japanese administered government – through credit, licensing approvals and other measures (El Kahal, 2001). After the Japanese occupation ended, and especially during the tenure of President Park Chung Hee, the system was extensively revamped and further developed. Park's regime selected a few companies which received preferential treatment and applied a range of subsidies designed to promote their growth and prosperity. These companies, later known as *Chaebol*, can be classified into three groups:

- The late 1950s *Chaebol* such as Hyundai, Samsung and LG, which were created by self-made founders who benefited from the sale of government owned properties, preference in taxation and the preferential allotment of grants;

- The 1960s *Chaebol*, such as Hanjin, Korea Explosive, Hyosung, Sangyong, and Dong-A, which were formed with the help of foreign loans during the institutionalisation of the five-year plans proposed by the government; and finally,

- The *Chaebol* of the 1970s, which include Daewoo, Lotte, Doosan, Kolon and Sunkyung that were the offspring of the rapid growth in exports and local demand (Chen, 2004).

These oligarchic conglomerates have become the pride of the Korean economy and have enjoyed profits as a consequence of strong government support in the form of tax concessions, tariff barriers, and wage and labour movement controls in a wide variety of industries. They have over a million employees and led to a massive, and arguably excessive, concentration of economic power (Chen, 2004).

The characteristics of the *Chaebol*

A major difference between the Korean *Chaebol* and the Japanese *Keiretsu* is that generally, *Chaebol* do not have financial institutions (banks) as a part of the group. This makes them more dependent on government approval of large-scale financing, especially after the nationalisation of South Korean banks in the mid-1970s (El Kahal, 2001). The *Chaebols* are spread across numerous industries. They tend to have a more formalised organisational structure and apply more centralised managerial control than their Japanese counterparts. In contrast to the Keiretsu, the *Chaebol* are family-dominated, highlighting a fundamental conceptual difference in the notion of 'family members' which exists between the two national cultures (Lee and Yoo, 1987b). The Japanese concept of a 'family' consists of two distinct meanings – one is the concept of a 'family' based strictly on a blood relationship, and the other broader notion is conceived around the idea of a 'household' that is not restricted to blood relationship but also recognises adoption. By contrast, as indicated previously, the Korean concept is strictly based on a blood relationship. This inherent conceptual difference has important implications for both family inheritance and corporate ownership. In Korea, inheritance is strictly an outcome of blood relationship, with the eldest son enjoying priority over other family members (Lie, 1990). The previous discussion on Korean socio-cultural heritage emphasised the longevity and centrality of the family structure in the Korean world view and this specific family value is powerfully manifest in the contemporary economic structure.

Three types of family ownership of the *Chaebol* classifications are generally identifiable (Hattori, 1989, pp. 87–8) (see Figure 6.1):

1. Those with direct and sole ownership, where the founder or his family members own all the chaebol-affiliated companies. An example of this type is the Hanjin group.

2. Those dominated by a holding company, which in turn owns the affiliated companies. The Daewoo group fits into such a structure.

3. Those with interlocking mutual ownership, where the founder, or his family members, own the holding company and/or some kind of foundation, which in turn owns the affiliated companies. The Samsung group represents this type.

Figure 6.1 Ownership structure of Korean Chaebol

(a) Type I: Direct ownership structure

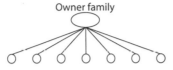

Owner family

Subsidiaries or affiliated companies

(b) Type II: Holding company structure

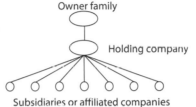

Owner family

Holding company

Subsidiaries or affiliated companies

(c) Type III: Mutual ownership structure

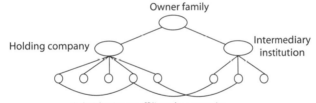

Owner family

Holding company

Intermediary institution

Subsidiaries or affiliated companies

Source: Greenwood Publishing Group.

The common evolutionary trend seems to be a progression from the first type to the third, as the *Chaebol* grows in size, though this transition may be a long and difficult process (Chen, 2004).

The family members of the founders have very important managerial roles in the *Chaebol* and the high value placed on family membership explains why the children of founders commonly hold key positions in the conglomerate organisational structure. More than 30 per cent of the executives of the top 20 *Chaebol* groups were the family members of the owners during the 1980s (Lee and Yoo, 1987a). Many Koreans value blood relationships so highly that they recognise an extended clan, or *chiban* which provides broad-based security for the family members. The larger the *chiban* the broader-based the security for the members of the clan (Song, 1990). Business founders are expected to not only take care of their own immediate family members but also their relatives. The term *hyul-yun* is used to describe the blood-related or kinship-based relationship with the owner. In Japan, by contrast, the major objective is to protect and expand the net worth of the family through the leadership of a capable individual rather than to bequeath only to a blood-related family member(s). Nevertheless, in both

Korea and Japan, professional executives and managers form an important elite power group in the conglomerate organisations. In some Korean companies, successful career managers promoted during their extended company service, can also exert networks within the company and foster them in the future (Chen, 2004).

Another distinguishing characteristic of the *Chaebol* is their high level of commitment to entrepreneurship. The strong entrepreneurial orientation that encouraged risk-taking is attributed to both the rapid growth of the *Chaebol* during the 'Asian Miracle' and to their sudden collapse during the Asian Financial Crisis (Morden and Bowles, 1998). This entrepreneurial spirit and higher risk-taking means that *Chaebol* management is regarded as more decisive and responsive than their Japanese counterparts. Their smaller size and family-dominated management structures mean that they pay less attention to building consensus across the different managerial levels (Ungson et al., 1997). 'This characteristic has proved valuable in riding the Asian crisis through the introduction of swift measures of restructuring and reforms' (El Kahal, 2001, p. 168).

The micro-organisational level: Critical traditional, transitional and transformational issues in Korean management

Inside the *Chaebol*

The previous discussion has identified why it is important for overseas companies, business partners and managers who liaise with Korean companies to understand the particular styles, patterns and processes applied at the micro-management level. It is noteworthy that Korean *Chaebol* management is at present undergoing a radical change owing to a massive corporate restructuring process. Despite these changes and the increasing influence of Western cultural and managerial approaches, Korean management maintains its unique characteristics. The following section briefly describes the characteristics of this unique management style.

Organisational culture

Korean companies have developed their own management style, often referred to as K-type management. This unique management style is underpinned by the Korean interpretation of Chinese derived Neo-Confucian ideas, along with additional Japanese and American management influences. The resultant approach to management represents a unique blend of Western and Eastern management philosophies and practices (England and Lee, 1971; Fukuyama, 1995; Morden and Bowles, 1998).

The Koreans are traditionally hard-working people. This trait traces back to the Confucian value system and is referred to as *eui-yok* which means 'will' or 'ambition' (Ungson et al., 1997). The concept of *eui-yok* provides an employee with an internal drive, or motivation, to succeed and to accomplish something of value. Arguably, this internal achievement-oriented drive exists in both Eastern and Western work ethics, but the fundamental focus of this drive is different in the two contexts. In Korea the 'Confucian' work ethic notion or the work effort of an individual employee is primarily group-oriented. *Eui-yok* entails the hard work of individuals so that the group or the company benefits. 'The goal of organisational growth is highly valued by Korean managers, relative to managers from other countries, and represents their strong desire for continued industrial development of Korea' (Davis and Rasool, 1988, p. 16). This Korean concept contrasts to the Western Protestant-derived cultural notion of work ethic that places emphasis on individual performance, which means employees place their personal goals as the highest priority. It is apparent that traditional Confucian-based notions for individual social responsibilities have a deep impact on the conduct of Korean workers. These are summarised as including:

- Absolute loyalty to the hierarchy within the structure of authority, whether the family, community, organisation, or nation;

- Trust between friends and working colleagues;

- Allegiance and respect to parents, incorporating love and gratitude;

- Orderly and clearly defined conduct between children and adults. Traditionally, all children are taught to be respectful to their parents and grandparents, to speak only when spoken to, bow when expected, and only used respectful language.

- Separation of husband and wife. Traditionally, the pair conducts their lives almost in total exclusion from one another. Men conducted their business affairs and women were responsible for running family matters (Adapted from Chong Ju and Wright, 1994, p. 41).

The corporate culture of Korean companies is often referred to as *sahoon*, meaning 'company credos'. Collectivism and loyalty, the traditional cultural values, are often stated in the *sahoon* of Korean companies (see Table 6.4). Drawing on the values which derive from Korean cultural heritage, the basic principles of K-type management include: top-down decision-making, planning and coordination; authoritarian and paternalistic leadership; *inhwa* (harmony-oriented cultural values); centralised management; flexible life-time employment; compensation based on seniority and merit; and high mobility of workers (Lee and Yoo, 1987a). Each of these features is now discussed.

Table 6.4 The corporate *sahoon* culture of Korean companies

Chaebol Group	Shared Values or Official *Sahoon*
Samsung	Respect for individual, pursuit of technology and empowerment
Hyundai	Diligence, thriftiness, trust and affection
Lucky Goldstar	Value creation for customers, respect for individual and empowerment
Daewoo	Creativity, challenge and sacrifice
Sunkyong (SK)	Humanism, rationalism and realism
SSangyong	Trust, credibility and innovativeness

Source: Walter De Gruyter, Berlin.

Korean leadership and decision-making styles

Given the strong influence of family traditions, there is a tendency for Korean business leaders, especially founders, to manage on the basis of the socio-cultural values and principles governing the family, or clan system. As Confucian dynamism favours regimentation and authoritarianism, authority in Korean firms is concentrated at senior levels of managerial hierarchies with the chairman at the top, followed by the president, vice-president, senior managing director, managing director, department manager, section manager to the foreman and blue-collar workers (Morden and Bowles, 1998). A top-down decision-making style is common. Approximately eighty per cent of authority lies in the upper management levels, with middle and lower management having very limited residual authority (Lee and Yoo, 1987a). An authoritarian approach to leadership is a well-accepted managerial norm under the centralised structure of Korean companies with the reins of management generally being held by a central paternalistic figure (Fukuyama, 1995). The chief executive, or founder, usually accepts responsibility for the performance of every aspect of the company. It is expected that a supervisor, or manager, will assume responsibility for the development of his subordinates who, in turn, will respond with respect and obedience. A manager, or supervisor, also takes an active interest in his subordinate's family life, attending functions, and giving gifts on special occasions. This integrated family-work management approach contrasts with the separate work-life values underpinning the western US-based management norm. However, a traditional decision-making *pummi* (proposal submitted to deliberation) approach is still practised and predominantly used to diffuse responsibility (De Mente, 1991).

The paternalistic and authoritarian senior management approach is heavily influenced by the highly valued Korean behaviour *inhwa*, defined as harmony, and this emphasises the value of harmony between those of unequal in rank, power and prestige (Alston, 1989). Korean managers cherish good interpersonal relationships with their subordinates and try to keep the needs and feelings of subordinates in mind. Another aspect of *inhwa* is that each party has mutual support obligations. Managers tend to make decisions in consultation with their subordinates. The process of informal consensus-formation (*sajeonhyupui*) is similar to the Japanese *nemawashi*, but Korean subordinates are normally reluctant to express their opinions to their supervisors (Byung-Nak, 1995). Managers maintain various informal interactions with subordinates to achieve and sustain a harmony-oriented model of leadership based on building mutual trust and acceptance of benevolent authoritarianism.

Centralised planning, coordination and communication

Most Chaebol have a planning group, known as the planning and co-ordination office, the central planning office, or the office of the chairman (El Kahal, 2001; Chen, 2004). The central planning group works closely with the group chairman in major decision-making which includes the design, development and implementation of strategic plans for future corporate actions. The planning group gather and analyse information, and prepare reports for the chairman and other core members as a basis for future decision-making. The planning group also plays a major human resource management role in personnel decisions and is mainly responsible for screening, hiring and assigning newly recruited staff, with a view to ensuring continuity and quality across the various business units. The group also oversees the transfer of personnel between functional units and companies, as well as the overall salary structure and bonus remuneration system.

Formal communication in Korean businesses is mainly achieved along vertical hierarchies, which is a feature of organisational communication (Lee, 1989). The organisational communication process depends largely on the hierarchical relations, which are determined by a combination of factors ranging from formal authority and informal social status to length of employment and age (Morden and Bowles, 1998; Chen, 2004). In the vertical communication process, superiors are expected to give directives to their subordinates who are then expected to comprehend and implement them. The directives are often vague and general, rather than specific and detailed, and subordinates apply their own interpretation instead of pursuing clarification from superiors. A study across twenty seven Korean organisations concluded that lower levels of centralisation and conflict in Korean organisations were associated with positive employee perceptions of organisational climate (Sommer, et al., 1995). Another feature of communication in Korean companies is that employees attach more importance to upward formal communication process on hierarchical lines, rather than to communication on horizontal interdependent lines which may derive from the high centralisation of authority. Poor horizontal communication between vertically structured departments has been identified as a major barrier to efficient organisational performance (De Mente, 1991).

Motivation

Korean employees are highly motivated and known for their long working hours which are attributed to the Confucian values of diligence and harmony combined with a strong survival instinct. While specific motivations vary depending on the size and structure of the company and the level of seniority, high wages and job security tend to be the most important motivational factors (Chen, 2004). In a 1984 study executives of large companies cited 'environment for voluntary participation' as the most effective incentive, while CEOs of small companies regarded the management-by-objective (MBO) system as the best motivational technique. It was also reported that workers over sixty years of age cited wages as the most important incentive for hard work, while new management staff under thirty years of age viewed 'environment for voluntary participation' as the most effective means of motivation and increasing productivity (Kim and Kim, 1989). Korean employees working as a group emphasise extrinsic factors including wages, working conditions and job security much more heavily than intrinsic factors like creativity (*changjo*), achievement and recognition for high enthusiasm and motivation (Lee, 1989). Nevertheless, with an increasingly complex global market environment in which Korean companies operate, more and more are shifting their emphasis to intrinsic motivation factors in order to establish a worldwide status and brand name (Chen, 2004).

Human resource management (HRM)

Korea has a well-educated, skilled and highly motivated workforce. Literacy levels are at ninety eight per cent (CIA World Factbook, 2005) with English widely taught in junior high and high schools. More than eighty per cent of Korean teenagers finish high school studies and a majority of high school graduates attend university, vocational or professional training schools. This vast talented pool of fresh graduates provides a rich recruiting resource for Korean companies whose human resource management priorities include recruiting the best candidates from this pool, designing and operating on-the-job training programmes, instituting reward and appraisal programmes, determining severance and retirement policies and determining industrial relations policies while dealing with trade and labour unions.

Recruitment and training

Most large Korean companies classify employees into three distinct categories: core (top management), basic (permanent staff) and temporary. Most Korean companies hire employees through word of mouth or reference checks, a test for knowledge in specialised areas, tests for English proficiency, a personal interview and a physical/medical examination. Korean companies prefer either talented new college graduates or experienced professionals (Lee, 1989; Chen, 2004). Recruitment for the large *Chaebol* companies is very competitive and campus recruitments in June and November often attract the brightest graduates from prestigious Korean universities.

Though individual jobs are not clearly structured and often do not have clear position descriptions, once hired, new staff are assigned to core departments for an in-house training program, where their individual responsibilities tend to be decided by the supervisor on a needs basis. Korean companies place heavy emphasis on in-house training programmes which are routinely utilised for employee development (Lee and Lazarus, 1993). This employee development emphasis derived from the Neo-Confucian high value for scholarship and learning. The large *Chaebol* have their own employee training centres where the staff receive formal training on a regular basis with development of employees at all levels. The focus is more on moulding and nurturing current and potential managers to blend in with the company's core values and corporate culture rather than attaining new job-related knowledge. Conventionally, the emphasis is on developing positive attitudes rather than professional skills, on the assumption that loyalty, dedication and team spirit are more important than current job skills (El Kahal, 2001). The company's aim is to develop and nurture an all-round person who possesses general abilities, and whose unreserved commitment is to the company and his co-workers, and training is seen as a means of instilling this attitude in employees across the organisation (Ungson et al., 1997). A study of labour productivity across four hundred organisations in the United States, Japan, South Korea and Taiwan reported Korea as having the most productive labour force (Lee and Blevins, 1990). The highly motivated, educated and skilled labour force in Korea has provided organisations with the much needed impetus to propel Korea to be an economy of strategic importance.

Compensation and promotion: An emphasis on seniority and merit

Reward and promotion systems in Korean companies are traditionally based on seniority and merit. Increasingly, performance has become an important factor in reward and promotion-related decisions (Lee, 1989). Over time, Korean companies have gradually combined seniority with performance in their reward distribution rationale. Wages are generally based on seniority, but bonuses may be awarded based on performance in many Korean companies (Chen 2004). However, it is strongly believed that the seniority system contributes to the maintenance of group harmony and reduces competition between co-workers.

Performance appraisal is a rather difficult task in Korean firms. Promotion is regarded as extremely important both to employees and employers. Generally top management is actively involved in promotion decisions. Overall, promotion is based on a number of criteria: seniority, performance, personality, family relationships, school and region. In addition to job performance, appraisers are expected to evaluate employee personal qualities and to weigh their sincerity, loyalty and attitude towards work, which are rather difficult to quantify. Since subjective judgements may hamper an objective evaluation of job attitude and special ability, many managers are often unwilling to give their subordinates too negative an evaluation. Because of the emphasis on harmony between unequals (*inhwa*) in prestige, rank and power, a negative evaluation may undermine harmonious relations (El Kahal, 2001; Chen, 2004). Another Korean value *koen-chanayo* or 'that's good enough' also hampers critical evaluation, as it advocates tolerance and appreciation of other people's efforts. The integral part of *koen-chanayo* is that 'one should not be excessively picky in assessing someone else's sincere efforts' (Kang, 1989, p. 12).

Severance and retirement

Retrenchments are common in Korean companies. Moving with business cycles, Korean companies retrench staff during a general downturn in the economy when cost cutting initiatives are imperative. Korean employees are known to change jobs freely, though many of them work with one organisation until retirement. Job-hopping is quite common among skilled staff, and although Korean employees attach great importance to their companies they would not normally feel embarrassed to accept better position/pay offers from other companies (Chen, 2004). As the concept of loyalty in Korea is based on individual relationships, the loyalty of Korean employees is often devoted to a specific superior, and when a manager moves to another company on a better offer (position and/or pay), often the manager may bring many of his loyal subordinates to the new company (Song, 1990).

Most Korean companies do not have a uniform retirement age, though many require their staff to retire between 55 and 60 years of age (Chen, 2004). Retirement age depends on rank and senior managers and executives usually have an extended retirement age. Korean companies do not normally make a distinction between resignation and retirement age in calculating severance or retirement pay. Most Korean companies set aside one month's salary per year for severance or retirement whereas some companies grant an additional two or three months per year in calculating the total period of service (Chang, 1989).

Trade and labour unions

American style labour legislation guaranteeing the worker's rights to organise and to bargain collectively was enacted in Korea after the end of the Korean War. However, this legislation did not have any impact as the government had not developed any enforcement measures. Instead, the government-dominated Federation of Korean Trade Union (FKTU) was institutionalised and given the power that helped employers control workers (Lithgow, 2000). In 1960, oppressed workers joined radical students in overthrowing Syngman Rhee's government. Throughout the 1960s and 1970s, the Park Chung Hee government upheld the policy of 'growth first and distribution later', and suppressed the labour movement (Lithgow, 2000). The Special Act on National Security of

1971 required workers to obtain government approval before any labour confrontation. Though lifted in 1981, new restrictions were imposed to control the power of trade unions, and the Korean Government banned industry-wide national unions in 1980 and initiated 'enterprise unions' which were managed by labour management councils (Chung and Lie, 1989). This was institutionalised to promote common interests between management and labour. The councils had managers and labour representatives and were to meet on a quarterly basis to coordinate the conflicts between productivity and welfare. However, these councils tended to favour the interests of management with many labour representatives being appointed by management (Chen, 2004).

Political reforms from 1987 removed government intervention in labour-management relations and granted workers the rights to form unions. Industry-based unions were also allowed to be established (Chen, 2004). The amended Trade Union Act protects workers from unfair labour practices by employers and allows them to organise, negotiate, bargain and take collective action. Trade unions today actively promote increased wages and improved working conditions.

Competitive strategies

Before the Asian Financial Crisis of 1997, many Korean companies had already achieved rapid economic growth and development by improving their manufacturing and service capabilities and diversifying their businesses. With radical reforms institutionalised by the government enabling foreign companies to directly invest in the Korean economy and supported by a well-established infrastructure, Korea's economic progress was unstoppable (Morden and Bowles, 1998). Foreign multinational companies increasingly recognised Korea's potential as an emerging economic powerhouse and made Korea part of their regional and global strategies. *Chaebol* corporate strategies also aimed at expanding their profile as the world class conglomerates that offer innovative products and services worldwide (Morden and Bowles, 1998). Competitive strategies have a strong influence on organisational structure, processes and managerial efficiency. Analysis of the competitive strategies commonly adopted by Korean companies helps to explain the positive turnaround and development of Korean businesses.

Manufacturing development and product/service strategies

Pre-1997 many Korean companies took advantage of the trade liberalisation policies institutionalised by the government, especially the import-substitution policy, and purposefully focussed on the manufacture of products in the growth or maturity stages of their lifecycle (Hahn, 1989; El Kahal, 2001). As unskilled labour was inexpensive and in abundant supply, most companies concentrated on labour-intensive light manufacturing industries. A number of cement and fertiliser industries were also developed to assist the agricultural development initiatives. This approach created a win-win situation for the government as it saved much needed foreign exchange through the focus on domestic investment. Individual companies were strongly backed by the government and quickly developed into worthy competitors for labour intensive products in the global marketplace (Lee, 1992; Chen, 2004).

As the government increased its investment in infrastructure and telecommunications technology transfer, duplication incentives were also promoted (Cho, 1993; Gywnne, 1993). The large intermediate goods manufacturers of, for example, cement, fertilisers and chemicals, relied heavily on support from foreign entities via turnkey plants, licensing and consultancy (Kim and Kim, 1989). Technicians and engineers received training which enabled them to apply this expertise in the area of maintenance and development. Smaller manufacturing companies without sufficient financial resources to negotiate with foreign technology suppliers resorted to alternatives such as applying reverse engineering to imitate locally available foreign products and so upgrade their products/services and technologies. This approach was prevalent in the early period of the technology transfer initiatives (Chen, 2004). Korean Steel Pipe, for example, successfully duplicated and improved the Japanese model through a competitive imitation strategy.

With an increasing western influence on Korean consumers and increasing per capita disposable income, foreign MNCs recognised export potential in the Korean market. MNCs adopted product and service modification strategies to suit Korean consumers' tastes and preferences. For example, competitive electrical/ electronic good company Phillips is well accepted in Korea with its prestigious brand name, design, state-of-the-art technology and worldwide after-sales services for all their products. Mercedes Benz adopts a global strategy under which premium cars produced in Germany are imported and sold in Korea (Jun and Yip, 2000). Motorola offers a wide variety of products and services in wireless communications and non-memory semiconductors and adapts to local market conditions. Hardware is imported, but includes the local frequency for personal cellular phones, with English expressions converted into Korean characters on pagers. Motorola also meets custom-made orders for large *Chaebol* like LG, Samsung and Hyundai. Proctor and Gamble and Unilever, two of the leading global consumer product giants, made inroads into the Korean economy by offering a wide variety of global products with little product adaptation.

Diversification and market participation strategies

Diversification strategies are crucial for gaining competitive advantage and are important for growth in any business. The larger *Chaebol* pursued diversification strategies until the mid-1990s. These strategies were well-supported by the Korean government which aimed to develop world class conglomerates that could compete successfully in the global environment. The *Chaebols* were encouraged to implement diversification strategies (Chen, 2004). In two to three decades this government-led strategy, coupled with a strong Korean entrepreneurial mindset, propelled the major *Chaebol* such as Samsung, Hyundai, LG and Daewoo, from locally based organisations to global businesses that underpinned the Korean economy.

The diversification strategies applied can be categorised as: single, vertical, dominant-constrained, dominant-linked, related-constrained, related-linked and unrelated (Cho, 1989). Large *Chaebol*, such as Samsung, tended to follow the strategy of 'unrelated' product diversification by entering into sugar and woollen textiles in the 1950s; electronics, fertiliser and paper production in the 1960s; shipbuilding in the 1970s and aircrafts, bio-engineering and semiconductors in the 1980s. Smaller companies generally pursued the strategy of a single, or dominant and well-established product structure. Medium-sized companies tended to adopt related product diversification, a strategy that was in-between that of the large and small companies (Cho, 1989). Table 6.5 outlines the Chaebol growth strategies. Diversification strategies also varied across industries with vertical diversification adopted by textile manufacturers owing to the critical survival issue of a continuous supply of raw materials and market outlets. Companies in the food and beverage industry tended to adopt a 'related-constrained' strategy whereby products closely related to each other in the use of raw material and distribution channels were manufactured. The 'dominant-constrained' strategy was popular in the metallic and non-metallic industries as it enabled management to focus on a few dominant product lines using the same organisational resources (Chen, 2004). The various diversification strategies, as indicated in Table 6.5, were applied to boost the profile of indigenous companies and relaxed its foreign MNCs' FDI market participation policies from the

Table 6.5 Growth strategy of Korean *Chaebols*

Business Group	Single	Dominant (%)	Related (%)	Unrelated (%)	TOTAL (%)
10 largest (213)	0	1 (10)	1 (10)	8 (80)	10 (100)
11–20 largest (123)	0	2 (20)	3 (30)	5 (50)	10 (100)
21–50 largest (206)	0	9 (30)	14 (47)	7 (23)	30 (100)
51–108 largest (246)	12 (21%)	21 (36)	19 (33)	6 (10)	58 (100)
108 largest (788)	12 (11%)	33 (31)	37 (34)	26 (24)	108 (100)

Source: Korean Chamber of Commerce, Korea.

early to mid 1970s in order to supply the market at a steady pace. Philips entered South Korea by establishing a marketing company Philips Industries Korea Ltd (PIKL) in 1976 and successfully competed against local giants Samsung, Daewoo and LG in the 'brown goods' market segment, where it accounts for a 40 per cent share in coffee makers and 27 per cent share in electric irons (Jun and Yip, 2000). Mercedes Benz was the first automobile manufacturer to enter Korea after government policy permitted the import of foreign passenger cars in 1987. Mercedes established an exclusive dealership with Hansung Motors to sell passenger cars and entered into a joint venture with Ssangyong in 1991 to produce engines for trucks and jeeps and later expanded operations to develop passenger cars and family vans. In 1996, Mercedes Benz sold 1121 units accounting for 12.6 per cent of the imported car market share (Jun and Yip, 2000). Global household consumer product leader Unilever commenced operations in 1982 through a series of joint ventures, first the Pacific Chemical Company, followed by Aekoyong, and then with Dong Bang Corporation to gain distribution and expertise in the Korean food business and in 1993 producing Lipton Ice Tea with Maeil Dairy Company.

Motorola made inroads into the Korean market in 1967 by establishing a 100 per cent owned manufacturing subsidiary Motorola Korea Industry (MKI) to take advantage of the cheap labour to assemble semiconductors. The company expanded its operations in 1980s to selling communications equipment in Korea through its second subsidiary Motorola Electronics and Communications Incorporated (MECI) with the result that it enjoyed a strong market position with 80 per cent of cellular phone market in the 1980s. This situation led to the Korean government to encourage the *Chaebol*, such as LG, Samsung and Hyundai, to apply diversification strategies to intensify local competition. With additional competition from foreign brands like Nokia and Ericsson, Motorola's market share tumbled in Korea to 19 per cent in 1996 (Jun and Yip, 2000).

Conclusion

Korea, always in the shadow of its powerful neighbours China and Japan, has had a remarkable political, economic and cultural history. Exemplifying a strong national identity and survival spirit following the pervasive destruction of the Korean War, the Korean Government utilised the *Chaebol*, clusters of family-dominated companies with family-oriented and Confucian-based management hierarchies, as a vehicle for rapid industrialisation and entry into international markets. Overall, the strategic approach adopted has been spectacularly successful. Contemporary Korea is undertaking reform and confidently expanding its industrial base, taking full advantage of globalising trends, especially in terms of access to foreign markets and the adoption of technology. Current Korean government policy, in contrast to the first phases of economic post Korean War expansion, continues to facilitate the international operations of the dominant *Chaebol* groups and is increasingly allowing foreign entry to the Korean domestic market to enhance competitiveness and efficiency in the deployment of human, capital and physical resources. The Korean management system, a unique hybrid of native and foreign influences, continues to adapt and evolve in the age of globalisation. The mainstay of the management system, the highly educated and motivated Korean workforce, nurtured by government economic, education and ICT policies, remains a fundamental source of competitive advantage.

The application of Korea's Confucian-based heritage, with its high value for education, the family as a structural basis for community and corporate governance and management, and a fierce competitive spirit have been effective across macro-, meso-and micro-societal levels at promoting South Korean economic development. Several regional geopolitical, policy and institutional reform, and human resource capability factors will determine the sustainable nature of the South Korean economy. Less positively, the Korean people remain divided with ongoing levels of hostility between the two countries. Recent nuclear threats from Pyongyang, the North Korean capital, have retarded conciliation efforts towards the formation of a unified Korea. However, now there is growing support for unification in the south amongst a young generation who have grown up in peace and prosperity, and are not mindful of Cold War historical perspectives (Fukuyama, 2005).

The future for South Korea will be significantly influenced by the actions of its powerful neighbours, China, Japan and Russia, but especially by the international political relationships between China, Japan and the United States. The high levels of economic growth in the region, with the exception of Japan, present Korea with both investment and market opportunity. Its focus on research and development as a basis for innovative product development will help to build a regional competitive advantage. For example, The Jakarta administration and an Indonesian development consortium are adopting a Monorail system for the city developed by South Korean Rotem Corporation over a Japanese competitor on the basis that it promises lower costs and better safety standards (Harsanto, 2005).

Regional power relationships are changing with the dramatic economic growth and global market influence of China. Shifting regional power relations are implicated in the recent anti-Japanese protests in China, Korea and Indonesia over recently published Japanese history texts which 'write-out' twentieth-century Japanese Asian region military imperialism (Economist.com, 2005b). Regionally, resolution of the tension between China and Taiwan, and the role of the United States and Japan, in that context will be crucial. Resolution of the tension between South and North Korea, and once again the role and responses of the regional powers of China, Japan and the United States is critical. Clearly, the outbreak of serious armed conflict in North East Asia would have a devastating effect on Korean society and economy, and it is very much in the interests of the Korean people to avoid such conflicts.

Until now a fierce competitive motivation to out-perform Japanese Kieretsu corporations drove the international business ambitions of many of the Korean *chaebol* corporations. For example, after the 1997 financial crisis, Korean Samsung reinvented itself to become an innovative competitor to Japanese Sony: 'Samsung wants to be not only *a* global brand, but *the* global brand, besting mighty Sony by 2005' (Larkin, 2002 p. 3). In 1996 Samsung was transformed from a 'copycat' company where the design staff were cut from 240 to 160 as the focus shifted from design to features and creativity was discouraged, when in the same year, Samsung Group Chairman Lee Kun Hee made an inspired decision: 'He eschewed "me-too" product lines, and admonished his foot soldiers to innovate or die at the hands of cheaper Chinese manufacturers' (Kang Yun Jem, Samsung designer cited in Larkin, 2002). This responsive strategic decision not only took into account the company's Japanese competition, but also incorporated a long-term vision of the rise of Chinese manufacturers. More recently however, Samsung and Sony have entered into a joint venture partnership for innovative high-tech TV manufacturing to be located in Tangjeong, South Chungcheon Province (*The Chosun Ilbo*, 2005) and this strategy indicates a dramatic shift towards collaboration whereby the pursuit of synergistic advantages build an alternative highly competitive 'win-win' global market approach.

In economic terms, South Korea's steady and impressive rise from the ashes of the Korean War was only interrupted by the Asian Financial crisis of 1997, and economic growth has resumed with noticeable shifts in government policy (El Kahal, 2001). The Asian Economic crisis highlighted the close relationship between the government and the chaebol industrial groups which resulted in the misuse of capital resources and corruption leading to an international confidence crisis in the Korean currency. However, reform since then has re-oriented towards an open and international economy, with a public focus on fiscal probity, and less direct government interference in the affairs of industry. The OECD Asian Centre for Public Governance is being established to share related information with Asian countries, which will hold meetings of high-ranking and working-level government officials of Asian countries. It will also conduct research and studies on government innovation on a regular basis, setting up a database by acquiring information from both OECD and non-OECD member countries in Asia (Jin-woo, 2005).

In addition, in promoting South Korea as the Northeast Asian business-hub and gateway to the region the government has designated three strategic areas – Inchon, Pusan/Jinhae and Kwangyang – for development as free economic zones. 'These zones will be fully equipped with state-of-the-art logistic facilities and an upscale living environment to create the freest and finest business hubs in Northeast Asia' (Hun-jai, 2004). The Kwangyang project consists of a top-of-the-line container port, high quality infrastructure, advanced manufacturing sites, logistic areas and recreational and cultural sites with a range of government investment incentive and support mechanisms in place. Once Kwangyang links with the trans-Siberian and Chinese railways, there will be cost-savings for companies operating in the area and it is predicted that in the near future the journey across the Siberian steppe will become the fastest way to ship to Europe from the region (Kyung-ae, 2004).

However, in general, provided the country is not interrupted by regional crises in international relations, it seems that the particularities of the Korean managerial approach with its Confucian-based collectivism, pragmatism and high familial and educational values, as articulated to Korean Christian cultural based individualist values provides Korean managers and the largely urban work-force with key managerial and human resource to sustain the economic future for South Korea. While ongoing globalisation of marketing and production will bring transformational challenges and opportunities to Korea, Korean products, especially motor vehicles and electronic products, will continue to find consumers in North America, Europe and Australia.

Nevertheless, globalising pressure expressed in current Korean government policies means that there will be increased competition in domestic markets. The expanding industrial colossus of North East Asia, China, will provide intense competition, especially at the lower end of the industrial market, in cheaper priced electronic and textile products, for example. Korean industrial managers will need to remain focussed if they are to build and sustain competitive advantage in the high technology area, and Korean Government policies in education and telecommunications will need to continue to facilitate knowledge acquisition and infrastructure development.

Korean society and its meso- and micro-level approaches to governance and management have been strongly influenced by its regional neighbours, and most recently America. Korean management offers a highly assimilative yet uniquely local system of management which clearly displays features of Chinese, Japanese and American approaches (Lee and Yoo, 1987a). Convergent globalising trends, in particular the information, communication and technology revolutions will continue to impact on Korean society. Despite these external forces, the individualism of South Koreans may yet provide the nation with the adaptive capacity to cope with ongoing and potentially disruptive and destabilising cultural challenges to traditional hierarchical authority. It seems most likely that Korean management will continue to learn, adapt and evolve from other systems, but the end result will remain uniquely South Korean.

Questions

1. Discuss the traditional and changing role of the *Chaebol* in South Korea's industrial development

2. Explain the 'unique' characteristics of South Korean management. What are its major socio-cultural influences?

3. What are the major legacies of foreign countries on management in South Korea?

URL linkages

Government and related information

Official Homepage of Government	http://www.korea.net/
Office of the President	http://www.cwd.go.kr/warp/ app/home/en_home
Ministry of Government Administration and Home Affairs	http://www.mogaha.go.kr/ webapp/home/en/home.action
Ministry of Foreign Affairs	http://www.mofat.go.kr/en/index.mof
Ministry of Information and Communication	http://www.mic.go.kr/index.jsp
Supreme Public Prosecutor's Officer	http://eng.sppo.go.kr/
Government Computerization Centre	http://www.gcc.go.kr/english/index.asp
National Statistical Office	http://www.nso.go.kr/eng/index.shtml

Economy, trading and technology

Korea Development Institute	
Korea Bank	http://www.bok.or.kr/
Korean Stock Exchange	http://www.kse.or.kr/webeng/index.jsp
Korea Trade Information Services	http://www.kita.org/
Korea Technology Transfer Centre	http://www.kttc.or.kr/e_kttc/ e_index.asp

News and information

Korea Infogate	http://www.koreainfogate.com/
The Korea Herald	http://www.koreaherald.co.kr/index.asp
The Korea Times	http://times.hankooki.com/
The Seoul Times	http://theseoultimes.com/ST/index.html
South Korea News	http://southkoreanews.net/
Yellow Pages	http://www.yellowpages.co.kr/

Search engines

Yahoo   http://dir.yahoo.com/Regional/
Countries/Korea__South/

Asiaco   http://search.asiaco.com/South_Korea/

Mochanni   http://www.mochanni.com/

Zip   http://en.zip.org/

References

Alston, JP, 1989, Wa, guanxi and inhwa: Managerial principles in Japan, China and Korea. *Business Horizons*, March–April, pp. 26–31.

Broinowski, R, 2003, New leadership in the ROK: President Roh's main challenge. *Asian Analysis*, March. Retrieved 20 April, 2005 from: http://aseanfocus.com/asiananysis/article.cfm?article!D=626

Byung-Nak, S, 1995, *The rise of the Korean Economy*, Oxford University Press, New York.

CIA World Factbook 2005, Central Intelligence Agency World Factbook. CIA Publication. http://www.cia.gov/cia/publications/factbook/

Chang, CS, 1989, Chaebol: The South Korean conglomerates. *Business Horizons*, March–April, pp. 51–57.

Chang, CS & Chang, NJ, 1994, *The Korean management system* Quorum Books, Westport, CT.

Chen, M, 2004, *Asian management systems* (2nd edn). Thomson Learning, London.

Cheong Wa Dae (Office of the President) 2005, 'The story of Roh Moo-hyun'. Retrieved 29 April, 2005 from: http://English.president.go.kr/warp/en/president/story/basis

Cho, KK, 1993, Manufacturing technology in Korea. *Journal of Manufacturing Systems*, vol.12, no. 3, pp. 216–22.

Cho, DS, 1989, 'Diversification strategy of Korean firms', In Kae H Chung & Hak Chong Lee (eds), *Korean management dynamics*, Praeger, New York.

Chung Ju, C & Wright, N, 1994, *How to achieve business success in Korea*. Macmillan, London.

Chung, KH & Lie, HK, 1989, 'Labor-management relations in Korea', In Kae H Chung & Hak Chong Lee (eds), *Korean managerial dynamics*, Praeger, New York.

Chung, KH, Lee, HC & Jung, KH, 1997, *Korean management: Global strategy and cultural transformation*, Walter De Gruyter, Berlin.

Davis, HJ & Rasool, SA, 1988, Values research and managerial behaviour: Implications for devising culturally consistent managerial styles. *Management International Review*, vol. 28, no. 3, pp. 11–20.

De Mente, B, 1991, Korean etiquette and ethics in business, In Chen, M, 2004, *Asian management systems* (2nd edn), Thomson Learning, London.

Economist.com. 2005a, 'Country briefings: South Korea, the political structure'. *The Economist* 27 January. Retrieved: 22 April, 2005 from: http:///www.economist.com/countries/SouthKorea/PrinterFriendly.cfm?Story_ID=361

Economist.com. 2005b, 'History that still hurts', *The Economist* 13th April. Retrieved 20 April, 2005 from: http:///www.economist.com/agends/PrinterFriendly.cfm?Story_ID=3856623

Economist.com. 2003, 'South Korea: Economic structure' (EIU) 10 April. Retrieved April 29, 2005 from: http://economist.com/countries/SouthKorea/profile.cfm?folder=ProfileEconomic%20Structure

El Kahal, S, 2001, *Business in Asia Pacific: Text and cases*. Oxford University Press, Oxford.

England, G & Lee, R, 1971, 'Organizational goals and expected behaviour among American, Japanese and Korean managers: A comparative study', *Academy of Management Journal*, vol.14, no. 4, pp. 425–38.

Fukuyama, F, 1995, *Trust: The social virtues and the creation of prosperity*, Hamish Hamilton, London.

Fukuyama, F. 2005, Re-visioning Asia, *Foreign Affairs*, February/March, pp.75–87.

Gywnne, P, 1993, 'Directing technology in Asia's dragons', *Research Technology Management*, vol. 32, no. 2, pp.12–15.

Hahn, CK, 1989, 'Korean manufacturing strategy', In Kae H Chung & Hak Chong Lee (eds), *Korean managerial dynamics*, Praeger, New York.

Harsanto, D, 2005, 'City, Jakarta monorail closer to deal with Korean Maglev', *The Jakarta Post*, 26 April. Retrieved 27 April, 2005 from: http://www.thejakartapost.com/yesterdaydetail.asp?fileid=200500426.G04

Hattori, T, 1989, 'Japanese zaibatsu and Korean chaebol', in Kae H Chung & Hak Chong Lee (eds), *Korean managerial dynamics*, Praeger, New York.

Hun-jai, L, 2004, 'Korea becomes top investment destination', *The Korea Times* 25 October. Retrieved: 20 April, 2005 from: http://www.times.hankooki.com/cgi-bin/hkiprn.cgi?pa=/1page/special/2000410/kt200410251

Jin-woo, L, 2005, 'Seoul to have OECD Centre for Public Governance', *The Korean Times* 19 April. Retrieved 20 April, 2005 from: http://www.hankooki.com/service/print/Print.php?po-times.hankkoki.com/1page/natio

Jung, KH, 1987, *Growth strategy and management structure of Korean business*. Korea Chamber of Commerce, Seoul.

Jun, Y & Yip, GS, 2000, 'South Korea: New prosperity and agony', In GS Yip (ed.) *Asian advantage: Key strategies for winning in the Asia-Pacific region*, Perseus Books, New York.

Kang, TW, 1989, *Is Korea the next Japan?* The Free Press, New York.

Kim, JL, 1996, 'Logistics in Korea: Current state and future direction', *International Journal of Physical Distribution and Logistics Management*, vol. 26, no. 10, pp. 6–18.

Kim, YH & Campbell, N, 1995, 'Strategic control in Korean MNCs', *Management International Review*, vol. 35, no. 1, pp. 95–108.

Kim, DK & Kim, CW, 1989, 'Korean value systems and managerial practices', In Kae H Chung & Hak Chong Lee (eds), *Korean managerial dynamics*, Praeger, New York.

Kim, E, Nam D & Stimpert, J. 2004, 'Testing the applicability of Porter's generic strategies in the digital age: A study of Korean cyber malls', *Journal of Business Strategies*, vol.21, no. 1, pp 19–45.

Korea National Statistics Office 2005, http://kosis.nso.go.kr/cgi-bin/SWS_1021.cgi?KorEng=2&A_UNFOLD=1&TableID=MT_ETITLE&TitleID=R3&FPub=4&UserID=

Korea.net. 2005, 'Gateway to Korea: Overview'. Retrieved 31 March, 2005 from: http://www.korea.net/korea

'Gateway to Korea: Colonial period'. Retrieved March 31, 2005 from: http://www.korea.net/korea

Kyung-ae. C, 2004, 'Free economic zones: One mesmerising zone, one global vision', *The Korea Times*. 25 October. Retrieved 20 April, 2005 from: http://wwwtimes.hankooki.com.cgi-bin/hkiprn.cgi?pa=/1page/special/soo410/kt200410251

Larkin, J, 2002, 'Samsung tries to snatch Sony's crown', *Far Eastern Economic Review*. 10 October, vol. 165, no. 40, p. 36. Retrieved 27 April, 2005 from http://proquest database.

Lee, CY, 1992, 'The adoption of Japanese manufacturing techniques in Korean manufacturing industry', *International Journal of Operations and Production Management*, vol. 12, no. 1, pp. 66–81.

Lee, HC, 1989, 'Characteristics of successful Korean firms, in Kae H. Chung & Hak Chong Lee (eds), *Korean managerial dynamics*, Praeger, New York.

Lee, J & Blevins, DE, 1990, 'Profitability and sales growth in industrialized versus newly industrializing countries', *Management International Review*, vol. 30, no. 1, pp. 87–100.

Lee, KU & Lee JH, 1990, *Business group and concentration of economic power*, Korea Economic Development Institute, Seoul.

Lee, YR & Lazarus H, 1993, 'Business meetings in giant Korean corporations – implications for executive development', *The Journal of Management Development*, vol.12, no. 4, pp. 4–12.

Lee, SM & Yoo, S, 1987a, 'The K-Type management: A driving force of Korean prosperity', *Management International Review*, vol. 27, no. 4, pp. 68–77.

Lee, SM & Yoo, S, 1987b, 'Management style and practice of Korean chaebols', *California Management Review*, vol. 29, no. 4. pp. 95–110.

Lie, J, 1990, 'Is Korean management just like Japanese management?', *Management International Review*, vol. 30, no. 2, pp. 113–118.

Lithgow, L, 2000, *Special blend: Fusion from Asia and the West*, John Wiley & Sons (Asia) Pte Ltd, Singapore.

Millet, A & Mason, RE, 1995, *Understanding is better than remembering: The Korean War, 1945–54*, The Dwight Eisenhower Lecture Series in War and Peace – a biennial series No. 7, pp. 1–20. Retrieved 7 June, 2005 from: http://www.kimsoft.com/2002/millet.htm

Ministry for Culture & Tourism (a) 2001, *About Korea: Religion*. Retrieved 20 April, 2005 from: http://www.mct/go/kr.8080/English/K_about/Religion03./html

Ministry for Culture & Tourism (b) 2001, *Korean history*. Retrieved 23 April, 2005 from: http:/www.mct.go.kr:8080/English/K_aboutt/history09.html

Morden, T & Bowles, D, 1998, Management in South Korea: A Review. *Management Decision*, vol. 36, no. 5, pp. 316–31.

Robertson, P, 2002, 'The pervading influence of Neo-Confucianism on the Korean education system', *Asian ELF Journal*, vol. 4, no. 2. Retrieved 20 April, 2005 from: http://www.asian-efl-journal.com/june2002.conf.htm

Sachwald, F, 2003, 'FDI and the economic status of Korea: The hub strategy in perspective', *Innovation and reform*. The Korea Economic Institute, Seoul. Retrieved 26 April, 2005 from: http:///www.keia.com/2-Publications/2–4Adhoc/Adhoc2003/7Sachwald.pdf

Sohal, AS & Ritter, M, 1995, 'Manufacturing best practices: Observations from study tours to Japan, South Korea, Singapore and Taiwan', *Benchmarking for Quality Management and Technology*, vol. 2, no 4, pp. 4–14.

Sommer, SM, Bae, SH & Luthans, F, 1995, 'The structure-climate relationship in Korean organizations', *Asia Pacific Journal of Management*, vol. 12, no. 2, pp. 23–36.

Song, B, 1990, *The rise of the Korean economy*. Oxford University Press, New York.

The Chosun Ilbo 2005, 'Samsung-Sony starts producing cutting-edge LCDs', [Digital Chosunilbo]. Retrieved 21 April, 2005 from: http://www.english.chosun.com. cgi-binprintNews?id=200504190017

Ungson, GR, Steers, RM & Seung-Ho, P, 1997, *The Korean enterprise: The quest for globalization*. Harvard Business School Press, Boston.

US Library of Congress (n.d.) 'Social structure and values'. Retrieved 1 April, 2005 (a) from: http://www.country-studies.com/south-korea/social-structure-and-values.html

US Library of Congress (n.d.) 'South Korea – Religion'. Retrieved 4 April, 2005 (b) from: http://www.country-studies.us/south-korea/43.htm

Whiteley, W & England, GW, 1977, 'Managerial values as a reflection of culture and the process of industrialization', *Academy of Management Journal*, vol. 20, no. 3, pp. 439–53.

Worldbank 2005, 'Korea: Key indicators' *East Asia Update Report*. Retrieved 29 April, 2005 from: http://web.worldbank.org/WBSITE/EXTERNAL/COUNTRIES/EASTASIAPACIFICEXT/ EXTEAPHALFYEARLYUPDATE/0,contentMDK:20467113~menuPK:550232~pagePK: 64168445~piPK:64168309~theSitePK:550226,00.html

Additional reading

Chang, CS & Chang, NJ, 1994, *The Korean management system*, Quorum Books, Westport CT.

Chen M, 2004, *Asian management systems* (2nd edn), Thomson Learning, London.

Chung, KH, Lee, HC, & Jung, KH, 1997, *Korean management: Global strategy and cultural transformation*, De Gruyter, Berlin.

De Mente, BL, 2004, *NTC's Dictionary of Korea's business and cultural code words*, McGraw-Hill, Singapore.

Lee, SM & Yoo, S, 1987a, 'The K-Type management: A driving force of Korean prosperity', *Management International Review*, vol. 27, no. 4, pp. 68–77.

Morden, T & Bowles, D, 1998, Management in South Korea: A review. *Management Decision*, vol. 36, no. 5, pp. 316–31.

Managing plurality, development, and modernisation in Malaysia

Chapter objectives

Introduction

Since independence in 1957 Malaysia has made the significant economic
transition from a dependence on the agricultural industries developed
by the British, to a diversified and modern economy with the nation
now pursuing the ambitious goal to achieve fully developed nation status
by 2020. The uniqueness of Malaysia lies in the particular ways the country's geography and history have shaped its multi-ethnic, multi-cultural
and multi-religious national characteristics. The presence of the three
largest ethnic groups – Malays, Chinese and Indians – are the result of
complex historical patterns of regional settlement and intermixing
based on trading patterns and resource exploitation. The various post-
independence governments have set in place an evolving range of strategic
political, economic and social policies designed to promote economic
development, to maintain political stability and to integrate the diverse
community groups into a unified, but pluralistic and modern Malaysian
Islamic nation. Thus, the successive government-led strategies have had
a significant impact on how the country's economic, political and social
institutions have been shaped. More particularly, the characteristic
multicultural Malaysian community, in conjunction with the various

development policies and management strategies implemented by the government, have together contributed to the resultant pluralist approaches to business and management in contemporary Malaysia. Nevertheless, the levels of economic and community development achieved to date indicate strong national conviction to continue to further pursue the requisite capacity and technology development needed to achieve fully-developed nation status. With the central leadership role played by the Malaysian government, often characterised as being a quasi- or partial democracy, achieving this national development objective will be as dependent on the political management strategies, as on the economic and business management strategies that are applied.

The macro-regional level: Local issues and external forces influencing the management context of Malaysia

The geography and history of Malaysia have played a key role in shaping the changing discourse on national identity and the unique characteristics of the nation's political approaches designed to promote economic development and modernisation. This section discusses how, from the macro-level perspective, its location and the legacy of its early, colonial and recent post-independence history have variously shaped contemporary Malaysia. Together these factors have contributed to particular human and natural resource characteristics, opportunities and constraints that have had long-lasting social, cultural, political and economic impacts which directly relate to the pluralistic nature of business enterprises and management in contemporary Malaysia. Malaysian history has not only shaped the pluralist characteristics of contemporary Malaysian society, but also the particular characteristics of the Malaysian political system and the strategic impetus given by the post-independence governments to achieve economic development and modernisation goals. This multifaceted approach aims to guide a deeper understanding of the internal Malaysian community governance and business context, and the particular pluralistic management approaches applied by the Malaysian corporate community in response to the realities of an increasingly integrated and competitive global economy.

The forces of heritage: Local and regional influences

The Malaysian territory, located on the Malay Peninsula (*Nusantara*), with the Straits of Melaka (Malacca) to the west, the South China Sea to the East, its northern border with Thailand, and to the east on the island of Borneo (Sabah and Sarawak), places Malaysia on important historical and inter-regional maritime trading routes. Just north of the equator, Malaysia experiences a hot and humid tropical climate and a rich natural resource environment. Limited references to the ancient history of the ancestors of the *Bumiputra* (indigenous) Malays generally attribute them as coming from external regional sources, with some evidence suggesting that the Proto-Malays came from Yunnan in southern China and moved onto the Peninsula in about 2000 BC (Church, 1995). Historically, many regional civilisations prospered on the Malay Peninsula and surrounding islands. The evolving maritime trading networks that involved the region's prized resource-based commodities, for example, gold, tin, timbers, resins, tortoise shell and importantly, spices contributed to the periodic waves of various peoples, who as a consequence moved to and through the region.

> The limited evidence suggests ... that both the Malay Peninsula and the north Borneo coast were important landfalls for merchant vessels involved in the great maritime trading networks that linked Southeast Asia with Africa, the Middle East, India and China. Port cities arose ... offering safe harbourage, transhipment facilities and collection points for the region's prized commodities. (Church, 1995, p. 66)

Along with this early resource exploitation and vibrant maritime trade, came important waves of diverse socio-cultural community influence that were to have both long-lasting influence and impacts.

This discussion gives a brief window into the evolving, but lasting nature of these impacts. The Buddhist Malay kingdom of Srivijaya (which centred on what is now known as Palembang, Sumatra) dominated the Peninsula from the ninth to the thirteenth centuries AD. In the fourteenth century, the Hindu kingdom of Majapahit, centrally located on the island of Java, took control and ruled the Peninsula. The development of these religious-based Buddhist and Hindu kingdoms meant that significant Indian cultural and administrative traditions became locally assimilated. In 1400, Parameswara, a Sumatran prince, settled on the peninsula and founded the Sultanate of Melaka, which was to become a great trading and cultural centre. Within 50 years it was the most influential port in Southeast Asia based on a number of factors: its excellent position on the key maritime trading routes; its rulers established efficient and secure conditions for traders both on the land and the sea lanes; and potential rival ports which were brought into a tributary relationship (Church, 1995). It is noteworthy that in light of developing contemporary ASEAN-based regional partnerships and expanding free-trade agreements Melaka ensured its own security by becoming a tributary of the important regional powers – China, Majapahit and the Thai state of Ayudhya (Church, 1995). Around this time Arab traders brought Islam to the region, and by the fifteenth century Malays were converting to Islam. The rising power and status of the Sultanate of Melaka at this time had a marked influence on the growing importance of Islam on the Peninsula. Both the Arab and the Chinese civilisations were ahead of the rest of the world in the development and application of science and technological knowledge. The religion of Islam was associated with the cultural sophistication and economic successes of Arab and Indian Moslem traders, and so became valued locally for being an important world religion of learning and advancement. For these reasons, those closely associated with, for example, the Sultanate of Melaka, took up the teaching of Islam. Hence, with the high community status of these people, the values of Islam spread and became assimilated with local Malay community *adat* (customary laws, beliefs, and social norms).

In addition, throughout this period increased numbers of immigrant Chinese and Indian communities settled on the Malay coastal territories that marked the trade route between China, India and the Middle East. These diverse ethnic peoples communicated through the Malay language. This early history explains:

● The strong cultural importance of local *adat*;

● The diverse Buddhist, Hindu and Islamic religions, coupled with

● The assimilation of Indian, Chinese and Arabic cultural influences;

● The wealth associated with the flow of trade through and from the region;

● The rising wealth and power of the various Malay Sultanates which together lay down the unique cultural, political and economic foundations for the Peninsula and surrounding island communities.

This early history emphasises the continuing cultural importance of an 'open market' model for the early development of the local economies of the Malay territories.

Colonial history

Arriving in 1511, the Portuguese were the first Europeans to strategically apply an imperial intent over the existing trading networks. Thus, their arrival brought an abrupt end to 'the golden age' of Melaka. However, despite an imperial intent, the Portuguese were unable to control the region, and so their presence in Melaka became instead a catalyst for the development of other trading centres on the Malay territories (Tarling, 2001). For example, both Johor, in the southern part of the peninsula, and Perak, in the north, remained key and expanding Muslim trading centres under indigenous rule. While the Portuguese had limited imperial success, nevertheless small residual pockets of Portuguese/Malay communities still exist within Malaysia today, for example, on the island of Penang and in Malacca (Goh, 2002). The next European nation to arrive with a strategic imperial intent was the Dutch. Indicative of their increasing regional influence, in 1641 the Sultanate of Johore gave support to the Dutch, who by then had replaced the Portuguese in Melaka. As a consequence, Johore became an outpost of the growing Dutch spice trading-based empire centred on Java. However, while the wealth of the Dutch empire grew, its resources were not enough to achieve complete control of the region:

> The Malay-Moslem trading world of the Peninsula and Archipelago thus persisted with considerable vigour ... The Dutch did attempt to monopolise the region's most lucrative

products, particularly the spices. They also took care to concentrate their naval and military resources against any state which emerged as a major threat to their monopolising strategies. Thus, no Malay state could ever hope to recreate the commercial power of fifteenth century Melaka. (Church, 1995, p. 70)

Moreover, this Dutch imperial 'divide-and-rule' strategy created internal instabilities between the Malay States.

With the growing power of the British in India, the British East India Company persuaded the Sultan of Kedah to allow the establishment of a fort on the island of Penang in 1786 to provide port facilities for their vessels on their way to China. Later negotiations between the Dutch and the British resulted in the Dutch handing over Melaka to the British in return for Bencoleen on Sumatra, and in 1819, assuming a greater regional role the British established a trading post colony on Singapore. This meant that by 1825 the British controlled the Straits Settlements of Penang, Melaka and Singapore. In 1874 the British took control over the northern areas of Perak and Selangor, and finally, took control over the whole of the Peninsula by 1930. Sabah was administered by the British North Borneo Chartered Company from 1882 to 1942. In 1841 after Englishman, James Brooke, supported the Sultan of Brunei in suppressing a local uprising, he was made the Rajah of Sarawak. His ancestors ruled until the 1941 Japanese invasion. After the Second World War 'the white Rajah' gave the territory to Britain. The local use of the term 'rajah', a Hindu Sanskrit term for ruler or prince, indicates the more limited nature of Arabic cultural and Islamic religious influences in Sarawak, in comparison to the Malay Peninsula Sultanates.

Throughout this colonial period, along with the flow of goods in the region, there were significant intra-regional movements and settlements of people between the islands of the archipelago and the Peninsula. For example: the Bugis, from Sulwesi, who were skilled sailors, navigators, fighters and traders, became the dominant force in states where they settled, such as Selangor; and Minangkabau groups from West Sumatra established communities that provided the basis for the state of Negari Sembilan (Church, 1995). Reflecting the resultant multilayered and pluralistic nature of cultural influences it is noteworthy that the Minangkabau community has a contemporary reputation of being adaptable, intelligent and economically successful people. While the Minangkabau are predominantly an Islamic society, conventionally understood to be patriarchal, under the powerful cultural influence of local Minang *adat* is strongly matriarchal and matrilineal (Singleton, 2002). Today, successful Malaysian women of Minangkabah ethnic origins will readily confirm this ethnic matriarchal community legacy (Mahmood, R. Managing Director, SMAS SDN BHD) 2002, pers.comm. March 7).

By the early 1900s, Britain controlled all the Malay states in the Peninsula as well as Singapore, and so by the end of the century had monopolised the region's tin supplies. In addition, the establishment of large rubber plantations by the British government meant that Indian and Chinese immigration was encouraged to provide workers for the tin mines and rubber estates. Augmenting the Chinese economic role as traders and merchants, a new wave of Chinese immigrants frequently worked in the tin industry. Indian immigration was encouraged to supply the increasing demand for labour in the rubber estates. The Malays, following traditional practice, were predominantly rice farmers and fishermen. This historical division of labour indicates how the natural resource-based occupations of the ethnic Chinese and Indians were incorporated into the modernising economic activities of the colonial administration. This characteristic pluralist workforce pattern, supported by a well-functioning British-based administrative system, supportive infrastructure systems and an export-orientation, laid the basis for the various natural resource-based industries of the Malay economy that remain important until today (Giroud, 2003).

During the Japanese occupation the pre-war economy was devastated, and the population was politicised and divided when the British returned in 1945 (Tarling, 2001). The Chinese made up the most significant number represented in the wartime underground resistance movement, and after the war, this community group became the communist-based political movement – the Communist Party of Malaya (CPM). The British returned to face the challenges of rebuilding the shattered economy and growing local but ethnically divided community calls for independence. Moreover, reform of the administrative system was required. In addition to the establishment of the CPM, the Malay-based United Malays National Organisation (UMNO) and the Malaya Indian Congress (MIC), representing the Indian community, were formed. After extensive discussions with the leaders of the ethnic Malay community, but not the other ethnic communities, a federated Malayan Union administrative system for the separate States (excluding Singapore) was proposed in 1946, with citizen rights for non-Malays based on meeting strict assessment requirements (Tarling, 2001).

Under this system, all foreign and military affairs were ceded to the British Crown, while other matters were still controlled by the pre-existing local ruler under the conditional advice of a local British advisor. However, the pro-independence activities of UMNO forced the British to replace the Union with a Malay States Federation in 1948. Unable to access political power, the CPM, with a Chinese majority membership, turned to violence. 'A spate of terrorist acts prompted the British to declare an "Emergency" in June 1948 and to even ban the Communist Party' (Tarling, 2001, p. 130). The banning of the CPM was a direct consequence of increasing international communist insurgency and an evolving communist and liberal democratic nation states- based 'bi-polar new world order'.

The British introduced the first local election in 1951 with the 1952 Kuala Lumpur elections demonstrating that the Malays and Chinese could work together, at least at the elite political level (Tarling, 2001). UMNO formed part of the Alliance with the Chinese (now a more politically conservative Malayan Chinese Association) and the MIC parties and the Alliance took power in the first federal elections in 1955. After ongoing inter-ethnic and pro-independence turmoil, in August 1957, the British finally gave into the Alliance's pressure and granted the new Federation of Malaya full independence. The political success of the Alliance testified to the pragmatic good sense, diplomatic skills, and political generosity of UMNO's leader, Tunku Abdul Rahman, who became the country's first Prime Minister (PM) until 1970 (Church, 1995). Nevertheless, 'one permanent result of the emergency was a highly centralized federation, the states having relinquished most of their sovereign powers so that the crisis could be handled efficiently' (Church, 1995, p. 77).

Malaysia was formed in 1963 through a federation of the former British colonies of Malaya, Singapore and the East Malaysian states of Sabah and Sarawak in Borneo. The two Malaysian territories of West Malaysia and East Malaysia were separated by the South China Sea. In 1965, Singapore ceased to be a member of the Malaysian federation and became an independent country. This brief view of Malaysia's colonial history highlights the ongoing importance of trade, the development of important resource-based industries and a supportive community and industry-based infrastructure, the entrenchment of a British-based administrative system and the intra-ethnic community tensions associated with the political achievement of independent nationhood.

Pluralist socio-cultural issues

More specifically, this background explains the characteristic multi-ethnic, religious, cultural and linguistic heritage of the post-independence Malaysian society. However, it is important to apply a cautionary note with regard to the limited value of characterising the nature of Malaysian society through over-emphasis on the discrete and stereotypical distinctions between the three ethnic Malay, Chinese and Indian communities. It is pertinent to note that within these various sub-cultural communities there is often greater intra- and inter-community complexity and multilayered facets to cultural community identity, values and behaviour than is commonly acknowledged (Fontaine et al., 2002; Mandal, 2003). Nevertheless, the very pluralist nature of Malaysian society indicates the necessity to understand how that sub-cultural diversity variously impacts the shared values and behaviour of individuals and groups.

The current distribution of the key ethnic communities is relatively stable. In 1991, the Malays (*Bumiputra* – or 'sons of soil') accounted for 60.4 per cent of the population, and 65.1 per cent in 2000; the Chinese 28.1 per cent and 26 per cent; and the Indians 7.9 per cent and 7.7 per cent, respectively (Department of Statistics, 2004a). In the 2000 census, the distribution of religious affiliations was closely linked with ethnicity: Islam 60.4 per cent; Buddhism 19.2 per cent; Christianity 9.1 per cent, Hinduism 6.3 per cent and Confucianism/Taoism and other traditional Chinese religions 2.6 per cent. This ethnic and religious pluralism has significant implications for the evolving post-independence national discourse, and the design of political and economic governance and management strategies.

The ethnic Malays (*Bumiputra*)

The largest indigenous community in Malaysia is the swiddening (hill rice cultivation) Iban, or Dayaks of Sarawak, who live along the rivers of the interior hill regions and in traditional longhouse villages. Some moved to coastal or urban areas of Sarawak. The second largest group, also a swiddening community, is the Bidayuh, who were once a coastal/lowland Dayak community of the south-eastern Sarawak, but moved to the inland mountainous areas when other immigrant groups took over their land. On the Peninsula, the *Orang Asli*, or aboriginal peoples, comprise a number of different ethnic communities and are mostly found in the central states of Perak, Pahang and Selangor. These indigenous communities continue to be involved in swiddening, fishing and rubber, palm oil and cocoa production (Nicholas, 1997). In 1954 the Department of *Orang Asli* Affairs was established and this department protects indigenous peoples' interests and appropriate community development strategies, under the Ministry for National Unity and Social Development (http://www.jheoa.gov.my/e-background.htm 2004). Traditional animist-based religions and traditional *adat* are still practised by some indigenous communities. Animists believe that everything in the environment – organic and inorganic – has a powerful spiritual dimension which must be respected. Many others have taken up Buddhism, or become Christians. These communities speak a variety of dialects that belong to the same Austronesian family of languages as Malay (Nicholas, 1997).

The Malays are the largest ethnic group, representing more than half of the population. The assimilative characteristic of Malay culture means that diverse external cultural influences can be incorporated into society along with prevailing cultural values. This assimilative characteristic has it roots in the flexible and tolerant cultural legacy of the Austronesian heritage (Fox, 1999). The early regional Indian cultural and religious influences, which were incorporated into Malay culture, derive from Hindu cultural logic and the Sanskrit language. From the fifteenth century onwards, when many of the Malay Sultanates and their nobility took up Islam as a religion that highly valued learning and scholarship, the values and beliefs of Islam were assimilated into the ethnic Malay community, while continuing to maintain many traditional *adat*-based practices and beliefs. This assimilative and adaptive cultural process accounts for the strength of a more open approach to Islam in Malaysia today, while marriage, burial customs and many other aspects of contemporary Malay life now conform to Islamic (or *Shari'ah*) Law.

Religious freedom is guaranteed by the national constitution, except for those born as Malays, who are by law Muslim. Since independence, ongoing debate on Malaysian national identity, and the key political and economic policies associated with this revolve around affirmative concerns to strengthen the socio-political position of the ethnic Malay community in association with the promotion of a Malaysian Islamic religious worldview. Within this affirmative *bumiputra* national governance strategy there is ongoing internal debate between modernist and more traditional perspectives on Islam. Nevertheless, being Islamic also means being a part of a global religious community, and more recently Malaysian leaders have taken an active and vocal international Islamic community leadership role.

Essentially, all Muslims follow the Koran-based teachings of Islam and observe its Five Pillars of Faith which include: the *shahada*, of statement of faith; *salat*, daily prayers; *zakat*, giving alms to the poor; *saum*, fasting during the holy month of Ramadan; and the *haj*, the pilgrimage to Mecca, which Muslims must try to make once in their lifetime. For Muslims the main day of worship is Friday. The following list includes values and behaviour that reflect an Islamic worldview: Belief in Allah, the extended family, respect for the elderly, conservatism, gender differentiation, generous hospitality, a hunger for education, the desire for justice, sincerity, an acute sense of honour, integrity, protection of the weak and a desire for praise and oratory (Lewis, 2003). Together these values and beliefs contribute to a culture that values the pursuit of learning, and a hierarchical and paternalistic leadership style dependent on a leader's inspirational rhetorical capacity, which is a legacy of both Islamic Koran and ethnic Malay *adat* oral-based cultural transmission traditions.

The Malays speak *Bahasa Malaysia* (Malay language) (which has the same regional origins as *Bahasa Indonesia* – the official language of Indonesia). This language was the historic linguistic medium for regional trade. As stated previously, the majority of Malays have been historically involved in agriculture and fishing activities, and this rural-worker background underpinned early government concerns for the Malay community's low level of education and low-status economic activity in the newly independent nation. Nevertheless, in sharp contrast to the poor social conditions of the Malay rural worker, under the colonial administration, the Malays, whose high ascriptive status and elite educational and economic opportunities derived from their associations with the powerful Sultanates, were incorporated into senior administrative positions in the bureaucracy. This elite Malay group, many of whom received a British-based university education were to become the repository for the post-independence political leadership and the bureaucracy.

Traditionally, Malay community life is centred on the rural village, or *kampong*, and the increasing drift of Malays to the towns and cities in search of employment has meant that these kampong community structures are also found in urban areas. In the kampong the *adat*-based maintenance of law, order, and the consensus-based approach to community decision-making are all mediated through the respected local village leader. The collectivist community-oriented culture and the associated family ties to the kampong are still an important part of national discourse and identity. In the context of globalisation, romanticising socio-cultural community notions of the *kampong* often plays an important political role in localising contemporary identity discourse on 'Malayness' (Goh, 2002). Hence, in this context, the political issue of poverty reduction and elevating the development of economic opportunities in the rural and urban kampongs remain crucial. At the same time, this underdeveloped

Malay ethnic community reality highlights a characteristic culture of dependency on the government.

Juggling the often contradictory societal dynamics, between traditional and modernist ethnic Malay community values in association with similar traditionalist and modernist religious interpretations of Islam, means that the complex socio-cultural characteristics of the *kampong* community (whether rural or urban) must be sensitively addressed in political discourse on economic development. The following example illustrates the complexities associated with managing the implementation of new technologies. After a recent pre-feasibility impact assessment for the proposed introduction of a high-tech environmental waste disposal system, the consultants cautiously noted the disruptive impact that the project would have on existing labour-intense community waste gathering and recycling systems, and the importance of this manual waste collection activity for the *gotong-royong* (mutual obligations) associated with day-to-day kampong community life. Hence, the consultants noted the crucial requirement of providing for alternative appropriate community-based economic activities if the new technology-based system was to be introduced (Singleton, (Principal Consultant, URS Corp) 2002, pers.comm., 24 August).

Under Prime Minister Dr Mahathir's leadership (1981–2003) there was an ongoing Islamisation process strategically applied to Malaysian society. The ultimate goal of this process was to infuse Islamic values across all the individual and institutional levels of the society (Tayeb, 1997). Hence, Islamic values have increasingly been politically embedded in the legislative and administrative systems during the last twenty years (Othman, 2004). In addition, in the early 1980s Dr Mahathir made a commitment for Malaysia to become a regional hub for Islamic Banking. Islamic banking is based on the Koranic beliefs that prevent the charging of interest (*Riba*) on loans on the assumption that both the lender and borrower must equally share the risks associated and the profits associated with the venture (*Nida'ul Islam* 1995). This government-led political and economic Islamisation process has played an important transformational role in shaping the cultural domination of the national discourse by Malaysian Islamic values and behaviour.

Notwithstanding this Islamisation process, pluralist approaches to Islam do apply within Malaysian society. This means that conservative or fundamentalist, and modern or reformist, interpretive approaches to Islam are acceptable. For example, there is not a uniform approach by Malaysian Islamic women to the more conservative value of the wearing of headscarves, or fuller outer garment (the *chador*). However, reflecting this increasing Islamisation of Malaysia (especially since the 1979 Iranian Islamic Revolution), whilst twenty to thirty years ago few Malay women wore the head scarf, today it is commonplace (Othman, 2004). In more cosmopolitan contexts, such as the capital of Kuala Lumpur, a more flexible approach applies. By contrast, in the two northern states of Terengganu and Kelantan, where the Pan-Malaysian Islamic Party (PAS) have greater political power, an Islamic State based on strict Islamic Laws had been proposed and a more devout, and conservative Islamic culture is practised.

Despite the adoption of diverse modernist and traditional interpretive approaches at both state and ethnic Malay community levels, being an Islamic State means that all Malaysian companies have to organise their activities and manage their employees in accordance with Koran teachings (Tayeb, 1997). International corporations must responsively address this specific local cultural and religious reality in their local corporate and human resource management strategies.

The following are examples of Islamic practice that have management implications for the workplace. For instance, Muslims are prohibited from drinking alcoholic beverages. This may limit their after-work social activities, especially when working with Western-based multinational companies. They must also observe limitations when interacting with the opposite gender. Muslim women are not allowed to shake the hands of the opposite gender, or be alone in their presence. Muslims must observe the practice of praying five times daily. This means that management must provide employees with a suitable prayer room for the women and another for the men, and allow them some time away from work during those prayer times. In addition, during the month of *Ramadhan*, when workers are fasting during daylight hours, productivity may be reduced. These values and practices have significant implications for management. The increasing politicisation of Islam since independence means that understanding Islamic approaches to business and management is crucial to understanding and operating in the Malaysian corporate environment.

The ethnic Chinese

While the ethnic Chinese have had a long local presence, it was not until the nineteenth century with the numbers increasing that they began to make a significant impact on the socio-cultural and religious landscape of the country. Their increased numbers during the nineteenth century related to rising colonial demands for labour in the tin mines and rubber plantations, along with appalling living conditions in China (Tarling, 2001). Initially, these immigrants made their livelihood as labourers, before many of them ventured into trade and industry. In the coastal towns, developed over the centuries through the flow of trade through the Straits of Melaka, the ethnic Chinese communities became locally embedded through intermarriage with Malay women and developed a characteristically distinct Malay–Chinese culture.

The majority of the ethnic Chinese are Buddhists and Taoists, and many are Christians. Hence, Buddhist and Confucian religious philosophy and culture play an important role in shaping Chinese Malay worldviews and practice. Buddhism is a practical religion that emphasises a way of life rather than a deity. In this sense it blends well with the code of ethics underpinning Confucianism (Lewis, 2003). Buddhist values are based around 'The four noble truths' which are that: All life is sorrow; Sorrow is the result of unchecked desire; Cessation of desire ends sorrow; and One must follow the middle way, avoiding extremes. Practice is guided by an eightfold path to follow: right understanding, right purpose, right speech, right action, right livelihood, right effort, seek the truth and contemplation (Lewis, 2003, p. 52).

The ethnic Chinese dominate the business community and collectively have made a significant contribution towards development. The majority trace their ancestry back to the southern provinces of Guangdong and Fujian. During the twentieth century, Chinese clans, with their membership based on dialect and regions of origin, were a prominent feature of society and they gave newly arrived immigrants a sense of belonging in a strange environment (Ngui, 2001).

> Over the decades these bodies have evolved to become formidable business entities, as well as advance the educational and cultural interests of a fast progressing community (p. 24). They hail from six major clans – Hokkien, Fuzhou, Cantonese, Teochiu, Hakka and Hainanese. (p. 25)
>
> In the past, we could see the association acting as a nucleus for clansmen in areas of information, capital accumulation and business networking; today they [clans] have no direct impact on business. It is the individuals within the associations that make the business impact. (Ching, cited in Ngui, 2001, p. 25)

During the early twentieth century particular clans dominated certain sectors of the economy – Hokkiens the banking sector, Hakkas the mining sector and Fuzhous the rubber trade (Ngui, 2001).

It is noteworthy that Malaysia is the only regional country that not only tolerated clans but formally recognised them. Today clan associations are mainly charitable economic associations and cultural organisations. 'Education being the top priority in a Confucianist society, clan associations are strong proponents of Chinese education' (Ngui, 2001). Historically, clans have been an important institutional resource for individuals to build important *guangxi* (reciprocity network) relationships. Mandarin is increasingly becoming the unifying language of the Chinese in Malaysia, and this trend is decreasing the old importance of Chinese regional dialects (Ngui, 2001). The limited political impact of the Chinese in Malaysia means that they have a more localised cultural community orientation than, for example, the Chinese in neighbouring Singapore who, having significant political control, identify more with their nation and are less interest in maintaining traditional Chinese culture (Wang, cited in Lockard, 2003/2004).

The ethnic Indians

The Indian community, the smallest of the three main ethnic groups, historically came to Malaya to trade their goods with other traders using the barter system. However, labour shortages during the colonial period resulted in Indian labourers being sent to work on the expanding sugar cane and coffee plantations, and later, in the rubber and oil palm estates. Additionally, some Indians worked as labourers on infrastructure construction and higher caste Indians were recruited by the British for the army or the police (Osborne, 1995). The labourers were mostly Hindu Tamils from Southern India supervised by *kanganis* (overseers) and *mandurs* (foreman) who were from the upper-caste Tamils. Sri Lankan Tamils came to Malaya as white-collar workers, holding jobs like clerks and hospital assistants. Most of the Punjabis from Punjab (North India) joined the army in Malaya while others handled the bullock-cart services in the country (Osborne, 1995).

The Indians brought with them the Hindu religious philosophy and cultural way of life. The various occupational types reflected the hierarchical social order of the Brahmanist-based Indian caste system. However, because they came in small numbers and did not live in ethnic enclaves, the rigid caste system was not transferred. The majority are Hindus with some Christians and Buddhists. Hinduism holds to a set of beliefs that promote a hierarchical notion of the social order. Reincarnation enables individuals to move through the social order. The pursuit of the Hindu moral ideals of non-violence, truthfulness, friendship, compassion, fortitude, self-control, purity and generosity enables reincarnation. Thus, Hinduism covers a 'whole of life' approach that integrates a large variety of heterogeneous elements: religious, social, economic, literature and artistic (Lewis, 2003), and so 'an Indian's everyday behaviour in social and business life is strongly affected by Hinduism' (p. 44).

The languages spoken by Indians, mainly Tamil, Malayalam, Telegu and some Hindi, reflect their diverse Indian sub-continent regional origins (Osborne, 1995). Many live in the larger towns on the west coast of the Peninsula and this settlement pattern reflects the ongoing flow of trade through the Straits of Melaka. Many ethnic Indians are still involved in the palm or rubber plantation industries. There is growing concern that, despite rapid Malaysian economic development, the Indian ethnic community is fast developing into an underclass (*The Economist* 22 February 2003). The problem is attributed to the decline of the rubber plantations and the fact that:

> [T]hey are not eligible for any of Malaysia's lavish affirmative-action programs ... Over the past few decades of breakneck economic growth, developers have ploughed up many rubber plantations to plant less-labour intensive oil palms, or to build shopping malls and housing estates. The displaced workers have wound up in shanty towns on the outskirts of Malaysia's cities. (p. 67)

Moreover, there is significant internal economic disparity in the Indian community with the high income levels of many professional Indians driving the average Indian incomes higher than those of average Malays. Small numbers of 'Indian immigrants and their first-generation descendents became successful businessmen, lawyers and doctors. ... Indian commercial success ... appears to have been very much at the family level' (Osborne, 1995). However, the majority of Indian labourers remained poor. 'But unlike poor [Malay] farmers ... they have to buy their own food, pay rent, and travel to work – all at inflated prices' (Jayasooria, cited in *The Economist*, 2003(a)). 'Furthermore, the sheltered life of plantations imbued Indians with a culture of dependence' (Partiban, cited in *The Economist*, 2003(a)).

A multilingual society

The previous section highlights the multi-ethnic, multi-religious and multi-linguistic heritage of Malaysian society. This reality means that being able to communicate in more than one language is commonplace in Malaysia. *Bahasa Melayu* (Malay Language) is the official national language of Malaysia, and hence, the primary medium of the state education system, as well as the public sector administration. However, the British colonial legacy of English is important in the context of the global economy and now, as the language of international business and diplomacy, English literacy gives Malaysia a key regional competitive advantage. Government recognition of this means that English is now a compulsory subject in state secondary schools and it is becoming increasingly important in the tertiary education sector. Furthermore, in light of the increasing economic importance of China and the economic strength of the Malaysian Chinese business community, their Mandarin skills, and regional ancestral and *guanxi*-based network relationships with China are also increasingly important factors for creating competitive advantage. Similarly, the growing economic strength of India means that the linguistic and socio-cultural background of the Indian business community offers important regional business resources and market opportunities for the Malaysian business community.

While this ethnic, cultural, religious and linguistic pluralism now presents Malaysia with regional opportunities in a global market, this socio-cultural complexity has presented the successive Malaysian administrations and the business sector with crucial management challenges associated with nation-building and economic development. For the government the key post-colonial challenge was to set in place policies that would unify the various sub-cultural communities under a collective Malaysian national identity while encouraging specific economic community development. As indicated previously, an outcome of this government-led development approach is the fundamental dependent socio-cultural characteristics associated with the economic development strategies applied to both the Malay and Indian communities. This dependency contrasts strongly with the longstanding independent and entrepreneurial cultural approach found in the Chinese community. Notwithstanding the potentially divisive nature of ethnic community based pluralism, the very same pluralism also presents a valuable intra-national socio-cultural community resource. The value-adding potential of this characteristic intra-community pluralism is reflected in the contemporary international tourism promotion catch-phrase 'Malaysia – truly Asia'. To promote wider societal recognition of the enriching and value-adding potential of this community plurality, the government encourages open multicultural display, such as ceremonies and celebrations.

The political and economic management framework

The previous section indicates how at the macro-level the forces of the Malaysian pre-independence heritage lay down the key legacies of: cultural pluralism, an assimilative cultural approach amongst the elite, an openness to trade, the British colonial natural resource-based economic production and export system and the British-based institutionalised administrative system supported by resource-based industry infrastructure as a community basis for building the newly independent nation (Giroud, 2003). More particularly, the various inherited British-based institutional systems and policies, which included the civil service, public education, transportation, infrastructure and healthcare, would become the foundations of the administrative systems guiding the post-independence Malaysian political approaches to community governance.

The British administration's employment and immigration policies laid the basis for the multi-ethnic, multi-cultural and multi-religious sub-cultural nature of the contemporary Malaysian national community. Nevertheless, the economic disparities that resulted from this ethnic plurality contributed to tensions and hatred among the Malays towards the other more economically advantaged ethnic groups, and an ongoing and potentially divisive ethnic tension underpins the evolving political and economic national policy discourse. This complex socio-cultural, economic and political circumstance as tied to a dynamic international macro-environment meant that the post-independence Malaysian leadership faced complex political and economic governance and management challenges at the meso-societal level, which continue to be important until the present.

The Federation of Malaysia, made up of thirteen states (*negeri*) and three federal territories (*wilayah persekutuan*), is a constitutional elective monarchy nominally headed by the king (*Yang Di-Pertuan Agong*), who is selected for a five-year term from amongst the nine hereditary leaders of the sultanate states. The Malaysian Parliament comprises the Senate (*Dewan Negara* – 'National Hall') and the House of Representatives (*Dewan Rakyat* – 'People's Hall'). The Senators, whether appointed or elected, serve a six-year term. All of the Peninsula Malaysian states have hereditary rulers except Melaka, Pulau Pinang (Penang), Negeri Sembilan, Sabah and Sarawak, which have governors (*Yang di Pertua Negeri*), or Chief Ministers, appointed by the Malaysian Government. Executive power is vested in the parliamentary cabinet which is headed by the Prime Minister.

Initially during the 1960s, the post-independence government was very democratic with the development of vigorous opposition parties such as PAS (*Parti Islam Se-Malaysia*), who aimed to build an Islamic State, and the Democratic Action Party (DAP) supported mainly by unhappy Chinese voters. However, political passions exploded into violent clashes between the Malays and Chinese during the general election campaign in Kuala Lumpur in 1969. After four days of riots several hundred people had died and extensive property was destroyed. A state of emergency was declared with the government placed under the coordinated military and police control of the National Operations Council until 1971 when the government was restored after elections.

> The level of political freedom allowed to critics of government policy in the 1960 did not return. Conciliation and consensus-building were to remain a key feature of the Malaysian political scene, but now non-Malays were left in no doubt that their bargaining position was weaker. … Malay interests became paramount in the formulation of government goals and policies. UMNO became unapologetically the dominant political party … and was to increase its power further over the next two decades. (Church, 1995, p. 79)

Since independence, the Malaysian federation government has been in the hands of a coalition of parties, known as *Barisan Nasional* (the National Front), representing the three main ethnic groups, with the Malays as the predominant ethnic group. UMNO is the dominant political party in the *Barisan Nasional* and has been ruling the government through an accommodation system with the other parties.

During colonisation an expanding natural resource-based economic production and export system was established, involving largely rubber and tin, which contributed to nearly 40 per cent of the nation's total employment, 70 per cent of total export earnings and 30 per cent of total revenue (Economic Planning Unit, 2004). Several clearly delineated strategic and government-led economic planning periods mark out post-independent economic development. The primary aim of the first phase of government policies was to promote the development of natural resource industries, reduce dependence on imported consumer goods, attract foreign investment, and create new employment opportunities (Giroud, 2003). Attracting foreign investment was a key issue for economic expansion.

> Foreign investment is a very old phenomenon in Malaysia; in the 1920s, there was already substantial British investment, mostly concentrated in the plantation and mining sectors (90% of the total). In the 1960s the government established measures to attract FDI into export activities … Major interventions were found in the promotion of rural development and in the development of infrastructure. A laissez-faire attitude was adopted in industry, yet with the endeavour to create a favourable investment climate. (Giroud, 2003, pp. 103–4)

Initially, economic growth in manufacturing was primarily the result of import-substituting industries and this approach concentrated on light first-stage manufacturers such as textiles, footwear and garments (Giroud, 2003).

Government intervention was largely limited to the provision of tariff protection, infrastructure facilities, tax exceptions and other incentives. 'The strategy sought to encourage foreign investors to set up production, assembly and packaging plants … to supply finished goods previously imported from abroad' (Jomo, 1997, p. 95). This investment strategy resulted in most import-substituting industries being subsidiaries of foreign companies. However, the inter-ethnic social conflict, based around Malay (*Bumiputra*) dissatisfaction with their poor economic circumstances, erupted in 1969. This conflict became a catalyst for a much stronger interventionist and a government-led strategic economic development approach involving a range of affirmative *Bumiputra* economic, political, and social policies which were incorporated into the New Economic Policy (NEP).

The new economic policy (NEP) (1971 to 85)

The NEP, which was implemented by a new government under the leadership of Tun Abdul Razak, ambitiously aimed to restructure Malaysian society, and redress disparities between the various ethnic communities (Church, 1995). The NEP policy set two basic goals to be achieved by 1990: to reduce and eventually eradicate poverty; and to disassociate economic function and race (Church, 1995). The strategic approach was to achieve these twin political and economic goals through building high levels of growth, coupled with a range of institutional and community development policies that would favour the economic development of the Malays. The economy was monopolised by the Chinese, with the Malays, who were largely rural-based and involved in agriculture, owning only 1.5 per cent of the capital share of companies and accounting for only 4.9 per cent of the country's registered professionals (Church, 1995). This economic disparity derives from the unique history and socio-cultural characteristics of the two ethnic communities. The ethnic Chinese community had the ongoing benefits of becoming economically 'embedded' (Granovetter, 1985) in the British colonial period of the evolving modern Malaysian capitalist system (Wee, 2002). The affirmative policies of the NEP aimed to create opportunities that would enable the Malay community to more readily become embedded in a diversifying and expanding Malaysian economy.

The strategic successes associated with the government-led national economic management and community development approach significantly increased UMNO's political power and influence. Key NEP development strategies included:

- Significant increase in public investment and expenditure;

- The establishment of major public enterprises (Government Controlled Industries – GCI) established to take up share capital to be held 'in trust' for the *Bumiputra* until they were in a position to purchase share capital privately;

- The affirmative promotion of *Bumiputra* education and training;

- Access of *Bumiputra* to all levels of the public service and private sectors;

- Modernisation of the rural economy (largely the *Bumiputra* workforce); and

- Planned expansion of urban areas (Church, 1995).

The Malaysia Industrial Development Authority (MIDA) played a major role in the identification of specific industry development opportunities, such as the automotive and electronics industries.

> In parallel, foreign investment continued to be encouraged. With the Free Trade Zones Act, the objective was to attract TNCs within certain industrial estates … [Foreign firms] were encouraged to create joint ventures with *Bumiputra*-owned companies, and employ a specified share of *Bumiputra*-employees. (Giroud, 2003, p. 105)

Between 1971 and the mid-1990s the Malaysian economy was transformed from being a producer of raw materials into an emerging multi-sector and export-oriented economy. The NEP strategy contributed to significant increased numbers of *Bumiputra* in business and the professions, with poverty dropping from 49 per cent in 1970 to 16 per cent in 1990 on the Malaysia Peninsula (Jomo, 1997). In urban areas in 1987 poverty was recorded to be as low as 8 per cent, while in rural areas 17.9 per cent (Church, 1995). These figures indicate the challenge to address the ongoing disparity between urban and rural communities.

While the government aimed to increase Malay share of the economy to 30 per cent by 1990, by 1988 their share grew to 19.4 per cent from a low 4.3 per cent in 1971. At the same time, foreign ownership decreased from 61.7 per cent in 1971 to 24.6 per cent in 1988. However, Malaysian ownership of share capital in the corporate sector increased from 38.3 per cent to 75.4 per cent (Ariff, 1991, cited in Giroud, 2003). Nevertheless, during this period the ownership-share of 'other Malaysian residents' also increased from 34 per cent in 1971 to 56 per cent in 1988 (Giroud, 2003). The impact of this 'other Malaysian residents' figure needs to be interpreted in light of the fact that the ethnic Chinese represent a significantly smaller percentage of the population.

Along with the expansion of natural resource-based products, the emphasis on non-resource based export products such as electronics and machinery increased. Foreign companies were attracted to the stable and low-cost environments offered in the Malaysian Free-Trade Zones (FTZs) (Jomo, 1997). The export-oriented industries generally involved higher levels of investment, employment, and output growth (Rasiah, 1996 cited in Jomo, 1997). However, a decreasing inward flow of foreign investment by the early 1980s is attributed to the introduction of a range of increasingly interventionist government policies, which included a strengthening of *Bumiputra* participation measures, both as a percentage of employees and in company ownership, and the restrictive features and increasing emphasis on joint-ventures of the Industrial Coordination Act (ICA) (Giroud, 2003).

With the specialist nature of the industry focus of TNCs, which were concentrated in the enclave setting of the FTZs, the linkages between foreign firms and the local economy were virtually non-existent (Giroud, 2003). The Malaysian government directly intervened in the manufacturing industrial sector in order to ensure the development of local content, for example, the state-owned

Proton Saga car manufacturer, HICOM (Heavy Industries Corporation of Malalysia), and the government controlled industries related to a strategic resource, e.g., Petronas – oil and gas production (Lasserre and Schutte, 1995). These specific industries were a part of a new heavy industries-based industrial diversification and development model, which was based on Prime Minister Mahathir's 'Look East' Korean strategic development policy measures (Jomo, 1997). Between 1971–90 average growth in GNP was 6.8 per cent. In addition to the rubber and tin resource production, the country became an important exporter of oil/LNG, palm oil, and timber, along with the manufacture of electrical, electronics, chemicals processed foods, textiles, and processes rubber and timber products (Economist.com, 2004).

The New Development Plan (1986–95)

Nevertheless, these economic successes were not without criticism.

> Very importantly, by the mid-1980s there was growing dissatisfaction with the government among some of the more capable *Bumiputras* ... By this point large Malay-controlled business groups had already emerged ... and some were to call for a less regulated economy ... the government could no longer even claim an ethnic mandate for its role in the economy. (Jomo and Gomez, 2000, pp. 291–2)

Moreover, with this economic success and diversification came population drift away from the rural villages to the industrialising and urbanising towns where there were new employment opportunities. In response to growing destabilising criticisms regarding the circumstances of the poor Chinese and Indians, the NEP was replaced by the NDP (New Development Policy), which was enacted in 1986 and sought to introduce additional governance and development strategies to redress the balance between economic growth and equity. The disparity related to uneven levels of development in some states and regions raised further critical concerns with additional implications for political stability (Jomo and Wee, 2003). In the least developed states (i.e., Terengganu and Kelantan) there is a more fundamental approach to Islam and politics dominated by PAS.

Over the ten-year period (1986–95) the NDP strategies were more outward-looking and liberalisation-oriented. Acknowledging the need to improve economic performance and become more competitive in the international market, Malaysia adopted a trade neutrality policy (equally export promotion and import liberalisation) (Okamoto, 1994, cited in Giroud, 2003). Selected strategies designed to strengthen existing competitive advantages and provide incentives included: targeted skills, training, technical support, finance and quality improvement, together with more import protection (Giroud, 2003). Thus, the new Industrial Restructuring Plan encouraged easy access to finance for some industries, protected infant industries, and additional policies refocused on attracting export-oriented TNCs to invest in the production of high value-adding enterprises. Together, these other measures contributed to a favourable investment climate which resulted in significantly increased levels of both foreign and local investment (Giroud, 2003). Malaysia then became an attractive manufacturing environment for both domestic and foreign investment, which included Japan, Taiwan and South Korea (Jomo, 1997), and this regional investment continued to flow in until the1997 economic crisis.

By the 1990s the increased annual per capita income enabled Malaysia to be classified as a high-level middle-income country, and it was then referred to as a newly industrialising economy (NIE). By 1995, Malaysia with a per capita income of US$3930 Malaysia was in an even stronger regional middle income country (US$696-$8,600) position (*World Development Report*, 1995 cited in Savage et al., 1998). This NIE classification gave Prime Minister Dr Mahathir further impetus to elevate Malaysia's commitment to become a fully industrialised nation with a unified national community, or '*Bangsa Malaysia*' (Malaysian race), by year 2020. Strategies for achieving these economic and community development goals were outlined in Vision 2020 in 1991. Underpinning the vision was recognition of the inter-ethnic tensions still operating within the various communities and to some extent the characteristic dependencies that the previous affirmative-policy approaches had created within the *Bumiputra* community. Vision 2020 'sets the macroeconomic framework and long-term targets through which the vision of the society is to be achieved' (Mahathir, 1991).

Vision 2020 included an integrationist 'social engineering' national community development approach designed to build greater intra-ethnic tolerance towards the diverse values, beliefs, traditions of the various cultures, and to universally promote proactive, hard working, and knowledge seeking values and capacities across the whole community, in order for Malaysia to become unified. It was conceived that through this social engineering policy approach Malaysian society would deterministically evolve into *Bangsa Malaysia* (a Malaysian race). Achieving this ambitious transformational societal outcome in the conceived time-frame may be unrealistic, and the deterministic and top-down nature of the policy approach may fail to acknowledge the deeply embedded nature of sub-cultural community identity and worldviews, and how these diversely shape the various pluralist values and behaviour of individuals and groups.

The second Industrial Master Plan (1995) continued to promote reinvestment, industrial linkages, export and training, and focussed on applying an 'industry cluster' approach framed around further developing resource-based agricultural and mining industries, automotive, aerospace, and machinery industries, electronics, electrical appliances and textile industries (Giroud, 2003). Associated with this cluster industry approach 'the eighth Malaysia Plan (2001 to 2005) aims at deepening the knowledge content of the economy and pays particular attention to the human resource enhancement, as well as the development of R&D facilities' (MIDA 2001, cited in Giroud, 2003, p. 111). By 2002 the economy was dominated by manufacturing and services, with manufacturing accounting for 30.6 per cent of nominal GDP and with the share of services at 50.7 per cent.

In October, 2003, Dr Mahathir stepped down and was replaced by his Deputy, Dato Seri Abdullah Badawi, who was elected with a large majority in March 2004. Under the high Islamic credentials of Badawi's UMNO leadership of the *Barisan Nasional* (the National Front), the coalition not only won a two-thirds majority in the parliament, but also recaptured the previously PAS-controlled state of Terengganu. The quietly spoken Prime Minister Badawi avowed to maintain the previous leader's strong economic development approach and fight corruption.

Strategic management responses to global imperatives

The previous section indicates how in less than 50 years since independence, Malaysia has transformed from a country that relied solely on tin and rubber, and a small traditional primary product economy, to an industrial-based economy and the sixth largest exporter of manufactured goods in the world (Economic Planning Unit, 2004). Malaysia has shifted its economic development direction, and has made significant progress in various industry sectors such as tourism, education, services, construction, manufacturing, agriculture, finance, information technology and telecommunication. However, like other neighbouring countries, Malaysia suffered severely from the financial crisis which swept across the region in 1997. Reasons for the high impact on the Malaysian economy include a combination of excessive investment; high borrowings, much of it in dollar-dominated debt; and a deteriorating balance-of-payments position (Giroud, 2003).

Nevertheless, its resilience, stable political system, strong and effective leadership, and good economic management are attributed to have led the nation to its recovery. Malaysia's rapid success is attributed significantly to Dr Mahathir's ability to resist the prescriptive 'one-size-fits-all' development hegemony recommended by the powerful 'Washington-consensus' institutions, such as the IMF and The World Bank. Instead, Malaysia charted a unique course for economic recovery conceived to be more appropriate to address the specific needs of Malaysia. Malaysia was the only crisis-affected country to peg its currency and it erected the most stringent capital controls to support the pegged rate (Cook, 2003). The successes of this recovery strategy, largely condemned at the time by the international community, are attributed to the strident leadership qualities of Dr Mahathir and his deeply held personal commitment to fulfilling the vision of Malaysia in becoming a leading modern and progressive Islamic State.

Following the crisis, the National Economic Recovery Plan (NERP) (1998) was introduced which recognised the loss of efficiency in the economy. The efficiency in the utilisation of resources in the economy is indicated by estimates of total factor productivity (TFP) and the incremental capital-output ratio (ICOR). Computations of TFP growth as illustrated in Figure 7.1 show that it had been declining over the years.

Figure 7.1 Total factor productivity growth (%) 1987 to 1997

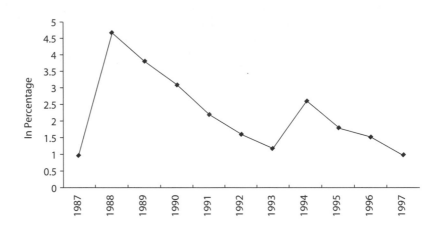

Source: National Economic Action Council, Malaysia.

The NERP policies contained measures to reduce current account deficit, to strengthen balance of payments and fiscal account, to improve competitiveness, and to increase monetary and financial stability. Malaysia recorded an economic growth of more than eight per cent in 2000 (Mahathir, 2002). Further strengthening the country's international position, PM Badawi, in the 2004 election promised continuing support to increase Malaysian economic competitiveness through policies that would enhance political stability, assist Malaysia's development as a knowledge society and the counter corruption associated with the privatisation of former state-owned-industries (SOIs) (Burton, 2004).

In the second quarter of 2004, real GDP was predicted to be eight per cent, following seven per cent in the first quarter (World Bank, 2004). The Institute for Management Development ranked Malaysia the fifth most competitive country for countries with a population greater than 20 million, ahead of countries such as Germany, the United Kingdom, Japan and Mainland China (MIDA, 2004(a)). In its Off-shore Location Attractiveness Index, global management consultant company AT Kearney placed Malaysia among the top three contenders for offshore services based on its low costs (particularly for infrastructure support) the most attractive business environment among emerging markets, and high levels of global integration (MIDA, 2004).

With the country's rapid recovery from the economic crisis Malaysia has continued to attract FDI. However, while Malaysia is still an attractive destination for FDI, its relative performance has slipped with a steady deceleration from a peak of $3.9 billion in 1999 to $3.2 billion in 2002, and $2.5 billion in 2003 (World Bank, 2004). 'Over the last decade, the share of inflows to the oil and gas sector increased sharply from 4 per cent in 1995 to 24 per cent in 2002, while the share of inflows into manufacturing declined from 53 percent to 38 per cent' (World Bank, 2004). The following figures indicate the share of total gross annual inflow of FDI (BIO data) by country of origin:

- USA (31.5%);
- EU (30.7%);
- Japan (12.1%);
- 4 Asian NIEs (17.6%); and
- Other (8.2%) (Giroud, 2003).

These figures highlight the sustained international attractiveness of Malaysia for business investment and the diverse sources of this investment. The high levels of Asian regional investments are noteworthy. Arguably, the development of regional complementarities has important implications for the continuation of this regional investment and the competitive position of Malaysia. The ongoing diversity of sources of FDI has further ramifications for the diverse cultural nature international management systems imported into Malaysia and the issue of how these 'fit' with pluralist local management systems.

Malaysia has been particularly successful in retaining overarching conservative Islamic values while pursuing modernisation and economic development goals, and maintaining the primacy of the Malays and the indigenous people in a multi-racial, religious and cultural environment (Shome, 2002). The terrorist events of September 11 and subsequently in the region have meant that the Malaysian leadership has had to re-evaluate Dr Mahathir's often strident anti-western rhetoric and forthright Malaysian political discourse on modernisation, economic development and Islamic statehood. With the onset of the invasion of Afghanistan and later the Coalition's invasion of Iraq, once again the Straits of Melaka played an important international strategic military and entrepot role as both the Malaysian and Singaporean governments approved the safe passage of the first American Naval fleet from the Pacific Ocean through to the Middle East. Moreover, increasing global economic integration and the rapid economic development of China and India have meant that, while the subsequent flow of goods and services have increased the strategic importance of the Straits of Melaka, Malaysian industries now face increasing international competition.

Furthermore, it is apparent that the inequities between the various sub-cultural communities and the different levels of economic development between the states, and between rural and urban communities, set additional corporate and community management challenges.

The fact is that the two communities [Chinese and Malay], though relations between them are civil enough, live their lives largely apart, attending different schools and universities, speaking different languages and working for different employers. Malaysia's political parties are uniformly race-based. The government's vision of a 'Malaysian race' by 2020 looks widely premature. (*The Economist*, 2003)

The management of these contemporary macro-environmental international and intra-national governance and management challenges now face the government of the more softly spoken and diplomatic leadership style of PM Badawi. In continuing the overarching political, economic and religious nature of national discourse, PM Badawi presented his national vision in a paper outlining his modernist Islam *Hadhari*, or Civilisational Islam approach (Hassan, 2004).

The meso-societal level: The management of Malaysian institutional infrastructure

Interconnected and government-led public and industrial infrastructure

The previous sections indicate how Malaysian heritage shaped the pluralistic ethnic, cultural, religious and linguistic nature of Malaysian society. The legacy of the British-based political, institutional, administrative and legislative systems is explained, along with the increasingly Islamicised (*Shari'ah*) and affirmative *Bumiputra* national political and administrative approach to governance and national cultural identity and specific Malaysian strategic responses to global imperatives. Evolving responses to these issues have contributed the fundamental characteristics that shape the unique features and culture of Malaysian society and its particular approach to management. This background indicates:

- How the evolving interventionist and government-led discourse on economic development have developed a progressive and unifying Malaysian national identity, while

- The various distinct streams of ethnic community-based enterprise activities are still clearly visible and arguably problematic;

- Why the government continues to face the management challenges related to the inter-Islamic community tensions associated with the sometimes syncretic pursuit of modernist and traditionalist Islamic community values and goals, and

- In applying a reconciliation strategy between modernist and traditionalist approaches to Islam the new leadership now promotes for example, Malaysia as a regional financial hub for Islamic banking (MIDA October, 2004; BankIslam January, 2005) and popular media discourse on Islam *Hadhari*, but more specifically,

- Why no one unifying Malaysian management paradigm has yet emerged, but instead pluralist cultural management structures, systems and management styles directly articulate to the ethnic-based business communities which operate in different fields of activity, and

- the paternalistic, authoritarian, and interventionist nature of the government's leadership role, and in particular that of the Prime Minister, which has been paramount in driving Malaysian economic and community development.

In this government-led development context the pivotal role of the *Bumiputra* dominated civil service cannot be underestimated. The international nature of the national business environment that derives from a longstanding dependence on the presence of foreign firms, which generally import the home-based management systems and styles, contributes further to managerial complexity. Hence, there are three distinct types of business enterprises operating in Malaysia:

- State-owned enterprises (now dramatically reduced in numbers and referred to as government-linked companies – GLCs);

- Joint or foreign owned international enterprises; and

- Local private Malay (*Bumiputra*); Chinese and Indian businesses.

Within the joint or foreign-owned businesses there will inevitably be additional managerial complexity related to the national origin of the investor company. Each of these types of business enterprises incorporates particular management structures, systems of styles. This plural systemic reality creates both opportunities and challenges for management. More particularly, this corporate diversity represents a valuable resource on which Malaysia can draw on in order to facilitate greater global economic integration and sustain economic growth through collaborations. However, in understanding the business and management context in Malaysia, it is crucial to understand the role and management culture of the Malaysian bureaucracy.

The key managerial role and Malaysianisation of the bureaucracy

Independent Malaysia inherited a British-based administrative system that included a comprehensive bureaucracy based on characteristic functional departments with a hierarchical career structure and mobility based on education levels, experience and performance. This bureaucratic structure importantly laid down the Western Anglo and European-based cultural foundations for the development of a civil service that was to play a key role in the future of the nation. The subsequent evolving 'Malaysianisation' of the civil service had some unique, important and evolving characteristics:

The Malaysianisation program was carried out in stages with generous compensatory terms, thus preventing an exodus of expatriates. In many cases, an expatriate was requested to retire only when there was an understudy to replace him/her. This process ... while enlarging the bureaucracy made for a smooth transition, and the

Malaysianisation process was less painful than the experience of other former colonies where no such preparations were made. (Ahmad, 2004)

British-owned companies and investors also had vested-interests in the business advantages of a smooth administrative transition. With limited human resource capacity, the process of localising the technical and professional fields took longer. The first PM Tunku Abdul Rahman inherited the export-oriented and resource-based economy. By the mid-1960s, consultants (under the Ford Foundation) undertook a review 'to improve the administrative system and achieve efficiency and administrative leadership in the public service to meet the needs of a dynamic and rapidly developing country' (Montgomery & Milton 1966, cited in Ahmad, 2004). The major government actions recommended were:

● The creation of a Development Administration Unit in the PM's Department, staffed by professional management analysts;

● Improvement of the government's education and training programmes for all levels of the civil service (e.g., the creation of a graduate study programme in development administration at the University of Malaysia, mid-career university-level education for professional officers; and an expanded in-service training facilities for technical and clerical staff); and

● Strengthening of professional competence of the civil service to provide the requisite leadership capacity (Ahmad, 2004)

While the development of the bureaucracy was not without major problems, by 1980 its size had increased by almost 900 per cent (Ahmad, 2004). This figure highlights the key managerial role of the elite cadre of the bureaucracy in the development processes.

Coupled with the historical advantages created by this British-based bureaucratic system, the broad natural resource-based business activities of Western companies established in Malaya and their associated management agencies laid down an important foundation on which to further develop and diversify business in Malaysia. For example, the German engineering and manufacturing company Bosch proudly claims to have been operating as a part of the evolving development of the country since 1958 (see www.bosch.com.my). These Western companies had been largely responsible for the establishment of the important economic infrastructure – the organised plantation industries, a complex network of trade, institutions of scientific research and technical training, banking, insurance, harbour installations and a wide range of public utilities.

To support the modernisation of resource-based production systems, government research institutes, such as the Rubber Research Institute, the Malaysian Agricultural Research Institute, the Palm Oil Research Institute of Malaysia, and the Forest Research Institute of Malaysia, were established (Shah, 2004). The establishment of these R&D institutions indicated the government's acknowledgement of the key role of science and technology in pursuing economic development. A pattern of government investment in science and technology and R&D-based institutions continued to be a part of Malaysia's futurist and modernist-orientation (Shah, 2004). As a result, the production expansion successes of these commodities have meant that they continue to be economically important until the present. For example, palm oil and palm oil-based products account for six per cent of total exports, timber and timber-based products 4.1 per cent, and crude oil and liquefied gas, together account for 7.7 per cent (Department of Statistics Malaysia, 2004b).

Structural transition: State-owned-enterprises (SOEs) to government-linked corporations (GLCs)

With fluctuations in world market prices of agricultural commodities, PM Tun Razak's NEP response was the expansion of the *Bumiputra* business and employment opportunities through a government-led corporate management approach to an industrial diversification strategy. This policy continued under the leadership of Hussein Onn, who was PM from 1976 to 1981. The implementation of the NEP meant that the civil service management and functions became increasingly politicised, and the elite *Bumiputra* of the bureaucracy increasingly took on SOEs' senior business management roles and functions. 'Both Chinese and foreign companies began to actively solicit business ties with the politically influential, but co-operative Malays' (Bowie, 1991, cited in Jomo and Gomez, 2000, p. 290). This cross-community business networking pattern at the elite level has become an important senior management characteristic. By 1990 economic activities and occupations broadly reflected ethnic community demography, except for the *Bumiputra* domination of agriculture and government services, and the Chinese-dominated wholesale and retail trade (Jomo and Gomez, 2000). However, while the government held up the large numbers of the SOEs to corroborate diversification and growth, the poor co-ordination and accountability of the SOE sector became apparent. 'For instance, of more than 900 identified SOEs in 1984, the Ministry for Public Enterprises could report annual returns for only 269, which recorded an accumulated loss of RM 137.3 million' (Supianh, 1988, cited in Jomo and Gomez, 2000, p. 289). Since then the issues of 'rent seeking' (Jomo and Gomez, 2000) and good governance have regularly arisen and a corresponding response for the implementation of reform advocated.

When Dr Mahathir came to power in 1981 the government interventionist policies gave greater impetus to increase industrialisation, and to further develop the manufacturing sector. Mahathir believed that the development and modernisation of Malaysia went hand-in-hand with the development and modernisation of the civil service. The slogan 'leadership by example' underpinned the administrative approach of his vision (Ahmad, 2004). This period saw the strengthening of a tripartite relationship between the civil service, the political sphere and business, and how as a result 'administrative reform and political leadership priorities are inter-supportive and complementary' (Ahmad, 2004). Malaysia became the most attractive site for labour-intensive manufacturing activities in the early 1980s, with electric/electronics and textile/garment manufacturing activities dominated by foreign ownership accounting for 63.3 per cent of manufactured exports, and over 30 per cent of manufacturing value-added (Rasiah, 2003). In addition, the automotive industry was to become an important industrial role model for Malaysian manufacturing.

Regional Asian manufacturing business partnerships

Under Mahathir's assertive and charismatic leadership style the 'Malaysianisation' cultural process took an 'Asianisation' redirection. Under the 'Look East Policy' Malaysians were encouraged to change their traditional views of Western countries as being role models and instead look towards Japan and South Korea as an Asian blueprint for economic success (Ahmad, 2004). Pro-Malay affirmative *Bumiputra* policies, coupled with a modernist Islamic nation state cultural vision, confirmed the particular Malaysian characteristics of this shift towards an Asian business development management model. Policies encouraging foreign investment in manufacturing operations supported this Malaysianised strategic development approach, and this resulted in a considerable inflow of Asian regional investment.

As a result of the affirmative policy the Malaysian public sector grew from only ten SOEs in 1957 to over 1100 by 1990 (Salazar, 2004). Between 1970 and 1990, the Bumiputra share of eight well-remunerated professional categories rose from 6 per cent to 25 per cent (Jomo and Gomez, 2000). Together these various policies contributed to the expansion of an intricately interconnected political, business and technological *Bumiputra* community-based civil service elite, which became the important professional and managerial class required to mobilise further development opportunities.

The micro organisational level: Critical traditional, transitional and transformational issues in Malaysian management

The Japanese, South Korean and Taiwanese foreign manufacturing companies establishing operations in Malaysia brought with them the national cultural particularities of their home-base organisational management systems and home country strategic development agendas. Hence, joint ventures took on an increasingly important role in not only developing the nation's manufacturing base, but also in establishing their particular management structures, systems and cultural styles which had additional implications for Malaysian managerial and HR capacity development. The industries associated with the production of the Malaysian Proton cars were a result of these 'Look East' policies. Reflecting the diversity of managerial and manufacturing approaches of these key investor nations it is generally accepted that:

> Japanese firms excel in process technology, a competence which enables them to produce competitively high quality, complex products in large scale and great variety. Korean firms employ economies of scale to drive down the production costs of standard products, while Taiwanese firms are quick to churn out down-scaled innovative products at lower costs. Japanese firms are also good at turning new developments into marketable products, and all of them are better at marketing their own products in their home markets. (Lasserre and Schutte, 1995, pp. 214–15)

Thus, these regional partnerships provided Malaysian management with key professional managerial and industrial technology learning opportunities, and experiences in diverse organisational strategic and operational management structures and systems.

'While experience, administrative efficiency and customs co-ordination have been important, the continued presence of assembly and test operations ... since the late 1980s has also been due to the changing dynamics of production driven by competition and technological evolution' (Rasiah, 2003, p. 45). In light of the diversity of foreign investment made in Malaysia, it is apparent that as a consequence of the multinational investment companies maintaining high levels of managerial and ownership control, the development of a cohesive Malaysian management model has not occurred. It does, however, indicate a characteristic and overarching 'appropriative, adaptive and assimilative' Malaysian management principle. In a pluralist and competitive global-market context this 'open and flexible' approach can be a valuable asset.

In response to increasing regional competition and the need to improve local efficiencies and quality, there has been a steady privatisation of the SOEs, and in an increasingly privatised and market-based business culture, now referred to as government-linked corporations (GLCs). However, the early privatisation process was criticised for concentrating wealth in the hands of small group and perpetuating many of the inefficiencies that the policy aimed to address (Salazar, 2004).

> The government awarded privatisation contracts under concessionary terms, and offered special privileges such as soft credit, state-back guarantees for loans, and in some cases secure monopoly status. This led to the establishment of conglomerates that amassed totally unrelated businesses. (Salazar, 2004)

The NERP, Vision 2020, and the 1997 economic crisis accelerated the process of increasing industry privatisation, efficiencies and responses to regional competition. However, ironically in the aftermath of the Asian crisis, no successful Malay capitalist has emerged despite the extensive state patronage through privatisation (Salazar, 2004). A new cluster industry approach shifted focus to the greater need for specialisation, innovation, and R&D. In other words, there was increasing recognition that for Malaysia to remain competitive, both the community and industry need to evolve towards the value-adding advantageous opportunities offered by becoming a knowledge-based society. This new direction now sets ongoing bureaucratic and corporate institutional reform and HR-based capacity development challenges for the country.

Critical management challenges: Organisational constraints and opportunities

Many of the critical contemporary management challenges and opportunities arise from a continuing need to address and reconcile the gap between the ambitious visions of the nation's leadership, and between the elite business and bureaucratic class and the day-to-day realities of ordinary Malaysians. At the elite level there is consensual understanding of the need to improve the productivity and competitiveness of industry and of the need to diversify and build more sophisticated and value-added business opportunities. Moreover, significant political good will has been given to improve corporate governance and accountability.

Bumiputra and *non-Bumiputra* divisions

Despite the enormous interventionist effort to achieve national unity, the Malaysian society is still marked by polarised *Bumiputra* and non-*Bumiputra* divisions. For instance, the divisions in the Malaysian education environment are of concern. At primary school level, the non-*Bumiputra* tend to attend the national school system while the *Bumiputra* attend religious school. Affirmative tertiary sector education policies mean that most *Bumiputra* attend public universities, while large numbers of Chinese attend private and often international universities.

> [I]n public universities, students with different ethnic descent do not interact closely due to a variety of reasons, such as differentiation in the courses pursued, language barrier and non-participation in multiethnic societies and clubs … [E]thnic segregation continues into the workplace and other social functions. The civil service is dominated by Bumiputra, while the non-Bumiputra tend to take up jobs in the private sector. Urbanisation of the Malays also has not contributed significantly to forging closer ethnic interactions, as different ethnic groups tend to concentrate in certain housing estates. Moreover, with individualistic lifestyle and the 'rat-race' of urban living, people do not have the time to socialise with their neighbours. (Tey and Yeoh, 2004)

This divisive institutionalised practice means that the two different ethnic communities have very different formational backgrounds; that the differences between the communities are emphasised; and that the result is diverse intra-community world views involving different values and practices. This pluralist societal 'streaming' continues to have ramifications across all sectors of the society. In other words, it is at the day-to-day life and business operational level that Malaysian society remains 'divided by the reinforcing cleavages of language, religion, customs, education, areas of residence and type of occupation' (Yeoh, 2003, cited in Tey and Yeoh, 2004).

HRM strategies: Reform and capacity development

The fundamental human resource development goal of Vision 2020 is to have a cadre of well-trained people managing the nation's key assets by the year 2020. However, Malaysian management and worker practices need to be understood in the context of interposing Confucian, Islamic and Western values (Mansor and Ali, 1998, cited in Mellahi and Wood, 2004). The government-led and corporate elite assumptions underpinning Vision 2020 are that both work practices and skills levels have to be changed and developed, on the understanding that in the competitive context of globalisation human capital must continuously be upgraded to keep abreast with the relevant modernisation changes required for sustainable economic growth and development. However, changes in institutional and social practice across the society are necessary to support this broad societal change at both the collective and individual level. The pluralist cultural reality has significant operational and HRM implications, such as the cross-cultural nature of communications, the performance of teams, diverse notions of productivity, particular performance statements of duty, decision-making and leadership.

Many of the elite have received international education at the tertiary level, and this international background gives them increased cross-cultural and cosmopolitan 'multiliteracy' (professional, managerial, technical and communications) capacity, which in turn supports an open and responsive approach to intercultural community mixing and the development of important cross community networks. For example, there are some 20,000 Malaysian students currently studying in Australian universities (Anderson, 2004). This international education experience not only builds cross-cultural understanding and capacity in individuals and groups, but also creates the potential for intra- and international community networks. Hence, through these networks, the synergistic nature of interests can be emphasised and opportunities created. Nevertheless, at the broader societal level cultural difference and economic and opportunity disparities can breed mistrust and distain. This interposing plurality needs to be further addressed if Malaysia is to build the important cross-sectoral and cross-community networks between individuals and communities in order to build the innovative and problem-solving capacity now required of a knowledge-society as conceived in Vision 2020.

Transition to a knowledge society (K-economy)

Vision 2020 focuses on science and technology, particularly on high technology and knowledge-intensive activities in areas such as information and communication, microelectronics, biotechnology and life science, advanced manufacturing, advanced materials, food, environment and energy (MOSTE, 2003 cited in Saloma, 2004). Within the Multimedia Super Corridor, the Kuala Lumpur International Airport (Petaling Jaya), Technology Park Malaysia, Universiti Putra Malasyia-MTDC, the Putrajaya (Parliamentary Houses of government) and Cyberjaya have been built to house the international and local technology and multimedia companies that will undertake the research and innovation that is conceived to lead to the nation's high value-added goods and services. The focus on information technology (IT) has taken attention away from the key socio-cultural and institutional societal factors that impact on key areas such as the process of knowledge acquisition, and the creation and utilisation activities in the production processes within the industrial economy that indicate elements of a knowledge society (Saloma, 2004, p. 5).

> A knowledge society ... relies not only on knowledge work that is centred in universities or laboratories of science, but also in knowledge work found in research institutions, industries, business entities, development agencies and 'open source' communities, technical and scientific work culture. A corresponding distinction between knowledge-based economy and knowledge economy is ... not being made in Malaysia. (Saloma, 2004)

PM Badawi, rhetorically made the *all*-important relevant national diagnosis: 'First World infrastructure, Third World Mentality' in identifying the country's inhibiting development malaise (Siang, 2004). Structural industry issues such as the high level of foreign ownership and investment mean that the nature of the transition is not only in Malaysian hands but also in the hands of the multinational corporate sector. This reality reflects increasing global integration across economic societal spheres and the Malaysian business manager is not alone in grappling with the challenges that this creates.

Competitive corporate leadership

Issues of leadership and the importance of individual and corporate role models have been an important component in the Malaysian interventionist approach. Petronas, the state-owned oil company, presents a valuable organisational role model for the home-based and international corporate community for Malaysia to promote its developed nation-status ambitions. In light of the power associated with the political sphere in Malaysia, analysts recognise the crucial issue of keeping Petronas free of politics, and the government has conceded the importance of this. In particular, international praise and credit is given to Petronas' strong and low-profile senior management team.

> In a country where state-owned companies and politically connected business are at time known for scandals and mismanagement, Petronas stands apart ... [as being a] sure-footed example of integrated approach top nature resource management ... Foreign investors have ploughed some ... $10.5 billion into Petronas' joint ventures in

everything from oil exploration to refineries and petrochemical plants. In addition to being a strong regional player in refined-product sales, Petronas as been a leading proponent of large financially complicated liquefied-natural-gas projects. That strategy has made it one of the most important sellers of LNG in Japan, Taiwan and South Korea. (Lopez, 2003)

Moreover, Petronas has made a success of its overseas venture work, operating in countries that its international rivals have shunned or have been barred from entering. Petronas is involved in operational projects in 32 counties including Iran, Algeria, Turkmenistan, Sudan, Pakistan and China where political risk, or anti-western sentiment have frightened off many big international companies (Lopez, 2003). CEO Hassan, a British-trained accountant, states that the company's overseas push has helped to brand Petronas as a truly global company. This competitive and sustainable approach to success has been built not only on high-level technical and business competencies, but also high-level corporate and international relationship-building capacities.

With increased international focus on Malaysian industry performance and efficiencies, the emphasis is now addressing the quality of partnerships and relationships between the public and private sectors. Greater attention is being placed on the restructuring and enhancement in the values and performance of GLCs:

There are approximately 40 GLCs with a combined market value of US$61 billion, accounting for 34 per cent of the market capitalisation [or five per cent of the total companies] of the Bursa Malaysia; the new name for the demutualised Kuala Lumpur Stock Exchange. The government is also consolidating its investment holding institutions. More than 30 publicly-listed companies under the Minister of Finance Inc will be transferred to the Government's investment arm, Khazanah Nasional Bhd. (PriceWaterhouseCoopers, 2004)

Standard and Poors has affirmed Malaysia's foreign currency rating of 'A-/A-2' and local currency rating of 'A+/A-1' with a stable outlook. This investment-grade rating reflects the country's strong external liquidity and the competitive export-oriented and open economy which after restructuring is now more resilient to shocks (Chong, 2004).

In May, 2004 PM Badawi announced measures to make Khazanah Nasional Bhd into one of the leading investment houses in Asia. The revamp of Khazanah into a premier market oriented investment house is similar to that of the Singapore government investment arm, Temasek Holdings (Chong, 2004). Enrik Azman Mokhtar, the new leader at Khazanah has been set the task of using Khazanah to remake Malaysia Incorporated.

The task ahead is threefold: to remake the GLCs that Khazanah controls; to remake Khazanah itself; and to add to the overall development of the Malaysian nation. It is not about pure free markets: Khazanah is going to stay at the heart of Malaysia, but the intention is to get the heart beating more forcefully. (Lord, 2004)

The management strategy to be applied involves reform of the GLCs and the implementation of a 'Key Performance Index' (KPI) to create a more comprehensive corporate culture that includes a performance-based management compensation system and the elevation of shareholder value (http://www.khazanah.com.my).

Malaysia's Third Industrial Master Plan (IMP3) (period 2005–20) is in development with the areas to be addressed including: innovation, research and development, links between manufacturing-related services, adoption of information and communications technology, logistics infrastructure, industry clusters, participation of local suppliers and services providers in the global supply chain, and the skills of the Malaysian workforce (Chong, 2004). This strengthening economic position reflects growing international confidence in the leadership abilities of the new PM Badawi. With leadership taking a key historical role in determining the political, economic and socio-cultural nature of the interventionist strategies designed by the government, and applied to Malaysian community, institutions, and corporations indicate the value of a closer look at the ideas of Prime Minister Badawi to determine the future direction of the country.

The future: A new internationally diplomatic and 'civilised' Islamic leadership and community model

There has been a generally positive response from both within Malaysia and the international community that PM Badawi is developing a progressive governance agenda that will challenge entrenched interests on the political and business establishment (EIU Newswire, 2004(a)). Essentially, the Badawi leadership and governance strategy is to promote moderate Islam, tackle corruption and money politics, and accelerate the dismantling of special privileges for the *Bumiputra*. The implication is that this is the only way for Malaysia to become more competitive, and to transform from a culture of state-dependency. Badawi has called for Malays to rethink affirmative action and has stated that they must improve their knowledge and skills to compete in a global economy: 'A continuing reliance on crutches will further enfeeble (Malays), and we may eventually end up in wheelchairs', he said calling for a 'mental revolution' (EIU NiewsWire, *Financial Times*, 23 September 2004(b)). In speaking of his first year he likened it to that of farming:

> It is only sowing the high-yield seeds. In the second year, the seeds will have grown and I expect to see big and leafy trees. If they bear fruit, I hope they will be of high quality. Leafy trees under which we can find shade. (Bernama.com, 2004)

His agricultural metaphor for advocating a more sustainable position for the nation would not be lost on the imagination of the rural and urban Malay population.

His personal and academic background promote high Islamic credentials to the *Bumiputra* sector of the national community, while a moderate approach to Islam, and vocal denouncement of terrorism and violence promote a characteristic progressive and reformist Islamic leadership model and diplomatic role to both the local and international community.

> These credentials are already allowing him to cultivate good relations with the West – even advocating some Malaysian role in the reconstruction of Iraq – without significant risk of being criticised domestically for undermining Muslim values. At the same time, his moderate stance gives him greater freedom to attack the West over issues such as Palestine–Israeli relations without unduly alarming the US as a key trading partner. (EIU Newswire, Sept 24 2004)

Badawi's vision of *Hadhari* Islam (or Civilisational Islam) to the UMNO General Assembly 23 September 2004 marks out his conceptualisation of *the* future direction for the country. Importantly, he contextualised his outline of Islam *Hadhari* within the Malay community's historical struggle for independence and development, with an emphasis on the goal of enhancing the quality of life (Hassan, 2004).

> This would be achieved through the acquisition of knowledge, the development of the individual and the nation and the establishment of a dynamic economic, trading and financial system. Such a balanced development would produce an ummah or community of knowledgeable and pious people with noble values like honesty and trustworthiness, and who would be able tot take on global challenges. (Hassan, 2004)

This progressive and reformist Islamic rhetoric reflects back to the very historical reasons why the Malay Sultanates took up Islam by the fifteenth century.

According to PM Badawi, Islam *Hadhari* involves ten principles which range from faith and piety in God and a just and trustworthy government, to the protection of the rights of minority groups and women, the need for strong defences and a balanced development, on the basis that the adoption of this approach will enhance Malaysian competitiveness (Hassan, 2004). There is also an implicit shift in emphasis in PM Badawi's rhetoric from one where the state paternalistically oversees an interventionist and collective responsibility for the community, to one that places more responsibility on individuals to practise Islamic *Hadhari* values. Commentators indicate that more elaboration and explanation of what is meant by the concept of balanced development is needed – what constitutes the balance between *fardu ain* (individual obligation) and *fardu kafayah* (collective obligations). However, importantly: 'It provides a benchmark for people to assess, evaluate or scrutinise current practices as well as a reference point for reform' (Hassan, 2004). In responding to the PM Badawi's emphasis on moderation on all aspects in life and what modern Malaysia needs: 'It is about working hard, hunger for knowledge and information in science and technology' (Badawi, cited in Sim, 2004), a Chinese Malay notes that:

> This middle path means that it is up to each individual to build a more comprehensive understanding of religion. Beginning from this platform, issues such as multiculturalism, religious tolerance, and development goals can be debated and discussed at a national level. (Sim, 2004)

Nevertheless, critics note that Islam *Hadhari* has little to say about the empowerment of civil society, liberal democracy, freedom of speech and human rights, since potentially divisive issues are rarely deemed progressive by Asian states (Chong, 2004). A comparison can be made with former Deputy PM Anwar's *Madani* Islam approach that draws its intellectual impetus from the humanist post-classical Muslim scholar Muhammad Iqbal (1877–1938) in which self-discovery, intellectual empowerment, and personal liberties are considered to be an integral part of notions of progress (Chong, 2004). This discussion indicates that allowing a plurality of voices in the political sphere is still a crucial governance issue that Malaysia must address. The country's political system is increasingly referred to as a 'half' democracy, or 'pseudo' democracy. Hopefully, the unfolding of PM Badawi's discourse on Islam *Hadhari* represents the beginning of a more open, accountable and equitable discourse on national development.

Contemporary pluralistic micro-level management approaches for Malaysian national development and global integration

In the pluralistic Malaysian business context, international and local organisations aspiring to develop corporate partnerships and/or alliances need to carefully analyse and reflect on the managerial and human resource implications of this diversity. This local corporate and community diversity has significant implications for pluralistic local cultural approaches to key managerial issues, such as leadership, motivation, decision-making, communication styles, plus additional human resource performance and capacity issues associated with technical, professional and interpersonal skills. While this chapter has drawn attention to the streamed nature of the *Bumiputra*, ethnic Chinese and ethnic Indian managerial context, in a dynamic and evolving socio-cultural setting, caution must also be drawn on the limitations of essentialising ethnic community characteristics. Closer analysis of the participants and stakeholders of a micro-organisational context will identify the prevailing collective and individual managerial specificities. Community pluralism results in high context-based behaviour. Hence, in multicultural settings sub-cultural groups and individuals hold and develop diverse multicultural and multilingual capabilities, and hence, a high-level capacity to 'code-switch', and appropriately adapt their behaviour depending on the expectations of the context.

As noted previously, amongst the elite cadre of senior level bureaucrats, senior managers and senior technocrats there is high-level, and often internationalised, education attainment. Moreover, in response to the government's highly concerted effort to promote its modernisation and development vision there has been significant internationalisation of higher education, especially in the area of business management. By 2002 more than 50 different types of MBAs were offered by the pubic and private tertiary sector, which included growing numbers of twinning or franchised programmes, predominantly with Australian, United Kingdom and the United States of America universities (Zabid and Ling, 2003). Hence, there is a growing pool of managers and employees who have sophisticated local and internationalised corporate and professional workplace capacities. This local and internationalising professional education trend will contribute to managerial cross-vergent as local and international values and practices are adapted to the Malaysian managerial context.

Furthermore, in recognition of the need to competitively build more internationalised human resource capacities in the Malaysian workforce the Malaysian Minister for Education recently announced official support for the national promotion of English beyond the previous government initiative to teach maths and science in English, by declaring 'English to be a Malaysian language' (Levett, 2005). In this pluralistic and streamed cultural and linguistic national context, English language usage can promote national integration, while becoming a community socio-cultural resource for global integration. This binding-linguistic strategy will have additional implications for ongoing convergence and cross-vergent of western and Malaysian managerial approaches. This strategy, coupled with PM Badawi's modernising Islam *Hadhari* vision will further contribute competitive advantages to Malaysia while sustaining a distinctive Malaysian corporate and managerial context.

In general terms, Malay, Chinese and Indian ethnic businesses do share common overarching 'Asian' cultural values and approaches. International companies and international managers pursuing corporate partnerships in Malaysia need to be mindful of how the following socio-cultural variables impact upon local organisational systems and workforce managerial and behaviours expectations in particular managerial contexts:

- *Hierarchy* – The three communities do share a hierarchical notion of the social order and, hence, this hierarchical value is transposed to the cultural notions that frame managerial approaches to leadership.
- *Leadership* – All Malaysian ethnic business communities share a hierarchical approach to leadership as a managerial strategy to achieve organisational objectives and motivate employees. 'Authority is not usually questioned or challenged. Effective leaders ... must have a "vision" as well as the expertise and technical competence to get the job done' (Ahmad, 2004). This Malaysian emphasis on 'vision' is a characteristically ethnic Malay notion of leadership.

● *Collectivism* – These communities also share a collectivist organisational approach whereby the cultivation and support of good vertical and horizontal relationships is crucial to workplace functioning. Hence, the emphasis is on the maintenance of harmony and the building and maintenance of relationships achieved through consensual, 'face-saving', indirect and context-dependent interactive strategies. Mutual obligation and responsibilities are associated with this Malaysian gotong royong collectivism. Thus, values such as tolerance, respect for elders, courtesy, and compromise guide behaviour between seniors and employees. Adler (2002) notes that aligned with this collectivist culture, the group orientation in Malaysia means that historically organisational charts tended to specify only section, departments and divisions except for one or two top divisions with functions and reporting relations assigned in collective terms. Distinctively, more pragmatic outcome oriented and entrepreneurial ethnic Chinese business and workplace behaviour may be interpreted as being too direct, rude, and ambitious to collectivist ethnic Malay sensibilities.

● *Paternalism* – Culturally, paternalism can be understood as being symbolised in two ways: the first is the strict, and all knowing authoritarian father, and the second the wise, but 'caring/nurturing' father. Underpinning the hierarchical and collectivist Malaysian community model is the assumption that the leader adopts a 'caring parent' behavioural model, addressing both the private and public dimensions of the subordinate's needs, and hence, building a leadership model based on trust and respect. Hence, paternalism in this context is inclusive. There are moral and mutual obligations between employer and employee, whereby the employer will traditionally protect the employee in return for loyalty (Ahmad, 2004). Drawing together these cultural characteristics the Malaysian perception of the ideal manager is someone who is always calm, polite, compassionate and unhurried (Ahmed, 2004).

● *Family status* – The family and family status play an important cultural role in the pluralistic organisational models and employee behaviour. For the ethnic Chinese the institutional importance of the family is paramount. Conventionally, the family-based business model, their intra-community networks and associated Confucian-based values have been inter-linked to explain ethnic Chinese enterprise successes. Historically, kinship ties were an important consideration in hiring staff and acquiring funds to get enterprises started in the early years after migrating (Gomez, 2004). Networks are not formed in a single dimension but are primarily production chains or subcontracting ties that undergo processes of change and operate at multiple levels (Gomez, 2004). Hence, arguably the family kinship business model is framed on pragmatic immigrant ethnic Chinese community logic, as much as Confucian familial cultural logic. Contemporary SMEs are more concerned that their children become professional than simply hand the firm on to them (Gomez, 2004). For the Indian ethnic community family status is associated with the hierarchies of the caste system, which in this context has evolved into three distinct social levels: rich businessmen, professionals and wage earners (Ahmad, 2004). High social status in the *Bumiputra* community has traditionally been associated with noble families. More recently, wider education opportunities and the promotion of Islamic notions of equality mean that wider attainment of community status beyond family is now possible (Ahmad, 2004). Ordinary Malay concepts of the family draw heavily on the reciprocal kinship traditions of the kampong.

In the contemporary business context, despite these shared assumptions it is possible to differentiate between the subtle qualities and attributes valued by the respective ethnic communities. For example, the Chinese prefer a competent and professional leader who can be trusted and in return has the trust of his/her employees. The Malays prefer a socially conscious leader who is both a friend and a boss, and the Indians a boss-centred relationship provided that they are fair and equitable (Ahmad, 2004).

While Malaysians exhibit a strong need for group affiliation, and in general, derive their identity from group membership, additional sub-cultural distinctions that have behavioural and organisational managerial implications can be made.

- *Motivation* – The Malays are motivated by their membership of family, *kampong* and religious communities. Status is associated with these affiliations along with property and other material assets. Driven by a collectivist community logic they are motivated by organisational efforts that result in productivity gains not just for the company, but also for the family, their community and the nation as a whole (Ahmed, 2004). Similarly, employees may be more motivated by having extra time with family and friends than in earning overtime bonuses (Adler, 2002). However, as success is measured in the Chinese and Indian community by one's capacity to support the family, pragmatically the Chinese value monetary rewards, while Indians value well-being and personal development opportunities (Ahmed, 2004). Additional organisational and behaviour differentiations can be made between the 'doing' cultural orientation of the ethnic Chinese who prefer performance-based appraisal systems and largely monetary reward systems and the 'being' orientation of the Malays, which means that output and performance depend on individual needs and they value rewards that reinforce membership, benefit community, and hence, give status (Ahmed, 2004).

Despite these distinctions, the convergent influence of international corporate practice and the local status of employment opportunities with MNCs means that many young professional Malaysians are highly adaptable and comfortable with more individualised western performance appraisal and monetary remuneration systems.

It is noteworthy however, that some practical attempts to build collective intra-ethnic employee and workplace relationships can be problematic because of the diversity of belief systems, and cultural practices. For example, while reciprocity around the sharing of food is an important relationship building strategy for traditional Islam, the practice of eating pork is taboo, alcohol is forbidden, and for Hindu religion followers the slaughtering of cows is taboo, while the Chinese may enjoy both pork and alcohol. This can make a simple communitarian meal sharing strategy with an intra-ethnic workforce problematic. With the high value placed on relationship building and the need for strong links between the public and private employee work/life dimensions reconciling the intra-community differences associated with integrating pluralism can and will be challenging. In order to address the challenges associated with the need to better integrate and align Malaysian organisations and managerial and workforce approaches it is apparent that some cultural convergence, adaptation and innovation will be required. Nevertheless, in light of the ethnic and religious plurality in the Malaysian workforce, the increased opportunities for a more internationalised education, and the promotion of a unique and more modernising form of Islam in Malaysia means that considerable transformation of management in Malaysia will continue in response to local and regional influences and global imperatives. In light of the pluralistic and transformative nature of the Malaysian managerial context, undertaking research and analysis into the resources and capacities of potential business partners, employees and managers becomes essential to enable the design and development of appropriate managerial and workplace responses that enable the alignment of sustainable approaches to local and international development.

Conclusion

Malaysia has made a remarkable economic transformation in the forty years since independence. Considerable progress has been made in achieving the nation's long-term quest for developed nation status. The successive governments have played a key role in guiding this multifaceted and government-led corporate and community development processes. A more competitive and integrated, global market economy has highlighted the necessary ongoing corporate and institutional reform processes required to attract foreign investment in Malaysia and sustained levels of economic growth. It is apparent that in order for Malaysia to continue to make the transformation to a knowledge society a more open management and governance-based approach to the political sphere is now required. In addition, strategies need to be set in place to address the economic disparities that exist between and across the ethnic-based sub-cultural communities. Malaysia is now placed in an important international leadership position to promote a reformist Islamic approach to economic and community development. It appears that the current leadership is mindful of this opportunity and the responsibilities that go with this leadership role and the challenges it presents. Furthermore, the nation needs to view its existing intra-societal plurality and pluralist business streams as being an important cultural and economic repository with which to create valuable inter-regional and international networks and linkages to build synergistic and competitive industry advantages and sustainable levels of economic growth.

Questions

1. Discuss the importance of religion and culture in Malaysian management.
2. Explain the origins and nature of the different managerial styles of *Bumiputra*, Chinese and Indian managers.
3. What are the major management challenges facing Malaysia in its attempt to achieve fully developed nation status by 2020?

URL linkages

Government and related information

Prime Minister's Office	http://www.smpke.jpm.my
Department of Statistics	http://www.statistics.gov.my
Ministry of Finance	http://www.treasury.gov.my
Ministry of Home Affairs	http://www.kdn.gov.my
Ministry of Foreign Affairs	http://www.kln.gov.my
Ministry of Information	http://www.kempen.gov.my
Ministry of International Trade and Industry	http://www.miti.gov.my
Ministry of Education	http://www.moe.gov.my
Ministry of Science, Technology & Environment	http://www.mastic.gov.my

Economy, trading and technology

Bank Negara Malaysia (Central Bank of Malaysia)	http://www.bnm.gov.my
Malaysian International Chamber of Commerce & Industry	http://www.micci.com/
Malaysian Science & Technology Information Centre	http://www.mastic.gov.my/

News and information

Sultanah Bahiyah Library, Universiti Utara Malaysia	http://www.lib.uum.edu.my/merdeka/2003/index.htm
The World Factbook	http://www.odci.gov/cia/publications/factbook/geos/my.html
The Nation: History	www.windowstomalaysia.com.my/nation
Malaysian National News Agency	http://www.bernama.com/bernama /index html
The Star Online	http://www.thestar.com.my/
New Straits Times	http://www.nstp.com.my/
Utusan Malaysia Online	http://www.utusan.com.my
Encyclopedia – Malaysia	http://www.nationmaster.com/encyclopedia/Malaysia

CIA World Factbook	http:www.cia.gov/cia/publications/ factbook/geos/my.html
The Economist: Country Briefings	http://www.economist.com/countries/ Malaysia/
Virtual Malaysia	http://www.virtualmalaysia.com/
New Malaysian Free Press	http://www.newmalaysia.com.my/news/

Search engine

Yahoo Malaysia	http://www.yahoo.com.my
Malaysia Directory	http://www.malaysiadirectory.com
Malaysia Cari	http://www.cari.com.my

References

Adler, N, 2002, *International dimensions of organisational behaviour*. South-Western, Cincinatti, Ohio.

Ahmad, SA, 2004, *Public administration reforms in Malaysia: A developing country perspective*, Asian Development Bank. Retrieved 11 November 2004 from: http://www.adb.org/Document/Conference/Governmance/chap6.pdf

Anderson, J, 2004, Deputy Prime Minister, Australian Federal Government Parliament, *Question Time*, ABC TV, 3 December, Canberra.

BankIslam, 2005, 'The future of Islamic banking', *News*, 15 January. Retrieved 17 February 2005 from: http://www.bankislam.com.my/berita_Jan1505_e.htm.

Bosch in Malaysia, Who are we – and what do we do', Available [on-line] http://www.bosch.com.my/content/language1/html/867.htm

Burton, J, 2004, 'Malaysia politics: Badawi signals ending of law favouring Malays', 23 September, New York. Source: *Financial Times*, EIU Views Wire. Retrieved 22 January 2004 from Proquest Database.

Chong, T, 2004, 'Pak Lah's Islam Hadhari and Anwar's Islam Madani compete for mantle of "progressiveness" ' *Straits Times*, 14 November. Retrieved 16 November 2004 from: http://www.mggpillai.com/print.php33?artid+8422.

Cook, M, 2003, 'Ringgit Pressures', *Asian Analysis*, November. Retrieved 6 September 2004 from: http://wwwaseanfocus.com/asiansnaysis/article.cfm>articleID=689.

Church, P (ed.) 1995, *Focus on Southeast Asia*, St. Leonards, NSW: Allen & Unwin.

Department of Statistics Malaysia, 2004a, *Key statistics*, Department of Statistics, Putrajaya, Malaysia. Retrieved 20 October 2004 from: http://www.statistics.gov.my.

Department of Statistics Malaysia, 2004b, *Malaysian External Trade Statistics* June 2004 Retrieved 20 October 2004 from: http://www.statistics.gov.my/English/rpm/rpmaugusto4.htm.

Economic Planning Unit, Prime Minister's Department 2004, *Malaysia: 30 years of poverty reduction, growth and racial harmony*, EPU, Prime Minister's Department, Putrajaya, Malaysia.

EIU NewsWire, 2004(a),' Malaysia politics: Badawi signals reformist intent', 24 September New York. Retrieved 22 November 2004 from Proquest Database.

EIU NewsWire, 2004(b), 'Malaysia politics: Badawi signals ending of law favouring Malays', 23 September, New York, source *Financial Times*. Retrieved 22 November 2004 from Proquest Database.

Fontaine, R, Richardson, S & Foong, Y, 2002, 'The tropical fish problem revisited: A Malaysian perspective', *Cross cultural management*, Partington, vol. 9, No. 4, pp. 60–71, Retrieved 22/10/04 from Proquest Database.

Fox, J, 1999, 'The Austronesian heritage'. In Fox J (ed.) *Indonesian Heritage: Religion and Ritual*, Archipelago Press, Singapore and Jakarta.

Giroud, A, 2003, *Transnational corporations, technology and economic development: Backward linkages and knowledge transfer in South-east Asia*, Edward Elgar, Cheltenham, UK.

Goh, B-L, 2002, 'Rethinking modernity: State, ethnicity and class in the forging of a modern urban Malaysia'. In CJW-L. Wee (ed.) *Local cultures and the new Asia: The state, and capitalism in Southeast Asia*. Institute of Southeast Asian Studies, Singapore.

Gomez, ET, 2004. 'De-Essentialising capitalism: Chinese networks and family firms in Malaysia.' *NIAS Nytt*, Copenhagen, No. 3, September, pp. 8–11. Retrieved 22 August 2005 from: http://proquest.umi/com.dbgw.lis.curtin.edu.au/pqdweb?index+13&sid=1&srchmode.

Granovetter, M, 1985, 'Economic action and social structure: The problem of embeddedness,' *American Journal of Sociology*, vol. 91, November, pp. 481–510.

Hassan, M, 2004, 'Islam Hadari: Abdullah's vision for Malaysia?' *IDSS commentaries*, Institute of Defence and Strategic Studies, NTU, Singapore. Retrieved 16 November 2004 from: http://www.malaysia.net/dap/lks3153.htm.

Jomo, KS & Gomez, ET, 2000, 'The Malaysian development dilemma' In MH Khan & KS Jomo (eds), *Rent, rent seeking and economic development: Theory and evidence in Asia*, Cambridge University Press, Cambridge, UK

Jomo, KS & Wee, CH, 2003, 'The political economy of Malaysian federalism: Economic development, public policy and conflict containment', *Journal of international development*, vol. 15, no. 4, pp. 441–56.

Jomo, KS, 1997, *Southeast Asia's misunderstood miracle: Industry policy and economic development in Thailand, Malaysia and Indonesia*, Westview Press, Colorado, USA and Oxford, UK.

Lassere, P & Schutte, H, 1995, *Strategies for Asia Pacific*, Macmillan Business, South Melbourne, Vic.

Levett, C, 2005, Colonial English back in Malaysian favour. *The Age*, 17 August. Retrieved 23 August 2005 from: http://www.theage.com.au/news/world/colonial-english-back-in-malasyian-favour/20.

Lewis, R, 2003. *The cultural imperative: Global trends in the 21st century*, Intercultural Press, Yarmouth, Maine, USA.

Lockard, C, 2003/2004, 'Ethnic Chinese in Singapore and Malaysia: A Dialogue between tradition and modernity' (Book Review), *Pacific Affairs*, vol. 76, no. 4, pp. 671–72.

Lopez, L, 2003, 'A well-oiled money machine', *Far Eastern Economic Review*, March 13, p. 40.

Lord, N, 2004, 'Khazanah's quiet revolution', *Finance Asia*, November. Retrieved 22 February 2005 from: http://www.khazanah.com.my/latest.asp.

Mandal, S, 2003, 'Transethnic solidarities in a racialised context', *Journal of Contemporary Asia*. Manila, vol. 33, no. 1, pp. 50–69. Retrieved 22 October 2004 from Proquest Database.

Mellahi, K & Wood, G, 2004, 'Human resource management in Malaysia', In PS Budhwar (ed.), *Human Resource Management in Asia Pacific* (pp. 201–20), Routledge, New York.

Mahathir, Bin Mohamad, 2002, 'Minister for Finance', *The 2002 Budget Speech*, The Dewan Rakyat, Kuala Lumpur, Malaysia. Retrieved from: http://www.mir.com.my/lb/budget2002/pmspeechpdf.

Mahathir, M, 1991, *Malaysian: The way forward (Vision 2020)*. Retrieved from http://www.epu.jpm.my/

Mahmood, R. Managing Director, SMAS SDN BHD, 2002, pers. comm. March 7.

MIDA, 2004(a), 'Economic Strength', Malaysian Industrial Development Authority. Retrieved 23 November 2004 from: http://www.mida.gov.my/beta/print.php?cat=1&scat=16.

MIDA, 2004(b), 'Malaysia set to become key Islamic banking hub' *Industry News*, 22 October. Retrieved 17 February 2005 from: http://www.mida.gov.my/beta/new/views_newsphp?id+1225.

Ministry for National Unity and Social Development (http://www.jheoa.gov.my/e-background.htm 2004).

Nicholas, C, 1997, *The Orang Asli of the Peninsula Malaysia*, Centre for Orang Asli Concerns, pp. 1–14. Retrieved 26 October 2004 from: http://www.xlibris.de/magickriver/oa.htm.

Nida"ul Islam, 1995, 'Principles of Islamic Banking', November–December. Retrieved 11 February 2005 from: http://www.islam.org.au/articles/older/BANKING.HTM.

Ngui, C, 2001, 'Clan power', *Malaysian business*, 16 June Kuala Lumpur, p. 24. Retrieved 22 October 2004 from Proquest Database.

Othman, N, 2004, 'Political Islam and Women's Rights: Southeast Asia and the Middle East', *Conflict, security and political regimes in Asia*. A Public Seminar Series Murdoch University's Asia Research Centre and Politics and International Studies Program, Perth, WA, 4 November.

Osborne, M, 1995, *Southeast Asia: An introductory history*, (6th edn) Allen and Unwin, St. Leonards, NSW.

PriceWaterhouseCoopers, 2004, *Malaysia*. Retrieved 30 November 2004 from: http://www.pwch.com/home/webmedia/10905734884/m&abulletin_ap_june2004_my.pdf

Rasiah, R, 2003, 'Manufacturing export growth in Indonesia, Malaysia and Thailand', in KS Jomo (ed.), *Southeast Asian paper tigers? From miracle to debacle and beyond*, RoutledgeCurzon, London and New York.

Salazar, C, 2004, 'The legacies of Mahathir's privatisation policy', *Asean focus group Asian analysis*, ANU, Canberra, March. Retrieved 26 November 2004 from: http://www.aseanfocus.com/asiananalysis/article.cfm?articleID=721.

Saloma, C, 2004, 'How Malaysians create cars and information technology products: Specifics of an emerging knowledge society', Paper presented Fourth International Malaysian Studies Conference, Universiti Kebangsaan Malaysia, Bangi, 3–5 August.

Savage, VR, Kong, L & Neville, W, 1998, *The Naga Awakens: Growth and Change in Southeast Asia*, Times Academic Press, Singapore.

Shah, M, 2004, *The Malaysian experience in science and technology development and its relevance for OIC countries*. Paper presented at the Fourth International Malaysian Studies Conference, UKM, Bangi, 3–5 August.

Shome, T, 2002, 'Malaysian leadership unique', *Massey News*, Massey University, New Zealand. Retrieved 6 October 2004 from: http://masseynews.massey.ac.nz/2002/masseynews/sept/sept30/stories/malysia_leadership.html.

Siang, L, 2004, Speech, DAP National consultant on "Agenda for First-World Parliament", 16 May. Retrieved 30 November 2004 from: http://www.malasyia.net/dap/iks3024.htm.

Sim, R, 2004, *MCA: Islam Hadhiri and PM's aspirations*, 28 June Retrieved 16 November 2004: from: http://wwwmca.org.my/services/printerfriendly.asp?file+/articles/commentary/2004/6.

Singleton, H, 2002, *Frameworks for the management of cross-cultural communication and business performance in the globalising economy: A professional service TNC case study in Indonesia*, PhD thesis, Schools of Management, & Languages & Intercultural Education, Curtin University of Technology, Bentley WA. Available http://adt.curtin.ed.au/theses/available/adt-wcu2005111615421/

Tarling, N, 2001, *Southeast Asia: A modern history*. Oxford University Press, South Melbourne, Vic.

Tayeb, M, 1997, 'Islamic Revival in Asia and HRM', *Employee Relations*, vol. 19, no. 4, pp. 352–64.

Tey, N & Yeoh, E, 2004, 'Ethnic relations amongst University of Malaya undergraduates', Paper, Research carried out for the Centre for Economic Development and Ethnic Relations (CEDER), Faculty of Economics and Administration, University of Malaya, Kuala Lumpur, Malaysia.

The Economist, 2003(a), 'Asia: No breaks; Malaysia', 22 February, vol. 366, no. 8312: p. 67. Retrieved 22 October 2004 from: Proquest Database.

The Economist, 2003(b), 'Survey: The guard', London, 5 April, vol. 367, no. 8318, p. 4. Retrieved 22 October 2004 from Proquest Database.

Wee, CJW–L., 2002, 'Introduction: Local cultures, economic development and Southeast Asia', In CCJW–L. Wee (ed.), *Local cultures and the New Asia: The state, culture and capitalism in Southeast Asia*, Institute of Southeast Asian Studies, Singapore.

World Bank, 2004, *Doing business 2005 report: Removing obstacles to growth*, Co-publication Worldbank, International Finance Corporation and Oxford University Press, Washington. Retrieved http://www.rru.worldbak.org/doing business (pdf version).

Zabid, AR & Ling, CN, 2003, Malaysian employer perceptions about local and foreign MBA graduates. *Journal of education for business*, Washington vol. 79, no. 2, pp. 111–18.

Additional readings

Cheam, J & Cheam, GJ, 1998, *Malaysia*, APA Publications, London.

Church, P (ed.) 1995, *Focus on Southeast Asia*, Allen and Unwin, Sydney.

Edwards, R, Nyland, C & Coulthard, M (eds), 2000, *Readings in international business: An Asian perspective*, Prentice Hall, Sydney.

Navaratnam, R, 1999, *Healing the wounded tiger: How the turmoil is reshaping Malaysia*, Pelanduk Publications, Malaysia.

Rodan, G, 2004, *Transparency and authoritarian rule in Southeast Asia: Singapore and Malaysia*, RoutledgeCurzon, New York.

Smith, W, 1999, 'Management in Malaysia', in M. Warner (ed.), *Management in Asia-Pacific*, Business Press Thomson Learning, Melbourne (pp. 244–59).

Tarling, N. 2001, *Southeast Asia: A modern history*, Oxford University Press, Melbourne.

Managing the entrepreneurial culture of Singapore

Chapter objectives

Introduction

Over a short period of 40 years the small island state of Singapore has progressed to become one of the fastest growing economies through the application of a government-led and pro-business strategic economic development plan. International support for the strategy has meant that Singapore has attracted substantial foreign investment through the activities of powerful multinational corporations (MNCs). The government assumed an entrepreneurial role through the establishment of state enterprises, known as government-led companies (GLCs). The Singapore government applied a paternalistic and entrepreneurial political approach to manage the development of both the economy and the society, and from independence in 1965 until 2000, this approach provided full employment and prosperity to most Singaporeans. However, the terrorist attacks of September 2001 were the catalyst for a severe economic downturn, which exposed the key structural weaknesses and the vulnerabilities of the economy that were further emphasised by the negative regional impact from the SARS outbreak. The economy's heavy dependence on the electronic sector, and a lack of entrepreneurial culture amongst individual Singaporeans, were made all the more apparent by significant competition from Chinese manufacturers. Increasing levels of unemployment resulted and significant community disorientation.

The contributor wishes to acknowledge Meldref Publication, USA for allowing some material from his article titled 'Developing an entrepreneurial culture in Singapore: Dream or reality' published in the *Asian Affairs journal*, vol. 36: 3(2005), pp. 361–73.

Individual creativity, risk-taking and entrepreneurship had not been encouraged by the socio-political system giving support for the cultivation of a new entrepreneurial culture in Singapore. To achieve a more sustainable approach to economic management critical focus is now on the paternalist style of governance, the process of privatisation of the non-strategic GLCs; and the encouragement of a more open society to institutionalise creativity and innovation into the social fabric of the nation.

The macro-regional level: Local and external forces influencing the management context of Singapore

This section identifies the particular local issues and external forces that over time now constitute the heritage of Singapore, a heritage which in more modern times underpins both the identity of Singaporeans and the specific governance and management approaches incorporated in the society at the macro-management level. The local history and the influence of important external forces played a pivotal role in shaping the key political, economic and cultural governance and management approaches that successfully frame the modern development of Singapore. The following discussion highlights how the island's heritage has contributed to the socio-cultural logic behind the specific Singaporean corporate and community governance and management strategies applied in response to the complex challenges set for the island community by rapidly changing macro-environmental realities.

The forces of heritage: Local and regional influences

Singapore has a unique history, and geography. The island state, located 137 kms north of the Equator, consists of one large island and some sixty smaller ones, which together make up only 647.5 sq kilometres. Half of the territory is set aside for forests, marshes and other non-built uses, while the remaining half is allocated for residential, commercial and industrial planning uses. With a population of some 3.5 million people, this means that there is a high density of some 4702 head of population per square kilometre. Despite this environmental limitation, the strategic location on the Straits of Malacca at the foot of the Malaysian Peninsula has provided both a unique heritage and unique development opportunities for the people of Singapore. The following material briefly explains the key local influences that have shaped modern Singapore and so aims to promote understanding of why particular management approaches prevail in Singapore at the macro-, meso- and micro-corporate and societal managerial levels.

A brief history

Many aspects of the contemporary management challenges now faced by the government and citizens of Singapore resonate with the particular and inter-related economic, political and social circumstances faced by the island's population throughout its history. In framing a contemporary societal response to current and future macro-global and local business and management issues, the Singapore government and its people inevitably draw on their rich and particular political, economic and socio-cultural history and the resources available in order to develop a sustainable development model that makes sense to the Singaporean community.

Earliest records indicate that the small island has had a long history as a trading post. Its maritime geographic location at the foot of the Malaysian Peninsula on the Straits of Malacca, which was for many centuries an important trading route between China, India, the Middle East and later Europe, meant that the small island's history and economic development has been embroiled in the changing military power and trading fortunes of other nations and empires. As a small island with limited natural resources this reality meant that historically a pragmatic and outward orientation was fundamental to the survival of the community. The longevity of this circumstance and the resultant pragmatic and outward community orientation resonate with the contemporary Singapore strategic management challenges in the context of globalisation. Moreover, this circumstance and local community orientation implies that the island's geography and history have additionally contributed to a flexible community characteristic framed on the basis of recognition of the need to adapt and change in response to the dynamic influences of fluctuating external realities.

The earliest reference to Singapore was a third-century Chinese account in which it was described as *Pu-luo-chung* (island at the end of the peninsula). The earliest history places the island as a geographic stop between the winds of the monsoon seasons for traders between China and India. The history of the island has been constructed from travellers' accounts and the court inscription of other lands which include Chinese, Malay, Javanese, Sumatran and Indian sources. Between the seventh and thirteenth centuries the island was caught up in the regional activities of the powerful Buddhist *Srivijayan* Empire centred at Palembang on Sumatra. During the fourteenth century the Thais briefly took control of the island, but soon had to relinquish control to the Javanese-based *Majapahit* Empire rulers. Accounts at this time refer to *Temasek* (or Sea Town) and by the end of the fourteenth century the Sanskrit name *Singa Pura* (Lion city) was in common use. These shifting historical empires reflect an evolving socio-cultural heritage framed on early Buddhist and Hindu influences derived from the Indian sub-continent. Early Chinese records from this period also indicate that Chinese were living on the island seeking their fortune through trade. This early Chinese influence also indicates the arrival of Confucian and eastern Buddhist cultural and religious influences. By the sixteenth century, with the rising wealth and power of the Islamic Sultanate of Malacca the island, Singapore's importance decreased as a major trading post. The early sixteenth century also saw the first European imperial force – the Portuguese – sail into the Straits of Malacca and subsequently they took over Malacca. Singapore then became caught up in the territorial quarrels between European empires and in 1613 was set on fire by the Portuguese, with the Dutch capturing the city in 1641: 'Aside from a fortification wall and a royal gravesite, there was hardly any visible evidence of Singapore's ancient history' (Singapore: A history of the Lion City', 2004).

By the second half of the eighteenth century the British were extending their colonial domination of India, expanding trade with China, and needing to address the growing Dutch colonial presence in the region. Hence, they recognised the strategic need to establish a trading port and refurbishment facility for their merchant fleet. Thus, Penang was established in 1786, Malacca taken from the Dutch in 1795 and in 1819, Singapore was established as a British colonial trading post with Sir Stamford Raffles acting as the governor. Within three years, Singapore's revenue earnings had surpassed that of Penang.

By the 1860s, the attraction of a tariff-free port, a flourishing colony and naval base meant that the population, then made up of 61.9 per cent Chinese, 13.5 per cent Malays, 16.05 per cent Indians and 8.5 per cent others including Europeans, had grown to 80,792 (ASNIC, 1994). The development of steam ships, the opening up of the Suez Canal, and the development of rubber plantations on the island and the Malay Peninsula, along with the development of tin mining, meant that by the end of the nineteenth century Singapore experienced unprecedented prosperity. Trade expanded eightfold between 1873 and 1913 (ASNIC, 1994). While the growth of Singapore continued under British colonial rule, it was not until the Japanese invasion in 1941 that the limited strength of British colonial power was revealed to the people of Singapore.

While the British returned after the defeat of the Japanese, the 1950s saw a burgeoning of nationalism across the region with new local and charismatic political leaders emerging. Lee Kuan Yew, a Cambridge university graduate and leader of The People's Action Party (PAP), was elected Prime Minister in 1959, and finally Singapore gained independence in 1965. Lee Kuan Yew was to guide Singapore for the following 31 years and he continues to influence the development of Singapore sas a Minister Mentor after his official retirement. It is noteworthy that the multifaceted personal Chinese ethnic background and British university education of Lee Kuan Yew, with their both local and outward looking orientation, have together played a critical role in shaping the specific governance and development strategies designed to modernise the independent island state. The Prime Minister's personal background suggests that both western and eastern influences played a paramount role in shaping the future of the nation. These influences continued with the Prime Ministers who followed Lee Kuan Yew – namely, Goh Chock Tong, and the current Prime Minister, Lee Hsien Loong.

This brief introduction indicates how the pre-independence history, the geographic location, and the consequences for the island community that were associated with the shifting fortunes of external empires were to lay down the important foundations that were to characteristically guide the evolving strategic governance and management responses to develop a post-independence Singaporean society.

Socio-cultural issues

The geographic island and trading route location of Singapore have significantly impacted on the diverse ethnic and religious make up of the population. Under Raffles' British colonial town plan for Singapore, separate areas were set aside for the various ethnic groups at the time: Chinese, Malays, Arabs, Indians, Bugis (from Sulawese) and Europeans (Leitch LePoer, 1990). Many of the largest group, the Chinese, came from earlier settled parts of the Malay Peninsula. Many Chinese settlers later came in search of economic opportunities from the south eastern provinces of China (Guandong and Fujian) bringing with them various ethnic Chinese dialects, religious and cultural practices. Some Chinese played an important middleman role for the merchant European community. In the mid-eighteenth century Indians were Singapore's second largest ethnic community. Some Indians, like the Chinese, had simply come to make their fortune, others were sent as troops, and another group were sent as convicts. These Indian convicts were trained in skills such as brick making, carpentry, rope-making, printing, weaving and tailoring, and on their release these skills were valued by the community. By contrast, the Malays usually worked as fishermen, boatmen, or artisans such as woodcutters, or carpenters (Leitch LePoer, 1990).

This historical ethnic diversity, coupled with more than 250 years of British cultural legacy accounts for the religious diversity of the island population which includes Buddhists, Christians, Muslims, Daoists and Hindus (Leitch LePoer, 1990). Government statistics reveal that the religious affiliations of the people of Singapore were relatively stable over the period 1990–2000 (*Singapore census of population*, 2000). Buddhism and Taoism accounted for 51 per cent of the fifteen years and over resident population; Christianity 15 per cent, Islam 15 per cent, Hindu 4 per cent, with other religions accounting for less than 1 per cent, and some 15 per cent nominating no religious affiliation. It is noteworthy that government statistical analysis reveals that Christianity is associated with the better educated Chinese with post-secondary and university qualifications (*Singapore census of population*, 2000). Similarly, the Chinese account for the bulk of persons reporting 'no religion'. Nearly 100 per cent of the ethnic Malay community have Islamic affiliations, whereas within the Indian ethnic community 55 per cent have Hindu, 25 per cent Islam and 12 per cent Christian affiliations.

The issue of home language is also associated with the religious affiliations of the various Singaporean ethnic communities.

Cultural factors, as manifest through the home language, have a strong influence on the religious affiliation of the resident population. Singapore residents who have adopted English as their home language appear to have greater exposure to the influence of Christianity. Thus, in 2000, Christians formed the largest group among the English-speaking population, Buddhism and Taoism, the traditional Chinese religions, were the main religion of the mandarin- and dialect speaking populations. There is also a strong correlation among ethnicity, home language and the religion among Malays and Indians. Almost all Malay-speaking residents were Muslims while more Tamil-speaking residents were Hindus in 2000. (*Singapore census of population*, 2000)

It is additionally noteworthy that the government statistical analysis also identifies a link between the larger representation of Christians and those with no religious affiliation who are residents of private flats and houses in comparison to the bulk of high density built (HDB) flat dwellers who are Buddhists and Muslims. This statistic points to how economic disparities within the Singapore community are associated with ethnicity and religious affiliation. Moreover, this ethnic and religious diversity now gives Singapore a range of potential competitive advantages on which to draw in an increasingly interconnected and interdependent global economy.

More particularly, links can be made between this early socio-cultural community plurality and the kind of nation building governance and economic development challenges faced in 1965 by the newly independent Singaporean government. For example, after independence, integrated community housing developments, designed to build social cohesion, were one of the key public infrastructure development strategies of the new government designed to promote social-cohesion (ANSIC, 1994). Thus, the importance of introducing a range of policies that would build and contribute to an overarching collective sense of Singaporean community identity was recognised as being crucial to bind the ethnically diverse community. In addition, a massive industrialisation programme was initiated to build economic development and a new modern national identity. Today, this rich ethnic, cultural and associated religious diversity is celebrated and promoted as being one of the island's key exotic and cosmopolitan 'life-style' attractions.

However, with ethnic Chinese community making 72 per cent of the island's population, it is apparent that this 'off-shore' Chinese cultural legacy would dominate the development logic of a national discourse. Hence, Chinese Confucian and Buddhist cultural values were to play a key role in shaping the modern management system, structures and culture of Singapore. The incorporation of a Confucian-based high work-ethic has been fundamental to the cultural development model framing of modern Singapore (Lewis, 2003). The Singaporean Government has set in place a unique range of strategic policies, administrative institutions and business development structures that together have built a cohesive national identity and a successful national economy.

The Singaporean governance and development model shares many 'Asian cultural model' characteristics with those of other Asian nations: a collective entrepreneurial spirit, an emphasis on education, high saving rates, positive government involvement in export expansion, dynamic community sprit, unanimous directional effort inside companies, loyalty to firms, a comforting focus on people, a high duty-consciousness, professional obedience among employees, basic trust as opposed to mere observance of legalities and vigorous reinvestment of profits in research and development and improvement of resources and infra-structure (Lewis, 2003). While the government has been highly successful in building a cohesive modern and collective Singaporean identity, it is noteworthy to point out that, drawing on the diverse values of their multi-ethnic backgrounds, individuals and groups within the community have multifaceted identities that incorporate both their shared national Singaporean identity along with other diverse ethnic sub-cultural identities. This multifaceted and pluralistic character particularly applies to the offshore ethnic Chinese communities, who are too often bundled together under a universalist notion of a Chinese diaspora (Wang, 2003). It is apparent that these historical, geographic and cultural issues interweave together to have important political and economic governance and management implications for both contemporary and future business activities and human resource issues in Singapore.

The political and economic management framework

At the time of independence, the island-state was 'weak in industrial bourgeoisie and lacked any significant manufacturing base' (Yeung, 1998, p. 400). Subsequently, the government embarked on a watershed direction that trans-formed Singapore in just four decades into one of the world's most competitive nations. Prime Minister Lee Kuan Yew (2002), who is often singularly credited with Singapore's economic success, explained in a *Leadership in Asia Pacific Lecture* that as 'we did not have enough entrepreneurs, and those we had lacked the capital of interest, government ministers undertook the task of starting new ventures'. This pro-business government development stance became widely known as Singapore Incorporated (Inc.). Over the past forty years, Singapore Inc. increased to involve hundreds of government-owned enterprises (GOEs). These organisations are run by an elite cadre of highly efficient civil servants, or technocrats in numerous key industries (Schein, 1996; Haley and Low, 1998). To ensure that these state enterprises were run efficiently, the PAP implemented a deliberate recruitment strategy to attract the country's brightest talents through incentives such as high salaries, long-term career opportunities and overseas university scholarships. This resulted in the nation's best talent com-peting to work in the government, rather than in the private sector.

During the 1960s and 1970s, a scarcity of local capital and entrepreneurs provided the catalyst for the government to assume the role of state entrepre-neurialism. Since then, the island-state government has been relentless in pursuing an industrialisation programme that included aggressively attracting foreign MNCs with strong technological capabilities to further expand the country's manufacturing and industrial infrastructure (Haley et al., 1996). In 1997, about 5000 MNCs operated in Singapore and about half maintained regional head-quarters in the island-state (*Economic Development Board*, 1997). The World Economic Forum's World Competitiveness Report and the US-based Business Environment Risk Intelligence (BERI) Report have repeatedly cited Singapore as one of the best places in the world to do business together with a world-class labour force (Haley, 1998). It is not surprising then that Singapore citizens are grouped amongst the highest gross national income per capita in the world.

This success in attracting MNCs into Singapore has been due to the government's strategic 'open-door' approach aimed to make the island-state both investment and employer friendly through a combination of generous incentives schemes, policy measures and labour laws. To demonstrate the government's commitment to its open-door policies, it regulated the labour market by disciplining the labour force through the Trade Union (Amendment) Bill in 1966, the Employment Act in 1968 and the Industrial Relations (Amendment) Act conferring increased power to employers (Rodan, 1989; Low et al., 1993; Huff, 1995). The government justifies this employer-oriented approach to the local community through the argument that the pursuit of economic growth is the only rational, non-ideological, pragmatic course of action to bolster Singapore's otherwise fragile and exposed position. These labour market regulations resulted in a corporate culture that consisted of a 'hierarchical, disciplined (and) materially successful' labour force (Haley and Low, 1998). Furthermore, the Singaporean culture is shaped by the government's deliberate coercive strategic approach of 'social re-engineering' justified through the promotion of the national interest, fashioning a suitable social order through the development of language, discipline and education and by controlling incoming cultural messages through direct control of the media (Haley and Low, 1998). This socio-political engineering strategy interlinks with the government's environmental landscape and infrastructure engineering strategy which includes extensive reclamation and landfill to expand the island's strategically important modern first class shipping port and airport hub facilities supported by first class digital information and communication technology.

Several scholars highlight the incorporation of Confucian ideologies and social institutions by the PAP in shaping the Singaporean culture (Cho, 1994; Low, 1994; Tremewan, 1994; Chua, 1995; Dolven, 1998). These authors suggest that Confucian ideology underpins the government's paternalistic and coercive management of the nation and its people through the application of the following strategies:

- The identification of socially desirable and undesirable values;

- Definitions of ethnicity and the nature of ethnic inter-relationships;

- Promotion of the use of English as the 'lingua franca' in addition to the use of one's mother tongue;

- The enforcement of a subsidised public housing policy;

- Compulsory national service in the Singapore Armed Forces;

- The promotion of the value of education for both individuals and the community;

- The imposition of compulsory savings rates;
- The implementation of workplace and labour laws; and
- Significant restriction on public political and social campaigns.

The government justifies its ubiquitous presence and high level of intervention at every level of Singaporeans' lives, such as from speaking Mandarin, to having more children, and to demonstrating courteousness as being necessary, as a means to sustain political stability and economic growth (Clammer, 1985; Haley et al., 1996). It is apparent that many of the underlying socio-cultural values framing this predominantly successful coercive and paternalistic governance strategy will have significant implications for the future development and success of the local private sphere and its management structures, systems and styles.

In August 2004 former PM Lee Kuan Yew's son, Lee Hsien Loong was appointed Prime Minister, with former PM Lee Kuan Yew acting as senior State 'Minister mentor'. 'Singapore's economic success, based on an odd mixture of free markets and state meddling, looks set to continue. But will its new leader allow a bit more social and political freedom?' (*The Economist*, 2004, 12 August). The new PM's wife, Ho Ching, manages the government's main industrial-holding company, Temasek, which owns a stake in diverse industry sectors that include airlines, banking and the country's main telecommunications firm. The new PM's leadership style resonates with that of his father. 'His speeches are full of stern injunctions to Singaporeans to tighten their belts against the hard times ahead' (*The Economist*, 2004).

Singaporean responses to global imperatives

The Singaporean government has been credited with successfully building the country to achieve an advanced developing nation status. However, paradoxically, its highly paternalistic and state entrepreneurial ideology has also been attributed with a contemporary economic decline under the global influences of terrorism, the SARS outbreak, and increased competition from China. In attempting to better understand Singapore's success, comparisons have often been drawn between the country and the type of MNCs it aggressively attracts (Caplen, 1993). Managed like a big corporation, Singapore has always placed significant value on strong leadership, meticulous planning and discipline. Furthermore, the range of paternalistic governance strategies, discussed previously, work collectively towards rallying all of the society's energies towards achieving defined goals and objectives. However, this top-down development approach is also seen to have restricted its citizens' spirit of creativity and risk-taking. These are the very characteristics that are needed to prosper in an increasingly dynamic and competitive global market context. Hence, the contemporary challenge for Singapore is to build the innovative and risk-taking of its citizens in order to have the more flexible and creative capacity now required for a dynamic and competitive global market context.

In response, Singapore leaders now openly acknowledge that the citizens must develop an entrepreneurial culture for the island-state to remain competitive (Saywell and Plott, 2002). Furthermore, it is acknowledged that, lifelong employment in GLCs, or in the civil service, can no longer be taken for granted. Instead of promoting dependence and the acquiescence of the people for the past 40 years, the government is now changing its tack by encouraging its citizens to think and act for themselves (Saywell and Plott, 2002). However, in a society where the coercive paternalistic influence of government has been so pervasive, and where the people have been accustomed to look to its leaders for direction, this more autonomous redirection will require a radical change in the national mindset.

With the exercising of control being fundamental to Singapore's political culture the government regulates many aspects of social and personal life (McNulty, 2000). While the government currently expresses a desire to foster an entrepreneurial culture, it is naturally somewhat reluctant to alter the foundations of a system that have worked so successfully in the past. As an outcome of the government's 'guiding social policy hand', management strategies include strong government in the economy, a high savings rate and an education system that has rewarded rote learning and examination results over critical and innovative thinking. Altering this institutionalised approach presents a serious challenge for the government as it looks for strategies to cultivate a new entrepreneurial culture in a social context where success is measured by having a well-paid position in the civil service, or in an MNC. However, to its credit the government has acknowledged key competitive shifts in the global economy and that it must also change in order to better prepare Singapore for participation in the knowledge economy.

The meso-societal level: The management of Singapore institutional infrastructure

A government-led approach to industrial infrastructure

The particular characteristics of the entrepreneurial culture of Singapore lie at the heart of managing the island's post-independence economic and community development successes. This section examines in more detail the entrepreneurial culture in Singapore at the meso-managerial level. Subsequently, the discussion focuses on the factors that have been widely identified to hinder the entrepreneurial culture, with particular reference to the dominance of GLCs and the entrenched risk-aversion attitude of Singaporeans, along with the historical development, financial performance and future role of GLCs. Two key factors that contribute to the risk-averse characteristics of Singaporeans: the safety net in the form of Central Provident Fund; and the education system are explored, and lastly, several approaches that the Singaporean government might undertake in order to cultivate a more entrepreneurial culture are considered.

The unique characteristics of Singapore's entrepreneurial culture

With the PAP ruling Singapore for the last thirty years, Singaporeans have not only enjoyed increasing living standards, but they have also experienced the emergence, consolidation and entrenchment of a strategic approach to economic and political management that has resulted in the island having a unique paternalistic and state driven business and community managerial structure and system. The success of the PAP business and community governance and management strategy is evidenced in the fact that Singapore enjoyed a remarkable per capita income growth between 1965 and 2000 to average 6.4 per cent per annum (Soon and Ong, 2001). This steady economic growth enabled Singaporeans to enjoy rapid increases in living standards equivalent to some developed nations.

The island economy managed to successfully weather the regional storm created following the 1997 Asian economic crisis. However, in 2001 the country suffered its worst recession since independence in 1965. The island-state's economy shrank by 2.2 per cent, which was the sharpest decline of any major Asian country (Saywell and Plott, 2002). This decline, which resulted in a 15 year high unemployment rate of about 5 per cent, was largely attributed to the global economic downturn and 11 September terrorist attacks in the United States. More importantly, the downturn revealed two major key structural flaws in the economy. One was the unhealthy reliance on the electronics sector, which made up 50 per cent of total domestic exports and the other, a lack of entrepreneurial culture amongst Singaporeans (Saywell and Plott, 2002).

There is currently a significant debate in Singapore about the issue of the development of an entrepreneurial culture. The ramifications of this issue had previously been examined by the government almost two decades ago. Following an economic recession between the years 1985 to 86, the Singaporean government realised the increasingly important role that small and medium-sized enterprises (SMEs) were playing in the country's long-term future (Tan and Tay, 1994). Consequently, the government set up a subcommittee on Entrepreneurship Development (Ang, 1985), which assessed how the government's development policies had affected the entrepreneurial environment in Singapore. The report findings produced pointed out that:

- The government's continuing efforts to attract MNCs and establish large GLCs had stifled local entrepreneurship; and that

- The high employment levels, high salaries and high job securities have led to Singaporeans becoming accustomed to the associated high security levels.

These circumstances contributed to the reluctance of Singaporeans to start their own businesses. Essentially, under the existing system and structure there were no incentives and motivations to venture into the risks associated with developing their own businesses.

It is noteworthy that the government has, over the years, actively expressed and committed government support to assist the development of SMEs as a key strategy to enhance local entrepreneurial culture. This strategic approach is consistent with the government philosophy to play the dominant role in the economy, as was the case in its previous strategic efforts designed to attract MNCs and to develop GLCs in order to spur employment levels and to develop the economy. Several of the leading government agencies include: the Economic Development Board (EDB), the Standards, Productivity and Innovation Board (SPRING), the Intellectual Property Office of Singapore (IPOS), the Infocommunications Development Authority (IDA), the Agency for Science, Technology & Research (A*STAR) and the International Enterprise Singapore (IE) (Lee et al., 2004). Nevertheless, despite the far-reaching government role applied to assist local businesses and to promote the spirit of entrepreneurship in Singapore, the island-state remains less entrepreneurial than many other countries in the world.

According to the latest Global Entrepreneurship Monitor (GEM) (2003), an annual survey carried out jointly by London Business School and Babson College on entrepreneurial activity, Singapore ranked twenty-first out of 31 nations based on the proportion of adults active in starting a new business. The level of entrepreneurship activity has been declining for two consecutive years. Only 5 per cent of Singapore's adult population in 2003 engaged in entrepreneurial activity, down from 5.9 per cent in 2002 and 6 per cent in 2001. The GEM (2003) offers some interesting explanations on the declining entrepreneurial activity in Singapore (Wong et al., 2004). In particular, the report highlights two dimensions that have provided barriers to developing an entrepreneurial culture. The first relates to the difficulty experienced by SMEs in entering markets due to the presence of established firms such as GLCs and MNCs. The second relates to Singapore's national cultural norm, which does not support entrepreneurial risk-taking, creativity and innovativeness.

In summary, it is apparent that the government has not been as successful as it had hoped in its effort to foster an entrepreneurial culture in Singapore. This is in spite of the numerous initiatives and reforms that the government has developed to provide the incentives and infrastructure to produce more entrepreneurs. These efforts have had little impact on the pervasive influence of the government in the economy through its vast network of GLCs and the entrenched risk-adverse propensity of Singaporeans. Hence, these two factors will now be examined in more detail to better appreciate the key issues and challenges.

The historical development of Government-Led Companies (GLCs)

After independence in 1965, the PAP inherited an economy from the British Administration that lacked any significant industrial or manufacturing infrastructure (Yeung, 1998). The country also faced a shortage of indigenous entrepreneurs who had the capital, or interests, to industrialise Singapore. More particularly, at that time the government was suspicious of indigenous Chinese capitalists, and was fearful of their pro-Communist and pro-China attitudes (McVey, 1992; Menkhoff, 1993). This associated ethnic-Chinese and pro-communism logic relates to fears at the time based around 'the domino theory', which postulated a model for the regional territorial expansion of Communist China. At the time in the region, the domino theory underpinned America's anti-communist involvement in the Vietnam War and similarly, a British military presence in Borneo on the Indonesian border. Many Chinese ethnic communities across the region suffered extraordinary levels of reactionary local violence against them as a response to this perceived Communist threat. Hence, to 'jump-start' local industrialisation, the Singaporean government took up responsibility for the provision of public infrastructure such as roads, electricity, transport and communication services, through GLCs and state-controlled statutory boards. A company is referred to as a GLC when the government holds at least a 20 per cent stake directly, or with an intermediate holding.

Pioneer GLCs included the Keppel, Sembawang and Jurong Shipyards, which positioned Singapore as a major ship building and repair centre; the Development Bank of Singapore (DBS), which was set up to undertake the risks of lending to new manufacturing ventures; and Neptune Orient Lines (NOL), which was formed to leverage on the island's strategic location (Ramirez and Tan, 2003). Some GLCs were strategically set up to develop a defence industry, notably the Chartered Industries and Allied Ordnance. Many of the early companies were joint ventures with foreign investors, e.g., the Singapore Refining Company, which provided the catalyst for the growth of the oil refining industry, was a joint venture with Caltex and British Petroleum, while the Petrochemical Corporation of Singapore, which launched Singapore's entry into the petro-chemicals industry, was a joint venture with Shell and a Japanese consortium. The historical development of GLCs reflects the 'government's thinking that the question of industrial structure should not be left solely to the market, especially given the absence of a domestic industrial bourgeoisie of any consequence' (Rodan, 1989, p. 77). Hence, the government assumed the role of an entrepreneur through its GLCs by taking up the task of starting new ventures.

Rapid economic growth over the past two decades has provided GLCs with opportunities to invest in a broad range of industries. During the 1980s and 1990s a number of statutory boards became GLCs. Over the years the total number of GLCs has grown rapidly and is estimated to now be in the hundreds. Their reach is so broad that it includes several of the largest public-listed companies in Southeast Asia, for example:

- Singapore's national airline (Singapore Airlines);

- Two leading telecommunications operators (SingTel and ST Telemedia);

- Southeast Asia's biggest banking group (DBS);

- A semiconductor producer (Chartered Semiconductor);

- The main shipyards (Keppel and Semb Corp);

- The port operator (PSA);

- A shipping company (Neptune Orient Lines);

- The subway operator (SMRT);

- Property developers (Keppel Land and Capital Land); along with

- A number of other non-listed businesses (Burton, 2002).

The various purposes of these particular GLCs reflect the government's long-term strategic intent to develop Singapore as an economy based around modern high-tech science and technology industries, a regional finance centre, and a high performance regional shipping and aircraft hub, the development of which in turn would attract more diversified industries. GLCs account for nearly half of the 20 largest listed companies and 41 per cent of the local *Strait Times* index, although some big state companies remain unlisted.

In 1974, the government established a limited holding company, Temasek Holdings, to manage its investments in GLCs (Ramirez and Tan, 2003). At that time, 36 companies were transferred to Temasek's control. Since then, its holdings have penetrated every key segment of the economy from ports, telecommunication, stockbroking and shipping to power, food, the media, logistics, airlines, engineering, property, healthcare, education and even zoos and aviaries (Webb and Saywell, 2002). Its asset stakes alone in 70 listed companies represented almost US\$35 billion in market capitalisation (Saywell and Plott, 2002). Recently, criticisms have been directed towards Temasek for 'crowding out' competition for the private sector caused by its ownership of competing companies within industries. The telecommunications industry is a good example. Temasek has holdings, directly or indirectly, in all three of the major telecommunication operators. It holds a 67.5 per cent stake in SingTel while at the same time has equities in the other players such as StarHub and MobileOne through its vast network of subsidiaries or associate companies (Saywell and Plott, 2002).

State Entrepreneurship

The Singaporean government has always claimed that the GLCs, whether wholly or partly owned, operate fully as for-profit commercial entities, on the same basis as private sector companies. They are expected to take a similar level of risks to provide commercial returns to their shareholders, subject to the same regulations and market forces as private entrepreneurs, and they do not receive any subsidies, or preferential treatment from the government (Ramirez and Tan, 2003). The main advantage of government ownership appears to be the positive signal of confidence this sends out to the market. The following statement by a GLC manager, cited in Low (1994), illustrates this perception:

> Being linked to government is of course useful. It gives the company credibility and nobody will think you are a 'fly-by-night' operation. But the company has to justify itself

and earn its keep by marketing the right products at the right place as no favours are given or expected. (p. 65)

This state entrepreneurial business model articulates to the Confucian-based collective entrepreneurial spirit and high work ethic values characteristic of the Asian business model described earlier.

A global downturn in the 1980s resulted in Singapore experiencing a serious recession (Yeung, 1998). This recession exposed the vulnerability of the country's economy due to an overdependence on foreign capital and the lack of a vibrant SME sector. Private entrepreneurship was directly discouraged by various state policies in the earlier phases of industrialisation. At the time a major strategy to overcome this structural weakness was to promote the growth of entrepreneurship by encouraging both state-owned and private sector enterprises to regionalise their operations in order to capture the growth potential of the surrounding countries. Consequently, the state took up the role of a 'quasi-entrepreneur' by assuming the risks of spearheading regionalisation in two specific ways:

1. The regionalisation of GLCs and companies set up by statutory boards.

2. The opening up of overseas business opportunities for private capitalists and negotiating the institutional framework for such opportunities to be tapped by Singaporean firms (Ministry of Finance, 1993).

With their substantial financial resources, specialised expertise, and commercial experience, these GLCs and companies of statutory boards would form partnerships with private sector companies. In large infrastructure projects, the GLCs were even prepared to take on a greater proportion of the risk by holding majority equity in the joint ventures. In most other projects, the private sector entrepreneurs were expected to bear the primary risks and to take on the majority stakes (Yeung, 1998). However, most of Singapore's outward foreign direct investment went into real estate projects and industrial parks rather than small, manufacturing footholds as was the Taiwanese strategy.

Over the years, public criticisms swelled as GLCs sought to expand their influence by moving into industries that appear to have no strategic significance to Singapore and could be left to the private sector. Not content with running airlines, banks, shipping, telecommunication, petrochemicals and utilities, at one stage GLCs also operated fast food restaurants and pubs. 'The role of the state in business has become at best unnecessary and at worst dysfunctional. It has warped the development of the private sector. For a bright young person, the system has been totally biased against entrepreneurship' (Lim, cited in Mellor 2001). The GLCs' activities leave little room for small businesses. This view is shared by others. 'The Singapore government has been very effective in eradicating entrepreneurs,' said Jeffrey Goh, who in 1998 started a company called Lightspeed Technologies to provide inexpensive intra-company e-mail services to small firms.

> The government is the single biggest economic actor here, and by virtue of being there it squeezes out the opportunities. All the things that make Singapore so successful today, particularly its ability to marshal talent and resources into government will make it unsuccessful in the twenty-first century. (Goh, cited in Dolven 1998)

This comment draws attention to the different kind of entrepreneurial spirit required in a globally competitive knowledge-based economy.

Financial performance

There have been various attempts to measure the role of GLCs in Singapore's economy. In 2001, the Singapore Department of Statistics (2001) estimated the contribution of GLCs to GDP at 12.9 per cent in 1998, with the non-GLC public sector (including statutory boards) accounting for another 8.9 per cent, for a total public sector/GLC share of 21.8 per cent. However, this more recent estimate is limited to GLCs in which the government's effective ownership of voting shares is 20 per cent or more (Feng et al., 2003). This estimate does not encompass the substantial number of subsidiaries of GLCs where the government's ownership level is calculated at below 20 per cent, even though the parent GLC may be the controlling shareholder. According to a July 2001 research report by the investment bank ING Barings, GLCs make up 41 per cent of the *Straits Times* Index. Estimates determine that GLCs make up about 33 per cent of the market capitalisation of the Singapore Exchange, the country's stock market, based on 2000 figures (Ding cited in Webb and Saywell, 2002).

Arguably, Singapore's GLCs may well be the most efficiently operated government-owned enterprises in the world. A study on the financial performance of 25 GLCs and 204 non-GLCs listed on the Singapore Exchange's main board (Ding and Ang, cited in *China Daily*, 2002, p. 6) revealed that from 1990 to 2000, the GLCs outperformed by 1.7 per cent on return on assets and by 10 per cent on return on equity. However, with Singapore facing its worst economic slump in 2000, the financial performance of GLCs attracted closer scrutiny from investors and analysts. Daniel Lian, an economist with Morgan Stanley, one of the more outspoken critics of the GLCs, claims that 'returns by GLCs have been poor in the past decade despite impressive economic growth and a substantial improvement in corporate governance' (Lian, cited in Webb 2001). A study conducted by KPMG Consulting in 1999 on listed manufacturing firms in Singapore included three GLCs among the top five 'destroyers of shareholder value', but no GLCs among the top five 'creators of shareholder value' (http://www.usembassysingapore.org.sg).

SingTel, which was run by chief executive Lee Hsien Yang, the younger son of Senior Minister, Lee Kuan Yew, is considered to be one such 'destroyer' of shareholder value. A recent study of shareholder wealth created by the world's biggest companies by consulting firm Stern Stewart ranked the company as one of the world's biggest 'value destroyers'. Stern Stewart argued that SingTel had wiped out nearly US$30 billion of wealth in the five years to June 2001 (cited in Webb 2001). Similar arguments were made about the performance of Singapore Food Industries (SFI), which supplies food to the armed forces, hospitals and schools (Webb and Saywell, 2002). Presenting another share value depreciation case, on 10 September 2002, SembCorp Industries offered to sell its stake in SFI to another Temasek Company, Singapore Technologies, at S$0.70 per share – a price that was 9 Singapore cents below the stock's trading price and 8 Singapore cents below SFI's original initial public offering price. As a result, the share price plunged 12 per cent in response to the offer, wiping about S$50 million off its stock market capitalisation.

Barriers to creativity

Recently, the rapid growth of GLCs, both in size and number, and the Singaporean government's role in business has attracted much debate. Critics charge that the pervasive influence of GLCs in most sectors is effectively 'crowding out' private investment and hindering the development of a critical mass of thriving local enterprises. Most Singaporeans, especially those involved in the SMEs, perceive that the government ownership or control in GLCs has created special advantages in the form of access to funds, tenders and other business opportunities. The Singapore Institute of Directors recently stated that corporate governance within GLCs lags behind international best practice (Burton, 2002).

One of the main reasons is attributed to the make-up of the executives or the directors of GLCs, who are very often relatives of senior government officials, current and former government officials, former senior military commanders and current and former MPs of the ruling PAP (Tan, 2002). The government blames the limited talent pool for its dependence on the political elite (Wong, 2002). Regardless of their being sourced from the political elite, as ex-civil servants, or military officers, they are predominantly risk-averse and lacking sufficient entrepreneurial drive (Krause, 1987). Furthermore, the same people sit on the many company boards and hence, tend to perpetuate similar styles of management. This senior management culture leaves little room for fresh and competitive ideas and innovation.

Over the past few years, a number of GLCs have pursued global strategies for growth and diversification. However, these firms have found that their close link with the government was often a hindrance to overseas expansion. Recently, some neighbouring countries have shown strong reluctance to allow Singaporean GLCs to invest in key local sectoral industries of national strategic importance. The most publicised case was the failed bid by the cash-laden SingTel for Cable & Wireless HKT to a 10-month old Hong Kong internet company (Shameen and Reyes, 2000). Singtel's later attempt to enter the Malaysian market through acquisition met with similar tough opposition. In another case major GLC, Singapore Airlines, faced strong opposition from neighbouring countries who feared for the loss of one of their key national strategic assets to a foreign government. Thus, Singapore's highly profitable national airline was not only unsuccessful in its bid to acquire a stake in an Australian airline, but also failed to secure the rights to launch new airlines in Cambodia and India (Tripathi, 2001).

In mid 2002, the Singapore government announced that it would divest some of its investment in sectors that were of no strategic significance, or had the potential to grow internationally (Webb and Saywell, 2002). Information on the timeframe for divestments, or the names of the companies that are up for sale remains unclear. However, the government has made it clear that it would still maintain a controlling stake in companies that provide public goods such as gaming, public broadcasting, subsidised services in healthcare, education, housing and public amenities such as the Singapore Zoo and Bird Park.

Moreover, the Singapore government has recently also made efforts to broaden the management of GLCs by hiring foreign executives and installing greater numbers of external directors. Several foreigners were appointed as chief executives to push through radical restructuring and to turn around underperforming GLCs such as DBS, NOL and Chartered Semiconductor (Wong, 2002). However, the resignations of several of these senior executives raise the question of whether outsiders (and their management approach) are suitable for Singapore Inc. The invisible hand of the state, witnessed in such activities as persuading local banks to merge ahead of the liberalisation of the sector, and pushing other corporations to expand regionally, indicate extra pressures that cause corporate management problems (Wong, 2002).

A risk-averse corporate and community management culture

Obviously, as the PAP has governed Singapore since independence in 1965, it has played the key role in shaping the political, economic and cultural characteristic nature of the prevailing Singaporean managerial style. These unique national community characteristics have implications for the behaviour and performance orientation of both senior management and individuals in the workplace. The leadership in PAP adopts an assertive and paternalistic style based on the values of efficiency and meritocracy (Chua, 1995). A 'nannying' leadership style results in Singaporeans looking to the government for guidance on solutions to many aspects of their public and private lives; from saving for their retirement, to providing housing and even to finding a marriage partner.

An entrepreneurial culture requires the willingness to risk failure, and as a consequence of the government's assertive and paternalistic cultural approach, in general Singaporeans are risk-averse. In an examination of the risk-taking behaviour of the Singaporean Chinese, who make up three-quarters of the population, Ray (1994) referred to the government's Subcommittee Report on Entrepreneurial Development (MITI, 1986). This report argues that contemporary Singapore has a low tolerance for failure. The prevailing Singaporean attitude is that failure on the job, or in business, will mean castigation and result in ruination

(MITI, 1986). This high failure cost atmosphere impacts on the behaviour of individuals and, hence, is not conducive to risk-taking for two reasons. First, the civil servants avoid risks by rigidly adhering to rules rather than by exercising discretion, and second, talented professionals tend to select safe well-paying jobs with large MNCs or GLCs (Ray, 1994).

Despite Singapore's economic success, the outcome of this risk-adverse managerial culture is a diminished supply of young entrepreneurs (Ray, 1994). With full employment, high salaries and job security in both the public and private sectors, there have been no motivational factors or policy incentives for graduates and professionals to start their own business ventures. Reflectively, the report (MITI, 1986) noted that in countries with great entrepreneurial flair, such as the United States and New Zealand, failure is taken as a lesson by entrepreneurs, who pick themselves up and keep trying until they succeed. Two key strategic factors contribute to this risk-averse nature of Singaporeans. The first relates to the safety net in the form of Central Provident Fund, which discourages Singaporeans from working for themselves and the other, the educational system, which places an extreme emphasis on passing exams and rote learning.

The role of the Central Provident Fund

Singapore has one of the world's highest saving rates, which is achieved through the state-run personal savings system known as the Central Provident Fund (CPF) (*Rethinking the Singapore model*, n.d.). This high savings rate is another political characteristic strategy employed in the Asian economic management model. This community saving fund enables Singaporeans to pay for a range of services such as health care, children's tertiary education, the financing of home ownership and retirement. Prior to the Asian economic crisis, the CPF system required that all workers, except for the self-employed, put aside 20 per cent of their gross monthly salaries, together with the employer contribution of an additional 20 per cent. This policy inadvertently rewards salaried employees and discriminates against entrepreneurs who have chosen to start their own business (Chew, 1996). Moreover, reduced profits and rising unemployment levels related to the recent economic downturn affected some organisations' fiscal performance and so the government reduced the employer's contribution to 10 per cent.

This government policy of state-enforced savings has resulted in Singapore achieving the world's largest savings ratio to GDP. It grew substantially from only 6.7 per cent between the 1960 to 1966 period to 28.8 per cent between the 1970 to 1979 period, and 42.7 per cent from 1980 to 1992 (Yeung, 1998). This enormous pool of domestic savings held by the CPF Board is invested overseas to assist in building Singapore's huge foreign reserves. This high saving level and foreign investment strategy buffered Singapore remarkably well during the 1997 Asian financial crisis. However, the channelling of a large share of potential investment capital from the private capital market to the CPF Board has made it extremely onerous for private entrepreneurs to obtain the necessary capital for domestic and overseas expansion. Thus inadvertently, this saving-investment strategy has hindered indigenous entrepreneurship initiatives (Tan, 1991).

Efforts by the government to redeploy some of the savings in the CPF have been resisted by the innate conservatism of the Singaporeans themselves. In an effort to promote the development of a mutual-fund industry, the government in 1997 allowed Singaporeans to invest a portion of their contributions to the CPF in approved private-sector investment vehicles (Saywell and Plott, 2002). Nevertheless, by the end of December 2001, Singaporeans had chosen to invest only about 28 per cent of eligible funds in the private sector. The remaining funds sit in the CPF, where the compound annual real returns between 1983 and 2000 averaged a meagre 1.8 per cent (Mukul Asher, cited in Saywell and Plott, 2002).

The educational system

Singapore's educational system places a high value on mathematics and the sciences. This curricula emphasis is partly blamed for a culture that discourages free thinking and instils a fear of failure (Saywell, 2000). Within the maths and science oriented educational system there is an institutionalised emphasis on the syllabus content, excessive attention to detailed performance in schoolwork and the attainment of good grades based on rote learning. Together, the resultant institutionalised educational culture is considered to be responsible for the lack of creative and critical thinking. These systemic educational characteristics are shared by other Southeast Asian nations. Indicating the perceived pressure to perform experienced by Singaporean children in particular, a survey of 1742 children aged 10 to 12 students found that they are more afraid of exams than of their parents dying (*Straits Times* 2000, cited in Saywell, 2000). These findings paint a grim picture of deeply depressed and overburdened children. In addition, the survey found that one in three appears to believe that sometimes life is not worth living, nearly four out of five spend as many as three hours studying after school, and seven out of ten receive extra classes tuition after school hours. Their pedagogical performance anxieties will inevitably spill over to a range of work-place performance and risk-taking anxieties.

Following public criticism, the government has taken steps to liberalise the island's education system by making it less results-oriented (Lee and Tsang, 2001). Even traditionalists admit that the current teaching methods and curriculum, which champions a discipline-oriented Confucian approach to learning and behaviour, is inappropriate to equip the students with the skills that are fundamental to a knowledge-based economy (Saywell, 2000). A knowledge-based economy requires human resources with analytical and critical problem solving and innovative capacities. There are now fewer tests, and the entire educational system is much less geared toward training children for the universities than previously. There is also now less emphasis on rote learning and more on creativity. Students are increasingly made to work collaboratively in teams on projects that 'range from researching the impact of El Nino on whales' migratory patterns to the use of insects in Chinese medicine' (Saywell, 2000, p. 64).

More recently, developing creativity has been considered one of the three priorities for Singapore's education system in the twenty-first century (Le Blond, 1997). This may be the most far-reaching change in Singapore today, but the full effects are unlikely to be felt for many years. A considerable effort and time-frame is required to change entrenched and institutionalised cultural values and behavioural patterns across a national community. Educators now agree that the system has emphasised test results at the expense of developing well-rounded individuals. Under the submissive characteristics of this education system, passive students took copious notes in order to be able to memorise everything the teacher presented. Beyond school hours students receive extra tutoring in the hope of achieving the required marks necessary to get into a prestigious school and, hence, to succeed in life (McNulty, 2000).

The Singapore government actively recruits the best and brightest talents into the civil service, offering not only high salaries, but also hundreds of lucrative scholarships that require students to serve obligatory terms in the public sector. This strategy results in the creation of highly skilled technocrats and bureaucrats instead of risk-takers and innovative entrepreneurs (Toh and Tan, 1998). These policies have significant management implications for leadership style, and culture-specific notions about human resource performance. In realising that this policy limits indigenous entrepreneurship, the government now intends to release more of its able and resource officers to the private sector after they have served their scholarship bonds (Lee 2002). Obviously, in a risk-averse cultural context, a range of policies will need to be implemented to support this intention.

Over the past three years, the Singaporean government has listened to the continuing criticism against the current educational system and responded to it. The office of Deputy PM Tony Tan, who oversees higher education, has drawn up plans to upgrade the universities and to bring them in line with world-class institutions (Cohen, 1997). As examples of this higher education upgrade strategy, two of the country's major tertiary institutions, the National University of Singapore (NUS) and the Nanyang Technological University (NTU) are now expected achieve the institutional objective of producing graduates who demonstrate independent thinking. A new institution, the Singapore Management University (SMU) has also been established in the central business district of Singapore.

However, at the same time, acknowledging the high political value placed on social cohesion, these universities have been careful not to encourage students to politically use this new approach to build intellectual independence to disrupt Singapore's collective community sense of tranquillity. Once again the prevailing cultural emphasis is on a collective entrepreneurial spirit and professional obedience. Nevertheless, at the same time as a liberalisation of business and education strategy is being implemented, many quality international universities have been encouraged to establish facilities in Singapore and, in response, many have set up independent and local partnership tertiary education facilities offering world-class undergraduate and postgraduate courses. This off-shore/ on-shore strategic educational approach has long-term implications for the assimilation of international cultural approaches to corporate and community management.

The micro-organisational level: Critical traditional, transitional and transformational issues in Singapore management

The previous sections indicate why, despite the considerable economic and community development successes of Singapore since independence, there is widespread recognition that, in order to maintain a competitive regional and global position, the particular patterns and processes applied at the micro-managerial level must evolve to responsively develop more effective pathways to sustain success. The dramatic economic downturn in 2001 has, in particular, shaken up the Singapore government and caused it to re-evaluate its strategic approach to the management of economic and community development. The downturn exposed the major structural weaknesses of an economy that provided one of the world's highest standards of living to its people over a short developmental history of almost 40 years. Until 2001, Singaporeans were living in an environment where it was taken for granted that there would be plentiful well-paying jobs in one of the many MNCs and GLCs in the country. As Singapore had experienced virtually negligible unemployment for the past decades, the pervasive influence of the political elite, who dominate GLCs, was tolerated despite its adverse impact on indigenous entrepreneurship. Together with institutions such as CPF and the exam-oriented education system, Singaporeans were discouraged from risk-taking and starting their own businesses.

However, the government now acknowledges that the world has changed and so it must also change to ensure Singapore's long-term prosperity. Following a conservative manufacturing approach to economic development the government has directly invested in further industry diversification beyond its traditional electronics industry base, especially in the pharmaceutical sector. 'Multinational drug firms, such as Pfizer and Schering-Plough are expanding their capacity ... attracted by its economic freedoms, reliable legal system, relative absence of corruption and well-educated workforce' (*The Economist*, 2004, 12 August). This diversification strategy is attributed to a significant improvement in economic performance, at 12 per cent per annum in the second quarter of 2004. However, there are still many questions hanging over the sustainability of this improved economic performance under increasing competition from Chinese manufacturers.

At the same time as the island's economy faces increasing competition from China, Chinese Singaporeans are increasing their investment in China. With the majority of Chinese Singaporeans being descendents of migrants from the Fujian and Guangdong Provinces, many share a common language and cultural background. After his visit to Singapore in 1979, esteemed former China leader, Deng Xiaoping, openly praised the island state's utilisation of foreign direct investment to improve its economy. In 1992 Deng indicated that 'Singapore enjoys good social order and is well-managed. We could tap on their expertise and learn how to manage better than them' (*Selected works of Deng Xiao Ping*, 1993, p. 378, cited in Wang et al., 1999). The long term implications of this statement should not be undervalued in assessing the future direction in the governance and management of Singapore, nor the current market-liberalisation strategies of China, and future regional strategic collaborations between the two nations.

Following formal diplomatic relations in 1990 the two governments have maintained a warm relationship at the highest level. 'The strong ethnic and political ties between the two countries have led the Singaporean government and businessmen to perceive that they would enjoy a competitive edge over western firms when investing in China' (Wang et al., 1999, p. 288). Overseas Chinese from Singapore, Hong Kong and Taiwan, now provide 80 per cent of the investment capital for the development of industry within China (Lewis, 2003). This suggests that the future of the Singapore governance and management strategy is now closely tied to economic developments in China.

This discussion indicates that, consistent with its paternalistic style of governing, the ruling PAP continues to adopt an Asian top-down paternalistic management approach in its strategic efforts to remake Singapore. However, many of the political elite have been educated in the West. For example, like his Cambridge University educated father, Lee Kuan Yew, the current PM, Lee, Hsien Loong was educated at Cambridge, as well as at Harvard University. His wife, and CEO of Temasek, Ho Ching, was educated at Stanford University in the United States. Hence, this international education of the political elite indicates their good understanding of western management strategies and techniques, and their specific Singaporean entrepreneurial approach reflects a selective and integrated Asian and Western management approach, designed to give them a competitive regional and international advantage. The educational background of the political elite is reflected in the government strategy to encourage first-class international education providers to operate in Singapore. This international education strategy provides a service not only for Singaporeans, but also offers a high quality, but cost effective international education service product to the regional community. In particular, this service addresses the educational needs of regional families of Chinese ethnic backgrounds. Hence, in the long run there will be more internationally oriented Singaporean human resources to manage business and the community at the micro-level, as well as significant regional *guanxi* reciprocity networks for building regional business relationships.

In line with international and local calls for greater community liberalisation, the administration has introduced a vast number of initiatives and reforms in the areas of education, bankruptcy rules and even zoning laws, to encourage Singaporeans to be creative and to take risks in starting a business. For example, the government has recently liberalised its rules to allow home-based businesses in public-housing developments where approximately three quarters of Singaporeans live. Moreover, the government is slowly loosening up its lifestyle restrictions on diverse issues such as chewing gum, tabletop dancing and the arts and cultural scene. Similarly, a diverse range of community and media activities have been introduced in order to liberalise many aspects of the lives of ordinary Singaporeans:

> Bans on everything from bungee-jumping to street-busking were relaxed. Singaporean television was even allowed to broadcast the salacious American sitcom *Sex in the city*. This cautious liberalisation partly reflects the government's realisation that Singapore must now move beyond manufacturing into 'knowledge-based' industries that depend on individual creativity. (*The Economist*, 2004, 12 August)

Moreover, the period of compulsory military service has been reduced and the community issue of poverty is under official review.

These wide reaching socio-cultural liberalisation strategies are attributed to government recognition of the need to move further away from a manufacturing economic orientation towards knowledge-based industries built on individual risk-taking and creativity. Increasing lower-cost based competition from Chinese manufacturers supports this new more liberalised redirection. This strategy reflects awareness of the need for political and cultural reform across a range of institutional and societal spheres, in order to impact on the behaviour of individuals and groups within the community, and hence, develop knowledge-based industries. The hope is to create a more relaxed, supportive and motivating socio-cultural environment for would-be local and foreign 'technopreneurs' (i.e., technology-oriented entrepreneurs).

The Singapore government is facing one of the biggest challenges since independence in its push to make Singaporeans more creative and entrepreneurial. While the government acknowledges that developing this represents a key pathway to sustainable development, it also realises that there is a limit as to what it can achieve, in spite of its efforts to provide the infrastructure and incentives, to encourage the people to innovate, to spot market opportunities and ultimately to take the personal risk of starting a business. An entrepreneurial culture requires individuals to possess a spirit of creativity and risk-taking propensity which cannot be entirely government mandated. This change in cultural norms, values and mindset, proves onerous in an environment where success in the society means having a well-paying job in the civil service or with an MNC. The key question is: 'How serious is the Singapore government in wanting to cultivate independent, risk-taking and creative entrepreneurs?' The price for doing so might be high. It calls for a bold move by the government in completely overhauling the institutions and the nature of society.

Currently, the government is taking a cautionary approach in trying to build on the strength and virtue it has developed over the past four decades. Although this stance is understandable, the government must lead by example in breaking down the barriers or 'sacred cows' in its drive towards building a more creative and risk-taking society. The world is changing, and the drivers that have propelled Singapore into an economic success story are ill-equipped and cumbersome for the knowledge economy. Arguably, current liberalisation reform will be slowly implemented, in line with Asian management model cultural notions that place high value on an incremental approach to innovation, in order to maintain collective cohesion and stability, in preference to more radical and individualised Western cultural notions for creativity and innovation (Westwood and Low, 2003).

Contemporary micro-level approaches for managing the entrepreneurial culture of Singapore

The intermixing of the unique geographic, historical and socio-cultural forces of Singapore heritage, coupled with Singapore's comprehensive government-led political and strategic national development policies, has resulted in the particular control-based managerial approach to drive the Singaporean entrepreneurial model. A consequence of this approach is high bureaucratic organisational emphasis with significant managerial focus on micro-level operational details. Arguably, this managerial approach is a cultural consequence of the Confucian-based values as strategically and sometimes coercively applied through the Singaporean state government-led social engineering development strategy. The performance criteria in both the education system and the world of work places a high value on the efficient performance of routine decisions and tasks. Nevertheless, these skills do not fulfil the creative and innovative managerial and human resource requirements of knowledge-based industries and a risk-taking entrepreneurial organisational model. The material presented in this chapter highlights government recognition of the need to transform the education system and the limitations of a 'nanny state' managerial approach. Nevertheless, investment in this kind of societal and managerial transformation will take time.

Notwithstanding, there is a high community value placed on education and with increasing local opportunities for internationalised education (off-shore and through international twinning programmes), and with the high number of MNCs now operating in Singapore, this internationalising corporate and community trend will increase the number of local managers and professionals with internationalised managerial and workplace capabilities. However, internationalised managerial systems do not indicate universalism. MNCs bring with them their home office managerial systems and styles and, in diverse MNC employment contexts, locals come face-to-face with the practical and often-alienating consequences of foreign managerial values and practices. These convergent and divergent managerial challenges indicate that training and development in these pluralistic workplace contexts will be complex. Moreover, multinational companies setting-up operations in Singapore and/or seeking partnerships and alliances with Singaporean companies need to be mindful of local Singaporean managerial organisational and workplace approaches when recruiting and setting up local training and development programs for both their home country and local Singaporean employees.

More particularly, attention needs to be paid to how the Singaporean managerial approach has characteristic consequences for the strategic level and day-to-day issues associated with, for example, leadership, decision-making, communication styles, motivation and team and individual problem solving capacity and performance. The Singaporean managerial approach shares many common characteristics of the Asian management model. A strong hierarchical notion of the social order is shared by Singaporeans and this assumption guides a hierarchical command approach to organisational management with senior management in an all-powerful top-down authority position. It has been suggested that fear of losing control (being risk-averse) and a low tolerance of failure (the influence of 'face-saving') by Singaporean business leaders underpins a low creative and innovative entrepreneurial corporate approach (Ang and Hong, 2000).

Under the logic of this prevailing hierarchical leadership there is a strong cultural assumption of strict respect for leadership. This means that conventionally senior managers and employees function in a high power-distance organisational context. In other words, leaders are expected to be strong and have a top-down and pervasive approach to directing command and control mechanisms, communication, decision-making and problem solving. A paternalistic 'father knows best' cultural assumption is applied to justify the authoritarian and hierarchical nature of the management model. These overarching values frame the Singaporean government-led 'nanny-state' approach to corporate and community development and modernisation. In accord with a strict parent family leadership model, the same party has ruled the country since independence and with this governance strategy serving to strengthen the power of the ruling elite, the government can make unpopular decisions regardless of the majority's opinion (Li, cited in Li and Karakowsky, 2002). At the organisational level this opaque approach to decision-making may be associated with collusion and corruption. The shift towards knowledge-based industries and a more risk-taking entrepreneurial corporate approach requires a more open, empowering and participative managerial approach.

A pragmatic Buddhist and Taoist-based cultural approach frames a collectivist Singaporean managerial ethos. This means that guided by the vision of a hierarchical and paternalistic leadership, through the collective application of a high work ethic and a shared moral framework, mutually agreed goals can be achieved to the advantage of all. The Singaporean government's restrictive western media and popular culture policies were designed to strengthen the particular Singaporean collectivist vision and approach. Hence, the overarching goal to value collective harmony has significant micro-level value and behaviour implications for wide-ranging interaction and interpersonal managerial and human resource issues, such as, high levels of courtesy, politeness, indirect styles of communication; concealed emotions and non-confrontational feedback approaches to 'save-face'; the ongoing need for clarification of functions and tasks; and intermixed public and private work/life dimensions. These collectivist micro-organisational approaches contrast to the egalitarian, direct, affective, intuitive and separate public and private work/life dimensions of the western micro-organisational approach. These contrasting managerial systems account for local workplace alienation and managerial perceptions of poor performance.

The family and kinship ties have played a crucial role in framing Singaporean organisational management and key human resource issues. As a significantly migrant-based community throughout its history, the family has provided a basis for the typical organisational structure. Thus, the family, coupled with a high work ethic and high saving rate, became the entrepreneurial basis for financial and human resource investment for business development. The survival and success of family-based businesses were further secured through the strengthening of wider kinship and community-based relationships. The pragmatic logic of this diaspora legacy underpins the overseas Chinese 'guangxi' networks. This micro-level approach is still an important managerial strategy for small-to-medium family-based enterprises in Singapore.

More broadly applied in this government-led and -owned corporate context, high family status is associated with the elite cadres of civil servants, senior managers and technocrats associated with the all-powerful and interlinked political and corporate sphere. Hence, the senior management and recruitment strategies of key Singaporean successful multi-industry organisations are drawn from key elite high status and powerful families. More negatively, managerial decision-making and recruitment practices associated with elitism practice can be associated with corruption and nepotism.

The risk-averse and high saving rate for wealth creation, which logically frames the Singaporean government-led managerial approach, means that security is an important motivating factor. Hence, a collective approach to this long-term and risk-averse oriented management approach underpins the CPF, which now involves community-wide and birth-to-death funds management strategies for healthcare, home ownership, family protection, assets enhancement and retirement. Thus, employment security, improved employment opportunities and monetary rewards with wider family benefits are important issues for HRM to address.

Within the Singapore managerial context, local community diversity and significant levels of multinational corporate investment mean that at the individual level pluralistic approaches to organisational management and behaviour co-exist. Nevertheless, the above discussion highlights the complexity of challenges Singapore now faces at the micro-level in transforming managerial approaches and workplace practices, to address the community's need to build the more creative and innovative managerial and professional human resource capacities, now associated with a more sustainable and competitive 'knowledge society' entrepreneurial approach framing the government's vision for the future of Singapore.

Conclusion

The innovative capacity of Singapore should not be underestimated. Reflecting the ways in which the small island's local, regional and international history, geography, politics and culture frame its governance and economic development strategies, then Deputy PM Lee HL (2004a) recently stated in a speech to the Singapore International Foundation that:

> As a small country, Singapore depends heavily on external demand and trade to survive and prosper. Our linkages with our neighbours, our region and the world are the arteries that keep the heart of our economy and society pumping. Over the years we have steadily strengthened these external linkages to establish ourselves as a key node for commerce, business, information and talent. We have developed ourselves into a major physical hub. We operate one of the busiest seaports and one of the best airports in the world. We are also a key node in the region's telecommunications network. Beyond physical connections, we have also developed strong external linkages at the Government-to-Government, Business-to business, and People-to-People levels.

This political rhetoric does indicate the multifaceted strategic political, economic, cultural and technological dimensions to Singapore's success story. With reference to international strategies, the PM also refers to the government establishment of network platforms, such as Network China and Network India, as a key technological infrastructure facility designed to encourage exchange between countries, business and individuals. Complex local, regional and international networking capacity between individuals and organisations is fundamental to a knowledge economy. This strategy suggests that the government realises the potential network resource and capacity embedded in its pluralistic national community.

Based on the current trends of political, economic and social changes, it appears that the Singapore government is moving towards adopting greater political and economic liberalisation in its strategic and operational management approach. Rhetoric from community leaders indicates that the government is reviewing the paternalistic style of governing that has arguably worked well in nation building so far. Critics argue that Singaporeans must be allowed to grow and develop in their own ways. The government needs to feel more comfortable with a more trusting relationship with the people. In other words, the Singapore government must learn the difficult task of letting go. Everyone needs to be allowed to make their choices and not to be considered as unsupportive, or a failure, for not following the convention. Learning from mistakes and thinking for oneself are essential ingredients to cultivating an entrepreneurial culture.

Acknowledging the need for this revision PM Lee HL (2004b) recently stated in a speech to the Harvard club of Singapore that:

> The Government will … continue to do its utmost to build a civil society. We will promote a political culture which responds to people's desires for greater participation in a

manner which supports Singapore's growth as a nation. But we will not ape others blindly and do something simply because it appears fashionable. We value diversity. As we engage one other and wrestle with our problems, we will encounter different views, but far better for us to manage these honest differences than become an apathetic society with no views.

In line with the paternalistic Singaporean management approach the PM then outlined his notion of 'Guidelines for public consultation'.

In addition, some argue that the government should hasten the process of privatisation by selling off its stakes in its vast network of non-strategic GLCs. This will send a very strong message to the investment community that the government is serious about making these companies more commercially accountable. Therefore, the merits of the chief executives, senior managers and directors, will be objectively assessed by the share prices of the companies. This is considered as likely to have an immediate effect on lifting the creativity and management skills of these executives.

Critics call for the incumbent ruling PAP to be more tolerant of criticisms and diversity if creativity is allowed any chance to grow and survive. The Singapore government needs to find ways within its overarching collective Asian and Confucian community assumptions to celebrate diversity and individuality. From within the society there is growing recognition that as a whole it will never fully reach maturity if it is intolerant of differences and freedom of expression. Being creative takes opportunity and practice, and for it to become second nature, Singaporeans must be encouraged to question everything, to be inquisitive, and to challenge the norm. However, emphasising that regardless of what critics say Singapore will build and manage its own economic and political future, the new PM states: 'we will have to feel our way forward, crossing the river stone by stone, to use Deng Xiaoping's phrase. But the strategic intent is clear' (Lee, 2004b). In recognition of this strategic intent, the Heritage Foundation in association with the Wall Street Journal released its annual 'Economic Freedom Rating 2005' (www.heritagefoundation.org) based on a comprehensive evaluation of the various tax and regulatory condition imposed by particular government. Singapore was the second most liberal global economy after Hong Kong (Miles et al., 2005).

Questions

1. What have been the most significant positive and negative impacts of active government intervention in Singapore?
2. Discuss the relative importance of Western and Asian management paradigms in Singapore.
3. Explain the future challenges for Singapore management, at macro-, meso-, and micro-levels.

URLs

Government and related information

Singapore Parliament	http://www.gov.sg/parliament/
Prime Minister's Office	http://www.pmo.gov.sg/
Ministry of Foreign Affairs	http://www.mfa.gov.sg/
Ministry of Home Affairs	www.mha.gov.sg
Ministry of Finance	http://www.mof.gov.sg/
Ministry of Law	http://www.minlaw.gov.sg/
Ministry of National Development	http://www.mnd.gov.sg/
Ministry of Trade and Industry	http://www.mti.gov.sg/public/home/frm_Mti_D efault.asp
Ministry of Information, Communication and the Arts	http://www.mita.gov.sg/

Economy, trading, technology

Singapore Economy	http://www.contactsingapore.org.sg/work/economy.htm
Singapore Statistics	http://www.singstat.gov.sg/PRESS/press.html
Singapore Finance	http://www.singaporefinance.com.sg
Yahoo Finance	http://sg.finance.yahoo.com/
Online Technology	http://www.online.com.sg/
Singapore Stock Exchange	http://www.ses.com.sg

News and information

Singapore News	http://www.singaporenews.com/
Straits Times	http://straitstimes.asia1.com.sg/home
Electric Newspaper	http://newpaper.asia1.com.sg/local.html
New Malaysia	http://news.newmalaysia.com/
News – Singapore	world/singapore

GLCs

Temasek Holdings	http://temasekholdings.com.sg
SingTel	http://www.singtel.com
Singapore Airlines	http://www.singaporeair.com
Singapore MRT	http://www.smrt.com.sg
Neptune Orient Lines	http://www.nol.com.sg
DBS Bank	http://www.dbs.com
SemCorp Industries	http://www.sembcorp.com.sg
Singapore Technologies	http://www.st.com.sg

Search engines

Yahoo! Singapore	http://sg.yahoo.com/
Singseek	http://www.singseek.com/
Search beat	http://www.searchbeat.com/Regional/Asia/Singapore/
E-guide	http://www.eguide.com.sg/eGuideGlobal/index.asp
Singapore Window	http://www.singapore-window.org/

References

Ang, KH, 1985, *Subcommittee report on economic development*, Economic Committee, Singapore.

Ang, SW & Hong, DGP, 2000, 'Entrepreneurial spirit among East Asian Chinese', *Thunderbird International Business Review*. vol. 42, no. 3, p. 285. Retrieved August 2005 from: Proquest Database.

ASNIC, 1994, *Singapore: History*. Retrieved 1 September 2004 from: http://recnic.utexas.edu/asnic/countries/singapore/Singapore-History

Burton, J, 2002, 'Doubts grow about the value of state businesses: Government-linked companies,' *Financial Times*, 12 April, p. 4. Retrieved 21 May 2004 from: Proquest Database.

Caplen, B, 1993, 'Putting the risk back in Singapore', *Asian Business*, vol. 29, no. 6, pp. 22–26.

China Daily, 2002, 'Gov't role in business takes new twist' 5 September, p. 6. Retrieved 21 May, 2004 from: Proquest Database.

Chew, R, 1996, 'Safety nets for entrepreneurship in Singapore', in AM Low & WL Tan (eds) *Entrepreneurs, Entrepreneurship & Enterprising Culture*, Addison-Wesley Publishing Company, Singapore, pp. 244–52.

Cho, S, 1994, 'Government and market in economic development,' *Asian Development Review*, vol. 12, no. 2, pp. 144–65.

Chua, BH, 1995, *Communitarian ideology and democracy in Singapore*, Routledge, London.

Clamer, J, 1985, *Singapore: Ideology, Society and Culture*, Chopmen Enterprises, Singapore.

Cohen, D, 1997, 'Singapore wants its universities to encourage more creativity', *The Chronicle of Higher Education*, 5 September, pp. A71–2. Retrieved 1 June, 2004 from: Proquest Database.

Dolven, B, 1998, 'Taiwan's trump', *Far Eastern Economic Review*, 6 August, pp. 12–15. Retrieved 1 June, 2004 from: Proquest Database.

Economic Development Board, 1997, *EDB Yearbook 1996/97*, EDB, Singapore.

Economist, 2004, 'Global agenda: From father to son'. 12 August, Retrieved 2 September 2004 from: http://www.economist.com.agenda/PrinterFriendly.cfm?Story_ID=3082824

Economist 2002, 'Business: Whither Singapore Inc? Face Value', 30th November, p. 68. Retrieved 3 June, 2004 from: Proquest Database.

Feng, F, Sun, Q & Tong, WHS, 2003, 'Do government-linked companies under perform?' *Journal of Banking & Finance*, article in press. Retrieved 1 June 2004 from: Science Direct.

Haley, UCV, Low, L & Toh, MH, 1996, 'Singapore incorporated: reinterpreting Singapore's business environments through a corporate metaphor', *Management Decisions*, vol. 34, no. 9, pp. 17–28. Retrieved 1 June 2004 from: Proquest Database.

Haley, UCV, 1998, 'Virtual Singapore: shaping international competitive environments through business-government partnerships', *Journal of Organizational Change Management*, Special Issue on Strategic Management in the Asia Pacific, part 1, Strategies for Foreign Investors, vol. 11, no. 4, pp. 38–56.

Haley, UCV, & Low, L, 1998, 'Crated culture: Government sculpting of modern Singapore and effects on business environments', *Journal of Organizational Change*, vol. 11, no. 6, pp. 530–47. Retrieved 21 May 2004 from: Proquest Database.

Huff, WG, 1995, 'The developmental state, government, and Singapore's economic development since 1960,' *World Development*, vol. 23, no. 8, pp. 1421–38.

Krause, LB, 1987, 'The government as an entrepreneur', in Koh AT, Krause LB & Lee TY (eds) *The Singapore Economy Reconsidered*, Institute of Southeast Asian Studies, Singapore.

Le Blond, R, 1997, 'The priorities for S'pore education system,' *The Strait Times*, January, p. 31.

Lee, DY & Tsang, EWK, 2001, 'The effects of entrepreneurial personality, background and network activities on venture growth', *Journal of Management Studies*, vol. 38, no. 4, pp. 583–602.

Lee, HL, 2004a, Speech by Deputy Prime Minister at the Third International Foundation Award. 25 April, Singapore

——, 2004b, 'Building a civic society', Speech by Deputy Prime Minister, at the Harvard Club of Singapore's Thirty-fifth Anniversary Dinner, June.

Lee, KY, 2002, 'An entrepreneurial culture in Singapore', *The Ho Rih Hwa Leadership in Asia Pacific Lecture*, 5 February, 2002. Retrieved 1 June 2004 from: http://www.mendaki.org.sg.

Lee, L, Chua, BL & Chen, J, 2004, 'Antecedents for entrepreneurial propensity and intention: findings from Singapore, Taiwan and Hong Kong', *NUS Entrepreneurship Centre Working Paper*, 2004/01.

Leitch LePoer, B, 1990, 'Singapore history'. Retrieved 1 September, 2004 from: http://www.reenic.utexas.edu/asnic/countries/singapore/Singapore-History

Lewis, R, 2003, *The cultural imperative: Global trends in the 21st century*. Intercultural Press, Yarmouth, Maine USA.

Li, J & Karakowsky L, 2002, 'Cultural malleability in an East Asian context: an illustration of the relationship between government policy, national culture and firm behaviour', *Administration and Society*. vol. 34, no. 2 pp. 176–202.

Low, L, Toh, MH, Soon, TW & Tan, KY, 1993, *Challenges and responses: Thirty years of the Economic Development Board*, Times Academic Press, Singapore.

Low, L, 1994, 'A market system with Singapore characteristics', *Master in Public Policy Working Paper Series*, Centre for Advanced Studies, National University of Singapore, November.

McNulty, S, 2000, 'Equipping a nation for the new economy', *Financial Times*, September 15, p. 12. Retrieved 19 May 2004 from: Proquest Database.

McVey, R. 1992, 'The materialization of the Southeast Asian entrepreneur', in McVey R. (ed.) *Southeast Asian Capitalists*, Cornell University Southeast Asia Program, Ithaca, pp. 7–33.

Mellor, W, 2001, 'Singapore: The risks of playing it safe; Singapore's long struggle to create an entrepreneurial environment', *Asiaweek*, 4 May, p. 1. Retrieved 19 May 2004 from: Proquest Database.

Menkhoff, T, 1993, *Trade routes, trust and trading networks – Chinese small enterprises in Singapore*, Verlag Breitenbach Publishers, Saarbrucken, Germany.

Miles, M, Feulner, E & O'Grady, M, 2005, *Executive summary*, Economic Liberalisation Rating 2005, The Heritage Foundation (pdf file). Retrieved 25 January 2005 from: www.heritage-foundation.org

Ministry of Finance, 1993, *Interim report of the committee to promote enterprise overseas*, MOF, Singapore.

Ministry of Trade and Industry, (MITI) 1986, 'The Singapore economy: new directions', *Report of the Economic Committee*, February, Singapore National Printers, Singapore.

Prystay, C, 2004, 'Singapore warms to entrepreneurs', *Wall Street Journal*, January 28, p. B. Retrieved 19 May, 2005 from: Proquest Database.

Ramirez, CD & Tan, LH, 2003, 'Singapore Inc. versus the private sector: are government-linked companies different?' *IMF Working Paper*, WP/03/156. Retrieved 17 June 2004 from http://www.imf.org.

Ray, DM, 1994, 'The role of risk taking in Singapore', *Journal of Business Venturing*, vol. 9, pp. 157–77.

'*Rethinking the Singapore model*' (n.d.). Retrieved 1 June 2004 from: http://www.sprint.net/~rwb/singapore.htm.

Rodan, G, 1989, *The political economy of Singapore's industrialization: national, state and international capital*, Macmillan Press, London.

Saywell, T, 2000, 'Thinking outside the box', *Far Eastern Economic Review*, 14 December, pp. 62–4.

Saywell, T & Plott, D, 2002, 'Re-imaging Singapore', *Far Eastern Economic Review*, 11 July, pp. 44–8.

Schein, EH, 1996, *Strategic pragmatism: The culture of Singapore's Economic Development Board*, MIT Press, Boston, MA.

Shameen, A, & Reyes, A, 2000, 'What Singapore has done right', Special Report, *Asia Week*, March 24, vol. 26, no. 11. Available at http://www.pathfinder.com/asiaweek/magazine/2000/0324/cover.2rightwrong.html

Singapore: A history of the lion city (n.d.). Retrieved 21 September 2004 from: http://hawaii.edu/cseas/pubs/Singapore/Singapore.html

Singapore census of population, 2000. 'Advanced data release no. 2 – Religion'. Retrieved from http://www.singstat.gov.sg/papers/c2000/adr-religion.pdf

Singapore Department of Statistics, 2001, *Occasional paper series – contribution of government-led companies to gross domestic product*, DOS, Singapore.

Soon, TW & Ong, LH, 2001, 'First world per capita income, but third world income structure? Wage share and productivity improvement in Singapore', *Statistics Singapore Newsletter*. Retrieved 18 June 2004 from: http://singstat.gov.sg.

Tan, BS, 2002, *Why it might be difficult for the government to withdraw from business*, 10 February. Retrieved 1 June 2004 from: http://www.sfdonline.org.

Tan, H, 1991, 'State capitalism, multi-national corporations and Chinese entrepreneurship in Singapore', in GG Hamilton (ed.), *Business Networks and Economic Development in East and South East Asia*, Centre of Asian Studies, University of Hong Kong: Hong Kong, pp. 201–16.

Tan, WCM & Tay, RST, 1994, 'Factors contributing to the growth of SMEs: The Singapore case', *Proceedings of 5th ENDEC World Conference on Entrepreneurship*; Singapore, pp. 150–61.

Toh, MH & Tan, KY (eds) 1998, *Competitiveness of the Singapore economy: a strategic perspective*, Singapore University Press and World Scientific, Singapore.

Tremewan, C, 1994, *The political economy of social control in Singapore*, St Martin's Press, New York.

Tripathi, S, 2001, 'Innocents abroad', *Asiaweek* January 19. Retrieved 1 June 2004 from: http://www.Asiaweek.com.

US Embassy, 2000, Singapore Annual Report, Singapore. Available http://www.usembassysingapore.org.sg.

Wan, P, Wee, C & Who, P, 1999, 'Establishing a successful Sino-foreign equity joint venture: The Singapore experience', *Journal of World Business*, vol. 34, no. 3, pp. 287–305.

Wang, GW, 2003. 'Diaspora, a much abused word' *Asian Affairs* interview. Retrieved 3 January 2003 from: http://www.asian-affairs.com/Diaspora/wanggungwu.html

Webb, S, 2001, 'Government-linked companies in Singapore are under scrutiny', *Wall Street Journal*, 27 December, p.C.10n. Retrieved 21 May 2004 from: Proquest Database.

Webb, S & Saywell, T, 2002, 'Untangling Temasek', *Far Eastern Economic Review*, 7 November pp. 42–5.

Westwood, R & Low, D, 2003, 'Multicultural muse: culture, creativity and innovation'. *International Journal of Cross-cultural Management*, vol. 3, no. 2, pp. 235–60

Wong, PK, Wong, F, Lee, L & Ho, YP, 2004, *Global Entrepreneurship Monitor 2003 Singapore Report*, NUS Entrepreneurship Centre, Singapore.

Wong, J, 2002, 'Small talent pool squeezes Singapore Inc.,'*Reuters News*, 1 July. Retrieved 21 May 2004 from: Factiva.

Yeung, HWC, 1998, 'The political economy of transnational corporations: a study of the regionalisation of Singaporean firms', *Political Science*, vol. 17, no. 4, pp. 389–416.

Additional readings

Chan, KB & Ngoh, CS, 1994, *Stepping out: The making of Chinese entrepreneurs*, Prentice Hall, Singapore.

Hampden-Turner, CM, 2003, 'Culture and management in Singapore', in Warner M (ed.), *Culture and management in Asia*, Routledge Curzon, London, pp. 171–86.

Lee Kuan Yew. 2000, *From third world to first: The Singapore story (1965–2000)*, Harper Collins, New York.

Rodan, G, 2004, *Transparency and authoritarian rule in Southeast Asia: Singapore and Malaysia*, Routledge Curzon, New York.

Schein, E, 1996, *Strategic pragmatism: The culture of Singapore's Economic Development Board*, MIT Press, Cambridge, MA.

Toh, MH & Tan, KY (eds), 1998, *Competitiveness of the Singapore economy: A strategic perspective*, Singapore University Press and World Scientific, Singapore.

Wee, BG (ed.), 2004, *Government-linked companies and other organizations in Singapore*, Asian Business Case Centre, Nanyang Technological University, Singapore.

Yeung, HW, 2002, 'Transnational entrepreneurship and Chinese business networks: The regionalisation of Chinese business firms from Singapore', in Menkhoff T & Gerke S (eds), *Chinese entrepreneurship and Asian business networks*, Routledge Curzon, London (pp. 159–83).

The management challenges of complex Asian nations

Two critically important and complex Asian countries: Thailand and Indonesia

Whilst the two Asian nations included in this final section of the book share some common cultural traditions and values with the preceding countries, they are also arguably different in their recent histories and economic stages of development. Both are considered developing countries, and both suffered significantly in the wake of the 1997 economic crisis. Thailand is one of the few Asian countries which was never colonised, and which has benefited from more/or less continuous political stability; whilst Indonesia was a Dutch and then a Japanese colony, and in recent years has borne the brunt of almost ongoing political and economic turmoil. The economies of both countries have been buffeted severely by recent natural disasters, and significant terrorism activities.

On the one hand, the Republic of Indonesia is a large archipelago comprised of thousands of islands, with many different ethnic groups, dialects and sub-cultures, and it has been influenced by many Asian and Western ideas and practices due to its location on the historic trade routes. The Kingdom of Thailand, on the other hand, is largely homogeneous, and comprises a relatively small land mass with a few important tourist islands. Thailand is predominantly Buddhist, whilst Indonesia is largely Muslim, but with notable Hindu and Christian sub-groups. Thus, whilst both share some Asian values with their regional neighbours, there are also significant differences which have their consequent implications for their management styles and processes.

Indonesia has a balanced industrial structure, with an important agricultural sector (14.5%), a strong manufacturing base (45%), and an emerging services sector (40.5%); Thailand has a smaller agricultural sector (9%), a similar manufacturing sector, and a significant and growing services sector (47%). Both have recently suffered significant declines in their tourism industries – in Thailand due to the 2004 tsunami in Phuket, and Islamic activities in southern Thailand; and in Indonesia, due to the tsunami in Aceh combined with terrorist bombings in Bali and Jakarta. The 'quality of life' in Indonesia and Thailand, as measured by the Human Development Index (see Chapter 1), indicates that Thailand has a higher score (76, compared with 111); and the World Competitiveness Score also rates Thailand higher (29, compared with 58). Similarly, the level of corruption in Indonesia (133) is considered more than double that of Thailand (64), but there is clear evidence that this issue is being directly addressed by the new Indonesian government.

As the following chapters illustrate, the effects of the above national characteristics of Indonesia and Thailand on their particular managerial styles and processes contain many similarities and differences with both regional and global counterparts. The final chapter in this section concludes the book with an overview of dynamic Asian management within a global marketplace.

Managing the process of continuity-in-change in Thailand

Chapter objectives

Introduction

Managers in Thailand are struggling with a process of 'continuity-in-change'. A series of global shocks have created increasing impetus for change, while the Thai socio-cultural context provides a countervailing milieu for continuity, and the maintenance of the status quo. Economic development, based on the export of manufactured goods and tourism supported by relatively inexpensive unskilled labour, served Thailand well until the 1997 economic crisis. Indeed, economic development from the mid-1970s emerged not from good corporate governance, but through the use of cheap labour, a relatively stable government, and investment by developed countries pursuing greater production efficiencies and continued economic growth. This pragmatic based investment strategy of developed countries and their multinational corporations is currently acting against Thailand's future interests, since China, India and Vietnam are now more attractive for the production of manufactured goods.

Recent events such as the 1997 Asian economic crisis, the 11 September 2001 terrorist attack, the 2003 SARS epidemic and in 2004 and on-going the Asian 'bird flu' scare and the 2004 tsunami natural disaster have prompted the government to seek long-term measures to counter their impacts. In general, the local corporate response has been to seek short-term solutions to each specific shock. As each 'crisis' passed so have more reflective concerns to improve business management and community governance. The only real reform has come from government legislation, and the increased foreign ownership and control of Thai companies.

In the long term Thailand's economic development is linked to its transition to a knowledge-based economy, but this transition is likely to be hindered by inadequate IT infrastructure, human resource capacity and social capital. Ultimately, Thai organisations may embrace more effective management systems as a pragmatic response to failing corporate governance and performance, and inadequate management systems. This is likely to happen because the Thais are more utilitarian than ideological. However, in the meantime, Thailand will continue to leverage the export of commodities (especially by the way of bilateral trade agreements) into the foreseeable future, albeit with far less extraordinary economic outcomes than were evident prior to the 1997 Asian economic crisis. In addition, investment needs to be made to protect the valuable foreign income earning capacity of the tourism sector from the negative impacts of circumstances created by terrorism, SARS, 'bird flu' and the 26 December 2004 tsunami.

The macro-regional level: Local issues and external forces influencing the management context of Thailand

The forces of heritage

This section briefly discusses how the geography and history of Thailand have shaped key cultural, political and economic dimensions of Thai society. Moreover, the discussion explains how these historical and contextual issues shape the structural and socio-cultural dimensions of contemporary Thai society, and hence, have significant implications for Thai meso-societal and micro-organisational level approaches to corporate and community governance and management. In addition, the discussion identifies how this particular Thai heritage impacts on the ways in which the Thai government and its corporate sector respond to the external forces manifest by changing macro-environmental realities.

A brief history

Thailand is centrally located in Southeast Asia and Indo-China. Its immediate neighbours are Malaysia in the south, Burma (Myanmar) in the west and north, Cambodia and Laos, in the east. It has a land area of 513,000 square kilometres (approximately the same size as France) (ARC, 2004). There are two distinct climatic zones. These are the tropical monsoons of southern Thailand and the tropical savannah in the northern mountains and plains areas.

Its geographic location places Thailand in the centre of mainland Southeast Asia, but its modern history has been unlike that of its neighbours. Its unique history has resulted in the Thai community having unique cultural characteristics in the region. In addition, its location has meant that Thailand has been shaped both by its interactions with its immediate regional neighbours, and international interactions that derive from the key historical trading routes between the East and the West that lie on the country's coastal areas. Today its central regional location presents opportunities for Thailand to take a leading role in the development of regional trade and economic cooperation. Unlike the other states of South-East Asia or Indo-China, Thailand has never come under colonial rule throughout its recorded history. It has, however, been subjected to attack at various times by neighbouring Asian countries and people (especially the Burmese) and, at times, significant areas of Thailand have been occupied by these invaders. This history explains the powerful role played by the military in shaping modern Thailand, together with its bureaucracy, political system and administrative culture.

The first attempts at nation-building by ethnic Thai communities were thought to have occurred in the thirteenth century through a strengthening of the inter-relationships between several small kingdoms made up of 'wet' irrigated rice village communities. While these ethnic Thai communities were the principal ancestors of modern Thais, other ethnic groups, including the Lao people, the Shans of Burma, and a range of upland communities in mainland Southeast Asia, such as the Black, Red and White Tais of Lao and northern Vietnam, and the Lu of Yunnan in China also became part of Thailand (Wyatt, 1984; ASEAN Focus Group, 2004). The emerging Thai kingdom was strengthened by its adaptation and incorporation of the various beliefs, ideas and techniques of the empires and states encountered on a southward movement. Thus, at this time the Thai kingdom developed important trading networks and military leaders, and probably adopted Theravada Buddhism from the Mon states in what is now central Thailand, and from the Burmese kingdom of Pagan.

> This religion accommodated itself into Tai folk traditions and animist beliefs, but it was also an institutionalised religion with a universalist worldview and a transmitter of Mon, Burmese and Sinhalese civilisation ... The principal blueprint for Tai state-builders was, however, Ankor, the great Cambodian kingdom. (ASEAN Focus Group, 2004, p. 2)

From Ankor came ideas that incorporated Indian Hindu hierarchical societal concepts, a range of arts and technologies and administrative ideas for managing large, scattered populations. The assimilation of these various historical and regional influences has important socio-cultural and political implications today.

Although not colonised by the European powers, Thailand was certainly influenced by them (particularly by the British and the French), and it was forced, at times, to concede outlying territories to neighbouring colonised states. In the latter part of the nineteenth century, American influence also developed in importance. During the second half of the twentieth century this relationship was further strengthened with American involvement in the Vietnam War and its associated concern for the spread of Communism in the region.

Known as the kingdom of Ayutthaya (also written Ayadhya) until 1767, European reports from the time described a wealthy trade centre frequented by Portuguese, Spanish, Dutch, French and English traders who interacted with Chinese, Japanese, Persian, Indian, Malay and other Asian traders (Wyatt, 1984). This strategic international trade route location and openness to trade meant that the kingdom was exposed to wide-ranging ideas and technologies. In 1767 the Ayutthaya kingdom was devastated by Burmese forces, and in response two important military leaders, Taksin, and his general Chaophraya Chakri emerged, with Taksin declaring himself king and establishing a new capital at Thonburi on the west side of the Chao Phraya River not far from the modern capital of Bangkok. After a military coup, Chaophraya Chakri was offered the throne, and accepting, Rama I (1782–1809) inaugurated a dynasty of Thai monarchs which continues until today. Rama I set about building the new capital Bangkok and contributed important military and administrative capabilities.

> Labour control now involved mass registrations and the tattooing of subjects to indicate place of residence and administrative superior. Rama I gathered about him talented officials, jurists, scholars and artists. With them he revitalised Thai culture. Their achievements included the reconstruction and reform of the sangha [nobility] hierarchy, the production of a new, definitive text of Buddhist scriptures, the complete revision of the Kingdom's laws, and the translation of numerous literary and historical works including the Indian epic Ramayana. (ASEAN Focus Group, 2004, p. 5)

While the other States of Southeast Asian were being subjugated by colonial rule, the Bangkok court was laying down the cultural and administrative basis for modern Thailand.

This brief introduction to early Thai history indicates how the key components – nation building, Buddhism and the Monarchy – were established to lay the foundation for the modern Thai nation, to Thai identity, and many of the evolving governance and economic development approaches still applied. The implications of these foundations for the more contemporary history of Thailand are now discussed. The following sections discuss the socio-cultural context, and the political and economic influences.

Socio-cultural influences

This section discusses the ways in which diverse external and internal historical, religious and environmental influences have been assimilated to shape the contemporary Thai worldview and the nation's key socio-political and economic institutions. Understanding just how these influences impact on the Thai worldview gives an explanation for the various corporate and community management strategies used in Thailand, and why individuals and groups may behave in particular ways.

Thailand is primarily a Buddhist country with approximately 90 per cent of the population Theravada Buddhists, approximately four per cent Muslim (mainly in the south, near the Malaysian border) and 0.5 per cent Christians. The Thai socio-cultural milieu has evolved from the ubiquitous influence of Buddhism (Keyes, 1987; Komin, 1991), as well as a strong agrarian base focused on the rural village community (Hirsch, 1991). 'Buddhist values, conceptions, and attitudes colour virtually all aspects of Thai life, pervading the Thai attitude toward the world in which they live' (Kirsch, 1977, p. 245). Theravada Buddhism has been particularly intense as a socio-cultural determinant because it is more than just religious expression – it is the 'emotional container of ... [a] whole way of life' (Myrdal, 1968, p. 112). This is in contrast to Mahayana Buddhism in China, Korea and Japan where Buddhism 'enters a pattern of diversity and adds to this diversity' (Slater, 1968, p. 96). It is not a national religion homogeneously unifying the life of the people; 'In China, it takes its place beside Taoism and Confucianism and is modified by both. In Japan, there is Shinto' (p. 96).

Together, Theravada Buddhism and history have resulted in the values, attitudes, and behaviours evident in Thai society today. Researchers in the fields of anthropology, sociology and psychology, as well as social commentators, have noted a number of identifiable characteristics that imbue the cultural identity of Thai people and, hence, impact on all aspects of Thai business enterprise. These multidisciplinary ideas are incorporated into the following discussion. These cultural characteristics include: high individualism, high ego, conflict avoidance, high power distance, patron–client relationships, and a present-world orientation. Each of these characteristics will be discussed separately.

Key Thai socio-cultural characteristics

● *High individualism* – Thai people are highly individualistic (Embree, 1950; Komin, 1991). This cultural characteristic contrasts with the prevailing collective orientation of other nations in the region. In explaining this characteristic the link is often made between the tenets of Buddhism which are concerned with the journey to achieving individual spiritual enlightenment, and the historical reality of never having been colonised unlike neighbouring countries. This highly individualistic classification means that the Thai people are characterised by independence, self-reliance, distrust of others, and lack of interpersonal cooperation, and has been noted in the 'careless self-reliance' of rural villagers (Benedict, 1952, p. 22): 'From early childhood, the *Ku Daeng* villager is trained toward or accustomed to individuality and self-reliance' (Kingshill, 1991, p. 58); and, 'individual autonomy is highly regarded' (Moerman, 1969, p. 542) in rural Thai villages.

As a consequence, Thai individualism leads to a lack of community and group cohesiveness, unless there is a pragmatic reason for cooperation. Hence, there is a lack of durable social units in Thai village life, such as neighbour-hood groups or voluntary associations; 'Thai villagers do not voluntarily organize themselves into groups unless there is a specific job to do' (Phillips, 1969, p. 37). '[O]ther than the nuclear family, the kindred, and the Buddhist monkhood, there are virtually no durable, functionally important groups on the local level' (Piker, 1969, pp. 62–3). Consequently, a lack of teamwork has traditionally been a major impediment to the effectiveness of the Thai bureaucracy (Prachyapruit, 1986). Similarly, the focus is on the individual in preference to team development within business enterprises (Vance et al., 1992). Associated with this individualistic characteristic, the passivity and ambivalence of the villagers for collective action were attributed to the general failure of Thai agricultural cooperative movements (Tomosugi, 1980); and 'little cooperation among equals' could be found in large Thai companies (Mabry, 1987, p. 307). In essence, the Thai people share an overarching collective national Thai identity built through loyalty to the royal family, the State apparatus and its symbols, but they are unable to identify with smaller interest groups for the sake of cooperative action. This community characteristic has crucial implications for any societal attempts to move towards a more collaborative-oriented knowledge-based economy.

● *High ego ('Face')* – Another socio-cultural characteristic of Thai people is that they are egocentric (Blanchard, 1958; Komin, 1991), and do not tolerate any affront which may be perceived as causing a loss of 'face'. This 'high ego' characteristic, associated with Chinese Confucianism, has been assimilated into Thai cultural logic through the movement of ideas and people from the Northeastern Asian side of Thailand, along with the significant number of immigrant Chinese, who have historically always made up a large proportion of the population. Under the influence of this characteristic, Thai people have a propensity for 'form over content' (Mulder, 1994).

High ego manifests in behaviour such as the attainment of educational qualifications by rote learning, expensive cars and the acquisition of status clothes by the neo-middle class, and a national obsession with grooming, hair-style, and vanity. It is associated with the possession of something not for its intrinsic and utilitarian value, but for its ascribed status. As an example, an international solar water heater manufacturer identified that the way to create high sales volume of its product in Thailand was to colour it gold and install it on the most visible position on a building. From this Thai high ego perspective, society is viewed as a stage where the individual acts out his, or her, perception of self based on hierarchical position (Mulder, 1994). It is apparent that this characteristic links to the power of vertical structural management systems and the systemic nature of this structure has cultural implications for mobilising institutional and corporate reform.

● Social harmony and '*Krengjai*' – Closely associated with high ego, criticism is perceived as an attack upon the ego, and as such, is to be avoided at all costs.

The Thai find themselves psychologically uncomfortable with interpersonal conflict, instilling an innate desire for social harmony. This desire underpins a 'social cosmetic' of politeness, which has the effect of minimising a person's impact on another while maximising each person's 'sense of psychic independence and integrity' (Phillips, 1965, pp. 66–7). *Krengjai* is the Thai word used to describe the restraint applied to inherent individualism in order to avoid conflict with others – a 'culturally constituted defence mechanism' against the anxiety induced by social interaction (Mentzer and Piker, 1975, p. 36); a 'respect for superiors with humility and obedience to authority' (Mole, 1973, p. 74); a high value for social harmony stifles individual initiative, and involves an emotional repression which must ultimately find an outlet. Thus, if a Thai feels affronted, overt confrontation is typically circumvented by surreptitious techniques such as covert uncooperativeness, spiteful gossip, projected vilification or anonymous assault at night (Hanks and Phillips, 1961; Klausner, 1997).

Confrontation avoiding behaviour has implications for communication in Thai organisations. For example, effective communicators 'know how to communicate so as to avoid conflict with others, display respect, control their emotions, tactfulness, modesty, and politeness' (Sriussadaporn-Charoenngam and Jablin, 1999, p. 409). While this may have the effect of reducing organisational conflict (Sheehan and Huvanandana, 2002), it also stifles open communication. Moreover, this communication style is at odds with the open, collaborative and problem-solving orientation of knowledge-based economies.

- *High power distance* – Buddhist teaching promotes an inherent link between *karma*, goodness, right-to-rule, wealth, power and authority, which is symbolised and perpetuated in national discourse by the monarchy and the bureaucracy. These values percolate down from the top through all levels of Thai society to legitimise political aspirations and economic goals. A fundamental precept of Buddhism is that the honest acquisition of wealth and power is not immoral, provided it is used to altruistic ends. In Thai life power is the central manifestation from which wealth is perceived to deservedly emanate (Mulder, 1994).

The foundations for Thai social hierarchy were noted in the thirteenth century as being prominent (Kirsch, 1984). In the fifteenth century, King Trailok formalised a system of social hierarchy under the name of *sakdina*, which quantified social ranking into a measurable variable ranging from 100,000 for the *nai* (noble), to 25 to 10 for the *phrai* (commoner), and 5 for a *that* (beggar). The formalised *sakdina* system eventually broke-down after the Ayutthaya period (1767). Informal patron-client relationships skewed the accumulation of wealth and power held by the *nai*, and threatened the power of the monarchy (Phongpaichit and Baker, 1995). However, 200 years of the *sakdina* system has indelibly forged on the Thai psyche a fundamental belief that each person has a place in a hierarchy of unequals.

Importantly, however, those holding positions of power must carefully exercise their authority in accordance with the traditional concepts of *pradej* and *prakhun* (Sangchai, 1976). *Pradej* is the use of force, or influence used to induce fear, while *prakhun* is the use of benevolence to induce respect and gratitude. Balancing *pradej* and *prakhun* provides a leader with *baramee* that is the power and strength that derive from respect and loyalty. This interpretation of the role of power has implications for a benevolent-paternalistic Thai style of management.

● *Patron-client relationships (Boon Koon)* – Patron-client relationships are a common social force throughout East and Southeast Asia. They maintain the social order via networks of micro units of society, rather than via institutions, such as universal law. Thai patronage (described as superficial, affectively neutral and expedient) 'differs from the more diffuse, affective (though not necessarily harmonious), and value-based vertical relationships of traditional patriarchal Chinese social organisation' (Deyo, 1978, p. 69). Indeed, the patron–client system permeates all levels of Thai society. It is an integral part of rural village life (Piker, 1983), and of Thai politics from the national to the local level (Neher, 1979). Patron–client relationships exist because institutional links are weak, and much inequality in wealth and power exists. Consequently, people think in hierarchical terms; 'subordinates seek to please their bosses, and people expect to do and to receive favors' (Gohlert, 1991, p. 18). 'The coherence of Thai society rests largely on the value of becoming a client of someone who has greater resources than one alone possesses' (Hanks, 1962, p. 1249).

Vertically oriented patron-client relationships in business enterprises inhibit the formation of horizontal cooperative networks. They give rise to 'entourages' and 'circles' of conflicting interests (Hanks, 1975), which ultimately result in the segmentation of organisations based on departments, the absence of a performance orientation, and a major hindrance to effective group functionality.

● *Present-world orientation* – The ultimate doctrinal Buddhist goal of escaping *karma*, the extinguishment of life, and the attainment of *nirvana*, is the reason why Buddhism is often characterised as radically other-worldly (Kirsch, 1977). However, Thai people do not, in general, aspire to attain the abstract religious goal of *nirvana* in this life, but instead, aspire to a more proximate version of an enhanced rebirth status (Kirsch, 1977). It is *karma* and rebirth, not *nirvana* that forms the fundamental populist concept of Buddhism (Klausner, 1964; Mole, 1973; Keyes, 1977) inculcating an 'indestructible conviction that existence is good' (Benedict, 1952, p. 34). Hence, Thai people are secularly concerned and present-worldly, 'they are not mystically inclined, and the elaborate Indian physical techniques of inducing contemplation are absent' (Benedict, 1952, p. 35), and are 'little concerned with general abstractions; they live in the 'here and now', which they try to make as comfortable and free of problems as possible' (Barry, 1967, p. 121). This worldview results in narrow temporal interests with 'concern being expressed chiefly for the immediate past and the immediate future' (Sharp, 1950, p. 160) and highlights a 'lack of emphasis on long term obligations' (Embree, 1950, p. 105).

The present-world orientation leads to a high value placed on opportunism in Thai business. For example, Thais tend to take advantage of opportunities when they arise, but they would seldom take the trouble to create such opportunities or cooperate with others in such an endeavour (Ayal, 1963). Thus, opportunism pervades both Thai village life (Kingshill, 1991) and business organisations. Thai executives have been found to place little weight on synergy in evaluating the acquisition of target firms, looking rather at the short-term opportunity (Park, 1997). Likewise, career planning programmes are either non-existent, or unsystematic in most firms (Siengthai and Bechter, 2004).

This discussion on the various Thai socio-cultural characteristics is useful to understand Thai management structures, systems and styles, because, in general, these characteristics are shared by the population at large. While there will be individuals in most communities who hold diverse and idiosyncratic values based on diverse life experiences, together these widely shared socio-cultural characteristics contribute to a homogeneous collective Thai worldview. This Thai worldview gives explanation for the values and behaviour of individuals and groups in Thai society, the bureaucracy and the corporate sector.

Socio-cultural homogeneity

Much of the evidence of Thai society and culture discussed above has been derived from anthropological and sociological sources involving research on rural Thai villages. A high degree of culture pattern consistency is evident across the rural population (Blanchard, 1958; Mizuno, 1975). However, the question remains as to the degree of homogeneity evident in Thai society as a whole, including urban Bangkok with its large ethnic-Chinese base.

Urban Bangkok culture has been heavily influenced by the traditional rural base, and the ubiquity of Theravada Buddhism. Few differences identified in the value orientations of Thai Buddhists and Thai Christians support a general notion of Thai socio-cultural homogeneity (Sensenig, 1975; Hughes, 1984). More particularly, Buddhism has laid the foundations of a Thai socio-cultural worldview, and hence, Buddhist values underpin the social norms which frame individual behaviour. As a measure of the strength of the Buddhist societal underpinnings, Christians unconsciously adopt the social norms historically rooted in the dominant Buddhist ideology. It is, however noteworthy that increasing urbanisation, higher levels of education and rising affluence, have contributed to a greater diversity of attitudes towards religion, including ambivalence (ASEAN Focus Group, 2004).

The other issue that may impact on the homogeneity of Thai society is the presence of significant numbers of ethnic Chinese. Between 1882 and 1950, 1.11million Chinese immigrated to Thailand, mostly from the southern Chinese provinces of *Guangdong* and *Fukien*, and belonging to the *Teochiu* dialect group (Coughlin, 1960). While historically there has been constant regional movement and settlement by the Chinese, significant Western mercantile expansion provided commercial opportunities that were a catalyst for the Chinese diaspora to the Southeast Asian region. Other reasons for emigration include the regularity of natural disasters, overcrowding, and general economic adversity (Coughlin, 1960).

The Chinese diaspora to Thailand has resulted in 8 per cent of the population of the country, and 35 per cent of the population of Bangkok, being ethnic Chinese (Smalley, 1994). Despite early ostracism, the integration of the Chinese into Thai society has been highly successful because of religious compatibility, the high rate of intermarriage, and the Thai willingness to accept outsiders (Coughlin, 1960; Keyes, 1987). Intermarriage was historically accepted at the highest social levels. For example, Taksin, who ruled the kingdom from 1767 to 1782, had a Thai mother and a Chinese father, and Rama I (1782–1809) who replaced Taksin after a coup, had a Chinese mother and a Thai father. Indeed, in Thailand, the integration and assimilation has been far more complete than in most other Southeast Asian countries. By the 1950s, most third-generation ethnic Chinese had taken up Thai citizenship, had Thai names, spoke Thai as a first language, and practised Thai-style Theravada Buddhism (Skinner, 1957). Confucian values have also become far less prominent in Thai society than in other ethnic-Chinese countries, such as Taiwan and Hong Kong (Hofstede and Bond, 1988). This integration reduced the work values of the Thai ethnic-Chinese (Coughlin, 1960). The cultural, linguistic and regional links of the ethnic-Chinese in Thailand have implications for future strengthening of economic relations between Thailand and the Peoples Republic of China.

Socio-cultural change

Another important issue for consideration is the degree of socio-cultural change now evident since the early anthropological rural peasant village research was undertaken. Moreover, this early research was based on the methodological assumption of a closed system. Contrary to this assumption, rural peasant society was described as being a 'half-society' and 'half-culture' (Redfield, 1956) which suggests openness to external influences, and therefore, to socio-cultural change.

The discussion on the early history of Thailand indicates that rather than being a closed system, the assimilation and appropriation of external influences, ideas, technologies and people has been more characteristic. Utility has been the primary driving force in the Thai acceptance of Western culture (Phitakspraiwan, 1967). For example, medical practices, systems of administration and technology have been readily accepted, while Christianity has been firmly rejected as inferior. This indicates that borrowing has been selective – 'the Thai responded to Western ways pragmatically, not ideologically' (p. 199). This selective incorporation of external cultural influences underpins the notion that Thai socio-culture is evolving in a process of 'continuity-in-change', in which fundamental local cultural traits, while largely retaining their original function, are constantly being reinterpreted and loosely redefined (Cohen, 1991, p. 142) – 'Thai culture appears marked by the persistence of the traditional and not by any marked tendency to break with it' (Siffin, 1966, p. 150). Hence, a present-world Thai orientation uses past tradition and selected cultural externalities to adapt to modernity, while placing little emphasis on the future. Consequently, this social conservatism leaves little room for a dynamic model for change in Thailand. This conservative cultural approach impacts on governance and management issues, such as reform of the bureaucracy, corporate governance, the privatisation of the business sector and human resource capacity development.

Political and economic influences

As previously mentioned, while Thailand's regional neighbours were being shaped by European colonisers, Thailand was independently building a modern national identity and economic development. During the nineteenth century many of the nobility and royal court were studying science, mathematics, Western languages and military strategies and technology in the West, and so the country reoriented towards the West for both ideas and trade. This modernisation strategy and the incorporation of international business meant that, aside from territorial concessions to the colonial French in the north and the British in northern Malaya, the core of the kingdom's territory was secure. As an important primary producer for the world market by the early twentieth century the country was producing 70 per cent of the world rice and other products such as tin, rubber and teak (ASEAN Focus Group, 2004).

Thailand became a constitutional monarchy in 1932. The present monarch (1946 to the present), King Bhumipol Adulayadej (Rama IX), is the longest serving monarch. He is dearly loved by his people. On several occasions the king has interceded against the heavy hand of the government in support of the people – the most recent time being during the pro-democratic student protests for reform in the 1992 when the government ordered the military to fire on the students. The fact that the king still has to act as a mediator between the government and the people underpins both international and local concern for long-term political stability in Thailand.

The name of the country was changed from Siam in 1939 as a nation-building strategy because this was the name given to Thailand by Europeans. Since 1932, Thailand, while nominally being a democracy, has endured many benevolent and paternal, but at times extremely autocratic, military dictatorships. There were a series of successful and unsuccessful military coups, usually bloodless, however, not always so. In the 60 years since the establishment of constitutional monarchy in 1945, Thailand had only six or seven years of democratically elected governments (i.e., not under military control). In 1977 during student pro-democracy riots the King gave the students protection. In response, the largely military-based government leadership conceded to adopt a 'managed democracy' style of governance (ASEAN Focus Group, 2004). The Thai political system came under international criticism and scrutiny after international television audiences witnessed the Thai army firing on pro-democracy protesting students in 1992. In this case the more powerful weapon was private video cameras. Thus, since 1995 the governments have been elected democratically.

Over most of the last 30 years, until the Asian financial crisis of 1997, Thailand's economy was one of rapid growth and development, particularly in the late 1980s, and early 1990s. Initially, this growth was based on an economic policy of import replacement, but from the mid 1970s, an economic policy of export promotion took over. This economic policy still largely applies today. The seeds of this more recent economic development strategy link historically back to previous governance and management successes, also achieved through an international export-orientation. The Asian financial crisis, which became apparent first in Thailand in mid-1997, had a profound and a prolonged effect on the Thai economy, which saw significant negative growth in 1997 and 1998. It has only been since the election of the *Thai Rak Thai* party under the prime ministership of Dr. Thaksin Shinawatra in January, 2001, that substantial economy recovery has occurred. This success may be threatened by recent political disruption, including the unseating of the Shinawatra government in 2006, and ethnic unrest in southern Thailand.

Global imperatives: Macro environmental management issues

Thailand is divided into 76 provinces, although there are six major regions – the Northern Region, Central and Western Region, Southern Region North Eastern Region, Eastern Region and Bangkok and vicinities. The Thai landscape is dominated by a large and highly fertile rice-growing central plain, but the topography is varied from the relatively high mountains in the north west and north (the 'Golden Triangle' area), the dry plains in the northeast, and the forest areas (once extensive but now much reduced by over-logging) of the southern peninsula. Thus, a rich natural resource-base coupled with cheap labour costs built the successful agricultural productivity that underpinned Thailand's early successful export-oriented economic growth strategy. Today, 49 per cent of the total Thai workforce is still involved in the agricultural sector (*Bangkok Post*, September 2004).

In addition, the rich socio-cultural and heritage values of the Thailand provide the resources for the now important Thai tourism sector. This service industry sector has become a major contributor to foreign capital and the recent growth of employment in the services sector means that it currently employs 34 per cent of the total workforce. Only 14 per cent of the workforce is employed in manufacturing industries (*Bangkok Post*, September 2004).

Nevertheless, in the 1980s and early 1990s, in pursuit of a more intense manufacturing production strategy and on the basis of an export-orientation and cheap labour, the Thai economy boomed, so much so that for three to four years it had the fastest growing economy in the world (Phonpaichit and Baker, 1995). However, by the mid-1990s, Thailand had to face the competitive impact of the rapid growth and integration of the global economy which forced local firms to improve their production technological capabilities to meet international quality production standards. In addition, the comparative advantage of cheap labour rapidly eroded with the opening up of other Asian economies particularly, the People's Republic of China (PRC) where labour rates were initially one-sixth of those in Thailand.

The erosion of Thailand's competitive position eventually led to the financial crisis, which was instigated with the floating of the baht in July 1997. This resulted in a significant fall in foreign direct investment (FDI) in Thailand, and a significant repatriation of foreign capital. Finally, the International Monetary Fund (IMF) was called in. Although the IMF helped to improve the foreign reserves position and to stabilise the exchange rate, the enforced austerity measures also contributed to considerable stagflation and negative economic growth, many technical and actual bankruptcies of Thai firms and takeovers by foreign partners. The fall in the value of the baht led to cheaper local suppliers, but these suppliers were forced to meet international production standards in order to remain competitive. Factor productivity had begun to fall in the early 1990s. As a result, substantial investment in training to upgrade design and engineering skills is urgently required. This investment requirement includes increasing both Research and Development, and spending on the training of labour.

A World Bank (Pomerleano, 1998) comparative review of the interest coverage ratio for companies in 12 countries and Latin America concluded that Latin American companies were quite modestly indebted; companies in developed countries (e.g., United States, Germany, France and Japan) were moderately indebted; and companies in several Asian developing countries (e.g., South Korea, Indonesia and Thailand) were severely in debt. Debt levels were an important contributing factor to the Asian economic crisis of 1997, as illustrated in Figure 9.1.

The successive governments since 1997 have been forced to address these various economic management issues. In the immediate aftermath of the crisis, many Thai firms were closed or taken over by foreign partners, and significant

Figure 9.1 Average interest coverage ratio, 1996

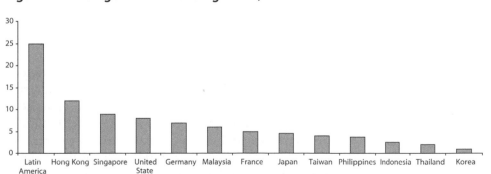

Source: World Bank staff calculations based on the Financial Times Information's Extel database.

Note: Ratio of operating cash flows (operating income before interest, taxes, and depreciation) to interest payable on loans.

unemployment resulted. In 1998, Thailand had a negative GDP growth rate of approximately 10 per cent, eliminating much of the country's earlier prosperity. After several years of low (or negative) economic growth, Dr. Thaksin Shinawatra became Prime Minister in January 2001.

Like the leaders in Malaysia and Singapore, Thaksin has an international education that includes Masters and PhD (Sam Houston State University, Texas) qualifications in Criminal Justice. After a career in policing in the late 1980s he successfully built a silk fabric business based in Chiang Mai, and later launched a range of telecommunications businesses that evolved into a huge telecommunications empire, supported by the accumulation of state monopolies. This background meant that he brought a CEO style of leadership to his government strategies, and hence, the range of economic policies introduced during his government are referred to as 'Thaksinomics'.

With increasing international concern for the impact of terrorism, the Thai government faces important security issues associated with uprisings in the southern region which borders with Malaysia where intelligence has identified the presence of fundamental Islamic terrorist cells. This region is where the majority of the Islamic people, who make up four per cent of the population, are located. A holistic examination of these potentially destabilising regional community issues is required.

> Southern Muslims are not stupid. They know that violence disrupts the lucrative tourism industry, oil exploration and grand plans for a canal across the isthmus (cancelled on March 30th after the Pattani massacre) ... Contrary to what may be the perception of some of the south, in Yala Province, one of the affected provinces, is Yala city – Thailand's only planned city, which is renowned for its cleanliness and order. The Royal Family has long been involved in encouraging southern social integration with frequent visits ... The regional Royal Palace was built in Narathiwas especially for this purpose. Scores of rural development schemes and economic plans, however, have failed to stem distrust of the central government. (Bodley, 2004b, p. 1)

These comments highlight the ways in which complex historical, cultural, political and economic issues interweave to create complex governance and management issues at the macro-societal level in Thailand.

They also highlight the pivotal and historical role of the Royal Family in placating unrest and acting as a 'neutral' mediator between conflicting government, corporate and community interests. Confirming the pivotal societal leadership role of the Royal Family, in the response to the ongoing unrest and violence in the South, Queen Sirikit recently 'urged people from all walks of life to unite in their efforts to douse the southern security inferno as an expression of gratitude to the motherland' (*Bangkok Post*, 17 November 2004): 'Please don't dump everything on the government. Every Thai has a duty to work for the country' (Queen Sirikit, cited by Reuters, 17 November 2004).

At the time academics called on the government to stop using military force to put down demonstrations and establish a national committee to draw up a long-term, non-violent strategy to establish peace. One university economics lecturer suggested that Prime Minister Thaksin go on a Gandhi-style three-day fast to protest the killings and urged him to state the date for a ceremony where all sides would apologise (*Bangkok Post*, 15 November 2004). These responses indicate the ways in which political, economic and cultural spheres are intermeshed together and how these societal spheres positively and negatively contribute to the complex environment of business and community management. Moreover, the increasingly deteriorating sectarian situation in the south confirms that in order to order for the nation to maintain political stability and sustain economic development, it is time for the government and people of Thailand to understand the ways in which traditional national and local corporate and community macro-level governance and management strategies either support, or hinder, these objectives.

The meso-societal level: The management of Thai institutional infrastructure

Industrial infrastructure

This section discusses some of the key governance and management structures, systems and styles currently operating at the meso-level in Thailand, and the kind of economic and political management strategies applied by the Thaskin government in order to rebuilt the rate of economic performance the country achieved prior to the 1997 economic crisis. The measures implemented since then have become popularly and interchangeably known as 'Thaksonomics' and 'Thailand Inc'.

Thasinomics and Thailand Inc.

Since PM Thaksin was elected in 2001 there has been strong revenue growth due largely to Thailand's continued success in the export sector. Economic growth was only 1.9 per cent in 2001, 5.3 per cent in 2002, 6.4 per cent in 2003 and 6.5 per cent for 2004 (NESDB, 2004). The Thaksin government's popularist economic management policies have successfully improved economic growth leading to an upsurge in producer and consumer confidence. However, growth is still uneven and not broadly based, with many industrial sectors remaining in a relatively weak economic state.

Thaksin was once personally ranked amongst the world's top billionaires by *Forbes* magazine. The telecom tycoon-cum-politician has already come to be regarded by foreign communities and the international media as the next leader of ASEAN (Maneerungsee, 2004). His outward looking regional and international economic policy approach 'aims to build up "Asianism", turning Asia into a huge economic bloc' (Maneerungsee, 2004) through the development of a range of cooperative political policy and trade agreements. He has been attributed with the coveted Asian catch phrase 'visionary' (Bodley, 2004a).

Table 9.1 Top 10 export sectors (2004) in Thailand

	Billion US$	% Change
Computers and components	9.3	7.3
Electrical circuits	5.7	29.2
Vehicles, accessories and parts	5.0	36.4
Clothing	3.4	2.3
Rubber	3.2	61.7
TVs, radios and parts	3.1	16.2
Gems and jewellery	3.1	13.6
Canned and processed seafood	2.7	10
Plastic pellets	2.6	18.2
Steel and related products	2.3	40
Total	**56.8**	**15.6**

Source: Thai Commerce Ministry.

Table 9.2 Farm sector outlook in Thailand

Sector	GDP by sector (million baht) *2003	2004F	Growth (%) 2004 F
Crops 484,704	510,051	5.28	
Livestock	61,879	66,205	7.60
Fisheries	179,268	192,557	7.41
Forestry	6,046	5,996	-0.83
Services	13,926	14,327	2.88
Simple processed products	69,874	75,329	7.83
Total (1)	815,698	864,465	6.07
■ Food and processed products (2)	274,255	302,719	10.38
Total (1) + (2)	1,089,954	1,187,185	7.15
■ Non-farm sector	4,886,924	5,266,015	8.19
■ Total GDP	5,956,878	6,433,200	8.00

Source: Thai Office of Agricultural Economics.
Notes: * estimates, F = forecast.

Exports have been the growth leader, increasing over 12 per cent in 2003. There has also been a significant growth in regional trade. Top commodity export sectors are shown in Table 9.1. The growth of the agricultural sector has also increased significantly in 2003 to 2004, largely due to higher world prices for agricultural products (see Table 9.2).

The tourism and hospitality industry is Thailand's second largest foreign income earner (in 2004), with 11 million tourists generating revenue of 340 billion baht (approximate US$8.5 billion) (ARC, 2004). Tourism throughout Asia suffered as a result of 11 September 2001 and following regional terrorist attacks, and then declined in 2003 with the SARS epidemic. An important political concern that intensified in 2003/2004 is the significant terrorism activity in southern (largely Muslim) Thailand. This recent terrorism intensity coupled with possible international terrorist group linkages are a worrying concern for business. If constructive dialogue between the Thai government and insurgent groups (such as the Pattani United Liberation Organisation – PULO) eventuates, then terrorism is unlikely to impact significantly on Thai business. However, if such activity escalates beyond the southern provinces, major economic impacts could eventuate – 'An incident like the Bali bombing, for example, would devastate Thailand's tourism industry, which accounts for more than 7 per cent of GDP' (Pongsudhirak, 2003, p. 29).

The devastating regional tsunami on 26 December 2004 dealt a significant blow to the tourist sector in the six affected coastal Provinces. The high numbers of Western tourists who were victims was widely profiled in the international media. At the same time media discussion highlighted widespread recognition of the importance of tourism for the local Thai economies and improving welfare of the local people. Hence, the importance of tourists returning to the region was promoted both internationally and nationally. The Tourism Authority of Thailand anticipated losses of 4 million baht per month across the six affected Provinces (*Bangkok Post*, 2005). This loss is expected to adversely impact on the overall economic growth of Thailand to the extent that the economic growth forecasts for 2005 have been cut from 6.3 per cent to 5.6 per cent. Apart from the community costs associated with the loss of life and the scale of human tragedy caused by the enormous natural disaster, the business perceives that the impact will only be short-term adversity in certain sectors. Moreover, there is a general feeling that economic growth in Thailand is unlikely to be affected beyond one year (*Bangkok Post*, 2005). With the diversity of external and local issues repeatedly impacting on the performance of the tourism sector over recent times, it is becoming increasingly apparent that both the Thai government and international and local business investors need to apply more sustainable development strategies for managing risk.

FDI in Thailand has continued to grow, although there are concerns about the continuation of this, given the high investment demands and investment attractiveness, of the PRC. Nevertheless, as Thailand's competitiveness has improved, so too has the investment outlook. The upsurge in consumer confidence has also

Table 9.3 Regional debt levels and household debt (2002)

	Thailand	Malaysia	S. Korea
Household debt to GDP (%)	27.2	66.3	73.6
Household debt to disposal income (%)	51.0	73.5	83.1

Source: Bank of Thailand

fuelled economic performance, despite concerns about the rapidly growing levels of consumer debt. While household debt has increased significantly, it is still lower than other Southeast and East Asian countries (see Table 9.3).

Thailand has been one of the most active countries in developing bilateral free trade agreements (FTAs), primarily as a strategy to further develop export growth. The following FTAs have been signed or are in negotiation:

● Bahrain in 2002 on the basis that it is expected to become a gateway to the Gulf countries;

● China concluded discussion in June 2003 only eliminating tariffs on vegetables and fruits and, paving the future way for a full FTA;

● India signed a framework in October 2003 with both countries agreeing to impose a zero-tariff rate of all goods and remove non-tariff barriers by 2010;

● Peru signed a framework agreement for closer economic cooperation in October 2003, and is expected to be concluded by 2005. Thailand sees Peru as a gateway to initiate bilateral trade talks with other Latin American countries;

● Australia signed a Closer Economic Relations and Free Trade Agreement (CER-FTA) in July 2004;

● Japan is negotiating a proposed Closer Economic Partnership (CEP), however, has been reluctant because of the inclusion of tariff cuts on some agricultural items (e.g., rice and chicken); and

● United States signed a Trade and Investment Framework Agreement (TIFA) in October 2002 with the two countries expecting to start negotiations for an FTA in early-2005. The FTA with the United States is expected to be more complicated than Thailand's FTA with other partners, because it will cover not only tariff reductions to all traded goods, but would also include an insistence that Thailand amend intellectual property rights, customs procedures, and foreign ownership laws.

Thailand has been involved in trade talks with Canada, Taiwan and New Zealand.

Critics note that the privatisation of state enterprises has moved at a snail's pace and that labour union resistance is growing (Parnsoonthorn, 2004). The government's privatisation plan aimed to apply the operational, financial and strategic restructuring of 59 state enterprises before they were privatised. More than three years into the government's term only three state enterprises have been privatised and have listed their shares (ibid). One of the key community concerns is the issue of transparency in the privatisation process.

Thailand has gradually improved its international ranking from fortieth in 2000 to twenty-ninth in 2004 and this improvement has largely been attributed to the government's macro-economic policies (IMD, 2004). Criticisms of Thaksin's 'CEO-Style' management of the country suggest that Dr Thaksin's style of administration does not fit the reality of Thai society, since the country is not a corporation where the employer always dominates employees (Anderson, 2004). The CEO administration cannot dismiss the citizenry, or shake the inert bureaucracy which can block executive orders in practice, despite the leaders' good intentions. Despite criticisms, Thailand was recently positioned at the twentieth easiest international country with which to do business in a World Bank report to be released in 2005.

Corporate governance

Capitalist development in Thailand from the 1960s was dominated by a 'tripod structure', including state-owned enterprises, multinational corporations and ethnic-Chinese private business groups (Akira, 1996). At the time of the economic crisis, about 150 leading Thai families controlled most Thai business activity, and most of these were ethnic Chinese. Indeed, Thailand follows the pattern of the dominance of business by the overseas Chinese in Southeast Asia. Thailand's population is eight per cent ethnic-Chinese (Smalley, 1994) and yet they control 60 per cent of trade (Chen, 2001). Hence, the vast majority of Thai business is controlled by ethnic-Chinese families, where corporate governance is the domain of family members.

A major factor contributing to the 1997 economic crisis has been attributed to poor corporate governance and 'crony capitalism'. Concentrated ownership of large corporations is considered to lead to inefficient investment, with excessive diversification and risk-taking (Alba et al., 1998). Furthermore, powerful *guanxi* and *boon koon* reciprocity networks pervade Thai commercial activity. This is often condemned as 'cronyism, collusion, corruption and complacency', and seen as expressing the 'dark side' of Thai business (Sila-On 1999, cited in Andrews and Chompusri, 2001, p. 80). Despite the economic crisis, about 80 per cent of the same leading ethnic-Chinese families and commercial groups still survive (Akira and Wailerdsak, 2004). However, one positive aspect of the crisis has been that it opened up many sectors of the economy to greater overseas investment, ownership and control. Many important commercial and industrial sectors are now substantially foreign owned, including retailing, some areas of banking and finance, and some of the major export industries, such as motor vehicle and computer parts manufacturing.

Since 1997, the Stock Exchange of Thailand (SET) has established audit committees, set provisions for independent directors and protection of minority shareholders, issued corporate governance guidelines, and set standards for performance-based evaluation of companies. In a recent scorecard on corporate governance in Southeast Asia (*Singapore companies top disclosure survey*, 2004) companies were graded according to international best practices, such as disclosure and the independence of the Boards of Directors. On a scale of 0 to 140, Singapore scored 80 (the highest in Southeast Asia), Malaysia 65 and Thailand 37. Despite the SET initiatives, the corporate scorecard results attest to the relative inadequacy of corporate governance in Thailand.

In summary, then, while significant government reforms have been implemented since the 1997 economic crisis, Thai management at the meso-level is still problematic in many respects. The period 2002 to 2004 has seen a sharply revived economy, with high export growth and high local demand. But the investment future is still uncertain, and there is a fear that strong economic growth will not be able to be sustained over the longer-term. There is also a fear that the need for fundamental reform to management practices, which became apparent in the economic crisis, will be largely ignored or forgotten as a result of the current improvements in economic performance, and that Thailand could face another economic 'crisis' in the not so distant future.

The micro-organisational level: Critical traditional, transitional and transformational issues in Thai management

It is apparent that there are a range of critical issues that Thailand must address at the micro-level of management in order to build pathways to greater effectiveness and so improve and sustain economic and community development in a dynamic and competitive regional and global market economy context. Key issues identified as being crucial in building both the infrastructure and capacity to build competitive advantages and facilitate the transition to a knowledge-based economy include: operational issues, financial management issues, human resource management issues, strategic government policy reform and development issues and information technology management. The development of this requisite infrastructure and capacity has significant implications for improving performance at the micro management level. This section discusses these key management and governance issues.

Operational issues

Ethnic-Chinese family businesses (the 'overseas Chinese') continue to play an important role in business in Thailand. Not only are many SMEs owned and operated as Thai–Chinese family businesses but some very large, partly public companies are still controlled by Thai–Chinese families (e.g., Charoen Pokphand, Siam Cement and Bangkok Bank). However, some commentators doubt the ability of such firms to survive or, prosper, in an era of globalisation. The role of the middleman, and the reliance on *guanxi* relationships by Chinese family businesses have been traditional strengths of business in Asia (Lobbato, 2000). However, for the success of these companies to continue, a change in mindset is required, since under the competitive influences of globalisation the historical environment in which they flourished is rapidly changing.

Since 1997, many Asian countries have learnt that they need to reform, restructure and strengthen their business models to cope with increased competition, and the opportunities offered by the new economy. Indeed, some of the larger Thai firms have embarked on corporate reform and introduced more Western-style decision-making processes, empowerment and transparency. Nevertheless generally, ethnic-Chinese family businesses have yet to adapt to issues such as globalisation, e-commerce, and liberalisation. Three criteria for ethnic-Chinese family businesses to survive and thrive in the coming years are suggested (Lobbato, 2000, p. 125):

- decentralise the decision-making process in order to move away from a command and control system to a people-centred management strategy;

- invest more in human resources and provide opportunities for staff who are not family members to be able to rise to the top of the management structure; and,

- embrace e-commerce to enable firms to reach global suppliers and customers at lower cost.

Financial management issues

Socio-cultural factors, as well as the ownership and control structure of Thai businesses, have meant that transparency of decision-making in financial operations is largely absent. Indeed, cronyism remains a prominent feature of Thai business, despite recent global shocks. Another aspect of the economic crisis was that the Thai banking sector was left with significant levels of non-performance loans (NPLs), and it has only been in relatively recent times (some years after the crisis) that NPLs have been brought under some sort of control. Nevertheless, there are still significant business debts, which still have not been settled. As a result of these high levels of NPLs Thai commercial banks have generally been reluctant to lend. The recent rise in credit and consumer spending has largely been due to credit card lending, and the Thai commercial banking sector has continued to be reluctant to lend for business and commercial operations. To some extent, this has been overcome by commercial lending from the government banking sector.

Liquidity conditions in the banking and financial sector remain unbalanced, with banks holding greater deposits than are needed to meet loan demand, resulting in low margins. Non-bank consumer finance providers are competing head-to-head with Thai banks in the personal loan and credit card markets. Foreign, and quasi-foreign banks, as well as the state-owned banks, are putting increasing pressure on Thai private banks to be innovative to keep market share. Further change is expected to come with the imminent passage of the government's long-awaited financial master plan. Authorities also plan to amend laws to expedite foreclosure and asset sales procedures, as well as to allow state-owned asset management companies to buy bad loans from local banks (*Bangkok Post*, 2003).

Human resource management (HRM) issues

One of the critical issues for Thailand is the development of human resources. Many of the key HRM issues relate to the prevailing values and attitudes discussed in the earlier sections. It is always easy to be critical in hindsight, but a criticism of successive governments has been that, in the late-1980s and early-1990s when the Thai economy had one of the highest GDP growth rates in the world, not nearly enough was expended to develop human capital. Unlike the governments of some of its neighbours (e.g., Singapore and Malaysia), Thailand's efforts to improve the capabilities and skills of its people have not so far been particularly successful in creating a workforce which can assist the country to cope with the challenges of globalisation and change. While Thailand's international competitiveness rankings have been gradually improving, it remains low in the area of human capital, even when compared to other countries in the region (Nirapattanasai, 2003). For example, a recent survey found that Thai companies were amongst the worst performers in the Asia-Pacific region for investing in human resource technologies (see Table 9.4). Table 9.4 indicates that Thai companies had poor HRM performance across a range of HRM issues.

Table 9.4 Human Capital Index (HCI) (%)

	Thailand	Best country in the region
HR function effectiveness	47	62
Collegial, flexible, customer-focused workplace	56	62
Clear total rewards and accountability	68	84
Recruiting and retention excellence	49	66
Communications integrity	54	68
Prudent use of resources	47	72
Overall Score	**56**	**79**

Source: http://www.watsonwyatt.com (retrieved March 12, 2004).

The survey found that some rewards paid by Thai employers were not flexible, and not linked to work performance. All employees had the same rate of bonus, and companies rarely offered staff stock options. In addition, the benevolent–paternalistic management style led to reluctance to adjust headcount during challenging economic conditions. Another area needing improvement was recruitment. New employees were often recruited in the hope that the companies could provide them with training courses to increase skills later. As well, work assessments were based more on *boon koon* network-based relationships rather than productivity. It is typical for Thai firms to develop a variety of training programmes without making sure they get value from them. Training is used as a form of reward or incentive, rather than being offered to meet real business needs. The survey also noted that Thai companies' human resource departments rarely participated in drafting business strategies:

> Most Thai firms have assigned their human resource departments to look after only the well-being of staff. They should change this concept as superior human capital management is one key to business success and can substantially increase shareholder value in the long term. (http://www.watsonwyatt.com)

There is some consensus that the greatest weakness of the Thai education system is its lack of market-driven training policies, which means that graduates are churned out regardless of whether there might be employment opportunities for them (Thapangachai, 2004). In the software sector a requirement of 40,000 graduates has been identified. Overall, there is a shortage of science-based professionals, but the education system has not kept pace with the increased need for an evolving economy (Thapangachai, 2004).

> Thai students continue to graduate from post-secondary studies without having been taught how to question, analyse and develop a structured response to a problem. This deficiency reduces their effectiveness in business, and more broadly, as contributors to a society as a whole. (Swift, cited in Sirpunyawit, 2004)

These human resource management and capacity development requirements need to be addressed if Thailand is to successfully evolve to a knowledge-based economy.

Contemporary micro-level managerial approaches for continuity-in-change in Thailand

The hierarchical, individualistic, high ego, high power distance and conflict avoidance and present-world characteristics that shape the unique 'middle-path' Thai cultural orientation essentially frame the 'continuity-in-change' assumptions of the Thai approach to management. This characteristic Thai managerial worldview means that conventionally both leaders and their employees value behaviour that manifests characteristic Thai cultural notions of preferred behaviour and etiquette: For example, interactions that avoid conflict with others, display respect, control emotions, and promote tactfulness, modesty and politeness. Moreover, Thai notions of effective managerial leadership involve a notion of hierarchical authority that includes the attainment of a paternalistic balance between the application of force, or fear (*pradej*) and a more benevolent approach (*prakhun*) to induce respect and gratitude, which together ascribes the leader with the power and strength (*baramee*) associated with respect and loyalty.

The previous discussion highlights how these characteristic Thai values frame Thai managerial responses to the dynamic consequences of global imperatives. In order to cushion the potentially destabilising consequences of the forces of global imperatives the material presented highlights how managerial approaches to reform are generally guided by these 'continuity-in-change' values. Hence, approaches to reform tend to be pragmatic, incremental and short-term oriented, and often fail to address the international reformist managerial concern for local cronyism and the need for greater transparency of decision-making. While the continuity-in-change approach sustains community harmony, and maintains the status quo, it may not be responsive enough to address the competitive economic development objectives of the nation. Nevertheless, under the convergent influence of global imperatives, characteristic Thai individualism and pragmatism offer a socio-cultural resource for both individuals and the society to meaningfully frame acceptable and more effective managerial and workplace responses to reform and change.

The core elements of Thaksinomics are controversial. It is a strategy for economic development that combines the traditional elements of Thai development (i.e., an outward orientation emphasising labour-intensive manufactured exports; and high rates of FDI), as well as a greater focus on domestic consumption (Looney, 2004). Prime Minister Thaksin envisioned these policies increasing domestic consumption from 55 per cent to 60 per cent of GDP, and reducing exports from 60 per cent to 50 percent of GDP (Looney, 2004). The rationale is based on GDP statistics from developed countries, and the current vulnerability of the Thai economy to external shocks, such as US economic fluctuations, terrorist attacks and the SARS epidemic. In practice, the Thai government intends to stimulate domestic demand in the short-term through increased government fiscal spending, while also promoting industries that move business up the value-added chain, and that move the Thai economy from manufacturing-based to knowledge-based.

Scholars now generally agree that the traditional elements of Thai economic development from the mid-1970s to 1997 cannot be leveraged for future long-term economic growth. Indeed, future economic growth must come from a transition to a knowledge-based economy (KBE) (Masuyama and Vandenbrink, 2003; Yusuf, 2003). The implications of this are immense, since the fundamental organisational and managerial paradigm and operational parameters associated with transforming to a knowledge-based economy challenge many prevailing 'continuity-in-change' managerial assumptions and practices. To transit to a KBE, countries need the necessary information and communication technology (ICT) infrastructure to promote information exchange and e-commerce, human resources with both technical and innovative talents, and the re-organisation of traditional industry and corporate structures to an 'international production network' model (Yusuf, 2003).

In assessing each of the fundamental KBE parameters, the source of the problem that Thailand is facing for continued economic development becomes apparent. ICT infrastructure is the first problematic issue. Less than six per cent of the population use the internet (compared to about 50 per cent in OECD countries), and 70 per cent of users live in Bangkok (the geographical disparity is related to income inequalities and low telephone penetration outside the capital) (Tangkitvanich, 2003). A substantial factor quelling the growth of the internet is the statutory monopolisation by a state-owned enterprise (Communication Authority of Thailand) for interconnection outside the country. This has had the effect of making the cost of global internet connection 250 to 600 per cent more in Thailand than in Hong Kong, Japan, Malaysia or the Philippines. In other words, high cost, low income and poor infrastructure outside of Bangkok, has facilitated the low penetration of the internet in Thailand which has severely inhibited the possibility of information exchange and e-commerce.

Secondly, human resources are a critical component in the transition to a KBE. While the human resources needed for a KBE are substantially lacking in Thailand (Charoenwongsak, 1999), they are improving (at least quantitatively). In 1987, 97 per cent of Thai children attended primary school, while only 30 per cent attended secondary school (Komin, 1989). By 2000, secondary enrolments were up to 55 percent, due to the *National Education Act of 1999* that extended compulsory education from six to nine years (this figure compares to 99 per cent in Singapore). Table 9.5 demonstrates the beginning of an encouraging shift in focus from commerce to engineering/computer science, as well as a growth rate in

Table 9.5 University graduates (Thailand and Singapore) – comparative 1994 and 2001 figures

	1994	2001	%Change
Thailand:			
Eng/Comp Science	6,687 (11%)	13,915 (13%)	+108
Business Administration	13,153 (21%)	20,811 (19%)	+58
Total	63,749	107,996	+69
Singapore:			
Total	18,337	26,678	+45

Source: Watson Wyatt.

Table 9.6 Regional education statistics for year 2001

	PRC	HK	IND	MAL	PHI	SING	THAI
Expenditure (%GDP)	–	4.1	1.3	7.9	3.2	–	5.0
Tertiary enrolments (% from sec)	13	26	15	27	31	40	37
Tertiary education (% pop)	2.0	14.5	2.3	6.9	–	7.6	7.9

Source: Singapore statistics.

graduates exceeding that of Singapore. When compared to regional neighbours, Thailand exhibits expenditure and enrolment statistics that will contribute well to a longer-term transition to a KBE (see Table 9.6). Unfortunately, the statistical trends and snap shot comparisons mask the real nature of the requirements in the shorter term. For example, as indicated in the previous section it is unlikely that 14,000 engineering/computer science graduates per year will be sufficient to counter the current shortage of ICT professionals (Tangkitvanich, 2003).

There is another dimension to education besides enrolment statistics; that is, the way that culture and politics shape the education curriculum and the type of assessments used. The current Thai education model will not meet the country's short-term transitional requirements in becoming a KBE. There is a lack of substantive content in the Thai education system with '75 per cent of school time is used to explain 10 per cent of experience' that would be of any practical value to the student outside the classroom (Mulder, 1997, p. 58). The education system propagates morality as the basis of the family unit, and proceeds to project this notion onto the wider society. Thus, the majority of school time is used to reinforce the social system, and teach gratitude, deference and hierarchical position. Indeed, the characteristic pedagogy of the Thai education system promotes subservience and rote learning (Siengthai and Bechter, 2004), rather than the creative thinking required in a KBE.

The third fundamental KBE parameter issue is the reorganisation of traditional industry and corporate structures to an 'international production network' model. This model requires a move away from centrally directed and vertically integrated structures to horizontal organisation with decentralised authority and cooperative alliances to share information between producers and innovators (Masuyama and Vandenbrink, 2003). For Thailand, the incorporation of this KBE parameter will provide both opportunities and threats. While the traditional *guanxi* networks of the overseas Chinese positively promote international cooperative alliances, more negatively, the nature of corporate governance based on authoritarian family control (Andrews and Chompusri, 2001) and the lack of the social capital characteristics of Thai society (Unger, 1998), are countervailing forces.

Thailand has traditionally relied upon the development of industries, and an export-oriented strategy, using the comparative advantage of cheap unskilled labour. This prevailing export-oriented approach to economic development, coupled with an inappropriate education model, a lack of technological capability and an inadequate ICT infrastructure are now counterproductive to the new prerequisites for establishing national competitive advantage (Porter, 1990). Simultaneously, Japanese and Asian Newly Industrialised Economies (NIEs) MNCs are abandoning Thailand as they seek out more competitive locations and conditions. As a result Thailand is being increasingly squeezed by competition from China, India and Vietnam, which maintain a comparative advantage in labour and land, and which are increasingly undermining Thailand's traditional export markets for low-cost commodities.

Technology management issues

Thai companies generally have low technological capabilities (Chareonwongsak, 1999; Intarakumnerd and Charatana, 2002), and while there are innovative activities in some Thai firms, those activities are not the products of formally recognised R&D. The formulation of a coherent and explicit national innovation and technology development policy is needed, and it should be an integral part of national trade, investment, industrial and macro-economic policies (Intarakumnerd and Charatana, 2002). Selecting technology policies to support specific sectors/clusters should be devised and implemented based on strict performance-based criteria. The government should make more effort to promote technology development within firms, rather than conducting technology development on behalf of firms. Government measures (financial and technological) also have to be specific enough to respond to companies' technological needs, in order to help them cross the thresholds of their capabilities. In order to strengthen the links between research technology organisations, universities and the private sector, the performance of these organisations should be evaluated, not only on the basis of academic excellence, but also on the intensity and success of interaction with the private sector.

Quality management issues

There are many examples of the efforts of Thai businesses to meet international quality standards. Many firms and organisations have promotional banners proclaiming that they are ISO-accredited in one form or another. However, it is not easy to measure the concept of quality within the Thai business and industrial sector. In comparing notions of quality in the same organisations with operations in Thailand and other countries, a rather different perception of the meaning of quality is identified (Hughes and Sheehan, 1993). In other countries, quality is measured in terms of achieving certain task-oriented goals, but in Thailand, apart from the actual technical measures of quality, it is seen as more as what pleases one's boss. This perspective has its roots ultimately in the nature of *boon koon* relationships, rather than the inherent benefits of 'quality' *per se*. In addition, a lack of customer focus in Thai companies has been noted (Egan and Sheehan, 1999). Managers were aware of the quest for quality of product, but the customer was not viewed as an element of quality of service. However, a substantial increase in the number of joint ventures and outsourcing in industries, such as computers, automobiles and tourism has meant greater external pressure for Thai firms to conform to international standards of product and service quality.

Conclusion

Management in Thailand at all three macro-, meso- and micro-levels is struggling with a process of 'continuity-in-change'. External shocks, such as the Asian economic crisis in 1997, the September 11 terrorist attacks in the United States in 2001, the SARS epidemic of 2003, the ongoing Asian 'bird flu' scare, and the 2004 tsunami have been and will continue to be forces for change in management patterns and processes. In response to these dynamic internal and external influences and forces, the Thai socio-cultural business milieu has predominantly counteracted to maintain a status quo approach to contemporary management systems. The Asian economic crisis of 1997 in particular had a profound effect on the Thai economy and business enterprises. FDI fell significantly, GDP growth became negative, and many Thai companies became bankrupt, or were taken over by foreign partners. The Thai government responded with measures to promote exports, to increase domestic consumption, and to improve corporate governance. For example, 'Thaksinomics' is an economic policy designed to increase domestic consumption, and to ameliorate the effects of external shocks on the Thai economy. Adopting a more effective long-term management approach, the SET has instigated initiatives to improve the transparency and diligence of corporate governance.

Despite these short and long-term initiatives, however, serious concerns remain about the very issues they were designed to counter. For example, while few would argue about the necessity of the Thai economy transiting to a knowledge-base (a major platform of the Thaksinomic policy), much evidence points to the practical difficulties of doing so in the short-term. These include a lack of IT infrastructure, inadequate human resources and social capital. Likewise, the SET initiatives have had little discernable effect on the quality and structure of contemporary corporate governance, traditionally built on *guanxi* and *boon koon* relationships.

At a more micro-level, contemporary managerial ethos remains plagued by characteristics inherited from Thai socio-cultural values. These characteristics include benevolent-paternalistic management, *boon koon* relationships, a lack of creative thinking and dysfunctional teamwork. While some of these managerial characteristics have been improved in companies with greater foreign ownership and control as a result of takeovers, the characteristics remain largely intact with little attention given to the operational inefficiencies that invariably result.

At present, too much of Thailand's industry is based on relatively low-skilled labour involved as subcontractors or outsources for international firms. Unlike its neighbours, Thailand has a long way to go to become a 'clever' country, but it must address the issues of technology, human resources and innovation if it is to keep pace with other Asian developing countries. In the short-term, Thailand will continue to leverage the export of commodities (especially by way of bilateral trade agreements), albeit with far less extraordinary economic outcomes. In the longer-term however, economic development will likely be undermined by more global shocks and continued adversity. However, the pursuit of a regional cooperative approach to trade and economic development, in association with the Thai utilitarian and pragmatic worldview, may lead to the adoption of more effective management systems, and a more transparent and diligent approach to corporate governance. This approach to transition would be an effective strategy for managing the processes of continuity-in-change in Thailand and building a more sustainable approach to development.

Questions

1. Explain Thailand's concept of 'continuity in change'. How has the concept both hindered and assisted the development of Thailand?
2. Discuss the unique socio-cultural characteristics, which have framed Thailand's managerial styles and practices.
3. How will Thai managers need to change in order to remain globally competitive?

URL linkages

Government and related information

Ministry of Foreign affairs	www.mfa.go.th
Office of the Board of Investment	www.boi.go.th
Office of the National Economic and Social Development Board	www.nesdb.go.th
Ministry of Export Promotion	www.thaitrade.com
Ministry of Foreign Trade	www.dft.moc.go.th
Ministry of Industry	www.mindustry.go.th
Ministry of Science, Technology, and Environment	www.moste.go.th
Ministry of Labour and Social Welfare	www.molsw.go.th
National Statistical Office	www.nso.go.th
Office of the Public Service Development Commission	www.opdc.go.th

Business organisations/research organisations

Stock Exchange of Thailand   www.set.or.th
Thailand Development Research Institute   www.tocdoc.or.th
KPMG Thailand   www.kpmg.com

News media

Nation Multimedia Group   www.nationmultimedia.com
Bangkok Post   www.bangkokpost.net
Business in Thailand   www.businessinthailand.com
Reuters   www.reuters.com

Government banks

Bank of Thailand (Central Bank)   www.bot.org.th
Export-import Bank of Thailand   www.exim.of.th

References

Alba, P, Claessens, S & Djankov, S, 1998, *Thailand's Corporate Financing and Governance Structures: Impact on Firm's Competitiveness*, Paper presented at the Conference on Thailand's Dynamic Economic Recovery and Competitiveness, Bangkok, 20–21 May.

Akira, S, 1996, *Capital Accumulation in Thailand 1855–1985*, Silkworm Books, Chiang Mai.

Akira, S & Wailerdsak, N, 2004, 'Family business in Thailand: Its management, governance, and future challenges', *ASEAN Economic Bulletin*, vol. 21, no. 1, pp. 81–93. Retrieved 6 April 2004 from ProQuest Database.

Anderson, B, 2004, *Statesmen or managers?* Address to seminar, Chulalongkorn University, Bangkok, 2 April.

ARC, 1996, *Pocket Thailand in Figures*, (2nd edn.) Alpha Research Company, Bangkok.

ARC, 2004, *Pocket Thailand in Figures*, (7th edn.) Alpha Research Company, Bangkok.

Andrews, TG. and Chompusri, N, 2001, 'Lessons in 'cross-vergence': Restructuring the Thai subsidiary corporation', *Journal of International Business Studies*, vol. 32, no. 1, pp. 77–93, Retrieved June 5, 2004 from: ProQuest Database.

ASEAN Focus Group, 2004, 'Thailand', *History of South East Asia* (2nd edn.) Retrieved 9 September 2004 from: www.aseanfocus.com/publications/historythailand.html

Ayal, EB, 1963, 'Value systems and economic development in Japan and Thailand', *Journal of Social Issues*, vol. 19, no. 1.

Bangkok Post 2005, 'SOS to the world: Please visit', 17 January, p. B1

Bangkok Post 2004, 'Midyear 2004: Thailand facts and figures'. Retrieved 9 September 2004 from: http://bangkokpost.net/midyear2004/graphics/factsandfigures01.gif

Bangkok Post 2004 November 15, 'PM 'studying scholars' ideas'. Retrieved 22 November 2004 from: http://www.bangkokpost.com/151104_News/15Nov2004_news05.ph0

Bangkok Post 2004 November 17, 'Queen urges unity, peace: Feels compelled to speak out on South'. Retrieved 22 November 2004 from: http://www.bangkokpost.com/171104_News/17Nov2004_new04.php

Bangkok Post 2003, 'Economic Review, Year End'.

Barry, J, 1967, *Thai Students in the United States*, Data Paper no. 66, Southeast Asian Program, Cornell University, New York.

Benedict, R, 1952, *Thai Culture and Behaviour*, Data Paper no. 4, Southeast Asian Program, Cornell University: New York.

Blanchard, W, 1958, *Thailand: Its People, Its, Society, Its Culture*, Hraf, New Haven.

Bodley, S, 2004a, Thaksin and Thai Inc., *Asian analysis newsletter* (May). Retrieved September 15, 2004 from: www.aseanfocus.com/asiananalysis/newsletter/archive

Bodley, S, 2004b, 'Bitter lesson for all', *Asian analysis newsletter* (August). Retrieved September 15 2004 from: www.aseanfocus.com/asiananalysis/newsletter

Charoenwongsak, K, 1999, 'Thailand must ready itself for conditions of intense global competition in the new millennium', *Insights into Thailand's Post-crisis Economy*, Success Media, Bangkok, Thailand.

Chen, M-J, 2001, *Inside Chinese Business*, Harvard Business School Press, Boston.

Cohen, E, 1991, *Thai Society in Comparative Perspective*, White Lotus, Bangkok.

Coughlin, G, 1960, *Double Identity: The Chinese in Modern Thailand*, Hong Kong University Press, Hong Kong.

Deyo, FC, 1978, 'The cultural patterning of organizational development: A comparative case study of Thai and Chinese industrial enterprise', *Human Organization*, vol. 37, no. 1.

Egan, V & Sheehan, B, 1999, 'Cultural Influences on Management Style', Proceedings of the 1999 *Asian Forum on Business Education Conference*, Hong Kong, 15–17 November, pp. 101–15.

Embree, JF, 1950, 'Thailand – A loosely structured social system', *American Anthropologist*, vol. 52, pp. 181–93.

Gohlert, EW, 1991, *Power and Culture: The Struggle against Poverty in Thailand*, White Lotus, Bangkok.

Hanks, LM, 1962, 'Merit and power in the Thai social order', *American Anthropologist*, vol. 64, no. 6, pp. 1247–261.

Hanks, LM, 1975, 'The social order as entourage and circle', in Skinner GW & Kirsh AT (eds), *Change and Persistence in Thai Society*, Cornell University Press, London.

Hanks, LM & Phillips, HP, 1961, 'A young Thai from the countryside', in Kaplan B (ed.), *Studying Personality Cross-Culturally*, Row, Peterson & Co., Illinois.

Hirsch, P, 1991, 'What is *the* Thai village?' In Reynolds CJ (ed.), *National Identity and Its Defenders*, Silkworm Books, Chiang Mai.

Hofstede, G & Bond, MH, 1988, 'The Confucius Connection: From cultural roots to economic growth', *Organizational Dynamics*, vol. 16, no. 4, pp. 5–21.

Hughes, P, 1984, 'Values of Thai Buddhists and Thai Christians', *Journal of the Siam Society*, vol. 72, no. 1 & 2, pp. 212–27.

Hughes, P & Sheehan, B, 1993, 'Culture and business practices', *Business and the Contemporary World*, vol. 5, (Autumn), pp. 153–70.

IMD, 2004, 'World competitiveness yearbook', *Institute of Management Development*. Retrieved June 10, 2004 from: http://www01.imd.ch/wcyl

Intarakumnerd, P & Charatana, P, 2002, 'Thailand's Economic Crisis and Its Impacts from the View of National Innovation Systems Approach', Paper presented at 8th Thai Studies Conference, Bangkok, 9–12 January.

Keyes, CF, 1977, 'Millennialism, Theravada Buddhism, and Thai society', *Journal of Asian Studies*, vol. 36, no. 2. pp. 283–302.

Keyes, CF, 1987, *Thailand: Buddhist Kingdom as Modern Nation-State*, Westview: Colorado.

Kingshill, K, 1991, *Ku Daeng – Thirty Years Later: A Village Study in Northern Thailand 1954–84*, Northern Illinois University, Illinois.

Kirsch, AT, 1977, 'Complexity in the Thai religious system: An interpretation', *Journal of Asian Studies*, vol. 36, no. 1, pp.137–60.

Kirsch, AT, 1984, 'Cosmology and ecology as factors in interpreting early Thai social organization', *Journal of Southeast Asian Studies*, vol.15, no. 2, pp. 253–65.

Klausner, W J, 1997, *Thai Culture in Transition*, The Siam Society, Bangkok.

—— 1964, 'Popular Buddhism in northeast Thailand'. In FSC. Northrop and Livingston HH (eds), *Cross-Cultural Understanding: Epistemology in Anthropology*, Harper & Row, New York.

Komin, S, 1991, *Psychology of the Thai People*, NIDA, Bangkok.

—— 1989, *Social Dimensions of Industrialization in Thailand*, NIDA: Bangkok.

Lobbato, J, 2000, *Beyond the Bamboo Network*, Anderson Consulting/EIU.

Looney, R, 2004, 'Thaksinomics: A new Asian paradigm?' *Journal of Social, Political, and Economic Studies*, vol. 29, no. 1, pp. 65–80.

Mabrey, BD, 1987, 'The labour movement and the practice of professional management in Thailand', *Journal of Southeast Asian Studies*, vol. 18, no. 2.

Maneerungsee, W, 2004, 'Thaksin: A new regional leader? Midyear 2004 *Bangkok Post*, September. Retrieved 9 September 2004 from: http://bangkokpost.net/midyear2004

Masuyama, S & Vandenbrink, D, 2003, 'The new industrial geography of East Asia under the knowledge-based economy', in Masuyama S & Vandenbrink D (eds) *Towards a knowledge-based economy: East Asia's Changing Industrial Geography*, Institute of Southeast Asian Studies, Singapore, and Nomura Research Institute, Tokyo.

Mentzer, EH & Piker, S, 1975, 'Personality profiles for two central Thai villages', *Contributions to Asian Studies*, vol. 8, pp. 19–43.

Mizuno, K, 1975, 'Thai pattern of social organization: Note on a comparative study', *Journal of Southeast Asian Studies*, vol. 6, no. 2, pp. 127–34.

Moerman, M, 1969, 'A Thai village headman as a synaptic leader', *Journal of Asian Studies*, vol. 28, no. 3, pp. 535–49.

Mole, RL, 1973, *Thai values and behaviour patterns*, Charles E. Tuttle, Tokyo.

Montreevat, S, 2004, 'Prospects of Thailand's bilateral trade pacts', *Viewpoints*, Institute of South East Asian Studies, Singapore. Retrieved 8 July 2004 from: http://www.iseas.edu.sg

Mulder, N, 1994, *Inside Thai Society: An Interpretation of Everyday Life*, Duang Kamol, Bangkok.

Mulder, N, 1997, *Thai Images: The Culture of the Public World*, Silkworm Books, Chiang Mai.

Myrdal, G, 1968, *Asian Drama: An Inquiry into the Poverty of Nations*, (vol. 1) Pantheon, New York.

Neher, CD, 1979, 'A critical analysis of research on Thai politics', in Neher CD (ed.) *Modern Thai politics: From village to nation*, Schenkman, Massachusetts.

NESDB, 2004, *National economic and social development board*. Retrieved 6 June 2004 from: http://www.nesdb.go.th

Niratapattanasai, K, 2003, 'The future is here', *Bangkok Post*, 10 January.

Pansoonthorn, K, 2004, 'The privatisation dilemma. Midyear 2004' *Bangkok Post*, September. Retrieved 9 September 2004 from: http://bangkokpost.net/midyear2004

Park, D, 1997, 'Executive and industry effects on acquisition strategy of Thai firms: Implications for multinational executives', *Multinational Business Review*, vol. 5, no. 1, pp. 85–91.

Phillips, HP, 1965, *Thai Peasant Personality*, University of California Press, California.

Phillips, HP, 1969, 'The scope and limits of the 'loose structure' concept', in Evers HD (ed.) *Loosely Structured Social System: Thailand in Comparative Perspective*, Cultural Report Series no. 17, Southeast Asian Studies, Yale University, New Haven.

Phitakspraiwan, T, 1967, 'The acceptance of Western culture in Thailand', *East Asian Cultural Studies*, vol. 6, no. 1, pp. 1–17.

Phongpaichit, S & Baker, C, 1995, *Thailand: Economy and politics*, Oxford University Press, New York.

Piker, S, 1969, 'Loose structure and the analysis of Thai social organization'. In Evers HD (ed.) *Loosely Structured Social System: Thailand in Comparative Perspective*, Cultural Report Series no. 17, Southeast Asian Studies, Yale University, New Haven.

Piker, S, 1983, *A Peasant Community in Changing Thailand*, Anthropological Research Papers no. 30, Arizona State University, Arizona.

Pomerleano, M, 1998, 'Corporate finance lessons from the East Asian crisis', *Public policy for the private sector*, note no. 155, The World Bank Group, October, p. 3.

Pongsudhirak, T, 2003, 'Behind Thaksin's war on terror', *Far Eastern Economic Review*, September 25, vol.166, no. 38, p. 29.

Porter, M, 1990, *The competitive advantage of nations*, Free Press, New York.

Prachyapruit, T, 1986, *Thailand's Elite Civil Servants and their Development-Orientedness: An Empirical Test of National Data*, Chulalongkorn University Social Research Institute, Bangkok.

Redfield, R, 1956, *Peasant society and culture*, University of Chicago Press, Chicago.

Reuters, 2004, 'Queen urges Thais to help govt. fight Muslim unrest'. Retrieved 22 November 2004 from: http://.www.abcnews.go.com/International/print?id=258798

Sangchai, S, 1976, *Coalition behaviour in modern Thai politics: A Thai perspective*, Occasional Paper no. 41, Institute of Southeast Studies, Singapore.

Sensenig, B, 1975, 'Socialization and personality in Thailand', *Contributions to Asian Studies*, vol. 8, pp. 109–25.

Sharp, L, 1950, 'Peasants and politics in Thailand', *Far Eastern Survey*, vol. 19, no. 15, pp. 157–61.

Sheehan, B & Huvanandana, O, 2002, *Strategic management in developing countries and local considerations – The need to develop 'hybrid' modules of strategic management*, Paper presented to The Asian Forum on Business Education, Beijing, June.

Siengthai, S & Bechter, C, 2004, 'HRM in Thailand'. In Budhwar PS (ed.) *Managing human resources in Asia-Pacific*, Routledge, London and New York, pp.141–72.

Siffin, WJ, 1966, *The Thai bureaucracy: Institutional change and development*, East-West Centre, Honolulu.

'Singapore companies top disclosure survey', 2004, *Bangkok Post*, 30 June.

Sirpunyawit, S, 2004, 'Joining the ranks of the unemployable? Midyear 2004', *Bangkok Post*. Retrieved 9 September 2004 from: http://bangkokpost.net/midyear2004

Skinner, GW, 1957, *Chinese society in Thailand: An Analytical History*, Cornell University Press, New York.

Slater, R, 1968, *World religions and world community*, Harper-Row, New York.

Smalley, WA, 1994, *Linguistic diversity and national unity: Language ecology in Thailand*, University of Chicago Press, Chicago.

Sriussadaporn-Charoenngam, N & Jablin, FM, 1999, 'An exploratory study of communication competence in Thai organizations', *Journal of Business Communication*, vol. 36, no. 4, pp. 382–418.

Tangkitvanich, S, 2003, 'Linking Thai "brick-and-mortars" to the global network economy'. In Masuyama S & Vandenbrink D (eds) *Towards a knowledge-based economy: East Asia's changing industrial geography*, Institute of Southeast Asian Studies: Singapore, and Nomura Research Institute, Tokyo.

Thapanganchai, S, 2004, 'Back to the classroom, Midyear 2004', *Bangkok Post* Retrieved 9 September 2004 from: http://bangkokpost.net/midyear2004

Tomosugi, T, 1980, *A structural analysis of Thai economic history: Case study of a Northern Chao Phraya Delta Village*, Centre for East Asian Cultural Studies for UNESCO, Tokyo.

Unger, D, 1998, *Building social capital in Thailand: Fibres, finance, and infrastructure*, Cambridge University Press, Cambridge.

Vance, CM, McClaine, SR, Boje, DM & Stage, HD, 1992, 'An examination of the transferability of traditional performance appraisal principles across cultural boundaries', *Management International Review*, vol. 32, no. 4, pp. 313–26.

World Bank News Release: Doing business in South Asia, 2005, 2004, email received 8 September 2004.

Wyatt, DK, 1984, *Thailand: A short history*, Silkworm Books, Chiang Mai.

Yusuf, S, 2003, *Innovative East Asia: The future of growth*, World Bank and Oxford University Press, New York.

Additional readings

Doyle, M, 2004, *Guide to Thailand business law*, Seri Manop & Doyle, Bangkok.

Emery, SL, Ellis, W & Chulavatnatol, M (eds) 2005, *Thailand: Competitive innovations Strategies*, National Innovation Agency, Bangkok.

Klausner, WJ, 1993, *Reflections on Thai culture*, Siam Society, Bangkok.

Lester, RC, 1987, *Buddhism: The path to nirvana*, Harper, San Francisco.

Niratpattanasai, K, 2004, *Bridging the gap: Managing the cross-cultural workplace in Thailand*, Bangkok: Asia Books.

Pongpaichit, P & Baker, C, 1995, *Thailand: Economy and politics*, Oxford University Press, Singapore.

Sheridan, G, 1999, *Asian values western dreams*, Allen & Unwin, Sydney.

Chapter 10

Managing complexity, paradox and transformation in Indonesia

Introduction

There is no country of such vital strategic importance that is less understood than Indonesia. In only six years Indonesia has transformed from an authoritarian military regime to the third largest political democracy in the world. As the world's largest predominantly Islamic nation, the implications are significant. The country's diverse geography, history, political and administrative systems, and the community's ethnic and religious diversity have complexly contributed to a characteristically assimilative, pluralistic and often paradoxical heritage. The resultant complex cultural and institutional nature of the society with its pluralistic approaches to governance and management frame the many complex challenges and opportunities now faced by the Indonesian government, corporations and the community. Since independence the country's autocratic government coercively applied a range of modernisation and development governance policies and management strategies that, by the 1990s, delivered economic growth levels that were the envy of the developing world. However, with the 1997 economic crisis the economy collapsed, the government fell, and a more educated population demanded a more democratic system of governance.

The economic collapse revealed that institutional reform and capacity strengthening was required across the society. Decentralisation policy was introduced to remove centralist power and wealth. The issues of terrorism, SARS and the 2004 earthquake and tsunami presented the nation with additional political, economic, administrative and community management and human resource capacity challenges. Now, under the democratic leadership of President Yudhoyono, there is deep administrative concern to maintain the necessary political stability required to attract foreign investment and develop appropriate economic and capacity development strategies that will build the increased and sustainable levels of economic growth to significantly improve economic opportunities of the nation's 220 million people.

The macro-regional level: Local issues and external forces influencing the managerial context of Indonesia

The title indicates the enormity of challenges and opportunities associated with governance and management in Indonesia today. The characteristically complex and paradoxical nature of Indonesian society and its approaches to governance and management derive from diverse macro-local influences and external forces that together contributed to the heritage of the islands of the Indonesian archipelago. While the nation continues to grapple with the economic hardships and reform instigated by the 1997 Asian economic crisis, the popular election of Susilo Bambang Yudhoyono (popularly known in Indonesia as 'SBY') as President of the Republic in September 2004 encapsulates the formidable nature of political change achieved by the world's fourth most populous nation. In only six years the nation's political system has transformed from a coercive military and authoritarian regime to a democratic political system of government. Indonesia is now the world's third largest democratic nation. As the world's largest predominantly Islamic nation the global implications of this development are significant. Since 1997, as the world watched the dramatic and traumatic political and economic events that have shaped the lives of the Indonesian people, it has become apparent that there is no country of such significance that is less understood than Indonesia. This section explores the development of the Indonesian heritage through the impact of a range of local influences and external forces.

The forces of heritage: Local and regional influences

The Indonesian national motto: *Bhinneka Tunggal Ika* (Unity in Diversity) is based on an old Javanese phrase meaning: *They are one, they are many*. This motto serves to bind together the diverse nature of the estimated population of 216.2 million (*Tradewatch*, 2004). The complex, interconnected and sometimes volatile political, economic and cultural dimensions to local and national business and community issues suggest that the development of a deeper appreciation of Indonesian society is fundamental to understand Indonesian management systems and practices. Without this deeper understanding the implication for individuals, businesses and communities pursuing economic development opportunities is continuing high levels of risk and poor performance. The complex nature of Indonesian society derives from the country's geography, history, diverse ethnicity, religions and languages. This section briefly discusses the dynamic and interwoven macro-impact of these as together they have variously shaped the peoples, institutions, and evolving approaches to governance and management in contemporary Indonesia.

A brief history

The Austronesian heritage

The 6000 habitable islands of the Indonesian archipelago stretch some 5000 kilometres across the tropics between the Indian and Pacific Oceans, to provide rich and diverse natural environments for the large population that today includes some 360 tribal and ethnic groups who speak an estimated 583 different languages and dialects (Rigg, 1996). Reflecting the long-term ways in which geography and climate shape culture, people inhabiting equatorial locations are less assiduous than colder climate cultures, but exhibit higher levels of optimism, openness and cheerfulness (Lewis, 2003). Transecting the important historic maritime trading routes between China, India, the Middle East and Europe meant that these diverse island peoples have been subject to ongoing external historical and cultural influences through trade and migration. This specific island geography and history have contributed to an overarching shared regional cultural legacy called 'the Austronesian heritage' (Fox, 1998).

This cultural heritage means that throughout history there has been a generalised tendency to assimilate, innovate and recreate external influences into local cultural and animist religious logic and in ways not to weaken local culture, but to enrich it. Hence, local *adat* (traditional, accepted codes of behaviour, and sets of norms and rules covering community etiquette and ceremonial behaviour, and customary laws concerning crime, property, inheritance, adoption, marriage and divorce) have maintained their legitimacy, while evolving in response to powerful external influences (Hill, 1996). Drawing on this rich environmental and cultural heritage, the traditional Austronesian worldview sees that all space is filled with life-giving and life-taking energies that need to be ordered and managed to maximise benefit and minimise harm (Rigg, 1996). Much of traditional *adat* was orally transferred from one generation to the next. That oral cultural tradition is still important.

The coastal regions have always been subject to the greatest outside influences as Chinese, Indian, Arabic, and later European traders passed through the predominantly natural resource rich islands which were an important source of spices, sandalwood, medicines and tropical foods. Together, the ebb and flow of the cultural influences of powerful empires and their associated world religions of Buddhism, Hinduism, Islam and Christianity, and the ongoing historical maritime trading variously shaped the pre-colonial nature of the island communities. The earliest kingdoms in the archipelago were Hindu/Buddhist. The Sriwijaya kingdom (seventh to twelfth century), centred on Sumatra, was the first Indonesian empire able to control much of the regional trade by virtue of its strategic position. At the time, Tamils and Chinese were the main traders (www.aseanfocus.com, 2004).

A more conservative agrarian-based culture developed inland on Java, and this is evidenced still today by the Hindu and Buddhist temples of Borobudur and Prambanan. During the late thirteenth century the great Hindu kingdom of Majapahit, often referred to as an Indonesian golden age, centred on East Java, achieved control over much of the archipelago. One hundred years later the Majapahit power started breaking down through revolt from coastal states, and by the beginning of the sixteenth century the empire collapsed. Settlements of Arab traders brought Islam to the islands from the seventh century onwards. By the end of the sixteenth century many Indonesian rulers declared themselves independent Muslim states. When the Europeans arrived in the middle of the sixteenth century there were longstanding trading networks, shipbuilding and maritime skills across the region, and hence, a constant flow of goods and people conversing in the Malay language (www.aseanfocus.com, 2004). Despite the power of these external historical influences, the longstanding authenticity of local culture is still today often highly valued over external worldliness. For example, the inhabitants of many eastern islands may claim their apparent poverty as subtle proof of their ancestral authority (Keanne, 1997).

The Dutch colonial era

The Dutch followed the Portuguese and Spanish to the region in search of wealth. The Dutch Republic amalgamated competing trading companies to form the East India Company, or Vereeniggde Oost-Indische Compagnie (VOC), enabling the government to monopolise the spice trade. With military support, by the seventeenth century the VOC had established its headquarters for the archipelago and renamed Jayakarta Batavia, the capital of the Dutch East Indies. The Dutch colonial government applied a divide and rule strategy, making the regional kings 'puppet rulers', building inter-ethnic mistrust through the use of local mercenaries, and using the Chinese as tax collectors (Antlov and Cederroth, 1994; Goodfellow, 1997). For over 350 years great wealth was extracted from the islands and sent back to Holland. Indicative of the wealth extracted, the VOC was able to buy spices for 1/320th of the value commanded in Amsterdam (Rigg, 1996). However, Dutch rule was always tenuous and there were many pockets of local resistance throughout the colonial administration (Grant, 1996).

The administrative system established by the Dutch, especially on Java, has had significant consequences for the administrative systems set in place up to the present day (Antlov and Cederroth, 1994). The Javanese agricultural system was transformed by the Dutch through a 'cultivation system' which forced the locals to do forced work (*kerja rodi*) for 60 days of the year, or to devote 20 per cent of their land to cultivate government-owned crops. Peasants were forced to grow more lucrative crops instead of rice, and famine often resulted. A consequence of this forced system of cultivation was a re-feudalisation of the political system (Kartodirjo, 1994).

Local district leaders (*burpati*), appointed by the Dutch, forced their people to produce more in order to please the Dutch. During the nineteenth century the Javanese aristocracy (*pryayi*) became entrenched in an administrative bureaucracy with a rigid hierarchical structure and a paternalistic approach to local culture (Kartodirjo, 1994). With the majority of the Dutch coming to the islands being males, many took native (*pribumi*) wives from the aristocracy and this intermixing guaranteed the ongoing loyal support of the local bureaucracy for the colonial rulers (Remmeling 1990, cited in Kartodirjo, 1994). Western education opportunities for locals were very limited and only available to a few of this privileged local class. Together these colonial administrative strategies built a semi-feudal agriculture-based economic system, a privileged and hierarchical administrative system and an agricultural 'coolie' labourer mindset for the masses.

By the end of the nineteenth century Java was the world's largest sugar producer (www.aseanfocus.com, 2004). While a subsistence economy was transformed and diversified, by the beginning of the twentieth century most Javanese no longer owned land, working as tenant farmers, share croppers or wage labourers. From the beginning of the twentieth century Sumatra was economically transformed through the development of large areas of tobacco and rubber plantations, and the discovery of oil in the 1920s led to the establishment of the Royal Dutch Shell Company (www.aseanfocus.com, 2004). However, the wealth created was held in Dutch hands. The drift of the rural poor to the towns and ports meant that most urban dwellers lived in appalling circumstances. A tropical and impoverished urban context meant that starvation and disease were rife. In response, a more 'ethical policy' framework for colonial administration was implemented by the Dutch who recognised their need for an expanded bureaucracy beyond the aristocracy, and this led to the creation of a new class of Dutch educated civil servants (*ambtenaar*) who pursued the same ideals of the old aristocracy (Antlov and Cederroth, 1994). This culturally mixed administration system was quite efficient in maintaining the colonial system (Kartodirjo, 1994).

However, by the beginning of the twentieth century a new intellectual local elite emerged and this group, together with an Islamic schools-based (*pesantrean*) youth movement, formed nationalistic organisations, such as *Syarikat Islam* and *Partai Nasional Indonesia* (PNI) (Grant, 1996). During the 1920s early nationalist leaders, such as Soekarno and Mohammad Hatta, led the ongoing struggle for independence. In the 1940s when the Dutch fled and the Japanese occupied the Islands, the nationalist independence movement leaders felt an initial sense of liberation by the Japanese from their European colonisers. However, they were soon imprisoned and came to understand that the Dutch colonial system had been replaced by a Japanese imperial force (Grant, 1996).

The Dutch returned in 1945 as colonial ruler after the defeat of the Japanese who occupied the islands from 1941. Only after four years of internal resistance and international diplomacy did the Dutch finally surrender the country and recognise Indonesian independence in 1949. At the end of the Dutch colonial era the literacy rate was lower than in any other European colony in Asia, with the exception of the Portuguese colony of East Timor (www.aseanfocus.com, 2004).

This complex early local and colonial history shaped the socio-cultural and political dimensions to the nationalist discourse developed by the new independence movement leaders and, subsequently, the kinds of political, economic and cultural policies and institutions first developed by President Soekarno, and later by President Soeharto. This brief glimpse into the complex pre-independence history of Indonesia indicates the important ways in which local geography, history, ethnicity, culture, religion and language have been interwoven with the powerful imported cultural, religious and institutional systems brought by traders, religious instructors, teachers and colonial administrators to shape pluralistic Indonesian worldviews.

Since Independence (*Merdeka* – freedom), a range of political, economic and cultural governance strategies have been institutionalised in order to build an overarching shared national consciousness and identity, and thus bind together the diverse peoples of the disparate island nation. Drawing on the shared nature of this geography and complex history, in just over half a century since Independence the various strategic nation-building policies set in place by Presidents Soekarno and Soeharto have by-and-large established successfully a strong collective national identity, while maintaining the local sub-cultural identity of community groups.

As a result of the multifaceted nature of the historical local, national and international cultural assimilation and appropriation processes Indonesians have complex and multilayered identity and worldviews (Singleton, 2002). This means that overall behaviour and values in Indonesian society are highly context-dependent, and that Indonesians have complex 'multiliteracy' (Cope and Kalantzis, 2000) that gives them the required multicultural and multilingual skills to 'switch' their behaviour according to national, and local cultural and sub-cultural community contexts. This has important implications for the particular management cultures and practices found in the contemporary Indonesian bureaucracy, institutions and business (Singleton, 2002).

The cultural evolution of a shared sense of place, in combination with the particularised and diverse religious, linguistic and socio-cultural ways of making sense of the many Indonesian ethnic and community groups is best understood by the concept of 'syncretism' (Slamet-Velsink, 1994). The concept of syncretism explains attempts to unify, or reconcile, differing schools of thought. Indonesian worldviews often appear to experience little conceptual discomfort in simultaneously holding contrasting and often paradoxical ways of thinking (Muldar, 1999). Hence, the concept of syncretism is a useful principle to apply to interpret the evolving and multilayered nature of Indonesian culture in which there is a fundamental capacity to incorporate new, often conflicting, cultural influences while maintaining strong local worldviews. Moreover, the adoption of the values of a new system of thinking does not indicate a rejection or throwing out of the old. Thus, for Indonesians, in practical terms, this syncretic cultural approach means that there may often be paradoxical contradictions in their everyday lives. The next section briefly discusses the key socio-cultural influences that shape the values and behaviour of Indonesians and, hence, have implications for Indonesian styles of management and performance.

Socio-cultural issues

The five world religions have variously shaped Indonesia and Indonesians, with 88.8 per cent following Islam, five per cent Protestantism, 2.9 per cent Catholicism, 2.4 per cent Hinduism, 0.7 per cent Buddhism, and 0.2 per cent other religions (Fox, 1998). Hindu and Buddhism were the earliest of the world religions assimilated into the islands. Many of the rulers of Javanese and Balinese Hindu kingdoms reinforced their power through their identification with a deity and through this appropriative cultural process divine rights were bestowed onto these local rulers (Proudfoot, 1996).

Islam was introduced through the settlement of Middle Eastern traders. The aristocracy initially rejected Islam. However, because it was a religion largely passed on through oral transmission, rote-learning and philosophical discussion, and hence placed high value on learning and scholarship, there was high status associated with this, they gradually became Islamicised. The high value placed on religious scholarship, within a Sunni orthodox framework, coupled with openness to external influences, has meant that Indonesia has drawn on religious inspiration from virtually the whole of the Islamic world (Fox, 1998). Hence, Islam in Indonesia has developed an exploratory philosophical tradition to learning that could serve as a model for the contemporary Islamic world.

Under Dutch rule, the Islamic schools (*Peasantren*) were the only access to upward social mobility for the Javanese. The basic curriculum consisted of the study of the Arabic language, and the progressive study of specific text books on jurisprudence, *Qur'anic* (Koranic) exegesis, theology, ethics and Sufi traditions. This assimilative and open historical approach to Islam accounts for the differences between Indonesian Islam and other Muslim countries, and the more diverse nature of Muslims within Indonesia.

Like Islam, Christianity in Indonesia involved similar assimilative patterns of intermixing Christian ideology with local animist worldviews and *adat* systems. While Protestant missionaries from Europe were active across the islands during the nineteenth and twentieth centuries, the Dutch colonial administration guaranteed freedom of religion. Protestant missionary societies established schools and so some indigenous ethnic groups – including Bataks, Dayaks, Torajans, Ambonese, West Papuans, Minahan and various groups in East Nusa Tengarra – became identified with Christianity (Garang, 1997).

Kebatinan, a Javanese form of spirituality that combines ancient Javanese beliefs and practices with the mystical traditions of Hinduism, Buddhism, Suffism and even some parts of Christianity, has an important influence in Indonesia (Muldar, 1999). Meaning 'inwardness', Kebatinan is concerned with the cultivation of the inner (*batin*) life of a person through various preferred forms of mediation. The journey associated with this inner spiritual life is contrasted with one's external (*lahir*) obligations (Howell, 1998). Indonesia is neither a secular nor a theocratic state. Indonesian religious plurality is a core national value with a monotheistic 'Belief in one God' being the key *Pancasila* national foundational principle.

Emphasising the predominance of oral communication in Indonesia, only eight of the nation's numerous languages and dialects have a written literature (McGlynn, 1998). In this pluralistic context oral communication styles are an important marker of socio-cultural identity. In other words, Indonesians can easy identify subtle aspects of an individual's background, such as ethnicity, regional origins, class and status, through oral interactions. All eight of the written languages have been influenced by the five world religions. The assimilative processes and influences of external culture, in association with the development of formal and informal written literacy, will inevitably have both historical and contemporary implications for Indonesian cultural styles of literacy and preferred styles of communication. The pluralistic nature of Indonesian society and the multifaceted nature of identities mean that diverse and context-dependent styles of communication have developed.

With religion and ethnicity being important identity markers in Indonesia, the impact of the ethnic Chinese is noteworthy. The historical settlement of Chinese was associated with the movement of trade. The Chinese were typically town-dwellers (Kumar and Proudfoot, 1998). Chinese traders often married local women, learnt Malay and often converted to Islam. The term *Peranakan* is used to describe those Indonesians of Chinese ethnic descent and *Totok* for those born in China. An estimated 90 per cent of all Chinese Indonesians are *Peranakan*. Importantly, being town dwellers, often wealthy merchants and often highly literate, the Chinese were well placed to gain entry to the higher levels of local societies, in particular the Javanese aristocracy and Dutch colonial administrative society (Kumar and Proudfoot, 1998). While the Javanese aristocracy were favoured by the Dutch for administrative positions, the Chinese had favours extended to them as merchants and tax collectors (Antlov and Cederroth, 1994; Goodfellow, 1997). This history contributed to local resentment, and the development of a 'deeply rooted, stereotypical view of the Chinese as clannish, aloof, subversive, opportunistic, disloyal and corrupt'

(Goodfellow, 1997, p. 80). At the time of the Asian economic crisis in 1997, the ethnic Chinese accounted for only 3 per cent of the population, but some 70 per cent of the nation's wealth (Schwartz, 1999(a)).

The complex, multilayered and pluralistic nature of Indonesian society means that it is classified as being uniquely culturally *hybrid*, or a mix of *multi-active* and *re-active* (Lewis, 2003). Multi-actives are emotional, loquacious and impulsive, attaching great importance to family, feelings and relationships, with the tendency to do many things at the same time while being poor followers of agendas. Conversation is circular and animated as everyone tries to listen and speak at the same time. Re-actives by contrast are listeners who rarely initiate action or discussion. Considerable reflection, or silence, occurs before a weighted response is given, with maybe a further question to clarify the speaker's intent, or aspiration (Lewis, 2003). Hence, multi-active and re-active intermixing appears paradoxical. This hybrid cultural classification links with the syncretic notion for Indonesian worldviews, and both categories emphasise the critical nature of context in association with particular values and behaviour in Indonesian society.

The reactive dimension to Indonesian society means a preference for 'outer-direction'.

> Outer directedness is preferred by cultures living in a crowded turbulent and potentially threatening terrain. By taking a circuitous route of positively altering the environment, one can in turn improve oneself. Outer directedness teaches survival disciplines that can become reactive habits and disciplines, minimising and deflecting violence. (Hampden-Turner and Trompenaars, 2000, p. 251)

This pluralistic religious and hybrid socio-cultural logic, coupled with the institutionalised colonial administrative legacy, explains why, for example:

● In Javanese society status is hierarchical and marked by prescriptive notions of highly valued and refined forms of etiquette, and why the Javanese dominate the civil service, where status and how you conduct yourself is more important than what you achieve;

● How the Mingankabah community of West Sumatra, while being largely Islamic maintains strong matrilineal values and institutional practices with high numbers of businesses being headed by Mingan women;

● Why the Javanese consider the patriarchal and predominantly Christian Batak community to be rude and outspoken, while the Batak consider themselves to be more extroverted, ambitious and hold a higher work ethic than the Javanese and

● Why the *Peranakan* dominate the business sector, yet in light of recurrent historical violence committed against them, are reluctant to confirm their ethnic Chinese background (Singleton, 2002).

These examples illustrate the complexity of challenges associated with management in Indonesia.

This discussion briefly indicates how history and geography have shaped the complex socio-cultural nature of Indonesian society and how this subsequent diversity within the population emphasises the complex, pluralistic, assimilative and often paradoxical characteristic nature of the Indonesian heritage. After more than three hundred years of colonial rule the socio-cultural legacy of the Dutch administrative system is still apparent. Since independence, Presidents Soekarno and Soeharto have set in place various political and economic institutional strategies to critically shape their modern vision of Indonesia.

The next section discusses the political and economic influences of the particular governance and management strategies implemented by these two leaders and their subsequent followers. Both leaders drew heavily on the culture of the largest ethnic-community, the Javanese, to culturally frame their particular political and economic strategic management approaches for the nation. The particular strategies that were applied have crucial implications for the important political and economic decisions to be made by the new President Yudhoyono administration.

Political and economic influences

The issue of leadership is pivotal in a post-independence context like Indonesia, which at the time was economically poor and underdeveloped. The background, qualities and style of the leadership would determine not only how national discourse would draw on the Indonesian heritage to design a range of strategic development policies applied to unify the people and modernise the nation, but the nature of Indonesian responses to complex international geopolitical and economic events. The leadership strategies of the two long-term leaders of Indonesia – Presidents Soekarno, and Soeharto have made an indelible mark on the nation and its particular approaches to governance and management.

The leadership style and management strategies of President Soekarno

The early nationalist leaders drew on nineteenth century European nationalist ideological and management notions and in keeping with the assimilative logic of the Indonesian heritage inter-mixed this with local historical, religious and ethnic-community cultural references. The Javanese kingdom of Majapahit served as the bounded national territorial model for the modern nation (Day and Reynolds, 2000). In 1945 Soekarno presented the five principles (*Pancasila*) that were to be the foundation on which the independent state was to be built. The five principles, designed to synthesise diversity and build an integrationist national model, include:

1. Faith in one God, meaning any god – Allah, Vishnu, Buddha and Christ;

2. Humanity, based on recognition of the place the diverse Indonesian peoples in the wider 'family of the nation';

3. Nationalism emphasising unity (one nation, one language – *Bahasa Indonesia*, and one flag) and mutual obligation (*gotong royong*);

4. Representative government based on the traditional village system of discussion (*musyawarah*) among representatives to achieve consensus (*mukafat*), and

5. Social justice, as represented in the nation's crest of arms – grains of rice and cotton – used to symbolise the individual's rights for basic provisions.

The intellectual development and the Javanese rhetorical style of delivery of these principles revealed Soekarno's powerful leadership capabilities (Grant, 1996). '[P]robably in no other exposition of principle can one find a better example of the synthesis of Western democratic, modern Islamic, Marxist and indigenous-village democratic and communistic ideas' (Kahin cited in Grant, 1996 p. 27). *Pancasila* ideology plays an ongoing central role in governing modern Indonesia. 'It has been – and often at the same time – both a forceful binding agent for the young nation and a powerful tool of repression' (Schwartz, 1999(a), p. 10).

Pancasila underpins the fact that Indonesia is neither a theocratic nor secular-based state. However, despite popular support for this integrationist strategy, the strength of local leadership often reinforced disunity (Antlov and Cederroth, 1994). Divisive political groups emerged based around religious belief and ethnic socio-cultural values and, later, various ideological-based (*aliran*) separatist movements developed. In response, the government allowed three political groups – the Nationalist, Islamic and the Communists – to compete with each other (McVey 1993 cited in Antlov and Cederroth, 1994). Indicative of the failure to find consensus between these factions between 1946 and 1958 there were seventeen cabinets, with an average change every ten months (Grant, 1996). Hence, in order to build stability Soerkarno implemented a firmer 'guided democracy' strategic governance policy. This coercive administrative strategy attempted to draw together the conflicting factions – the army, Islamic groups and the Communists – but instead resulted in ongoing conflict and rebellion in the regions.

Individuals had very little freedom, with loyalty being ensured by local leadership through both social and anti-social means (officially and unofficially). A syncretic approach to leaders prevailed, whereby villagers often supported more than one leader as a conscious political survival strategy. This style of approach and response to leadership still has relevance (Slamet-Velsink, 1994). Soekarno continued to re-organise the political system in order to gain greater control. He replaced an elected parliament with one appointed by the President, set up the Supreme Advisor council as a non-elected policy making body, nationalised many Dutch companies and pursued an aggressive expansionist foreign policy by instigating international battles for the remaining Majapahit 'Golden Age' empire territories. His powerful rhetoric called for Indonesians to throw-off the colonial legacy of being considered as only 'coolies' or agricultural labourers by the outside world. The consequences of this international image of the

Indonesian workforce are still regularly debated in the Indonesian media today. Through these 'guided democracy' political strategies he presented himself as the father (*Bapak*) of the nation through the many guises of general, president and king (Grant, 1996). Nevertheless, the military campaigns were costly, many companies collapsed due to mismanagement, and economic development declined.

Having offended the West by his military expansionist strategies, Soekarno turned more to Communist China for financial support. At the height of the Cold War, with America being drawn into the Vietnam War, Indonesian national politics became enmeshed in international issues while the economy was impoverished and inflation reached 500 per cent (Grant, 1996). On the 'long' night of 30 September 1965, an abortive coup, thought to be inspired by the Communists, and in which six army generals were executed, resulted in a counter-response by General Soeharto, head of the army's strategic reserve. This counter-coup was followed by a violent anti-communist purging of the country led by Soeharto, in which it is claimed that 500,000 suspect Communist sympathisers were killed. There were pro-Communist led responses and the nation erupted into savage conflict between pro-Muslim, and Christians and pro-communist groups, with the *Peranakan* Chinese Indonesians often ending up as convenient 'scapegoats' (Schwartz, 1999). The country was politically divided and economically impoverished. Despite this, both Soekarno's personal style and the various political and governance strategies he applied laid down an important hierarchical and paternalistic socio-cultural model for leadership for the young nation.

The leadership style and management strategies of President Soeharto

In 1967 Soekarno was forced to resign and Soeharto became the new President, ushering in the 'New Order' Regime which was to last for the next thirty years. Soeharto framed his vision for the modernisation of Indonesia through the twin goals of political stability and economic growth. To politically stabilise the nation the army was given dual socio-political and military functions (*dwifungsi*), the Communist Party (PKI) banned, and large numbers of suspected communists or communist sympathisers massacred. 'Estimates of deaths range from under 100,000 to more than one million. The most common and credible estimates are 300,000 to 400,000 killed' (Schwartz, 1999, p. 20). The local religious, ethnic and economic issues became embroiled in the political identity of victims (Schwartz, 1999(a)).

Economic support was given from the West, especially the United States. Western economists were recruited to help introduce modern economic and administrative procedures. Western academic and technical support was recruited for the human resource development required to administer the bureaucracy to attract foreign investment and to develop agriculture and industry. Educational policy and institutional commitment were made to build the nation's literacy levels and, in particular, to develop the nation's science and technology capabilities (Schwartz, 1999(a)). Between 1965 and the early 1990s basic literacy skyrocketed from 40 per cent to 90 per cent (Jones and Manning, 1992, cited in Hefner, 1999). Western trained Indonesian economists, known as the 'technocrats', were given the task to rein in inflation, stabilise the rupiah, get a 'handle' on foreign debt, attract foreign aid and encourage foreign investment. They succeeded on all fronts, particularly during the first period of dramatic economic growth (Schwartz, 1999(a)).

There was a steady rise in state-owned enterprises. By the beginning of the 1990s state enterprises focused on the areas of banking, plantations and the transport and mining sector, along with a range of manufacturing industries dominated the economy and accounted for 30 per cent of GDP (Schwartz, 1999(a)). SOEs were viewed by some as a needed counterweight to the large and growing Chinese-controlled and privately owned conglomerates. 'Culturally, the Chinese had a head start in the name of capitalism. Business and commerce have long been acceptable to the Chinese; for the *pribumi*, this idea is relatively new' (Schwartz, 1999(a), p. 107). Hence, this ethnic-based business ownership imbalance contributed to indigenous Indonesian (*pribumi*) business and community resentment.

Many of the capitalists (*peranakan* and *pribumi*), several of whom were generals and high ranking bureaucrats and their children, were close to the centre of political power.

> Soeharto is always consulted when major contracts are to be awarded by the largest of the state-owned enterprises: Pertamina [oil], the state electricity utility PLN, the telephone company Telkom, the national logistics board Bulog, the State tin-mining company PT Timah, the national flag carrier Garuda Indonesia, the state road agency Jasa Marha, and leading companies controlled by the minister of Transportation, Forestry and others. (Schwartz, 1999(a), p. 61)

The SOEs were designed to build *pribumi* business capacity. In reality they strengthened the power of the *pribumi* elite and failed to encourage support small-to-medium *pribumi* business (Schwartz, 1999(a)).

Soeharto drew on a mixture of traditional Javanese cultural assumptions, and linked these with a range of modernist development assumptions to frame his political and economic vision for the nation. In order to suppress the endless factionalism which he considered hindered the implementation of his modernist vision and strategic approach for economic growth, the military were given a coercive administrative and political role in the government. Soeharto set about building a centralised and authoritarian political architecture in which his power reached out to the rural areas through a massive bureaucracy, supported by a very visible paramilitary and military presence. The rural areas were of prime interest for economic development, and so this new bureaucratic administrative and military structure extended political control down to the village level, even in the most remote areas of the archipelago. As a consequence:

> Because village leaders are tied to the state by multi-strands, they became state clients; because state clients are a local noble [*burpati*] with legitimate authority, state policies are given the touch of compulsion and substance ... with up to 170 positions for officials in a single village. (Antlov and Cederrroth, 1994, p. 8)

A consequence of this political and administrative structure was that, together with a large and complex hierarchy of state-based officials, the New Order administration had almost unlimited power to regulate the activities of all corporations and persons within Indonesian society (Antlov and Cederrroth, 1994). The control and reach of the centralist government was further supported by the acquisition of a satellite television broadcast system and an institutionalised authoritarian approach to all information and media content (Sen and Hill, 2000).

In order to justify this coercive approach to governance the Javanese cultural notion of the family (*kekluaragaan*) was appropriated, to reconceptualise the national need for social harmony and the crucial role of the mutual obligations (*gotong royong*) in achieving this was emphasised. 'In social life harmony should occur like in a family, in the consciousness that common interests transcend the individual ... If the common good is fulfilled all individual goals are reached' (Muldar, 1994, p. 58). Javanese cosmology emphasises the inequality of these mutual obligations, and this cultural assumption morally underpins the hierarchical fact that there are some who are guided and some who lead. A leader must have the qualities of a guardian, or caretaker, and the leader's role is to stimulate, lead and guide the ones he has responsibilities for. Therefore, a leader is conceived of as the ideal father: 'He is a *Bapak*, a father, a reliable person who should be honoured and followed, whose whim and wish is a command and who cares for his subjects' (Muldar, 1994, pp. 60–61).

Thus, subjects are constructed as being child-like. Conflict is construed as individual weakness. As a consequence, such a stratified and paternalistic notion of the moral order justified the imposition of strict rules which demand obedience, and this moral order is tied to a prescriptive etiquette that also tied people to their specific societal status and duties. The assumptions of this cultural model have significant ramifications for the framing of the policies of various societal institutions such as the media (Sen and Hill, 2000), education in general and the higher education sector, (Singleton, 2002), and in particular, the many layers of bureaucracy, the military and the police, and the management of business and the economy. These various political, economic and cultural governance and management strategies supported significant economic growth and development.

During the 1990s, with the dramatic 'tiger' status rate of economic growth came a burgeoning of the middle class. Higher standards of living for the middle class brought increased levels of consumption, and under the influence of globalisation, many western consumer products. By the mid-1990s the Soeharto regime was experiencing international pressure to deregulate and open up Indonesia for market opportunities. Keen to attract international foreign investment, a range of deregulation measures were introduced. At the same time, pressure was mounting from the middle class within the country for the liberalisation of media control and, hence, some loosening of media policy occurred. Daily newspapers papers presented stories about the rich and cosmopolitan lifestyle of the political and business elite. A more open media encouraged more critical political community debate, which in turn focused attention on internal governance and management issues, concern for the impact of globalisation, and the increasing gap between rich and poor in Indonesia (Sen and Hill, 2000).

Soeharto's Presidency also left a hierarchical and paternalistic cultural style of leadership, but the authoritarian and coercive governance and management strategy and the concentration of wealth on the hands of a powerful few also left a systemic legacy of inter-community and institutional mistrust, fear and anger. This legacy has not only divisive ramifications which can be identified in the values and behaviour of groups and individuals, but also underpins the following community determination to collectively pursue national democratic political goals over personal and community economic development.

The post-Soeharto *reformasi* leadership and managing *transformasi*

Under the impact of the 1997 Asian economic crisis the nation's status changed from that of an enviable economic 'tiger' to a massive economic collapse, followed by political turmoil, and the dramatic downfall of the Soeharto New Order Regime. Economic chaos spilt over into political chaos. Riots broke out, ethnic chasms developed and the ethnic Chinese became victims of rioters. 'Comprising four per cent of the population, the Chinese control 70 per cent of the private, modern economy and are especially dominant in banking, trading and distribution' (Schwartz, 1999b, p. 2). Many Chinese Indonesians who could afford to, fled the country for Singapore, Australia and the United States. The many that remained lived in fear.

In response to the economic and political chaos, caretaker President Habibie introduced a further range of liberal political policies including: the withdrawal of the restrictive press laws, the release of political prisoners, the removal of the ban on new political parties, the removal of restrictions on trade unions and new electoral laws were announced that included a diminished political role of the military, and Indonesians were free to establish new media (Liddle, 1999; ICG, 2000). 'Two controversial pieces of legislation introduced early in the post-Soeharto period, Laws no. 22 and 25(1999), transferred significant administrative powers to the sub-provincial level and introduced new revenue-sharing arrangements between Jakarta and the regions' (Bouchier and Hadiz, 2003, p. 255). In 1999, after a general election which was conducted in an extraordinarily free and transparent manner (ICG, 2000) the People's Consultative Assembly elected Abdurrahman Wahid, leader of the country's largest Islamic organisation Nahdlatul Ulama (NU) president.

While Wahid enjoyed popular grassroots support, his unpretentious, indecisive and intellectual style of leadership, which may have appealed to his rural and urban support base, did not suit the wider expectation for a more hierarchical, paternalistic and formalised Javanese cultural style of leadership. Wahid's cultural style of leadership reflected a more open, learned and modernist Islamic religious teacher (*Ulama*) approach. Factional-based destabilising and coercive military activities, which stirred violent regional inter-ethnic and inter-religious clashes, plagued Wahid's fragile democratic reform (*reformasi*) aims. With this ongoing instability foreign investment failed to return and the economy continued to flounder. Wahid was impeached in 2001. Nevertheless, despite ongoing economic hardship national commitment to his democratic vision for reform continued. However, it is too simplistic to see democracy as something 'exported' from the West to Islamic countries, such as Indonesia (Hefner, 1999). While powerful international institutions, such as the IMF and the World Bank, imposed significant institutional economic reform, the *rakyat*, or the mass of Indonesian people, actively engaged in processes of building popular democratic reform and a strengthening of Indonesia as a civil society.

Wahid was replaced with the election of President Megawati Sukarnoputri, leader of the nationalist People's Democratic Party (PDI) and daughter of former President Soekarno. Her leadership was marked by silence and indecisions, but significant ongoing macroeconomic reform. Silence is a Javanese strategy for dealing with bad news and as such is a 'reactive' cultural management strategy (Lewis, 2003). Her passive, possibly over optimistic, but symbolic leadership role also conveyed the stabilising cultural role of a Javanese mother-figure (*Ibu*). Her time as President marked out the transition to political democracy. In addition, the nation became embroiled in the international terrorism events associated with Islamic fundamentalism which culminated in the Bali bombing (2002), The Hotel Marriot, (2003) and just prior to the 2004 Presidential election, the bombing of the Australian embassy. The economic costs of terrorism continue to be high as tourists and investors alike perceived the unstable situation to be too risky and costly to return in large numbers.

Megawati's popular power was associated with the legacy of her father Soekarno and her ongoing pro-democracy struggle under Soeharto's regime. The finance for her political success came from her Sumatran politician/businessman husband, Taufik Kiemas. Without any tangible proof or charges being laid, Taufik was accused of involvement in a wide range of large regional infrastructure development projects tainted with corruption (Guerin, 2002). Promises to address corruption, collusion and nepotism (*Korupsi, Kolusi, dan Nepotisme* – KKN) are seen to be meaningless by the masses that live with this characteristic elite intermixing of politics and business, and accusations of corruption. With little foreign investment from the West, just as her father had previously made strategic alliances with China, she and Taufik visited Beijing to meet with Chinese Prime Minister, Zhu Rongji to win LNG gas supply contracts. While they failed to win the contracts, this action strengthened perceptions of her associations with the Chinese Indonesian business elite.

Interestingly, when the overseas Indonesian ballot boxes were counted after the September 2004 Presidential elections, only two had a majority that supported Megawati – Beijing and Los Angeles (Brown, 2004).

However, former army General Susilo Bambang Yudhoyono (SBY) and a former minister in Megawati's Cabinet received more than 60 per cent of the vote, to be popularly elected President in September 2004. Both the parliamentary and presidential elections were reported by international observers as being orderly, peaceful and transparent, reflecting Indonesia' maturing as a democracy. President Yudhoyono has had significant military officer training in the United States. He has a Masters qualification in Management and recently completed doctoral studies in agricultural economics at the prestigious Bogor Institute of Agriculture. He speaks fluent English. SBY's electoral website identified his key national concerns as being:

● The elimination of poverty and the need to build an economy that works for the interests of all Indonesians;

● Law enforcement as this is vital for both business and national security; and

● To build prosperity to create employment opportunities through the development of the private sector supporting small and medium businesses through better policies and access to investment finance (http://www.sbyudhoyono.com/National.aspx).

Jusef Kalla, his deputy, is a powerful businessman from Sulawesi. This choice breaks with the political dominance of the Javanese. In general, the announcement of his new Cabinet received favourable response. However, his choice of ministers indicated that while a democratic system of election has been set in place the same elite political, business and former military maintain a pivotal decision-making positions in the future of Indonesia. With only 10.4 per cent of the popular vote by SBY's Democrat Party, characteristic Indonesian compromises guided the choice of the Cabinet. Particular international concern was expressed at the appointment of *pribumi* business, Bakrie Brothers' conglomerate head and member of Golkar, Aburizal Bakrie, as Chief Economic Minister. Bakrie's conglomerate defaulted on more than US$1 billion worth of foreign debt to international creditors following the Asian Economic Crisis (Kolesnikov-Jessop, 2004). Whatever the economic development approach adopted by the cabinet under his leadership, the achievement of democratic reform of the political system of government, is a huge transformation. While the other countries in the region have concentrated on economic reform as a post-economic crisis governance strategy, Indonesia took this alternative reform path. However, it is apparent that institutional reform, the fight against corruption and the strengthening of the rule of law must continue. Now the people will be keen for economic development opportunities and outcomes, and if there is ongoing political stability investment should return.

The impact of external forces: Economic stagnation, institutional reform and terrorism

Many, if not all industry sectors suffered the severe impact of ongoing economic stagnation instigated by the Asian economic crisis, especially the construction, manufacturing, banking and finance, tourism and hospitality sectors and SMEs (Tayeb, 1997). At the peak of the crisis many MNCs withdrew their staff and operations, and in a high-risk environment have not returned. The limited number that remained developed 'a comprehensive set of integrated contingency plans presented by terrorism, rising crime, labour unrest, and the need for better community relations' (Foster, 2002, p. 1) in an anti-globalisation backlash climate.

At the time of the crisis, a series of economic and institutional reform priorities that the Indonesian government needed to address were identified that included the following governance and management issues: prudent macroeconomic management, the restructure of the banking sector, the resolution of corporate debt issues, the promotion of good governance, addressing social impacts and maintaining political stability (Tayeb, 1997). In addition, it was suggested that Indonesian business needed more sophisticated managerial skills, venture capital, financial and information technology knowledge and skills, and new legislation covering legal aspects such as the protection of intellectual property and corporate governance (Tayeb, 1997). These institutional reform agendas have important requirements associated with human resource capacity development.

Since then a range of economic and institutional reforms was implemented that managed to restore macroeconomic stability. Economic growth of 4.1 per cent was achieved in 2003 (*Tradewatch*, 2004), with 4.7 per cent indicated for 2004 (World Bank, 2004).

> Under the tutelage of the IMF, they have slashed the deficit, mainly by reducing subsidies and selling the banks and associated assets that the government had taken over during the crisis. The subsequent appreciation of the rupiah has helped to reduce Indonesia's stock of public debt from over 90 per cent of GDP in 2001 to roughly 60 per cent today. Interest rates, in line with the global trend, have fallen steadily. All this propelled the economy to respectable growth of almost five percent. (*The Economist*, 25 September 2004)

A required six per cent growth figure is needed in Indonesia in order for the nation to be able to invest in the urgently required infrastructure, institutional strengthening and capacity development. Current growth is based on local consumer spending and investment, with little foreign investment to date.

The maintenance of political stability, the issue of terrorism associated with fundamental Islamic groups such as *Jemaah Islamiah*, and a more certain policy and legislative environment remain the dominant issues in encouraging the foreign investment required for higher levels of economic growth. The Asia Foundation Survey found only three per cent support for Islamic *shari'ah* law with the majority of citizens considering themselves to be Indonesians first and

Muslims second (Cochrane, 2004, p. 21). The new President has played a leading spokesperson role in the Indonesian response to terrorism and, hence, it may be likely that a concerted effort in this area will continue, along with a strengthening of regional intergovernmental intelligence and security cooperation.

One of the key corporate and institutional reform issues to emerge after the collapse of the New Order Regime was both international and national concern for the KKN associated with corporate and institutional business management and governance practices. This issue, associated with the power amassed by the political, bureaucratic and corporate elite, and coupled with critical international and local concern for the lack of institutional and corporate transparency, were considered to account for the depth of the economic crisis in Indonesia. Most humiliating for the country was the fact that President Soeharto was rated as the most corrupt international political leader ahead of nine others (*Press Release*, Transparency International (TI), 2004). TI research estimates that between 1967 and 1998 the President embezzled US$15 to 35 billion while the GDP per capita (2001) was US$695. A long way behind at number two rating was President Marcos of the Philippines who embezzled US$5 to 10 billion between 1972 and 1986.

The transfer of power from the centralist government to the regions has revealed the need for both institutional reform and the strengthening of regional governments. In addition, significant human resource capacity development is also now required in the regions. The local *burpati* leaders continue to play a key leadership role in the devolved economic and political system. The significant primary industry natural resource opportunities (agriculture, forestry, oil and gas, mining and maritime) now require investment and sustainable approaches to management. International developers now require a more uniform and transparent regulatory and legislative environment for development projects.

Table 10.1 below indicates the key trading partners of Indonesia, and it is apparent that the strengthening of these relationships will play a critical role in future development. These trading partners are important for future foreign investment, strategic alliances and market opportunities. In such a dynamic regional context the relationship with Japan may become more important.

Table 10.1 Indonesia's global trade relationships for year 2003

Indonesia's principal export destinations sources	Sources	Indonesia's principal import	
1 Japan	22.3%	1 Japan	13.0%
2 United States	12.1%	2 United States	12.8%
3 Singapore	8.8%	3 Singapore	9.1%
4 South Korea	7.1%	4 South Korea	8.3%
5 China	6.2%	5 China	5.2%
6 Australia	2.9%	6 Australia	5.1%

Source: DFAT, Australia.

Under the leadership of SBY the relationship with America will strengthen. However, it is also predictable that the relationship with China and the connection to local Chinese Indonesian networks will become increasingly important. Indicative of this, senior officials of the Indonesian Chamber of Commerce and Industry (KADIN) visited Shanghai in early November 2004 to try to increase investment and trade between the two countries' business sectors. Indonesian investment in Shanghai was US$1.74 billion in 2001, while Shanghai investment in Indonesia was much less (*The Jakarta Post* November, 2004).

In a democratic and politically engaged Indonesia there is now a powerful network of local and international non-government organisations (NGOs) scrutinising Indonesian and international business activities. The popular commitment to democratic political reform over the past six years, despite the extreme hardships imposed by the economic collapse and the Soeharto Regime legacy of a better educated middle class, indicates that there is a strong national desire to rise to the significant human resource and management challenges necessary to rebuild sustainable economic growth on a stronger institutional foundation and to create a new 'golden era' for Indonesia.

The meso-societal level: The management of Indonesian institutional infrastructure

Industrial infrastructure

The previous section explains how at the macro-level specific local and regional geography, history, religion and diverse ethnicity along with external international issues have complexly shaped the particular culture, economics and politics of Indonesian society. The next section discusses how the various management strategies applied in Indonesia at the meso-management level impact on the nation's industrial infrastructure. The corporate and community governance and management strategies applied at the meso-societal level have, in turn, critical implications for the management patterns and processes applied at the micro-level.

The prevailing Javanese approach to management in Indonesia

The various political, economic and cultural strategic policies institutionally implemented over the past fifty years by the national governments have successfully built a shared national world view that guides national behaviour and attitudes. The previous discussion indicates how the particular world view and cultural assumptions of the Javanese, the largest ethnic group, have been interwoven to dominate the cultural logic of national discourse. Hence, it is apparent that the Javanese and their cultural assumptions dominate the bureaucracy and many corporate and community organisations with their particular preferred management styles of command, motivation and communications, decision-making systems, human resource management, production values and approaches to technology and quality control. Yet at the same time, it is important always to be mindful of the diverse sub-cultural ways in which ethnicity and religion shape the behaviour and values of groups and individuals.

The single most important value dominating the Javanese managerial culture is the idea of the *pribumi* or indigenous 'sons of soil' and the power associated with this group is legitimised by a convoluted web of 'crony'-based management. The strength of this notion accounts for the historical discrimination against ethnic Chinese and their businesses and other ethnic groups, and the historical need for the ethnic Chinese to assimilate. The Javanese mutual obligation (*gotong royong*) concept, which emphasises the importance of social harmony, has additional management implications. Over the past fifty years these two concepts were used to perpetuate cronyism affirming *pribumi* power and status, while the issues of dissent and diversity were neutralised by *gotony royong* (mutual obligations) proclamations and a high value placed on social harmony. The key features that derive from the powerful Javanese-based *kekluaragann* family model for imagining the Indonesian nation include: a hierarchical structure, a patriarchal *bapak* manager and a conservative reactivism (*surat keputusan*).

In 2001 President Wahid introduced legislation that allowed the ethnic Chinese to overtly participate in Chinese cultural celebrations. Drawing on the cultural traditions of Confucianism, the Chinese place a high value on education, and as a consequence of their political vulnerability they tend to have a high saving rate, distrust strangers and depend to a great extent on personal relationships and family networks, all of which are conducive to the rapid growth of family-run businesses (Schwartz, 1999(b)). 'These alliances ... give Chinese firms "access to well-established networks of credit, market information, and domestic and overseas trading contacts, which enable the a stronger among them to ride out fluctuation of business cycles"' (Mackie cited in Schwartz, 1999(b), p. 107). However, most Chinese firms 'also have to rely on political connections, bribes and payoff to ensure immunity from arbitrary imposts' (Mackie cited in Schwartz, 1999(b), p. 107). With the increasing regional importance of China, its high rate of economic growth, the relationship of off-shore Chinese business to mainland developments and the need to attract foreign investment to Indonesia, it is predictable that *Peranakan* businesses will only increase in economic importance.

Types of enterprises

While there has been considerable political and economic reform since the collapse of the New Order Regime, its institutionalised legacy on the Indonesian economy and society is comprehensive. Enterprises in Indonesia can be categorised into private (*swasta*), government owned companies (*Badan Usaha Milik Negara*, BUMN) and cooperatives (*Koperasi*). Each of these is discussed briefly.

- *Private enterprises* – are organisations that are owned by a private individual, a family or a group of people. These enterprises can be local, national or international in scope. Local and national enterprises are normally managed by the owner(s), while many of those companies that have become international are normally managed by professional managers, many of whom are from overseas.

- *The BUMNs* – are fully owned by the government and are run by government or military officers. These companies have been grouped into 3 categories, namely *jawatan* (part of the government bureaucracy), *perum* ('perusahaan umum', public company), and *persero* (privatised companies). The *jawatan* is still part of the public service and the status of their employees is the same as that of other public servants. The status of the *perum* employees is variable, and their position is not as secure as public servants. The status of employees in the *persero* companies is very much the same as that of employees of private companies. Some of the *persero* companies have been privatised, listed on Jakarta Stock Market and run by professional managers. Examples include PT Indosat, PT Telkom and PT Timah. The structure of these companies is similar to that of the private companies, consisting of a Board of Commissioners (*dewan komisaris*), a Board of Directors (*direksi*) and various section/subsection heads (*pegawai yang berjabatan*), and finally, general employees (*pegawai biasa*). Members of the Board of Commissioners are normally relevant government ministers, high ranking officials and major shareholders. Members of the Board of Directors are also high-ranking government or military officers, as well as a few non-government professional managers.

The government significantly influences the decisions of these companies' professional managers who are often subjected to corrupt practices. Managers are powerless to reject 'memos' from powerful government representatives asking for favours or preferential treatment for family members and colleagues. Many instances involved Soeharto's sons and daughters. Such practices have often come at significant economic costs, including bankruptcy. There has been considerable popular debate within Indonesia on the issues of KKN and transparency. In the current politically engaged environment the business activities and wealth of the elite are widely known and critically discussed by the mass of Indonesian people (*rakyat*), who during the election period disseminated this information on a daily basis on 'backyard'-produced broadsheets read time and time again (Lane, 2003).

- *A Cooperative enterprise* – is an enterprise that is initiated by ordinary people and shareholders are members of the cooperative. Its office holders are called chairman, vice chairman, secretary, treasurer, section heads and general assistants. They are elected by members on a periodic basis. Cooperative enterprises are supposed to be the core (*sokoguru*) of the Indonesian economy, as instructed by the 1945 Constitution (UUD 1945).

Hence, there is a ministry dedicated to it. The Soeharto government claimed to promote cooperatives, and almost every village has a cooperative, known as *Koperasi Unit Desa* (KUD) and *Badan Usaha Unit Desa* (BUUD). However, they have not developed as rapidly as private enterprises.

The micro-organisation level: Critical traditional, transitional and transformational issues in Indonesian management

Organisational structure

Large companies normally have two boards, a board of commissioners (*dewan komisaris*) and board of directors (*dewan direksi*). The board of commissioners provides advice on the strategic direction of the company, but little or no involvement in the daily running of the company. Members of this board are normally major shareholders or influential people invited by the owners. However, this does not mean that owners are not involved in the running of the companies. In fact, most companies are run by principal owner(s) as heads of the boards of directors which run the daily activities of the company, or in Indonesian terms *direktur umum* (general director). Cooperative enterprises also have similar structures, but use different terms for similar positions. These include *penasehat* (board of advisors), *pengurus* (office holders) including the chairman, vice chairman, secretary, vice secretary, treasurer and vice treasurer, and *pembantu umum* (committee members). The number of deputies depends on the size of the cooperative. Some cooperatives also have a patron, who is the most powerful person in the area. For example, if the cooperative is in a village, the patron is the head (*burpati*) of the village. If it is situated in a government department, the patron is the minister of the relevant department.

A hierarchical structure indicates a top-down command and control system, with delegation within sections. The top leadership is seen as the supreme leader to whom everyone seeks guidance. He or she holds the position of the *Bapak* (father) or *Ibu* (mother) who will take care of, protect, and provide guidance, for everyone in the company. In turn, the Father or Mother figure is expected to be wise in leading the company, needs to treat every member of the family equally, to avoid anything that may affect harmonious relationships among the family members and be expected to adhere to moral values as an example for the whole big family (*keluarga besar*). Multinational companies operating in Indonesia, and employing Indonesians need to integrate this senior management *bapak* position into their particular corporate management system.

Organisational behaviour

Motivation

The modern Western notion of capital accumulation and the pursuit of economic growth is a relatively recently imported cultural value in Indonesia. Traditional Javanese society did not value trading as a respected career. Traders, or those involved in commercial activities, do not conventionally belong to the upper class. Senior civil servants have high ascriptive status. Thus, within the Javanese-based cultural model there has been limited entrepreneurial incentive. A Javanese world view considers that the purpose of a business enterprise is essentially survival, to meet needs such as food, clothing, housing and education. There is a Javanese saying, *makan tidak makan, yang penting kumpul* (Whether we can eat or not, it does not matter as long as we can get together) – that is, what matters is meeting or being together with family and relatives. Thus, a Javanese person might refuse a job offer if they have to leave their family, even though they may have to struggle to obtain food to survive. Hence, for the Javanese striving for excellence in business is not culturally valued. However, for the Chinese or the Batak manager, whose culture promotes a higher work ethic, the motivation for achieving business success will be higher.

Individual assertiveness and aggression, while disregarding the interests of fellow employees, is considered undesirable in Indonesian business culture. The prevailing collectivist community assumptions mean that self-promotion to a superior is considered too 'ambitious', and this egotistic individualism is resented by colleagues. The prevailing collectivist orientation partly explains why the Chinese dominate the Indonesian economy and why only a small number of *pribumi* Indonesians have become major capitalists. Soeharto's policy, (especially during the 1970s) of giving priority to Chinese businessmen close to him at the expense of the indigenous (Muslim) entrepreneurs, led to the rapid expansion of Chinese owned businesses and the demise of many indigenous enterprises (Robison, 1986).

Styles of communication

The dominance of Javanese cultural values has significant implications for Indonesian styles of communication. In stark contrast to the direct, linear and argumentative style of Western English language-based communication styles, Indonesian communication tends to be indirect, cyclical and based around conflict avoidance. Importantly, the culture has a strong oral tradition. Most Indonesians are multilingual. The choice of *Bahasa* Indonesia as the official unifying national language is a relatively recent phenomenon. It is the official language of education, administration and the bureaucracy. As such its official usage has become imbued with a formal and institutionalised Javanese bureaucratic logic, while on the streets of Jakarta a more colloquial and animated Javanese dialect applies. Hence, communication in Indonesia is highly context-dependent.

Moreover, conversation is an effective means of marking the complex and diverse socio-cultural identities.

Following are some specific examples of an Indonesian style of communication in a business context:

- *Indirectness* – A manager in Indonesia needs to give explanations to employees in plain language, but with sensitive issues they will avoid being direct. Sensitive issues may cause loss of face. When an employee makes a mistake blame will not be attributed, but instead the manager will use a 'good but' rhetorical pattern, whereby the employee is praised for their positive aspects, then implicitly an additional message is conveyed, or instead the message is buried in a long-winded speech, a trusted third party is used to deliver the message, or simply an 'unhappy' face is exhibited. Hence, Indonesians are very good at reading indirect communication and do not expect a manager to be aggressive (especially in public) because of the implied loss of face. If loss of face occurs the consequences could range from a simple guilt feeling, the refusal to admit to problems, revenge, or even resignation, depending on how serious is the loss of face implied. Tension in a confrontation or anxiety creating context may be expressed by nervous laughter (as often demonstrated in the trials of the Bali bombers) and physical attempts to render oneself as invisible, such as sliding down very low in a chair while sitting behind a desk or conference table (Singleton, 2002).

- *Circumlocution* (non-linearity) – As Indonesians are concerned about keeping face, circular logic is incorporated into both oral and written communication. A Javanese cultural notion of deliberation (*musyawarh*) underpins this circumlocutory communication style on the assumption that any decision (*mukafat*) must be collective and consensual. Sometimes the purpose of an interaction will not be directly referred to and metaphors may be used. Hence, the role of the Bapak as senior manager is affirmed as employees will need to constantly defer to this person for clarification that the collective decision-making process is heading in the right direction.

Thus, an Indonesian will never be the bearer of bad news to those in more senior positions, and will never directly say 'no' (i.e. confront). This style of communication has significant implications for Western notions of productivity, task performance and assessment. This characteristic circumlocutory style of oral communication is reflected in Indonesian written communication. Hence, a circular rationale is embedded in the cultural logic of Indonesian bureaucratic regulations, legislation and associated report writing (Singleton, 2002). Hence, the embedded nature of this cultural logic in Indonesian world views has critical implications for the areas of institutional strengthening and human resource capacity development.

The Indonesian way of doing business is characteristically very different from Western and other national and regional approaches. It is apparent that this particular Indonesian cultural approach coupled with complex and inter-related macro-global, regional, national and local environmental realities, create significant micro-environmental management challenges for business operating in Indonesia. Nevertheless, the current macro-political and economic reform achievements, and the decentralisation of administrative power to regional and local authorities in a complex and dynamic context, indicate that there is both a will and enthusiasm for further micro-reform with the long-term view to achieve more sustainable and equitable economic development. However, achieving this has crucial human resource development implications.

It is estimated that there are more than 40 million unemployed in Indonesia, half of these being university or college graduates, who have been a particularly volatile group. World Bank reports indicate that 50 per cent of the population is barely above the poverty line and 'very vulnerable' (National Committee on US–Indonesian Relations, 2003). Yet since the introduction of the laws in 2001 to devolve all powers, except justice, foreign affairs, defence and security, monetary and fiscal matters and religious affairs, to approximately 400 districts and municipalities, there has not been significant breakdown of service delivery. This devolution management process has, however, created a less uniform regulatory and more complex fiscal management environment for business investment and operations.

Case study examples indicate the need for international companies to adapt to the micro-environment of business in regional Indonesia. Considerable adaptability and responsiveness is required by international management. For instance, an MNC in addressing, for example, the project risk of a very large natural resource mining project in regional Indonesia may need to assess the potential impact on the project of controversy associated with local media and community stakeholder issues. Characteristically, a large mining MNC will have centrally designed global 'media and communications' public relations policies and guidelines conceived to be universally applied and strictly managed. These guidelines are premised to a large degree on a risk-averse approach to giving out information (say little and only when necessary, and even then only when authorised by corporate Head Quarters (HQ)), along a very developed nation institutional understanding of how the media operates. Should any community or stakeholder controversy arise from a specific mining project, assessing the risk aversion communication strategy to be applied in regional Indonesia on the basis of a centralised corporate HQ media and communications policy guideline could be disastrous. There are enormous challenges associated with culturally aligning the global corporate (often based on Western assumptions) and local community interpretations of the 'message content' of media releases from a remote home-base HQs for release in regional Indonesia. In addition, there is little international understanding of how media as part of local business operates in regional Indonesia.

First, the notion that local media in Indonesia support their business only through 'selling news' and advertising, like the Western press is to be naïve. Accessing other revenue streams is vital for business in Indonesia. Hence, from an Indonesian perspective if a corporation wishes to benefit from public relations-based exposure in the local Indonesian media (i.e., to gain fair and reasonable reporting) then like all business arrangements that 'service' mutually beneficial exchange is based on a business fee-for-service partnership. If the company is not prepared to pay for the service it cannot expect favourable local reporting. Moreover, from the Indonesian perspective there are costs associated with, for example a local journalist travelling distances to a MNC's project site, consuming resources and committing time to report honestly and favourably. Thus, there is an expectation that the MNC in question will amply support these costs in return for the access to media service. In Indonesia this is not corrupt practice, and arguably should not be judged in the context of western normative behaviour. The only way to manage the cultural difference in business practices in this example is for the MNC to recognise the difference and adapt its standardised global practices and accommodate to locally realities (Singleton, URS Corp, pers. comm. 2004, 29 October).

However, there are many microeconomic and institutional reforms necessary to create the certainty required to attract investment, and to improve the competitiveness of all industry in order to achieve higher and more sustainable levels of economic growth. The implementation of microeconomic reforms is essential to elevate the country towards higher economic growth (Standards and Poor cited in *The Jakarta Post*, September, 2004).

> In particular, measures to reduce pervasive corruption, increase the competence and integrity of the judiciary, create a predictable and fair commercial legal environment, create internationally competitive labour markets, and cohesive industry and trade policy, are urgently needed to reverse the country's declining competitiveness. (*The Jakarta Post*, 29 September 2004)

Standard and Poor emphasise that the difficulties encountered in implementing this ongoing reform cannot be underestimated. Strengthening the management and governance capacity of the nation is crucial to achieve on going microeconomic reform. Many critical management concerns relate to the ways in which the prevailing cultural norms and practices are imbued into institutional and professional life. The United States Ambassador, (Boyce, 2004) points to the Presidential mandate, the newly empowered parliament, a media that is playing a watchdog role, the growth of NGOs and a previously non-existent civil society as important catalysts for sustaining the ongoing management and governance reform. This reform is considered essential for business to manage and minimise risk and, hence, increase foreign direct investment.

Pt. Pertamina, the state oil company, presents a good case example of the complex management challenges that lie ahead in achieving ongoing corporate reform, efficiencies and productivity. As the largest company in Indonesia, Pertamina faces increased competition through deregulation of the nation's oil market and increased scrutiny from the government's Anti-corruption Commission and Antimonopoly Commission which have both begun investigations into an oil-tanker sale scandal (Mapes, 2004). In early August, 2004 the government fired the company president and most of the directors with the exception of the finance director, after a string of corruption allegations.

The shake up comes at a difficult time ... Indonesia's largest company is struggling to reverse a decline in crude-oil production that turned East Asia's only member of the Organisation of Petroleum Exporting Countries (OPEC) into a net oil importer during the first quarter this year. Thanks to a sharp drop in new investment in oil exploration and production over the past few years Indonesia's net export of oil during 2004 is expected to average 23,000 barrels a day, a plunge of 97% from 697,000 barrels a day in 1998. (Mapes, 2004)

Historically, investment, production and the export of oil have been crucial to the Indonesian economy. These current and dramatically reduced production figures must be viewed in a global context where both prices and demand are rising dramatically. As well as increased competition from the entry of foreign oil companies who will no longer be forced to cooperate with the state-run producer, the government is taking away many of the company benefits including a monopoly over domestic fuel sales. The newly appointed President does not come from an oil background, but from a successful company, Indosat, recently named as one of the country's ten best-managed companies. In addition, in light of elevated international oil prices and local price subsidies, one of the first unpopular actions that President Yudhoyono may have to address is the need to increase the price of fuel. In a national context where the population has already paid a heavy economic cost, price rises may be politically destabilising.

Complex and paradoxical patterns and processes

Culture influences the way people manage their business and this is particularly apparent in Indonesian management practice at the micro-level. More particularly, the management patterns and processes applied at the micro-level have significant implications for not only the corporate performance of particular organisations operating in Indonesia, but for the overall economic and social welfare of the nation as determined by particular organisational management strategies applied in response to an increasingly competitive and integrated global market context.

The following comments are generalised, however it is noteworthy to remember that while there is a strong collective management and workplace culture, the existing plurality within Indonesia means that individuals will often perform differently according to their religious, ethnic and educational backgrounds and the context in which they are operating (Singleton, 2002). Seven aspects of Indonesian culture are supportive of modern management and three are considered adverse (Prawirosentono, 1999, p. 136). The supportive aspects of modern management are: Indonesians tend to be helpful and friendly to neighbours, friendly to others including foreigners and loyal to friends, cooperative (*gotong royong*), tolerant, a preference for harmony, collective and collaborative decision-making and patient and hardworking (*Prawirosentono, 1999, pp. 299–301*). The crucial basis to *gotong royong* is the spirit of working together, the drive to combine everyone's effort to finish a job or to achieve a common goal.

Nevertheless, in practice, this collectivist approach can be counter-productive if it does not combine collective goals with individual responsibility. To avoid problems, everyone needs to be given clear responsibility so that their achievements can be assessed accurately in order to ensure that each human resource functions to achieve the common company goal. If promoted appropriately, the inherent team spirit can be an effective driving force to achieve company goals for at least two reasons: every team member will feel that they work for common goals, and each is prepared to help one another. Tolerance is usually a positive characteristic, although it may also be negative in relation to the tolerance of inadequate or inappropriate behaviour, or performance.

A preference for harmony is positive in that it prevents conflicts from developing. However, for the sake of harmony, people avoid conflicts. People hide their feelings if they are angry or unhappy, but such feelings can accumulate. The outcome may be withdrawal, 'backstabbing' or a lack of communication. For foreigners, in particular, it is difficult to discover the real issues underlying a situation. For example, Indonesians will always respond positively to a request, by predominantly saying 'ya ya'. This has important implications for tracking work performance, time management and the achievement of team goals. Responses to management queries suggest that everything is going according to plan when in fact it is not. Foreigners need to learn to interpret the many different and indirect ways of an Indonesian saying 'no'.

The three attitudes that may be negative for management are: lack of discipline, irresponsibility and lack of creativity (Prawirosentono, 1999, pp. 301–2). These attitudes are common in the region, but are especially characteristic in Indonesia. Indonesians may have incorporated planning and contract documents, but they are often disregarded. Western management notions of discipline and efficiency are problematic. Western corporate representatives should not be dependent solely on written contracts when working with Indonesians because they do not always rely on written contracts (Mann, 1998). To give greater local support to contractual arrangements foreign entrepreneurs should invest in and develop strong relationships with their Indonesian counterparts. The Indonesian use of time may imply a lack of discipline. Meetings almost always begin late and Indonesians use the term 'rubber time' (*jam karet*), which implies that time can be stretched. One may have to wait for hours to be able to meet a manager even though one has made an appointment (Mann, 1998). The cultural assumption underpinning this approach is that individuals, particularly those with high ascriptive status, have multiple public, private and religious responsibilities and so decisions around prioritising these must be judged by the senior individual. Those with less ascriptive status should not question this judgement.

Some Indonesians tend to avoid individual responsibility. They tend to diffuse responsibility through the group or through superiors due to a lack of confidence, and few people are prepared to admit guilt because of fear of the consequences. The lack of individual initiative in problem solving and innovation in general, is another issue. Even though the government spends millions of dollars every year for research, the outcomes are small compared to the amount of money spent.

The majority of big companies, either private or BUMN, have not shown significant innovation, or transfer of technology. For example, Indonesian automobile industries have received support and protection from the government since the first Five Year Development Plan (*Repelita I*) beginning in 1969, and since then have not been able to be independent from the 'mother' companies which supplied them with licences. By contrast, Malaysia, which began automobile manufacturing several years later than Indonesia, has been able to be independent. Similar situations are found in the manufacturing and service industries (Prawirosentono, 1999, p. 302).

The Soeharto government attempted to reduce these potentially negative attitudes through national discipline action (*Gerakan displine nasional*). Posters, brochures, radio and television stations were used to create a 'discipline' campaign. However, the government itself often did not demonstrate the discipline it was trying to instil. The government said that corruption must be eradicated, but many of its officials committed corruption. Nonetheless, some companies have improved performance and have become more efficient. For example, the Railway Company has significantly reduced the unpunctuality of trains, and the management has turned the company's significant losses into significant profits (Prawirosentono, 1999, p. 155).

The changing role of education

Significant collective investment has been made over the past thirty years in education as a part of the government's modernist national development vision. A range of government education policies was employed to raise literacy levels and to build the necessary technical and science-based human resources considered critical to modernise and develop the nation. Since the economic crisis many can no longer afford to send their children to schools or to cover minimal material and uniform costs. Between 1997 to 1999 primary school enrolments were at 84 per cent, secondary enrolments 85 per cent (41 per cent female and 44 per cent males), with tertiary enrolments between 1996 to 1999 being 10 per cent (*Earthtrends*, 2003). For many of the current generation economic hardship means that the opportunities created by education will be lost. There will be additional costs for the nation.

The vast majority attend state-run schools, but in addition there are Islamic (*pesantrean*), Protestant and Catholic private schools. Obviously, a religion-based education plays an important role in shaping its students' worldview and behaviour. The Western culture-based Protestant Christian religious tradition promotes 'individualistic' and 'inner-directional' values and motivations, whereas Islam promotes 'communitarian' and 'outer directional' cultural values and motivations, with Catholicism sharing many of the communitarian and outer directional values and motivations of Islam (Hampden-Turner and Trompenaars, 2000). Individualism encourages competition, self-reliance, self-interest and personal growth and fulfilment, with communitarianism promoting cooperation, social concern, altruism and public service and societal legacy.

> Individualism seeks to locate the origins of value in the creative, feeling, inquiring and discovering person who seeks fulfilment and is solely responsible for choices made and convictions formed. Communitarianism seeks to locate the origins of value within the social discourse of the living society, which nurtures, educates, and takes responsibility for the spirit engendered amongst its members. (Hampden-Turner and Trompenaars, 2000, pp. 69–70)

> Inner direction conceives of virtue as inside each of us – in our souls, wills, convictions, principles and core beliefs – in the triumph of the conscious purpose. Outer direction conceives of virtue as outside each of us, in natural rhythms, in the beauties and power of nature, in aesthetic environments and relationships. (p. 234)

Hence, graduates of a Protestant Christian-based education system develop more of an individualistic and inner directional cultural orientation in contrast to those who experienced an Islamic-based education, which are concerned with developing a collective, communitarian and outer directional cultural orientation in students. This fundamental cultural dichotomy has significant implications for the pluralistic pedagogical ways in which learning is promoted, decisions are made and educational performance is assessed.

With *Pancasila* principles being the blueprint for nationalist discourse it was included as an area of study in every year of schooling. This powerful cultural and educational policy was applied in order to integrate the culturally diverse ethnic and religious identities, values and practices through the acquisition of an overarching homogeneous cultural values system that built a cohesive and shared national identity. The implications for governance were that *Pancasila* would provide the socio-cultural basis for a well-ordered and highly civilised society. Soldiers, teachers, politicians, doctors and even overseas students were required to attend classes to better understand the meaning of *Pancasila* in Soeharto's Indonesia (Schwartz, 1999(a)). Thus, the teaching of *Pancasila* principles reinforced the communitarian, neutral, ascriptive status, diffusion and outer directional (Hampden-Turner and Trompenaars, 2000) basis for the national system of cultural logic. Hence, during the New Order the prescriptive teaching of *Pancasila* manifested itself in the society by:

> [T]he Great Teacher, displaying ceremony, election rituals, unanimous nominations, unity-in-diversity television shows, endless series of successful development projects, mantra-like speeches, uniforms and more uniforms, happy, family-planned families, cleanest villages, … grateful civil servants … Such manifestations are supposed to – and do – take the sights off political and economic decision-making. They obscure social cleavages and concede considerable freedom to those few who do indeed take the decisions. (Muldar, 1999, p. 123)

Similarly, collectivist *Pancasila* values became embedded in the way science and technology was taught in schools and the tertiary sector. They became the criteria for staff selection and promotion within schools and universities. However, the paradoxical gap between the ideological promotion and the promise, and the nature of reality experienced by ordinary Indonesians, underpinned the rapid collapse of the New Order. Yet since then, there has been little investment in revising the national education curriculum. One of the first agendas of the new Yudhoyono government is a review of the national curriculum. There is recognition that the New Order education system has not been able to produce sufficient graduates who are suitable for employment. Since the 1997 economic crisis, local Islamic schools with a narrow and often fundamentalist focus on Koranic interpretations have been the only educational opportunity for many of the poor. Seventy per cent of the workforce has had only primary education. Many companies still employ international managers, and foreign companies operating in Indonesia find it difficult to obtain adequate numbers of middle managers (Mann, 1998).

Many of the prestigious universities were established early in the twentieth century. During the 1970s American aid and teachers were used to boost educational capacity. Since then there has been significant growth in the tertiary sector including the establishment of numerous international tertiary facilities. Indonesians have made considerable investment in education, with many recognising the value of an international tertiary education in creating both personal career opportunities and greater competitiveness for the nation.

Often those who have pursued international education have made an early commitment to learn English. English language learning opportunities were available in the secondary and tertiary sectors, but with very limited numbers of native English speakers, the teaching approach failed to build competent levels of oral and written English literacy. Hence, there are limited numbers of business managers and professional staff who have the required international levels of oral and written competency in English (Singleton, 2002). Research identified that a common concern expressed by Indonesians employed in international companies and studying in Western universities is that they want to learn to 'argue' like the *bule* (Westerners) (Singleton, 2002). There is recognition of the critical importance of building this international language and literacy capacity for both business and diplomacy. However, there is currently community concern for the costs and availability associated with any English language learning materials (*Jakarta Post*, 2004). Many of the current business and government leaders, including President Yudhoyono, have received Western education along with their Indonesian education.

Islam and employment conditions

This chapter explains the complex shared and particularised nature of Indonesian cultural and social systems, and some of the overall characteristic values and behaviours that employees are likely to hold and practise. It describes the broad context within which businesses and their managers must operate, and the associated challenges and opportunities. As a predominantly Muslim nation the influence of Islamic values on work systems, HRM policies and processes is noteworthy. The major Islamic values requiring accommodation within the relationships between employers and their employees are summarised as equality before God; individual responsibilities within a cooperative framework; managers should treat their employees kindly; fatalism (or the acceptance of one's fate), but with a degree of personal choice; and consultation at all levels of decision-making (Latifi cited in Tayeb, 1997, p. 357). These Islamic values further link to universal characteristics such as trustworthiness, responsibility, sincerity, discipline, dedication, diligence, cleanliness, cooperation, good conduct, and moderation, are also important, and that employers should '... pay a reasonable wage, charge a fair price, and be decently restrained in the way (they) spend (their) profits ... (and) take care of the environment, God's handiwork' (Tayeb, 1997, p. 357).

In support of some of these values, and in response to international trends, consecutive Indonesian governments have (albeit slowly) introduced a series of legislative initiatives designed to provide a basic level of employment conditions for all employees. A minimum wage rate, defined as the level of minimum physical need (*Indonesia: Industry Government and Employment Opportunities*, 1997) which varies between regions was established by the Ministry of Manpower in 1989, and then increased in April 1996 by an average of 10.63 per cent across different regions. A Manpower Insurance Program (ASTEK) for civil servants was established in 1978 and extended to private sector employees in 1992. Additional employment related legislation or traditions include the following provisions: a minimum employment age of 15 years; a maximum work day of seven hours and a work week of 40 hours; 12 days annual leave, and a 13th month salary bonus; and female employees can take maternity leave (Hutching, 1996, p. 69) and up to two days a month 'menstrual leave' (*Indonesia: Industry Government and Employment Opportunities* 1997).

Occupational health and safety legislation is in its infancy in Indonesia, as in many regional countries. There is, however, a Basic Provision Respecting Manpower which allows for minimal employee protection, the implementation of safety and industrial hygiene standards and medical care and rehabilitation, but they are not supported by adequate government funding or sanctions. 'Culturally, [Indonesians] have no concept of injury other than the medically obvious wound, and even long-term injury from the lack of protective eye-ware will not be recognised' (Hutching, 1996, p. 66). While this conventional view may derive from the cultural fatalism of Indonesian traditions and values, with the current high activity of international and local NGOs and civil society organisations attitudes will be changing.

Industrial relations systems in Indonesia are non-adversarial, similarly to those in other regional nations such as Malaysia and Thailand although this situation is changing, and are based on negotiations between a single recognised union, the All Indonesia Union of Workers (SPSI), and government parties such as the Ministry of Manpower. Approximately 40 per cent of the workforce officially belongs to SPSI or the unregistered Indonesian Welfare Labour Union, but only 5 to 10 per cent are active members (Leggett and Bamber, 1996, p. 16).

Human resource management

In an international context human resource management (HRM) is understood as the process of placing the right person in the right job. Three groups of activities are included: HR planning, recruitment and retrenchment; orientation, development and training; and performance appraisal, career development and industrial relations. The objective is to provide an organisation with staff with appropriate required capabilities, to identify and address performance problems, and to assist employees to achieve their career goals. How do Indonesian companies organise these activities? The answer varies. Theoretically and rhetorically, there is always an intention to carry them out in order to be the best, but this does not always happen in practice. Some large companies adopt international HRM practice (e.g., Indosat) and some apply an ad hoc approach.

Most problems occur in the area of recruitment and performance appraisal. Family members and colleagues are often favoured in recruitment. Company owners do invest in staff education, but family members dominate companies. In BUMNs, for example, the selection criteria of directors are sometimes unclear. Powerful officials will use their influence in the recruitment process. The use of the 'memo' is well known as a means of influencing recruitment and dismissal decisions. Bribery may also be involved in the process. The 'rent-seeking' (Khan, 2000) practices of KKN have been strongly criticised both internationally and by the local 'reformasi' (reform) groups who question whether these activities contribute to sustainable economic growth or instead underpinned the dramatic regional economic collapse of 1997. President Wahid declared that he would not tolerate such practices, and he dismissed three of his ministers because of KKN practices, and President Megawati and President Yudhoyono have expressed similar views.

> It is our duty to jointly stage *jihad* against corruption, although it will be very tiring because *jihad* requires our preparedness to work hard to achieve our noble goal. There is no other way to ensure a good and respectable future for the nation … (Ahmad Dayafii Maarif, Chairman Muhammadiyah. [Islamic social and educational organisation] 2003)

Notwithstanding the consensual nature of these reformist community perspectives as a basis for policy, the newly fashionable discourse of good governance is still under-theorised and flawed (Dick, 2002).

> The challenge of sustainable development should be reconceptualised as a problem of 'search strategy' in which politics are an essential part of the process and institutions are formed to embody learning-by-doing … Institutional reform is not a politically disembodied 'quick-fix'. (p. 72)

The inference is that not that all employees are recruited through cronyism and nepotism. As in Western countries, most companies and BUMNs have proper recruitment procedures, such as completing applications and requiring resumes, interviews, apprenticeships and provisional periods. There is now greater concern for the appropriate selection of senior management in light of corporate failures and collapses. Loyalty is often an important HRM factor. Some companies try not to sack their loyal employees in hard times. PT National Gobel, for example, maintained its employees by selling the personal assets of the owner to pay for their wages. The idea of jobs for life is common. Loyalty to and seniority in the company are often more important than merit. An employee may not necessarily perform well, but because they have worked loyally for a long time, they are likely to be chosen over someone else who has just completed their higher degree.

HRM 'has historically not had an important role in Indonesian management [and has] been regarded as a personnel function, almost totally administrative in orientation' (Habir and Lasarati, 1999, p. 1). Three organisational case studies suggest that this focus may be changing, especially in the largest and most successful Indonesian businesses (Habir and Lasarati, 1999). A study of the Sinar Mas Group (SMG), the third largest Indonesian conglomerate; the Astra Group (automobiles, financial services, agribusiness and heavy industry); and PT Rekayasa, a government-owned engineering and construction enterprise, found considerable evidence of modern HRM strategies and processes linked with their business imperatives.

- SMG espouses corporate values (thrift, honesty, loyalty, perseverance) consistent with Islamic values, and is still influenced by its Widjaja family owners, but has introduced a modern performance management system (for example, its 'Management by Olympics System' – MBOS); uses work teams (for example, its 'Reaching the Sky Programme'), and attempts to be a global learning organisation.

- Astra separates ownership and management; has a clear non-discriminatory employment policy (a recent CEO was a female *pribumi*); and is regarded as a 'pioneer of Indonesian modern management' (Habir and Lasarati, 1999, p. 7) due partly to its comprehensive human resource development programme (for example, Astra Basic Management Programme, Astra Middle Management Programme, Astra Executive Development Programme). Post-1997, it has focused on diversification, debt restructuring and clear core competencies, as part of its business recovery strategy.

- PT Rekayasa Indonesia, unlike many other state enterprises which have been characterised by 'weak management, mismanagement, and poor performance' (ibid. p. 6), has increased employee pay, utilises a 'knowledge-based computer system' has extensive internal development programmes and encourages '100 percent empowerment' amongst its employees. The company expresses a belief that 'strong and capable people are the ultimate competitive advantage, and all efforts should be directed to its development' (Habir and Lasarati, 1999, p. 8).

These cases suggest that modern management and HRM techniques and tools can be successfully integrated with Indonesian social and cultural styles, but this integration needs to be facilitated by innovative and charismatic business leadership.

In 2000 Garuda broke with the conventional 'no-bad-news' culture by running a full page colour advertisement in *The Jakarta Post* (March) apologising for its poor customer service and asking for customer feedback on how it could improve the quality of services provided. In this way leading companies can play an important leadership role. At the same time, facing dramatically reduced demand Merpati shared the reduced volume of work between its pilot workforce, which meant that they were working only a few days a month rather than retrench employees – a very Indonesian cultural HRM strategy (Singleton, 2002). Whilst SMG, Astra and PT Rekayasa Indonesia appear to have risen to the difficult task of adapting modern management and HRM strategies and processes to Indonesian workplace characteristics and societal culture, other businesses may need to follow suit, albeit in more customised ways.

New technology and quality management

Despite economic hard times, there is widespread enthusiasm for the new information and communication technologies (ICT) in Indonesia, especially with the new urban middle class. The key issue with the uptake rates and usage patterns of new information and communication technology is the high cost of establishment infrastructure in the middle class residential estate areas beyond the CBD of Jakarta and other major cities. A key issue, as in many developing countries where there is a significant gap between the resources of the elite and the middle classes and the wider mass of the people, is the 'digital divide'. In many areas reliable electricity is an issue, with power failures being a regular occurrence. The popularity of western multimedia entertainment products with the young has given them access to colloquial English language skills. The pirating of software and entertainment media products in Indonesia is of critical international concern. The popular use of the internet, email and mobile phones have played an important role in the democratisation of the country. These ICTs gave protesters the capacity to instantaneously to organise political protests. Moreover, they have given local NGOs and civil society groups access to wider national and international shared community group networks, thus increasing their political power. Access to these technologies now underpins sustaining the Indonesian civil society sector.

Western social and economic notions of quality management are being incorporated into Indonesia through external international pressure and bottom-up local pressure. The international scrutiny by the IMF, World Bank and the ADB of the Indonesian corporate sector after the 1997 crisis highlighted the greater need for transparency and a more standardised regulatory environment. In 2002, President Surkarnoputri opened the Indonesian Quality and National Convention of Standardisation by rhetorically recognising the importance of standards and conformity in assessment in the global market. The objectives were:

1. to prepare Indonesian readiness on AFTA 2003 implementation in the field of standards and conformity assessment;

2. to enhance promotion of standards to consumers and academics;

3. to promote information on quality products and services supported by certification;

4. to enhance the role of national standards and conformity assessment; and

5. to enhance commitment of government officials on the maintenance of standards and quality assurance (http://www.aseansec.org/13838.htm)

A standards promotion was held in 26 cities between February and December 2002 to increase awareness and stakeholder participation. In addition training sessions on standardisation to improve knowledge and skills in ISO 9000: 2000, ISO 14000 and ISO 17025 were held. Similarly, multinational corporations operating in Indonesia have played a key professional development role for locals in building quality management and assessment capabilities.

Tsunami: A reform and capacity development catalyst

The enormity of the immediate and tragic local impact on the communities of Aceh and Northern Sumatra that resulted from the earthquake of 26 December 2004 and the subsequent island of Nias centred event cannot be exaggerated. Early impact assessments and the overwhelming international response to the natural disaster suggest that both the local and international crisis management responses will have repercussions not just for the immediate region affected, but for the nation as a whole. Importantly, the tragic event has elevated the issue of Indonesian economic development into global consciousness. The timing of this natural catastrophe towards the end of the first 100 days of President Yudhoyono's Presidency has meant that coincidentally the government was ready to announce its early national governance goals and development strategies to a more responsive international corporate and governance community. The coincidence suggests that more international engagement with Indonesians across a range of national and local organisational and institutional spheres may result in capacity development that has implications for a more positive economic future for the nation as a whole. Both Indonesians have voiced this perspective and the international community (Yudhoyono, 2005; Sjahrir, 2005; and Wolfensohn, 2005).The tsunami had an enormous impact on both the physical and human infrastructure of Aceh and Northern Sumatra. The bureaucracy in Aceh was effectively wiped out and the large number of deaths will have a huge effect on manpower (Sjahrir, 2005).

Planning for a rapid and comprehensive recovery programme is well underway with billions of dollar pledged by the international community to facilitate this. For example, a Memorandum of Understanding (MOU) for the reconstruction and rehabilitation of activities in Aceh and Northern Sumatra has been signed between the World Bank and the Government of Indonesia aimed at rebuilding communities and physical infrastructure through investments in housing health, education, roads and important social assets. The project expands the World Bank's support for the Government's community-driven-development program (*Kecamatan* Development Project (KDP)), the world's largest community-driven development programme, where communities make their own decisions about how assistance money is spent, and monitor the use of funds. Additional projects will focus on rebuilding health and education facilities and promoting private sector investment in reconstruction, along with province-level road, urban infrastructure, water supply and health-project based on the government needs assessment outcomes.

'Now we need a fast and transparent way to channel the billions of dollars' (Wolfensohn cited in World Bank, 2005). The entire programme is being designed to ensure that the people have the opportunity to closely monitor how reconstruction funds are spent in order to prevent corruption and enhance governance. 'This kind of transparency and citizen oversight is the best method to prevent corruption' (Wolfensohn cited in World Bank, 2005). PricewaterhouseCoopers is going to follow the crisis money for the United Nations (Wolfensohn, 2005). Having learnt from the failings of the characteristic top-down and externally conceived development project management strategies previously applied, the new approach is, for example, to put ten World Bank people in with BAPPENAS (The Government Planning Agency) with a view to strengthening the operations in each of the two organisations on the basis of collaboration (Wolfensohn, 2005).

At the same time as this international and local crisis response was unfolding, the government of Indonesia held an important Indonesia Infrastructure Summit 2005 with a view to establishing a new private sector/government local and foreign investment partnership. This strategy aims to address the decline and stagnation in infrastructure facilities (e.g., electricity, transport, communications and water) since the 1997 economic crisis. The assumption is that this lack of infrastructure is a barrier to domestic and international investment (Yudhoyono, 2005). Moreover, at the Summit the President announced the government was pursuing trade and industry policies that aim to increase competitiveness, decrease costs and remove those distortions that have obscured investment and economic activities as a whole. In addition, the Government claims to be developing a stable policy framework to better enable clear cost assessments, freedom from arbitrary political interference, increased deregulation, a more flexible workforce market and a more efficient bureaucracy. 'This Summit ... comes at a very critical time; and ... the outcome should be a shared commitment to improve the quality and efficiency of infrastructure services – in ways that will make a dramatic difference not only to the competitiveness of Indonesian businesses over the next three to five years, but more broadly, to the lives of millions of Indonesians' (Kassum, 2005). Diverse media rhetoric in

Indonesia now calls for a renewal of 'the Spirit of 45' to unite the nation in its pursuit of these economic development goals.

Contemporary Indonesian micro-level management approaches for national transformation

As in many other Asian nations, the philosophies, styles and practices of Indonesian managers are transforming in response to both the legacies of the past, and the challenges posed by the present and the future. Indonesia's ancient and more recent history, complex social and cultural traditions and relationships, religious influences, and especially its economic 'roller coaster ride' since the mid-1990s, have all contributed to an overwhelming management conundrum – how to engage successfully in the global marketplace whilst incorporating the multiple community contexts and values which both bind and divide this huge and disconnected archipelago. Unlike other Asian nations, with the possible exception of India, Indonesia's social and cultural diversity permeates every area of management, in both positive and negative ways.

Whilst 'unity in diversity' and *Pancasila* principles discussed earlier have been promoted by successive governments for almost forty years as the essential glue of social cohesion, there is ubiquitous evidence of contradictions, multiple layers of understanding and communication and sometimes outright hostility between different ethnic groups, urban and rural dwellers, and between the various islands which form the Indonesian archipelago (especially between Java and the other islands). Despite recent government attempts to restore unity, notably in Aceh, these tensions continue to simmer underneath the surface, reflected in industry in the segmentation of particular ethnic groups (for example, the Peranakan or local Chinese in the private sector, the Javanese in the public sector and Bataknese in entrepreneurial and semi-skilled occupations), and the continuance of nepotism and familism in many management hierarchies. These factors have often constrained the application of the principle of the best person for the job; restricted creativity and innovation; encouraged cronyism; and developed contradictory multiple management structures, systems and processes within individual organisations.

Whilst these issues may appear problematic, as discussed earlier in this chapter, Indonesian managers and their employees in general are adaptable and relatively comfortable with such apparent paradoxes, and have the ability to assimilate or incorporate innovative ideas and practices with their more traditional socio-cultural mindsets and work practices. However, some characteristics of Indonesian management bestride their differences, and have proven difficult to change, even in the face of the challenges of modern global business. As examples, hierarchical management structures and authoritarian management styles prevail, in both the public and private sectors, in Chinese and Javanese family companies, and whilst employees are involved in preliminary consultations, decision-making in most Indonesian companies is the responsibility of senior management. Both formal and informal communication is conducted, but at both levels it can be circuitous, obtuse, and often quite animated.

As in other Asian societies, harmony and cooperation are regarded as important in the Indonesian workplace, there is little industrial conflict and managers primarily adopt relational rather transactional perspectives towards their employees. These characteristics may have served organisations well in the past, but the combination of hierarchical management styles, limited employee participation in decision-making, and emphases on harmony and cooperation rather than productive conflict, have restricted innovation and creativity, and hence the development of the entrepreneurial or intrapreneurial activities, which are essential for Indonesian competitiveness in a global marketplace. As a reflection of the collectivist traditions of Indonesian culture, it has historically been difficult to recruit managers due to the unwillingness of employees to volunteer to become the 'first among equals', a situation which is exacerbated by the relatively less enthusiastic ambition for higher education, and especially management education, exhibited by Indonesians, as compared to their counterparts in Malaysia, Singapore, Thailand, China, India or Japan. Thus Indonesia suffers from a notable lack of well-trained and educated middle and senior managers, professionals, and technical specialists, and has not been able to attract significant levels of foreign investment and new venture capital to date, which might provide such opportunities, due to its continuing economic and political turmoil since the mid-1990s. It is expected that this situation may improve with the political stability promised by its new democratic regime, and there are signs in the coastal business regions that this is already occurring, albeit gradually.

Indonesia's history has encompassed significant changes, including Dutch and Japanese colonialism, and the sequential governments since Independence, together with its inherent societal diversity and segmentation, but despite these experiences, there is often considerable resistance to and difficulty with adapting to radical change at the workplace level. Inhibitors include overly relational management styles; a preference for harmony and consensus; and the unwillingness of employees to express their diverse opinions due to hierarchical structures, collectivist perspectives, and past bad experiences during the Soeharto era. Indonesian managers will need to address these issues in the future in order to ensure the global, regional and national competitiveness and profitability of their organisations into the future. In so doing, specific HRM systems such as HR planning, recruitment and selection, human resource development, career management, remuneration and termination, will require attention. Thus, the analysis and attraction of focused labour markets with more highly developed professional, technical and managerial skills and educational qualifications; the development of modern selection techniques based upon objective criteria and utilising multiple processes; employee access to in-house and external training and development; competitive and performance-based remuneration and career development programmes; and culturally appropriate retrenchment systems, are likely to be features of Indonesian management in the future.

Conclusion

This chapter outlines why complexity, paradox and transformation currently frame the corporate and community governance and management in Indonesia today. The last six years have witnessed significant reform of the nation's political and economic system. Both political and economic institutions have been subject to increased reformist scrutiny and accountability. Until recently political uncertainty meant that the reform of economic management has been more conservative and so only small levels of economic growth have been achieved, and the country's economic performance is still very dependent on its future ability to attract foreign investment. Significant human resource and institutional strengthening capacity development issues are implicated in the Indonesian quest for higher levels and more sustainable economic growth. Moreover, the dual national objectives of economic recovery and regional autonomy are resulting in increased tensions between the local, regional and central levels of government over interests and control. Exactly how these global, national, regional and local tensions will play out is uncertain. It is apparent that historically the country is at an important development crossroads and time will tell the direction in which the new leadership will take the Indonesian people. Furthermore, the international community, and international business in particular, has a responsibility to gain a deeper and more reflective understanding of the complex, paradoxical and transformational nature of Indonesian society and its approach to management.

Questions

1. Discuss the recent political and economic factors which have affected Indonesian management
2. Explain the dominance of 'Javanese' management in Indonesia, and its implications for local management styles and practices
3. What future challenges lie ahead for Indonesian management?

URL linkages

Government and related information

Indonesian Government   http://www.ri.go.id/
Indonesian House of Representatives   http://www.dpr.go.id/
Department of Foreign Affairs   http://www.dfa-deplu.go.id/
Ministry of Finance   http://www.depkeu.go.id/
Ministry for Research and Technology   http://www.ristek.go.id/
Ministry of Public Works   http://www.pu.go.id/

Ministry of Forestry	http://mofrinet.cbn.net.id/
Department of Justice and Human Rights	http://www.sisminbakum.com/ kehakiman/index.html
Central Bureau of Statistics	http://www.bps.go.id/

Economy, trading, technology

Indonesian Chamber of Commerce	http://www.kadin.net.id/
Indo Exchange	http://www.indoexchange.com/
Indonesia Business	http://www.indonesiamu.com/
Trade Indonesia	http://www.tradeindonesia.com/
Indonesian Business Directory	http://www.mencarialamat.com/ mca2/index.jsp
Jakarta Stock Exchange	http://www.jsx.co.id/

Other Useful Links	http://www.indobiz.com
	http://www.kompas.co.id
	http://www.indoscope.com/cfo

News and information

South East Asia Press Alliance, Jakarta	http://www.seapa-jak.or.id/
Indonesia Business News	http://www.suratkabar.com/c.shtml
Satunet	http://www.satunet.com/
Inilho	http://www.inilho.com/
Indonesia Raya	http://www.indonesia-raya.com/
Hukum Online	http://www.hukumonline.com/
Antara	http://www.antara.co.id/indonesia.asp

Search engine

Yahoo! Indonesia	http://dir.yahoo.com/Regional/ Countries/Indonesia
Search Indonesia	http://www.searchindonesia.com/
Master Web Indonesia	http://master.web.id/main.htm
Indowell	http://www.indowell.com/
Catcha	http://www.catcha.co.id/
Kopitime	http://www.kopitime.com/

References

Antlov, H & Cederroth, S, 1994, *Leadership on Java*, Nordic Institute of Asian Studies, Curzon Press, Surrey, UK.

Aseanfocus (2004), 'Indonesia: A brief history'. Retrieved 7 September 2004 from: www.aseanfocus.com

Bouchier, D & Hadiz, V, 2003, *Indonesian politics and society: A reader*, Routledge Curzon, London and New York.

Boyce, R, 2004, 'Global Partners: RI moving in right direction, although at "glacial speed" ', *The Jakarta Post*, 29 September, Retrieved 29 September 2004 from: http://www.thejakartapost.com/gpb07_1.asp

Brown, C, 2004, *Bombs and ballots boxes: The Indonesian presidential election* RUSSIC Seminar Series, September, Curtin University of Technology, Perth, WA.

Cochrane, J, 2004, 'Radical retreat', *Newsweek*, April 5, pp. 20–2.

Day, T & Reynolds, C, 2000, 'Cosmologies, truth regimes and the state in Southeast Asia', *Modern Asian Studies*, vol. 1, no. 1. pp. 1–55, Cambridge University Press, Cambridge.

Dick, H, 2002, 'Corruption and good governance', In Lindsey T & Dick H (eds), *Corruption in Asia: Rethinking the governance paradigm*, Federation Press, Annandale, NSW.

Earthtrends, 2003, *Population, health, and human well-being; Indonesia.* Retrieved 26 September 2004 from: http://earthtrends.wri.org/pdf_library/country_profiles/Pop

Foster, C, 2002, *A sea change for risk management in Indonesia.* Retrieved from: http://www.expat.or.id/business/riskmanagement.html (n.d.)

Fox, J, 1998, 'Religions in Indonesia'. In Fox J (vol. ed.), *Indonesian heritage: Religions and ritual*, Archipelago Press Inc. Jakarta.

Garang, J, 1997, 'Protestantism'. In Fox J (vol. ed.), *Indonesian heritage: Religions and ritual*, Archipelago Press Inc. Jakarta.

Guerin, B, 2002, 'Indonesia's first man', *Asia Times Online Co, Ltd* Retrieved 11 November, 2004 from: http://www.atimes.com/atimes/printNhtml

Goodfellow, R, 1997, *Indonesian business culture*, Butterworth Heineman Asia, Singapore.

Grant, B, 1996, *Indonesia* (3rd edn), Melbourne University Press, Carlton South, Victoria.

Habir, A & Lasarati, A, 1999, 'HRM as competitive advantage in the new millennium: An Indonesian perspective', *International Journal of Management*, vol. 20, no. 8, pp. 540–8.

Hampden-Turner, C & Trompenaars, F, 2000, *Building cross-cultural competence: how to create wealth from conflicting values*, Wiley & Sons, Chichester, England.

Hefner, R, 1999, 'Islam and nation in the post-Suharto era', In Schwartz A and Paris J (eds), *The politics of post-Suharto Indonesia*, Council of Foreign Relations Press, New York.

Hill, I, 1996, 'The cultural mosaic', In Rigg J (vol. ed.), *Indonesian heritage: The human environment*, Archipelago Press, Jakarta.

Howell, J, 1998, 'Kebatinan and Kejawan traditions', In Fox J (vol. ed.), *Indonesian heritage: Religions and ritual*, Archipelago Press Inc. Jakarta.

Hutching, K, 1996, 'Workforce Practices of Japanese and Australian Multinational Corporations Operating in Singapore, Malaysia and Indonesia', *Human Resource Management Journal*, vol. 6, no. 2, pp. 58–71.

Indonesia: Industry government and employment opportunities, 1999. Retrieved from: http://www.services.unimelb.edu.au (n.d.)

Indonesian quality and national convention of standardisation, 2002, Convention Jakarta, 30 September –3 October. Retrieved 30 September 2004 from: http://www.aseansec.org/13834.htm

International Crisis Group (ICG), 2000, *Report: Indonesia's crisis, chronic but not acute.* Retrieved 31 May 2000 from: http://www.crisisweb.org/projects/Indonesian/reports/indo02erep.htm

Kartodirjo, S, 1994, 'The development and demise of the Javanese aristocracy', In Antlov H & Cedderroth S (eds) *Leadership on Java*, Nordic Institute of Asian studies, Curzon Press, Surrey, UK.

Kassum, J, 2005, 'Mobilizing finance for infrastructure development in Indonesia', Speech, Vice President World Bank, Indonesia Infrastructure Summit, Jakarta January 17 & 18.

Keanne, W, 1997, Knowing one's place: National language and the idea of local in Eastern Indonesia, *Cultural anthropology*, vol. 12. no. 1, pp. 37–63.

Khan, M, 2000, 'Rents, efficiency and growth', In Khan M and Jomo J (eds), *Rents, rent seeking and economic development: Theory and evidence in Asia*, Cambridge University Press, Cambridge, UK.

Kolesnikov-Jessop, S, 2004, 'SBY Cabinet jockeying points to problems ahead', United Press International, 21 October Singapore. Retrieved 3 November 2004 from: http://washingtontimes.com/upi-breaking/20041021-081726-3977r.htm

Kumar, A & Proudfoot, I, 1998, 'Chinese manuscript in language', In McGlynn J (vol. ed.), *Indonesian Heritage: Language and literature*. Archipelago Press Inc, Jakarta.

Lane, M, 2003, *Understanding contemporary Indonesia*, Public lecture series, University of Western Australia Extension Services, Perth, spring.

Leggett, C & Bamber, G, 1996, 'Asia Pacific Two of Change', *Human Resource Management Journal*, vol. 6, no. 25, pp. 4–19.

Lewis, R, 2003, *The cultural imperative: global trends in the 21st century*, Intercultural Press Inc. Yarmouth, Maine.

Liddle, R, 1999, 'Indonesia's unexpected failure of leadership', In Schwartz A & Paris J (eds), *The politics of post-Suharto Indonesia*, Council on Foreign Relations, New York.

Maarif, AS, 2003, 'Online special: Can Indonesia survive until 2050?' *The Jakarta Post*, 25 February. Retrieved from: http://www.thejakartapost.com/special/os_26.asp

Mann, R, 1998, *The culture of business in Indonesia* (3rd edn) Gateway Books, Singapore.

Mapes, T, 2004, 'Jakarta overhauls top management at state oil firm', *The Wall Street Journal*, 12 August. Retrieved 31 August 2004 from: Proquest Database.

McGlynn, T, 1998, 'Writing traditions', In McGlynn J (vol. ed.), *Indonesian Heritage: Language and literature*. Archipelago Press Inc, Jakarta.

Muldar, N, 1998, *Mysticism in Java: Ideology in Indonesia*, Peppin Press, Singapore, 1994, 'The ideology of Javanese-Indonesian leadership'. In Antlov H & Cedderroth S (eds) *Leadership on Java*, Nordic Institute of Asian studies, Curzon Press, Surrey, UK.

National Committee on US–Indonesian relations, 2003, *Strengthening U.S relations with Indonesia: Toward a partnership for human resource development*, The Asia-Pacific Research Centre, Standford University, California.

Prawirosentono, S, 1999, *Manajemen Sumberdaya Manusia, Kebijakan Kinerja Karyawan: Kiat Membangun Organisasi Kompetitif Menjelang Perdagangan Bebas Dunia*, BPFE, Yogyakarta.

Proudfoot, I, 1996, 'Historical foundations of Buddhism', In Fox J (vol. ed.), *Indonesian heritage: Religions and ritual*, Archipelago Press Inc. Jakarta.

Rigg, J, 1996, 'Indonesia: People and environment', In Rigg J (vol. ed.), *Indonesian heritage: The human environment*, Archipelago Press, Jakarta.

Robison, K, 1986, *Indonesia: The rise of capital*, Allen and Unwin, Sydney.

Schwartz, A, 1999, *A nation in waiting: Indonesia's search for stability*, Allen and Unwin, St Leonards, NSW.

Schwartz, A, 1999b, 'Introduction: The politics of post-Suharto Indonesia', In A Schwartz & J Paris (eds), *The politics of post-Suharto Indonesia*, Council of Foreign Relations Press, New York.

Sen, K & Hill, D, 2000, *Media, culture and politics in Indonesia*, Oxford University Press, South Melbourne, Victoria.

Singleton, H, 2002, *Frameworks for the management of cross-cultural communication and business performance in the globalising economy: A professional service TNC case study in Indonesia*, PhD thesis, Schools of Management, & Languages & Intercultural Education, Curtin University of Technology, Bentley WA. Available http://adt.curtin.ed.au/theses/available/adt-wcu2005111615421/

Singleton, H. Personal communication with URS Corporation, 29 October 2004.

Sjahrir, Dr. 2005, 'Impact of the Tsunamis: New political and societal landscapes' USINDO Open Forum, 3rd January Washington, DC Retrieved 19 May 2005 from http://www.usindo.org/Briefs/2005/Dr.%Sjahrir%20the%20Tsunami%200

Slamet-Velsink, I, 1994, 'Traditional leadership in rural Java', In Antlov H & Cedderroth S (eds) *Leadership on Java*, Nordic Institute of Asian studies, Curzon Press, Surrey, UK.

Tayeb, M, 1997, *Islamic Revival in Asia and HRM*, Employee Relations, vol. 19, no. 4, pp. 352–64.

The Economist, 2004, 'Special Report: Indonesia's election, enter a new star', pp. 27–9, 25 September.

The Jakarta Post, 2004, 29 September, 'Business and investment: RI elections may be positive for reforms: S&P'. Retrieved 29 September 2004 from: http://www.thejakartapost.com/yesterdaydetail.asp?fileid=20040923.L01.

The Jakarta Post, 2004, 'Business news: Top Kadin officials visit Shanghai to lure investment' November, Retrieved 3 November 2004 from: http://www.thejakartapost.com/detailbusiness.asp?fileid=20041103.L03&irec=2.

Tradewatch, 2004, 'Country report: Indonesia', August. Department of Foreign Affairs & Trade, Canberra. Retrieved 25 September 2004 from: www.dfat.gov.au.

Transparency International (TI), 2004, *Press release: Plundering politicians and bribing multinationals undermine economic development, says TI*. Retrieved 30 September 2004 from: www.globalcorruption.report.org.

Wolfensohn, J, 2005, 'Press conference on the Tsunami', *News release*, 12 January, Worldbank, Washington, DC. Retrieved 19 January 2005 from: http://web.worldbank.org/WEBSITE EXTERNAL/NEWS/

WorldBank, 2005, 'World Bank President visits Aceh; Announces new reconstruction efforts', *News release No: 2005/275/S*, 7 January, Jakarta, retrieved 19 January 2005 from: http://web.worldbank.org/WEBSITE EXTERNAL/NEWS

WorldBank, 2004, *East Asia update report: Indonesia country brief*. Retrieved 9 November 2004 from: http://lnweb18.worldbank.org/eap/eap.nsf/All/ 2DA786CAE06BE84885256F460013F284?OpenDocument

Yudhoyono, S, 2005, 'Revitalising Indonesia: Opportunity, partnership, progress'. Keynote address President Yodhoyono, Indonesia Infrastructure Summit 2005 17 January, Jakarta. Retrieved 19 January 2005 from: http://www.antara.co.id/en/seenws/?id=294

Yudhoyono, S, 2004, 'SBY, 2004: National issues'. Retrieved 6 October 2004 from: http://www.sbyudhiyono.com/National.aspx

Additional readings

Bouchier, D & Hadiz, V (eds) 2003, *Indonesian politics and society: A reader*, London & RoutledgeCurzon, New York.

Chalmers, I, 2005, *Indonesia: an introduction to contemporary traditions*, Oxford University Press, Oxford.

Fox, J (ed.), 1998, *Indonesian heritage: religions and ritual*, Archipelago Press, Jakarta.

Goodfellow, R, 1997, *Indonesian business culture*, Butterworth Heinemann Asia, Singapore.

Hill, D & Sen, K, 2005, The internet in Indonesia's new democracy, Routledge, London and New York.

Mann R, 1998, *The culture of business in Indonesia*, 3rd edn, Gateway Books, Singapore.

Schwarz, A, 1999, *A nation in waiting: Indonesia's search for stability*, Allen and Unwin, Sydney.

Schwarz, A & Paris, J (eds) 1999, *The politics of post-Suharto Indonesia*, Council of Foreign Relations, New York.

Sen, K & Hill, D, 2000, *Media, culture and politics in Indonesia*, Melbourne: Oxford University Press.

Tsing, AL, 2005, *Friction: An ethnography of global connection*, Princeton University Press, Princeton and Oxford.

Conclusion

Dynamic and divergent Asian management responses to convergent global imperatives

Introduction

Prior to the 1997 Asian financial crisis, international management analysts attributed the dramatic regional economic successes to an 'Asian values' paradigm which encompassed such socio-cultural characteristics as a hierarchical social order, ascribed status, paternalism, collectivism, fatalism, family values, education, relationships, social harmony and high savings rates. Soon afterwards, the very same Asian values were blamed for the 1997 financial collapse. Similarly, attention focused on the shared characteristics of Asian communication styles and organisational patterns. These regionally convergent values and practices, associated with the shared 'forces of heritage', are identified in each of the foregoing chapters. This book argues pervasively for the value and application of a convergence–divergence conceptual model for building a deeper understanding of how these Asian socio-cultural values are manifested in the particularist strategies and practices of individuals and groups as leaders and managers within their various national contexts.

This convergence–divergence conceptual model, presented in Chapter 2, identifies the managerial characteristics of each of the nations through the exploration of how the important national, regional and global forces impact on the evolving managerial cultures and practices. More particularly, the model facilitates discussion on how, in an increasingly more integrated global market context, these local socio-cultural factors variously influence each nation's interpretation of its competitive strengths and weakness, and the various managerial strategies applied to improve the standard of living of their respective societies, and to achieve sustainable levels of development. The foregoing chapters reveal how, in each of the eight countries, the specific 'pull' factors derived from powerful regional, national and local forces impact upon its managerial orientation. For example, the reform of state enterprises has been a critical social imperative in China for the past decade, in response to globalisation forces. The required managerial 'catch-up' has replaced the former ideological education with a trend towards the completion of Western-style MBAs, even in the state-owned enterprises.

Convergence and divergence across the Asian region

Broadly speaking, preceding chapters bring to attention a number of interesting issues. These include a shared paternalistic and government-led approach to development, and the recognition that the charismatic and visionary role of their leaders and managers have been of paramount importance in the particular meso-level (societal) choice of development strategies. By and large, the various post-independence and modernising governance and managerial approaches applied over the last thirty years have resulted in dramatic levels of economic growth and community development in each nation. Each nation has at times had enviable levels of economic growth. The standards of living have improved considerably, and all have experienced a burgeoning middle class. This growing middle class has expanded domestic and international market opportunities for the diversifying local economies. The meso-level of development has resulted in greater urbanisation across the region and increased disparity between urban and rural communities.

Drawing deeply on their respective 'forces of heritage', each nation has developed modernising policy frameworks and infrastructure investment which has mobilised strong and cohesive national identities, and literacy levels across the region have risen. While the historical colonial and regional forces left foreign and imposed administrative and institutional systems, each chapter identifies how these have been 'localised' in each national context. Similarly, the particular ways in which significant but variable industry transitions have evolved from colonial agricultural and natural resource-based economies to diversified manufacturing and services economies are also identified. In association with these transitions, workforce capacities have also been elevated and diversified. Each nation in its own way reflects various perspectives on the generational implications of their transition to a new knowledge-based society.

Nevertheless, while these convergent managerial and development responses and processes are identified, each chapter explains the deeply felt and unique legacies of the forces of heritage in shaping the divergent and often esoteric societal and managerial cultures at meso- (societal) and micro- (organisational) levels. The various local religious and spiritual systems have left important and diverse community cultural legacies that still underpin local cultural logic. Buddhism, Islam, Hinduism and Christianity, and philosophies, such as Confucianism, have variously been 'indigenised' or localised to address particularist and evolving community needs and mindsets. The consequences of these socio-cultural influences at both the meso-societal and micro-organisational levels are clearly identifiable in the beliefs and practices of individuals and groups in particular corporate and community contexts. Moreover, they have significant ramifications for the esoteric nature of the managerial cultures in each nation.

Despite the remarkable economic successes of the region during the 1980s and 1990s, the dramatic regional and local impacts of events such as the 1997 Asian financial crisis, and subsequent issues such as terrorism, SARS, bird flu, the environmental consequences of forestry fires in Indonesia and the 2004 tsunami, all heightened recognition of the need for each nation to address the 'push' factors of global imperatives in order to improve economic performance, increase transparency and ameliorate risk. Simultaneously, the dramatic rise of China has highlighted the additional issue of increasing regional competition. These issues have generated a new transitional wave across the region as each nation grapples with the managerial challenges created by global integration and interdependency. In the context of this macro-(regional) level dynamism, the first years of the new millennium have seen the emergence of a new generation of leaders and managers across the region.

More specifically, each of the chapters reveals how national governments across the region are implementing variable economic reform and management strategies that distinguish their particular transition from a government-owned corporate model, conceived to 'kick start' the development process, towards increasing emphases on strengthening and expanding the private sector. This convergent privatisation trend links to regional agreements on the need to address the competitive 'push' factors of global imperatives. Macro-regional and meso-societal level managerial consensus can be identified across the chapters concerning recognition of the need to:

- Improve national competitiveness in order to sustain economic and community development;

- Maintain internal community stability in order to build the certainty required by foreign investors; and linked to this, to:

- Address the issue of intra-community disparity between urban and rural, or ethnic communities;

- Strengthen their particular human resource management and institutional capacities;

- Reform and improve accountability and transparency mechanisms;

- Design and implement government policy and infrastructure support for both community and industry development;

- Implement and enforce regulatory guidelines for more sustainable natural and community resources management;

- Address the pedagogical and institutional requirements associated with the transition to knowledge societies and information-based economies;

- Acknowledge the growing economic interdependencies between regions, nations and communities; and hence the need to:

- Identify the synergistic opportunities created by a more integrated global market economy.

Acknowledgement of these convergent strategic managerial actions has particular implications for the meso-societal and micro-organisational level approaches adopted in each of the countries in response to the 'push' factors of global imperatives. While there is a broad-based consensus regarding the merit of these strategic imperatives, each of the chapters reveals that there is considerable divergence between the eight nations as to how these performance-associated challenges should be addressed and implemented. The perspectives presented by each of the authors highlight the localised nature of the managerial tensions associated with responding to the countervailing reformist and status quo forces.

Each of the chapters reveals how the interplay of the convergent 'push' factors of global imperatives and the powerful 'pull' forces of heritage is developing unique national cultures which articulate to divergent and localised managerial approaches. Local forces play a powerful role in framing the unique and often countervailing socio-cultural values, worldview, ideological orientation and communication and decision-making styles of individuals and groups in particular community institutions and business organisations in particular national contexts. During key community and corporate development transition phases, as conceived by each nation to respond to these global/local push-pull factors, disparate, paradoxical and potentially destabilising consequences are identifiable. Each nation shares the complex leadership and managerial challenges associated with setting community governance and managerial parameters to reconcile these often paradoxical dynamic and status quo factors at the meso-societal and micro-organisational level in order to achieve the shared community development goals while maintaining social harmony and stability.

The region includes divergent political systems, including centrally-planned socialism, 'guided democracy' and Western-style democratic systems. Coupled with this, divergent political and ceremonial heads of state are represented (i.e., President, Emperor, Constitutional Monarchy and Prime Minister), and the differential nature of the socio-political assumptions of these political systems have additional implications for the conceptualisation of national governance and management models, values and behaviour. Since the 1997 Asian economic crisis, there has been evidence of broad-based regional concern about the adverse effects of cronyism amongst the political and corporate elite, and the consequent need for greater institutional transparency, propelled in large part by the influences of the ADB and the WTO.

Divergence, convergence and cross-vergence in particular Asian nations

The following discussion draws together some of the key convergence, divergence and cross-vergence pressures identified by the various authors, who emphasise the complex role of heritage in framing the particularist managerial approaches applied to address global imperatives in the various national contexts.

Large regional nations

Part two of the book examines managerial approaches in China, India and Japan. The transformation processes taking place in the three largest economies in the Asian region have wide-reaching macro- (regional and international) implications. While pragmatism underpins a cross-vergent international and local managerial approach, each of the chapters reveals the distinctiveness of managerial values and practices in these three nations. In China, for example, the long-term and more recent issues of heritage reverberate through the management practices of its macro-, meso-, and micro- level political and economic characteristics in its rapid transformation from a centrally planned socialist nation to a highly competitive global market-based economy. The phenomenal speed and economic success of this transition process has significant implications for future economic development across the region and the world.

The first stage of this government-led, market-driven, and manufacturing-based development strategy was initiated in the Special Economic Zones (SEZs) in the south, and then rapidly spread to Shanghai, Beijing and other coastal cities and regions. The success of this resulted in a dramatic drift of workers from rural regions to the cities and the rise of a new urban Chinese middle class. Currently, the government is implementing policies to encourage development in the interior and rural areas in order to maintain social cohesion in this context of growing regional, and urban and rural, disparities. In this highly dynamic context, the interwoven cultural dimensions of traditional, Marxist and Capitalist ideologies mean that ancient philosophical values and a socialist welfare-based political system coexist with the competitive values of market-driven economic forces. The chapter emphasises the new macro-, meso-, and micro-level management challenges associated with the next transition phase China faces to transform its economy for more effective and sustainable integration into the global economy, while simultaneously maintaining internal political and social stability.

Questions still remain unanswered as to how China will address its role in maintaining regional stability and developing synergistic economic opportunities with its regional neighbours. Leadership and management is likely to draw heavily on Confucianism and other ancient Chinese philosophies to reframe the paradoxes associated with these transformational challenges.

Considerable attention has been given to the economic success achieved by India in recent years. At least 300 million globally conscious consumers are placing demands of quality, service and innovation, leading to a new managerial imperative. India's GDP grew by 8 per cent in 2004, the strongest in a decade and double that of 2003. South Korean Chaebol, Hyundai, for example, announced the doubling of the capacity of its Madras (Chennai) plant by making an additional investment of Rs. 10 billion (US$300 million) in 2004. It is interesting that the stunning success of Korean companies such as Hyundai, LG and Samsung in India have been based on their cross-verging managerial emphases, in which indigenous Indian managerial culture has been blended with a number of uniquely Korean managerial techniques.

World-class competition has had a dramatic effect on managerial thinking in Indian companies, and the cross-verging strategic shifts have resulted in significant improvements in the quality of local products. The quest for quality was achieved for the first time in 1998, with one Indian company being recognised with the Deming Award for Quality. In successive years the numbers of such awards have steadily increased. In addition, the faith in India demonstrated by US company Texas Instruments over the last 20 years by setting up a Research and Development Centre (RDC) in Bangalore, has recently been strengthened with the establishment of more than a hundred global RDCs in the same city by General Electric, Microsoft, IBM, Cisco, Intel, AstraZeneca and Motorola, amongst others (Preiss, 2005). These global research centres have provided the opportunity for Indian managers to lead knowledge-intensive organisations without traditional bureaucratic formalism. Such regional and global linkages have been able to revitalise a number of moribund state-run enterprises, as the bureaucratic mindset is gradually being replaced by new learning and managerialism. For example, Nokia's success in penetrating the Indian market, especially amongst the middle class, has led to the growth of not only a number of private companies like Reliance, but also state-run Bharati Telecoms, which after years of loss making registered a net profit of Rs.6 billion (US$200 million) in 2004 (Nadkarni, 2004).

To maintain this impetus, considerable managerial attention in India will need to be devoted to the development of local infrastructures, such as power, transportation and the legal system, as in China, Thailand, Indonesia and parts of Malaysia. Even here there are differences between these countries. A recent Confederation of Indian Industries (CII) and World Bank study found, for example, that the hidden cost of unanticipated power shortages in India is as high as nine per cent, compared to only two per cent in China and one per cent in Malaysia (*India Today* March, 2004, p. 30). However, whilst the impediments for managers in India may appear formidable in contextual terms, the real challenge lies in the less visible area of rigid mindsets. Harvard Professor Tarun Khanna has suggested that the path to globalisation for Indian companies lies in the cross-vergence of local and global mindsets:

> In India too there are instances of companies leveraging local strengths. ITC and HLL have learned to work with the informal sector in the villages successfully and profitably. Across the developing world there are lots of opportunities to work in the informal sector which these companies can tap into ... Mahindra and Mahindra created a successful vehicle Scorpio from scratch in a market where all global auto giants are present. (Khanna, 2004, p.32)

In contrast to China and India, the development, role, and unique features of the Japanese heritage in the development of the two factors, which were pivotal in successfully mobilising the industrial development of Japan – (1) a high value for learning and (2) a highly disciplined approach to learning and problem solving. Both factors owe much to the philosophical legacy and the deeply embedded *Bushido*-based *Samurai* 'way-of-life' values. In addition, the incorporation of specific foreign expertise through an 'indigenisation'–assimilation process is a significant characteristic of Japanese leadership and managerial approaches. These foreign systems became imbued with particular Japanese cultural logic through a disciplined approach to learning and a localised appropriation process. The chapter explains why and how Japanese approaches to change and development mean that innovation is applied to managerial systems in both a disciplined and an incremental manner. This disciplined and incremental strategy means that deeply embedded traditional Japanese socio-cultural values remain predominantly stable, while particular dynamic contextual issues and needs are addressed often in response to destabilising external imperatives.

The Japanese economy grew dramatically using the multi-industry structural base of the *keiretsu* conglomerates. The application of this disciplined learning strategy enabled the Japanese to develop a highly competitive, innovative and cutting-edge approach to American management notions of quality with regard to manufacturing systems. More recently, this knowledge has expanded to create further competitive advantage though a deeper analysis of the management challenges associated with service. Similarly, learning from the foreign direct investment (FDI) strategies of western development models, the Japanese applied a macro-(regional and international) FDI strategy to gain access to natural resources, cheap labour and new markets. This macro-regional development strategy was and continues to be an important catalyst for Asian regional development.

However, the convergent push forces of global imperatives are imposing reformist pressures on Japanese institutions, corporations and society. In association with these competitive global forces, the key Japanese managerial principles of work-for-life, a high collectivist work ethic, and corporation-based education and training systems, are now under threat. With the characteristic corporate welfare safety net disappearing, Japanese society faces new organisational and community management challenges together with the changing regional symmetries associated with the dramatic expansion of the Chinese economy.

Smaller regional nations

Part three of the book examines the diverse approaches to management in the smaller nations of South Korea, Malaysia and Singapore. These chapters reveal the very distinctive nature of their national contexts and associated managerial approaches. For example, despite the open and coercive assimilation of significant external influences from China, Japan, and more recently the US, a uniquely Korean approach to management is clearly identifiable. Over time, the high heritage value placed on the family, in association with a high value for learning, have cemented the deeply held Confucian socio-cultural assumptions for a family-based social structure and a meritocratic culture in Korean society. These two socio-cultural concepts provide the structural framework for both the political and economic systems that were the modern basis for development.

A highly competitive spirit also underpins the unique characteristics of the Korean approach to management. This competitive characteristic is associated with the historical experiences derived from the intimidating geo-political reality of life on the Korean Peninsula surrounded by powerful regional nations. In this context, the evolution of cultural distinctiveness has been an important historical vehicle for both Korean subjugation and survival. The concerted application of these particular Korean values at the macro-(strategic), meso-(societal), and micro-(organisational) levels have provided South Korea with the basis for a systemic policy and institutional framework to successfully manage the significant economic growth and industrial development that has occurred since the end of the Korean War in 1953.

With the initial support of international aid, in particular from the United States, a government-led development policy framework developed focused on supporting and encouraging the growth of the family-based *Chaebol* manufacturers. Over a short period, the *Chaebol* evolved into powerful family-based multi-industry conglomerates that played a pivotal role in the rapid and highly successful of development of the Korean economy. The subjugating forces of colonial history meant that Koreans have also learnt to be flexible and adaptable in order to survive. Similarly, the drive to survive embedded a high work ethic in Koreans. Western Christian influences and predominantly American western influence reinforced Korean individualism. Like all the nations of the Asian region, a government-led approach to economic development prevailed, but the characteristic Korean managerial approach shaped the nation's unique strategic and operational development features.

As a result of the strategic and competitive application of Korea's governance and management approach the nation now has a powerful economy, is a major industrial and trading nation, and has one of the fastest growing economies in the Asia-Pacific region, with an average annual growth rate of more than eight per cent over the last three decades. The importance of understanding how the unique socio-cultural features of the Korean managerial approach are manifested in values and behaviour at meso-(societal) and micro-(organisational) levels, and the nation's vision to become a regional gateway and high tech investment hub, is emphasised. Korea now displays a high capacity for research and development and encourages innovation. However, less positively, the 'pressure cooker' nature of the highly competitive education system is questioned frequently, and curricula and institutional reform are now demanded. These particular Korean managerial approaches and reactive development strategies suggest that more than any regional nation South Korea displays a unique but cross-vergent Asian/global management model.

Malaysia provides a further example of a small regional nation which has made the significant economic transition from a colonial British-based dependence on agricultural industries to a diversified and modern economy now in pursuit of the ambitious goal of fully developed nation status by 2020. The pluralist Malaysian heritage explains how the multi-cultural, and multi-religious characteristics associated with the three largest ethnic groups – Malays, Chinese and Indians – are the result of complex historical patterns of regional settlement and intermixing based on evolving trading patterns and resource exploitation. This pluralism has contributed to a 'flexible and open' cultural approach to trade and innovation. As a democratic Islamic state, with the political sphere dominated by the ethnic Malays (*bumiputra*), a strategically managed, government-led and government-owned managerial approach to national development has prevailed. This meso-(society) level management approach has been dominated by an affirmative '*bumiputra* portfolio' policy approach designed to elevate the Malay community and to strengthen Malay business. Nevertheless, the ethnic Chinese community continues to dominate the economic sphere at meso-(societal) and micro-(organisational) levels. The divergent socio-cultural values and practices associated with each of the ethnic communities presents management with practical challenges at the day-to-day, organisation-to-organisation micro-level.

In order to build a more diverse economy and to strengthen local Malaysian industrial capacities the government has recently introduced a range of policy measures that have successfully attracted diverse FDI and MNC investment. With the MNCs bringing their diverse multinational Asian (predominantly Japanese and Korean), European and American ethnocentric approaches to management, further diversification has resulted. Hence, no one unified Malaysian approach to management has emerged. Thus, a highly pluralist and context-based managerial approach prevails. Nonetheless, this complex internal divergence presents Malaysia with both outward-looking opportunities and potentially destabilising internal community outcomes, which will no doubt call for careful management.

The post-1997 economic crisis environment means that Malaysia faces both internal and external pressure brought on by global imperatives. Malaysia needs to attract further investment, and this reality has forced the government to privatise previously government-owned businesses and to promote further institutional and organisational reform, in order to achieve greater corporate and institutional accountability and transparency. In pursuing the competitive advantages associated with the transition to a knowledge economy, further meso-(societal) and micro-(organisational) level reform is required to build HR capabilities, and the institutional research and innovation capacity needed for the foreign investment associated with the high-tech industries Malaysia now seeks. Moreover, in the dynamic and multicultural Asian regional context, Malaysian pluralism also presents the nation with the valuable community resources and off-shore networks necessary to attract diverse global-oriented industry partnerships and agreements, especially with the growing regional powerhouses of India and China.

The 'flexible and open' Malaysian cultural heritage offers a pluralist Malaysian corporate and community framework to build the requisite policy and industry reform and political transition strategies that will enable a deeper and more integrated achievement of the Malaysian branding strategy 'Malaysia – Truly Asia'. Prime Minister Abdullah Badawi's more 'open and flexible' *Hadhari* (civilisational) Islam approach may indeed represent recognition of the value of progressive reform to transform Malaysia to a fully developed nation that values its diversity.

Perhaps the most quixotic nation in the region, Singapore, has transformed itself from an entrepot trading port to a modern global player guided by an evolving but 'pragmatic and flexible' heritage that has enabled it to grow and sustain itself in response to the changing fortunes created by external forces. In the forty years since Independence, drawing on this pragmatic and flexible heritage, the Chinese dominated government has successfully applied a paternalistic approach to community and industrial development through a government-guided and -owned corporate management model. Its management strategies are designed to bind the people of Singapore through the promotion of a cohesive and modern national identity based upon the shared goal of national industrial development through a paternalistic and entrepreneurial culture. Open-door investment and highly-regulated labour policies, supported by state-of-the-art logistics and communications infrastructure facilities, were designed to attract high levels of foreign investment which provided Singaporeans with rising standards of living and promoted Singapore as an important global business and cultural hub.

In response to increasing international competition, and the impact of additional external forces, such as the 1997 Asian crisis, terrorism and SARS, the paternalistic leadership model and government-led cultural and business approaches have been subject to increasing criticism in light of the country's desire to become a highly competitive knowledge-based industrial society. In the context of global market complexities, the government, corporations and the people of Singapore have acknowledged the need to 'flexibly and pragmatically' face the reformist challenges associated with the transition to a more risk-taking and innovation.

Thailand and Indonesia

Part four examines the contextual and managerial characteristics of a further two regional nations which are distinguished from those previously discussed due to historical factors on the one hand, and more recent social and political issues on the other. Both of these nations have been more deeply affected than other regional nations by destabilising local political, economic, inter-ethnic issues and natural disasters, together with the shared consequences of a more competitive global environment and convergent managerial imperatives. Thailand is unique in being the only Asian nation never colonised by imperial powers, and Indonesia in the extent of social and political disruption experienced over the last decade.

The chapter on Thailand discusses the complex 'continuity-in-change' characteristics that underlie the responsive and resistive Thai managerial characteristics applied at meso-(societal) and micro-(organisational) levels to address national development imperatives. The Buddhist socio-cultural community characteristics derived from Thai heritage play an important role in framing the apparently contradictory approach underpinning Thai managerial pragmatism, which simultaneously aims to maintain socio-cultural continuity and the status quo, whilst acknowledging the crucial need to embrace the changes associated with global imperatives. Thailand shares similar circumstances with Malaysia with regard to the impact of changing regional development imperatives. Both nations have achieved rising levels of economic growth and standards of living, which means that they can no longer rely on the competitive regional advantages of cheap labour, relatively stable governments and simple production efficiency improvement to sustain foreign investment and economic development.

The pragmatic nature of the Thais means that, guided by a utilitarian approach at both the meso-(societal) and micro-(organisational) levels, management may embrace more effective management systems in the pursuit of greater efficiencies. The characteristic Thai individualism, in association with a group-orientation, suggests that the leadership role of management will be crucial in facilitating this transition. Conversely, short-term solutions are often applied to address the impact of the various international, regional and local crises mentioned above, while complex contemporary realities now call for long-term measures, long-term oriented reform and government and corporate investment to counter the impacts.

On the other hand, complex local and regional ethnic, religious and economic influences and forces have had both convergent and divergent impacts on Indonesia to form the basis of a unique and shared heritage. The Indonesian heritage is characterised by 'assimilative, pluralistic and often paradoxical' local and external values and behaviours. These characteristics have significant implications for both the contextual and complex nature of management approaches in Indonesia.

Since independence in 1945, and with a three hundred year Dutch economic and administrative legacy, the two previous Presidential leaders – Soekarno and Soeharto – drew variously on traditional and community heritages to infuse a unifying Indonesian national cultural logic into national discourse to guide community governance and organisational management strategies. Beneath a generally cohesive modern Indonesian national worldview, multi-layered and sub-cultural community identities and their related communicative, linguistic, and behaviour practices are found. This plurality has significant implications for the highly contextual nature of Indonesian values and behaviour, and there are considerable issues and challenges associated with managing this pluralism on a day-to-day basis in government, professional, technical and workplace settings alike. Hence, an understanding of Indonesian history, its cultural legacy, and the plurality of sub-cultural communities, is crucial to make sense of its particular esoteric national, regional and local approaches to management.

Following the economic and political collapse of the autocratic New Order regime, despite dramatic and ongoing hardship, Indonesia has demonstrated considerable collective resolve and tenacity in its pursuit of a new democratic political order. In just six years the nation undertook the remarkable political transformation to the largest predominantly Islamic democratic nation in the world. Throughout this political reform process additional economic hardships were brought on by inter-ethnic and religious conflict; terrorist bombings in Bali, Jakarta and other regional cities; SARS; and traumatic natural disasters such a earthquakes, floods and more recently the 2004 tsunami.

As a result of the cumulative influences of the 1997 Asian economic crisis, political transformation and more recent human and natural disasters, the governance and management of Indonesian institutions and corporations have come under increasing international and local scrutiny. Subsequently, both local and international agencies have called for increased transparency, institutional reform and the associated human resource capacity development, in order for the country to create the necessary political stability and regulatory certainty required for both local and foreign investment. The election of President Yudhoyono has focused political and community commitment on addressing the issues of corruption, collusion and nepotism (KKN), and undertaking further institutional reform.

The 'assimilative' dimension of the Indonesian heritage may provide the vehicle for the appropriation and adaptation of new ideas and practices in locally meaningful ways, so as to not to destabilise but rather to transform Indonesia as both a large global producer and a global marketplace. The managerial implications for Indonesia are that in light of the 'paradoxical' nature of the Indonesian heritage, Indonesians will be required to incorporate another international, but often paradoxical cultural layer of values and practices to their already syncretic and multilayered worldviews and identities.

Conclusion

This chapter, and the book as a whole, canvas the concept of an emergent Asian Management paradigm which embraces all of the countries explored, and which is transforming earlier socio-cultural traditions under the influences of global dynamism towards a new cross-vergence of Western and Asian values and practices. It is argued that not only are Asian management styles and behaviours being impacted by Western influences, but conversely, Western managerial approaches are also beginning to accommodate some of the Asian management agendas.

Over the past few years, optimism in Asia has replaced the negative business climate triggered by the financial meltdown of 1997. This resurgence has been achieved by a new boost in domestic demand and interregional trade and investment. One hundred and sixteen companies from the countries included in this volume were ranked in the *Fortune 500* leading companies in 2005 (Japan 81, China 16, South Korea 11, India 5, Singapore 1, Malaysia 1 and Thailand 1 (*Fortune*, 2005)). The growth of Asian multinationals will see Asia transform into the largest regional economy over the next two decades. If that occurs, it would be first region since the Industrial Revolution to be able to signal both its interdependence and its cross-vergence. The large-scale shift of high-tech manufacturing towards Asia has now been replaced by services and research and development. New Asian technology companies like Infosys and Wipro of India, Huawei and ZTE of China and Samsung of Korea indicate Asia's growing supremacy. It may be noted, for example, that half of India's population is under twenty five years of age and entry to some of the top management schools in India are 100 times harder than entry to United States 'Ivy League' universities. The Asian managerial scene is not without its problems, particularly in the area of transparency, but the book highlights how family, business and government structures are changing in favour of professionalism, creativity, innovation and development. However, far from a universalistic global amalgam of management philosophies and models, there is considerable evidence of a myriad of cross-vergence options, which may differ from country to country, and within particular countries, at macro-, meso- and micro-levels.

It remains to be seen how these issues will develop as the twenty first century unfolds.

References

Fortune, 2005, 'Fortune global 500', July 25, no. 13, pp.1–44

India Today, 2004, 29 March, p.30.

Khanna, T, 2004, 'Building 100 Indian MNCs', *India Today*, 29 March p.32.

Nadkarni, S, 2004, 'The rise of the tiger, biz quotient', *Journal of Singapore Business Federation*, October, pp.15–16.

Preiss, M, 2005, India: Welcoming the world, *Asia Inc.*, January, p.14.

Additional readings

Chow, I, Holbert, N, Kelly, L & Yu, J, 2004, *Business strategy: An Asia-Pacific focus*, Pearson Prentice Hall, UK.

Davies, G & Nyland, C, 2005, *Globalisation in the Asian region*, Edward Elgar, London.

Meyer, A, Mar, P, Richter, F-J & Williamson, P, 2005, *Global future: The next challenge for Asian business*, Wiley and Sons, Singapore.

Saee, J, 2005, *Managing organisations in a global economy – An intercultural perspective*, Thomson Learning, UK.

Williamson, PJ, 2004, *Winning in Asia: Strategies for the new millennium*, Harvard Business School Press, Boston.

Yeung, H (ed.), 2006, *Handbook of research on Asian business*, Edward Elgar, London.

Glossary of terms

Chapter 3   China

Buddhism	religious philosophy based on the teaching of the Buddha and holding that a state of enlightenment can be attained by suppressing worldly desires
danwei	mini society or local social unit
dyads	five hierarchical social relationships
guanxi	Chinese reciprocity networks
guoyou	state-owned enterprises
'iron-rice-bowl'	cradle-to-grave based welfare system
mianxi	face (pride)
renshi guanli	personnel administration
renzhi zlyuan guanli	HRM
suan pan	Chinese abacus
tie fenwan	lifetime employment
tie gongzi	centrally-fixed wage system
Taoism	Chinese philosophy that advocates a simple life and a policy of non-interference with the natural course of thing
yun dong	migratory movements (government or self-imposed)

Chapter 4   India

Licence Raj	protectionist and government–controlled corporate culture
Arthashastra	comprehensive forth century handbook of public administration 3 variables guiding public/private behaviour division
desh	1. site or location
kaal	2. timing
patra	3. specificities of context
caste	traditional Indian system of social hierarchies
brahmins	1. high status priests, intellectuals & teachers caste
kshatriyas	2. warriors & aristocrats caste

vaishyas	3. traditionally agricultural workers and merchants, now managers in business & commerce caste.
shudra	4. service people caste
guna	qualities
guna dynamics	workplace motivation concept based on a matrix of static and dynamic paradigms for human duties and roles in life formulated in ancient India.
sattava guna	1. virtue orientation (to reveal)
tamasik guna	2. positive orientation (to suppress) (lethargic/negative orientation/ignorance orientation)
rajas guna	3. action orientation (to make active)
zoroastrian	ancient Persian belief system based on spiritual contest between good and evil
nishkama	a balanced approach to endeavour or work (desireless) Hindu values: Four pillars to sustain individual and society
dharma	1. ethical framework (religious duty)
artha	2. practical challenge
kama	3. worldly motivation
moksha	4. self-actualisation
sradha	loyalty to seniors
sneha	reciprocal affection & acceptance of mentoring role
swamis	a title of respect for a Hindu saint, or religious teacher
gyana	knowledge
sadhana	training or dedication (a lifelong process)

Chapter 5   Japan

Amaterasu 天照	The sun goddess: The supreme god in mythology
Baigan Ishida 石田梅岩	merchant philosopher
Baigan Ishida & *Ei'ichi Shibusawa* 石田梅岩&渋沢 栄一	the spirit of capitalism
Bakufu 幕府	military-based government (1603–1867)
bubble economy	economic collapse of the early 1990s.
Bushidō 武士道	the code of honour and behaviour of the Japanese warrior class, emphasising self-discipline, courage, and loyalty
FREETERS フリーター	compound of English 'free' and German 'arbeiter' worker part-time worker or job-hopper.

Fukoku-kyōhei 富国強兵	nationalist slogan – rich country, strong military
Gen X	post-baby boomer generation (born 1961–79)
Han 藩	assigned land
Han shu 藩主	feudal lord
Hongyō kaiki 本業回帰	reform: refocus on the foundations of business
Japan Inc.	post-war industrial development model.
Jimmu 神武	1st Japanese Emperor, "Divine Warrior"
Kaizen 改善	system of production based on continuous improvement achieved through grass-root and company-wide approach.
Keidanren 経団連	Federation of Economic Organisations.
Keiretsu 系列	Post-World War II enterprises based around large bank & general trading company; basis of Japanese 'network capitalism'
Kigyobetsu kumain 企業別組合	enterprise-based unions
kogai system 子飼い制度	standardised in-house training
Kojiki 古事記	Record of ancient things, 712 AD
kyōzon kyōei 共存共栄	moral philosophy – holistic coexistence and co-prosperity – drawing on 18thc Shinto, Confucianism and Buddhist values
Meiji Constitution 明治憲法	modern constitution based on German model, retained emperor at the center
Meiji restoration 明治維新	end of feudal era (1867), new period of nationalism and bi-lateral trade agreements
mekkō hōshi 滅公奉私	self-indulgence with little consideration for costs to others
messhi hōkō 滅私奉公	ethos: service through self-sacrifice
NEETS	English acronym for Not in Employment, Education or Training
Nenkō joretsu chingin 年功序列賃金	seniority-based wage system
Neo-Confucianism	Assimilation of Japanese values with the teachings of Confucius, emphasising personal control, adherence to a social hierarchy, and social and political order

Nihon Shoki 日本書記	Chronicle of Japan. 720 AD
Nikkeiren 日経連	Japanese Federation of Employers Association.
oitsuke, oikose	slogan, catch up and overtake
Pacific War	(1941–45)
parasite shinguru	sociological category – parasite singles
ringi system 稟議制度	characteristic system for decision-making about complex operational and strategic issues
Ritsuryō 律令	code of laws
Samurai	warrior class
seclusion policy 鎖国主義	inward-looking 'closed-door' policy (1639–1858)
Shintō 神道	Ancient indigenous religion
Shogun 将軍	a hereditary military commander in feudal Japan who ruled the country under the nominal rule of an emperor between the years 1192 and 1867
Shōnindō 商人道	way of the merchants
Shukkō 出向	inter-firm employee transfer within the keiretsu system.
Shushin koyō 終身雇用	lifetime employment
Sino-Japanese War 日清戦争	(1937–45)
Taishō 大正	democracy period (1912–26)
Taiwa 対話	dialogue
Terakoya 寺子屋	temple school
Terauke system 寺受け制度	institutionalised Buddhist temples in local community
Toyota production system	global production manufacturing model: just-in-time, *kaizen* and automation principles, full optimisation of the system is not achieved without the commitment and empowerment of line workers under a paternalistic and collaborative labour relations management paradigm.
Uchi- soto 内外	we/they-group relations: concentric structure of layers to boundary.
Wa 輪	harmony in Japanese group relations.
wakon yōsai 和魂洋才	Development vision: Western capabilities under Japanese spirit

Yamato 大和	Ancient name for Japan
Zaibatsu 財閥	large family controlled financial and industrial conglomerate
Zaitech 財テク	financial techniques and risk-taking money games of the 1980s.
Zen 禅	school of Buddhism that emphasises enlightenment through meditation

Chapter 6   South Korea

ch'ommin	bottom class of society
chaebol	family-centred large scale industrial conglomerate
changjo	creativity
chinban	extended (family blood line-based) clan
Choson dynasty	1392 to 1910
chungun	middle class – technicians and administrators
eui-yok	value: ambition or hard work
hangul	Korean phonetic script
hyal-yun	describes an individual's blood-related or kinship-based relationship with the Chaebol owner
inhwa	harmony-oriented cultural value
koenchanayo	'good enough' value applied to maintain harmony
Korean War	(1950 to 1953) between North Korea, and its ally China, and South Korea, supported by United Nations Allied forces, especially from the United States
Koryo	ancient Kingdom formed AD918 – *Korea* anglicised version
K-type management	characteristic Korean interpretation of Neo-Confucian, Japanese & American management influences
kut	shaman ritual
kwageo	rigorous civil servant exams (enabled citizens to move up the social scale)
mudang	shaman female spirit
O Ryun	five relationships – hierarchical notion of the social order
pummi	traditional approach to decision-making
sahoon	shared company values
sajeonhyupui	process of informal consensus formation similar to Japanese *nemawashi*
sangmin	commoner class (75 per cent of population) traditionally farmers, craftsmen and merchants
sansin	shaman spirits
Seon	Zen Buddhist religion
Shammanism	indigenous Korean religion; unorganised pantheon of gods, spirits, and ghosts, ranging from the god

	generals who rule the different quarters of heaven to mountain spirits
won	Korean currency
yangban	traditional class of scholars recruited for government administration

Chapter 7   Malaysia

adat	customary laws, beliefs & social norms
Allah	God
ASEAN	regional country partnerships & free-trade agreements between Malaysia, Indonesia, Philippines, Singapore, Thailand, Brunei-Darussalam, Vietnam, Laos, Myanmar & Cambodia.
Austronesian heritage	appropriative and assimilative regional cultural traditions
Bahasa Melayu	official Malaysian language
Barasan Nasional	coalition of political parties that make up the federated government
bumiputra	native born 'sons of soil'
Bursa Malaysia	de-mutualised Kuala Lumpur stock exchange
chador	traditional garment worn by Muslim women covering the head and body.
Dewan Negara	Senate 'National Hall'
Dewan Rakyat	House of Representatives
fardu ain	individual obligations
fardu kafayah	collective obligations
gotong-royong	mutual obligations
guanxi	ethnic Chinese community reciprocity networks
Hadhari	reformist and 'civilisational' approach to Islam
haj	fifth pillar of Islamic faith – pilgrimage to the holy city of Mecca
hijab	headscarf worn by Islamic women
kampong	a village
kanganis	overseer of low caste labourers (Tamil southern India)
Khazanal Nasional Bhd.	Malaysian Government investment arm
laissez-faire	policy based on the principle that the economy works best if private industry is not regulated and markets are free
Majapahit	14th century Hindu kingdom centred on Java & ruled the Malay Peninsula
mandurs	foreman – high caste Tamil (Southern India)
Melaka	Malacca (not Straits)
negeri	Malaysian states

Nusantara	Malay Peninsula
Orang Asli	aboriginal peoples of the Malay Peninsula
Qur' an	Koran – the sacred text of Islam, believed by Muslims to record god's revelations to Muhammad
rajah	Hindu Sanskrit term for ruler or prince
Ramadhan	Islamic month of fasting and prayer during daylight hours
rent-seeking	corruption, collusion & nepotism
riba	the charging of interest in Islamic Banking based on shared risk between the lender and the borrower
salat	second pillar of Islamic faith – daily prayers
sanin	fourth pillar of Islamic faith – fasting during the holy month of Ramadan
shahada	first pillar of Islamic faith – the statement of faith
Shari'ah	Sharia Law – Islamic religious law, based on the Koran
sultanate	aristocratic ruler
swiddening	terraced hill rice cultivation
ummah	community of knowledgeable people
Vision 2020	initiated 1991 – policy plans outlining national economic & cultural development goals
Yang Di Pertua Negeri	State Governor
Yang Di-Pertuan Agong	The Malaysian King
zaket	third pillar of Islamic faith – giving of alms to the poor

Chapter 8   Singapore

entrepot trade	merchant activity gained from being seaport on major international trading routes
lingua franca	a language used for communication by people who speak different first languages
Majapahit	14th century Hindu empire centred on Java
Pu-luo-cuing	traditional Chinese name for island at the end of the peninsula
Singa Pura	Lion Town
Srivijayan	13th century Buddhist empire centred on Palembang, Sumatra.
Termasek	Sea town – early name for Singapore
the domino theory	The political theory postulating that events are interrelated and can trigger off a chain of others as applied to post-War II notions of Communist China's expanding Asia-Pacific regional sphere of influence.

Chapter 9   Thailand

Ayutthaya (Ayadhya)	historic name for Thailand
krengjai	restraint applied to inherent individualism to avoid conflict
Theravada Buddhism	The branch of Buddhism followed in Thailand that follows the teachings of the Buddha based on a morality underpinned by the principles of harmlessness and moderation
sakdina	traditional system of social hierarchy
rai	nobles
phrai	commoners
that	beggars
pradej	use of force to induce fear
prakhun	use of benevolence to induce respect and gratitude
baramee	power endowed on leader through the use of *pradej* & *prakhun*
boon koon	patron–client relationships
thaksonomics	reform measures taken by the Thaksin Government since the Asian economic crisis to rebuild the economy

Chapter 10   Indonesia

aliran	ideological streams related to separatist political movements
ambtenaar (amtenar)	official – Dutch educated civil servants
badan usaha milik negara (BUMN)	government-owned companies
bapak	father, father figure
pak	Mr.
batin	the inner spiritual life of an individual
Bhinneka Tunggal Ika	national motto: Unity in Diversity
bule	a Westerner
burpati	local noble or district leader
direktur umum	general director
dwifungsi	dual socio-political and military functions of the army
ibu	mother, or mother figure, Mrs.
jam karet	rubber (flexible) time
Jamaah Islamiah (JI)	transl. 'Islamic community' fundamentalist organisation
kebatinan	Javanese form of spirituality combining ancient beliefs & practices the Hindu, Buddhist, Sufi & Christian mystical traditions

kekluaragaan	Javanese notion of the family framed around the cultural notion of social harmony
keluarga besar	a big family (applicable to an organisation)
koperasi	cooperatives
lahir	external world obligations
merdeka	freedom, independence
mukafat	achieved consensus through discussion (musyawarah)
musyawarah	traditional village system of collective discussion
Nahdlatal (NU) Ulama	transl. 'Revival of religious scholars', Indonesia's largest Muslim organisation supported by over 30million centred on East Java formerly headed by Abdurrahman Wahid, the fourth President.
Pancasila	five fundamental principles of the Republic of Indonesia
penasehat	board of advisors
Peranakan	Indonesians of Chinese descent
persantrean	Islamic based school
pribumi	local natives
pryayi	Javanese aristocracy
rakyat	the people
reformasi	reform
surat keputusan	reactivism
swasta	private companies
syncretism	combining different, often paradoxical systems of belief or values
Totok	Ethnic Chinese not born in Indonesia
ulama	religious teacher

Index